Rolling Stone

THE DECADES OF
rock & roll

Rolling Stone

THE DECADES OF
rock & roll

••• BY THE EDITORS OF
rolling stone
•••
PHOTOGRAPHS FROM THE
MICHAEL OCHS ARCHIVES

CHRONICLE BOOKS
SAN FRANCISCO

A Rolling Stone Press Book

EDITOR: **holly george-warren**

ASSOCIATE EDITORS: **kathryn huck, nina pearlman**

ASSISTANT EDITORS: **wendy mitchell, jordan mamone**

EDITORIAL ASSISTANT: **andrew simon**

Library of Congress Cataloging-in-Publication Data:
Rolling Stone: The decades of rock & roll / by the editors of Rolling
Stone.
p.cm.
ISBN 0-8118-2978-2
Rock music—History and criticism. I. Title: The decades of rock and
roll. II. Rolling stone (San Francisco, Calif.)

ML3534.D43 2001
781.66'09—dc21
00-047506

Cover:

CHUCK BERRY: MICHAEL OCHS ARCHIVES

Case:

C. CHUCK KRALL/MICHAEL OCHS ARCHIVES

Front endpapers:

DAVID BOWIE: MICHAEL OCHS ARCHIVES

JAMES BROWN: MICHAEL OCHS ARCHIVES

MADONNA: KEVIN MAZUR

Page 1:

RUN DMC: STEPHANIE CHERNIKOWSKI/

MICHAEL OCHS ARCHIVES

Page 2:

BECK: SHERYL OLSON

Page 4:

BOB DYLAN: MICHAEL OCHS ARCHIVES

Page 288:

ADAM YAUCH (BEASTIE BOYS):
DANNY CLINCH/NASTY LITTLE MAN

Back endpapers:

DONNA SUMMERS: MICHAEL OCHS ARCHIVES

JIMI HENDRIX: MICHAEL OCHS ARCHIVES

PATTI SMITH: MICHAEL OCHS ARCHIVES

DESIGNED BY: **azi rad**

COMPOSED BY: **suzanne scott**

MANUFACTURED IN CHINA

Distributed in Canada by Raincoast Books
9050 Shaughnessy Street
Vancouver, British Columbia V6P 6E5
1 3 5 7 9 10 8 6 4 2

chronicle books llc
85 Second Street
San Francisco, California 94105
www.chroniclebooks.com

CONTENTS

introduction
11

section four: the eighties

section five: the nineties

contributors

acknowledgments

index

introduction

How do you sum up fifty years of rock & roll in less than three hundred pages? You don't! What we've tried to do here, within the covers of *The Decades of Rock & Roll*, is give a taste of the major movers and shakers and a flavor of the most important musical movements of each decade since rock & roll was born in the 1950s. Therefore, in these pages, you'll find words from those artists responsible for rock & roll's creation and those who've continued to add to its canon, as well as the work of writers who came of age with the music.

The idea for this book originated back in 1989, when the editors of ROLLING STONE began assigning some of the magazine's best journalists to write about the artists essential to each decade through the 1980s. The result: ROLLING STONE's "Celebration of Four Decades of Rock," consisting of "The Fifties" (April 19, 1990), "The Sixties" (August 23, 1990), "The Seventies" (September 20, 1990) and "The Eighties" (November 15, 1990). Looking back at the 1990s, we've added pieces from various issues of ROLLING STONE, and we've asked writer Rob Sheffield to comment on the musical maelstrom of the twentieth century's last decade.

Over the past fifty years, the music has "evolved" from Little Richard's "a-wop-bop-a-loo-bop-a-wop-bam-boom" to the Sugarhill Gang's "With a hip, hop, the hipit, hipidipit, hip, hip, hopit," from Jerry Lee Lewis's "Great Balls of Fire" to Beck's "The Devil's Haircut," from the Beatles' "Love Me Do" to Nirvana's "Lithium." Throughout, the music's essence— its feisty spirit—has remained intact, however, and lives on in the twenty first century.

Sadly, two of the most eloquent contributors to the original concept of *The Decades of Rock & Roll* did not live to see the new century. This book is dedicated to the memory— and musical passions—of writer Robert Palmer and hillbilly cat Carl Perkins.

HOLLY GEORGE-WARREN
Editor, Rolling Stone Press

the fifties

By ROBERT PALMER

For some of us, it began late at night: huddled under bedroom covers with our ears glued to a radio pulling in black voices charged with intense emotion and propelled by a wildly kinetic rhythm through the after-midnight static. Growing up in the white-bread America of the Fifties, we had never heard anything like it, but we reacted, or remember reacting, instantaneously and were converted. We were believers before we knew what it was that had so spectacularly ripped the dull, familiar fabric of our lives. We asked our friends, maybe an older brother or sister. We found out that they called it rock & roll. It was so much more vital and alive than any music we had ever heard before that it needed a new category: Rock & roll was much more than new music for us. It was an obsession and a way of life.

For some of us, it began a little later, with our first glimpse of Elvis on the family television set. But for those of us growing up in the Fifties, it didn't seem to matter how or where we first heard the music. Our reactions were remarkably uniform. Here, we knew, was a sonic cataclysm come bursting (apparently) out of nowhere, with the power to change our lives forever, because it was obviously, inarguably *our* music. If we had any initial doubt about that, our parents' horrified—or at best dismissive—reactions banished those doubts. Growing up in a world we were only beginning to understand, we had finally found something for us: for us together, for us alone.

But where did it come from? How did it get started? Forty-five-odd years after rock & roll first burst upon us in all its glory, we still don't have a simple, definitive answer to these questions. Of course, they are trick questions. Where you think rock & roll came from and how you think it grew depend on how you define rock & roll.

Fats Domino, the most amiable and pragmatic of the first-generation rock & roll stars, was asked about the music's origins in a Fifties television interview. "Rock & roll is nothing but rhythm and blues," he responded with characteristic candor, "and we've been playing it for years down in New Orleans." This is a valid statement: All Fifties rockers, black and white, country born and city bred, were fundamentally influenced by R&B, the black popular music of the late Forties and early Fifties. R&B was a catchall rubric for the sound of everything from stomping Kansas City swing bands to New York street-corner vocal groups to scrappy Delta and Chicago blues bands. As far as Fats Domino was concerned, rock & roll was simply a new marketing strategy for the style of music he had been recording since 1949.

But what about the rest of the Fifties rock front-runners? When we get down to cases, we find that several of the most distinctive and influential rock & roll performers of the mid-Fifties

were making music that could not, by any stretch of the imagination, be defined as a continuation of pre-1955 R&B. There was no clear precedent in R&B for an artist like Chuck Berry, who combined hillbilly, blues and swing jazz influences in more or less equal measure and wrote songs about teenage life and culture that black and white teens found equally appealing. (Louis Jordan, the early idol of both Berry and Bill Haley, came closest, but his jump & jive story songs were aimed as much at adults as teens, and any hillbilly flavor in his records was strictly a comedic device.) Certainly, mainstream popular music had never seen a performer whose vocal delivery, stage moves and seamless integration of influences as diverse as down-home blues, white Pentecostalism and hit-parade crooning remotely resembled Elvis Presley's. And where, outside the wildest, most Dionysian black storefront churches, had anyone heard or seen *anything* like Little Richard?

Sam Phillips, the rock & roll patriarch whose Sun label first recorded Elvis, Jerry Lee Lewis, Carl Perkins, Johnny Cash and other first-rate talents, has suggested that the true import of Fifties rock & roll had very little to do with musical content, let alone musical innovation. And it's perfectly true that once you strip the music down and analyze it, riff by riff, lick by lick, you find a mélange of blues conceits, prewar big-band and Western swing, gospel and other existing vocabularies.

For Phillips, rock & roll's real significance was twofold. First, it was the only form of popular music that specifically addressed and was tailored to teenagers—there had been adult records and kiddie records, but nothing for that burgeoning bulge of the baby boom population caught between childhood and adulthood. Second, rock & roll enabled "marginal" Americans—poor white sharecroppers, black ghetto youths and, not coincidentally, storefront record-label operators in out-of-the-way places like Memphis—the opportunity to express themselves freely, not as purveyors of R&B and C&W, whose audiences were limited, but as a dominant force in the popular marketplace. Elvis was transformed from hick truck driver to idol of millions in less than a year. Suddenly, it seemed, the sky was the limit, if there was a limit at all.

The coming of rock & roll in the mid-Fifties was not merely a musical revolution but a social and generational upheaval of vast and unpredictable scope. It also represented a major reversal in the *business* of popular music. There were no pre–rock & roll counterparts to Sam Phillips, who parlayed a tiny Memphis label with a staff of one into a company whose artists sold millions of records throughout the world. In record-business terms, rock & roll meant that small, formerly specialized labels like Sun, Chess and Specialty were invading the upper reaches of the pop charts, long the exclusive domain of the major corporate record labels and old-line Tin Pan Alley music-publishing interests.

Concentrating on high-volume sales and bland, lowest-common-denominator pop disposables, the majors were caught napping by an unholy coalition of Southern renegade radio engineers (Phillips), Jewish immigrant merchants (the Chess brothers), black ex–swing-band musicians and raving hillbilly wild men. These were the "marginal" Americans who had been recording for specialized audiences since the majors had virtually ceded them that territory at the end of World War II. The ghetto-storefront, nickel-and-dime record operation of 1949–53 suddenly emerged an industry giant in 1955–56, accounting for many and often most of the records at the top of the pop charts.

Because many of the same small labels that had taken over the R&B market were also dabbling in country & western music, and vice versa, these musics had been drawing closer together. The younger generation of C&W fans were also listening and dancing to black music, and as a result, white country musicians were encouraged to record R&B songs and play with a heavier, emphatically rocking beat.

Meanwhile, many blacks growing up in isolated pockets of the rural South listened to and were influenced by the country music on radio programs like the *Grand Ole Opry*, from Nashville. Black performers like Chuck Berry and Bo Diddley found that when they performed a song that was vaguely hillbilly in style or derivation, black audiences went for it. Despite the still-rigid racial segregation of the Fifties, the white and black underclass of music fans and performers was finding more and more common ground.

With the flowering of the postwar baby boom, teenagers, especially white teenagers with money in their pockets, represented a potentially enormous and largely untapped consumer group. It didn't take a genius to realize, as Sam Phillips and other early-Fifties indie label owners did, that more and more of these free-spending kids were listening to black records, spun on local radio stations by a new generation of black-talking but mostly white-skinned disc jockeys. If a white performer with an R&B style and teen appeal could be found ...

The runaway success of Bill Haley and the Comets, following the use of their "Rock Around the Clock" in a key sequence of the 1955 juvenile delinquent movie *The Blackboard Jungle*, was a clear signal that R&B and C&W (Haley's Comets were a former C&W band recording R&B tunes in a style resembling Louis Jordan's) weren't going to remain ghettoized from the pop-music mainstream much longer. Haley wasn't exactly teen-idol material, though. It took an assiduously groomed and promoted Elvis Presley—who, legend has it, walked into Sam Phillips's tiny office to make a record for his mother's birthday—to ensure the triumph of rock & roll.

1
5

‹HAIL, HAIL ROCK AND ROLL:
chuck berry in action
MICHAEL OCHS ARCHIVES/VENICE, CA

To succeed in the teen marketplace, the new music—new, at least, to the teenagers who embraced it—needed a name. Rhythm & blues was a dated term with exclusively black connotations. Alan Freed, the white R&B disc jockey whose move from Cleveland to a top-rated New York station in 1954 was as crucial to the emergence of rock & roll as the timely appearance of the Pelvis, came up with the name. It must have amused Freed and other insiders a great deal that the term rock & roll was black slang for sex—and had been as early as 1922, when blues singer Trixie Smith recorded "My Man Rocks Me (With One Steady Roll)." It was a secret shared by the disc jockeys, the performers and the kids: Astonishingly, "responsible adults" didn't seem to "get it." Certainly, nobody who was in on the joke was going to spell it out for them. Teenagers were developing their own codes of in-group complicity, expressed in clothes, in accouterments (from girls' earrings and pins to greasers' switchblades) and increasingly in their own slanguage. The medium that spread this underground teen culture was rock & roll.

From its earliest days the rock & roll label covered a broad musical terrain. The cliché is that rock & roll was a melding of country music and blues, and if you are talking about, say, Chuck Berry or Elvis Presley, the description, though simplistic, does fit. But the black inner-city vocal group sound—which itself was diverse enough to accommodate the tough, soulful Midnighters and 5 Royales, the neo-barbershop harmonies of "bird groups" like the Orioles and the Crows and the kid sound of Frankie Lymon and the Teenagers or Shirley and Lee—had little to do with either blues or country music in their purer forms.

The Bo Diddley beat—which, once Bo popularized it, began showing up on records by everybody from the former jazz bandleader Johnny Otis ("Willie and the Hand Jive") to the Texas rockabilly Buddy Holly ("Not Fade Away")—was Afro-Caribbean in derivation. The most durable (read "overused") bass riff in Fifties rock & roll, as exemplified by Fats Domino's "Blue Monday" or Lloyd Price's and Elvis Presley's "Lawdy Miss Clawdy," had been pinched by Dave Bartholomew, Domino's canny producer and bandleader, from a Cuban *son* record. The screaming, athletic saxophone playing that was Fifties rock's dominant instrumental voice, before the electric guitar moved front and center, was straight out of Forties big-band swing, as were such typical rock & roll arrangers' devices as riffing sax sections and stop-time breaks. Traditional Mexican rhythms entered the rock & roll arena through Chicano artists, most prominently Ritchie Valens. Rock & roll proved an all-American, multiethnic hybrid, its sources and developing substyles too various to be explained away by "blues plus country" or any other reductionist formula.

At the height of the initial pandemonium, in 1955–56, a select number of front-runners emerged, stars whose personalities and performing antics set the stage for all that was to follow: Elvis, of course; Chuck Berry, whose definitive guitar style (rooted in swing jazz and the uptown band blues of T-Bone Walker) was as widely emulated as his brilliant, vividly economical lyrics of teenage tribulations and triumphs; Little Richard, the archetypal rock & roll screamer and ambisexual striptease artist, with the toughest, most influential road band of the period, the mighty Upsetters; friendly, reliable Fats Domino, who mixed New Orleans blues and jazz with Tin Pan Alley pop and quietly racked up more hit records than anyone but Elvis; Jerry Lee Lewis, the prototype of the rock & roll wild man, his stage persona and lifestyle perfectly matched; Buddy Holly and the Crickets, the paradigm of the singer/songwriter–fronted guitar band; Sam Cooke, Ray Charles, the 5 Royales and a young James Brown, all of whom enacted Pentecostal religious ecstasies on the rock & roll stage and spawned the Sixties soul men in the process; and Eddie Cochran, who combined teen-idol looks with a probing musical intelligence and who understood early on that the recording studio was a musical instrument.

Certain behind-the-scenes figures were arguably as important as even the brightest singing stars in building and shaping rock & roll as a viable musical idiom, with a future as well as a spectacular, slam-bang present: the producer Milt Gabler, who applied what he learned producing Louis Jordan's Forties jump-blues novelties to Bill Haley's breakthrough hits; Dave Bartholomew, the New Orleans trumpeter, bandleader, songwriter and record producer, whose musicians powered most of the hits by Fats Domino and Little Richard; and Bartholomew's drummer, Earl Palmer, who defined rock & roll rhythm in New Orleans and moved on to first-call status among the Los Angeles studio elite, playing uncredited on a staggering number of the era's most influential records, from Richard's "Tutti Frutti" to Cochran's "Summertime Blues." If any single musician can be credited with defining rock & roll as a rhythmic idiom distinct from the jump, R&B and all else that preceded it, that musician is surely Earl Palmer. Yet, it was another drummer and Little Richard associate, the Upsetters' Charles Connor, who first put the funk in the rhythm, as even James Brown admitted.

Atlantic Records' Tom Dowd introduced true stereo and gave Atlantic singles by the Coasters, the Drifters and many others a unique clarity and presence. Sam Phillips was as significant for his ingenious engineering, his feel for echo and ambience, as for his talent spotting and genre mixing. And Phillips's multiracial populism, an unpopular stance for a white Southerner in the Fifties, to say the least, had a lot to do with defining what we might choose to call either the spirit of rock & roll or its politics. It was Phillips who expressed most clearly, through his recording policies and his public utterances, the vision of rock & roll as a dream of equality and freedom.

Much has been made of Sixties rock as a vehicle for revolutionary social and cultural change, but it was mid-Fifties rock & roll that blew away, in one mighty, concentrated blast, the accumulated racial and social properties of centuries. What could be more outrageous, more threatening to the social and sexual order subsumed by the ingenuous phrase "traditional American values," than a full-tilt Little Richard show? There he was, camping it up androgynously one minute, then ripping off his clothes to display for a packed house of screaming teenage white girls his finely muscled black body.

It is a measure of Fifties rock's genuine revolutionary potential (as opposed to the revolution-as-corporate-marketing ploy so characteristic of the Sixties) that while Sixties rock eventually calmed down, was co-opted or snuffed itself out in heedless excess, Fifties rock & roll was *stopped*. Cold.

Rock & roll's takeover of the pop-music marketplace in the mid-Fifties was as threatening to the entrenched old-line music and entertainment business as it was to professional authority figures everywhere. RCA had Elvis, but most of the early rock & roll hits were on regionally rooted indie operations. Most of the major labels, as well as the established music publishers that had been the industry's backbone for more than a century, reacted slowly to the rock & roll onslaught, and most were definitely not amused by it.

It took a coalition of these Tin Pan Alley interests and publicity-hungry congressmen to bring rock & roll to its knees with the payola hearings that so ingloriously capped a truly tumultuous decade. The payola hearings managed to pillory Alan Freed, who had always played original black recordings rather than the bland white "cover" versions being offered by squeaky-clean opportunists like Pat Boone.

At the same time, a combination of economic forces and the gradual takeover of record-distribution networks by major labels made running a small label more and more difficult. The indie labels that had launched the music and sustained it during the two or three years when it ravaged the land either caved in to the pressure and quietly wound down their operations, like Sun and Specialty, or diversified and became corporate giants themselves, like Atlantic.

On top of all this came a series of mishaps in the careers of some of rock's leading lights. The army and Colonel Parker conspired to make Elvis safe. Chuck Berry was busted and spent time in jail. Little Richard quit at the peak of his powers to preach the gospel. Jerry Lee Lewis married his barely pubescent cousin and was blackballed. Holly, Valens, and the Big Bopper went down in an Iowa field. Alan Freed's fall from grace ended at the bottom, with his death as an alcoholic recluse.

During the few brief years when high-octane rock & roll ruled unchecked, the possibilities seemed mind-boggling, even limitless. Viewed with hindsight, the whole affair turns out to have been the cultural vanguard of a movement toward racial, social and sexual equality that was then only beginning to assume an explicitly political form. It's no mere accident of history that Rosa Parks's refusal to move to the back of a segregated Alabama bus, the germinal act of what became the civil rights movement, occurred during the brief pop-music ascendancy of performers like Chuck Berry and Little Richard, black men whose every sound and sign communicated their refusal to respond to the racist's traditional "C'mere, boy!"

If Fifties rock & roll failed to realize the creative and social aspirations it so eloquently expressed, on a purely cultural level it succeeded beyond the wildest dreams *anyone* could have entertained at the time. Not only has it proved more than a passing fad or an episode of youthful folly, it has provided the model, the template, the jumping-off point for virtually every subsequent wave of pop-music innovation. The best of Fifties rock & roll may have promised a utopia that was not to be, but as long as the music survives, the dream will live on.

ruth brown

By LEE JESKE

If popular music handed out comeback awards, R&B singer Ruth Brown would have one more trophy for her mantelpiece.

After decades of obscurity, Brown—who racked up so many hits in the early Fifties for a fledgling Atlantic Records that the label was tagged the House That Ruth Built—rebounded in the Eighties. She starred in Allen Toussaint's off-Broadway musical *Staggerlee*, appeared as the jive-talking disc jockey Motormouth Mabel in John Waters's film *Hairspray* and hosted the National Public Radio series *Harlem Hit Parade* and *Blues Stage*. Brown's role in the Broadway play *Black and Blue* won her a Tony in 1989, and her 1989 album, *Blues on Broadway*, earned her a Grammy Award. Her quest to recover back royalties from Atlantic led to the formation of the nonprofit Rhythm & Blues Foundation. Brown continues to perform and record, and in 1996, she wrote with Andrew Yule, *Miss Rhythm: The Autobiography of Ruth Brown, Rhythm & Blues Legend,* which won a Ralph J. Gleason Music Book Award.

Born Ruth Weston in Portsmouth, Virginia, in 1928 (she became Ruth Brown after a teenage marriage to trumpeter Jimmy Brown), she was an aspiring jazz singer when she came to the attention of Atlantic Records in the late Forties. After a serious car accident sidelined her for a year, Brown recorded the ballad "So Long," backed by a traditional jazz band led by guitarist Eddie Condon, in 1949. The song hit the R&B Top Ten, the first of more than twenty of Brown's singles to make the R&B charts during the next decade.

But it was "Teardrops From My Eyes," in 1950, that set the course for her career. The uptempo million-selling single—to be followed by such monster hits as "5-10-15 Hours" and "(Mama) He Treats Your Daughter Mean"—established Ruth Brown as a hard-rocking R&B belter, and she became one of the most successful and influential singers of the Fifties.

Miss Rhythm, as she was nicknamed, finally crossed over to the pop charts in 1957 with Leiber and Stoller's "Lucky Lips." That record, and its followup, Bobby Darin and Mann Curtis's "This Little Girl's Gone Rockin'," moved her from the black tour circuit to Alan Freed's early rock & roll package shows.

Brown's career tapered off in the late Fifties, and she and Atlantic Records parted ways in 1962.

When did you notice black music starting to solidify into rhythm & blues?

I guess in '51 or '52. You started hearing it from a radio show called *Randy's Record Shop*, in Gallatin, Tennessee. In the East and North, the Top 100 stations weren't playing it—it was "race music"—but it was coming out of Gallatin, Tennessee, on *Randy's Record Shop*. What people didn't know was that Randy was a white man. [WCLA's *Randy's Record Shop Show*, sponsored by a local record store, was hosted by Gene Nobles.] *He* was the person who

really started that whole thing when the turnabout came for rhythm & blues. The station was strong: You could pick it up in California and in Virginia. You could pick it up practically everywhere.

Did you notice other stations jumping on the format?

Yeah. See, at that time in every major city, there was a black-oriented radio station. That was necessary. We didn't get the coverage, but in every local city, there was always your favorite black DJ. I grew up listening to Jack Holmes; he was the DJ who turned my ear. He had a program called *The Mail Bag*. He played Sister Rosetta Tharpe, Lucky Millinder, Buddy Johnson, the Charioteers, the Ink Spots. I could hardly wait for my daddy to get out of the house in the morning, so I could flip over to this station.

You began singing with Lucky Millinder's big band. How did you end up meeting Ahmet Ertegun and Herb Abramson of Atlantic Records?
I had been fired by Lucky Millinder, and I was stranded in Washington, D.C., without the price of a ticket to get back to Virginia. But because I was in a business that my daddy didn't want me in, I couldn't call home.

So I was introduced to Blanche Calloway, Cab's sister, who was running a club in Washington called the Crystal Caverns. She gave me a job there singing, and I was supposed to work long enough to earn enough money to go back home.

One night Duke Ellington was working at the Howard Theater, and he came with Willis Conover, from the Voice of America, and Sonny Til of the Orioles. I was singing Vaughn Monroe stuff, Andrews Sisters stuff, Bing Crosby.... This is the kind of junk I was singing.

Now, Sonny Til and the Orioles had this record called "It's Too Soon to Know." And when I realized that that was Sonny Til—*ohhhh!* I told the bandleader I wanted to sing "It's Too Soon to Know," and I dedicated it to him. I saw Duke Ellington's expression, and without his saying a word, I knew that he was pleased with what he was hearing.

Willis Conover was kind of fidgeting in his seat, and I thought he was being disrespectful to me. When he got up from the table and went to a pay phone, I was insulted. I thought, "That's how bad I am," but what he was doing was calling Ahmet Ertegun.

Ahmet sent Herb Abramson [an original partner in Atlantic] and a fellow named Blackie Sales, who worked for him; they were the ones that heard me. By then, Blanche Calloway had taught me some Ethel Waters things, and I was doing Billie Holiday's "Gloomy Sunday." I think they saw my versatility. I wasn't doing any real swinging, grooving things—I had a taste for torch ballads. I was doing everything except what I would end up doing.

You made a verbal agreement with Abramson to record for Atlantic and were on your way to New York City to sign the contract and perform at the Apollo Theater, when you were in a serious car accident.

Yes, in Chester, Pennsylvania. Atlantic Records actually signed me to a contract in the hospital bed.
Had you met Ahmet Ertegun before this?
No.
And you hadn't even recorded a demo?
Never.
And Atlantic paid for your hospitalization?
Yes. I was in the hospital for a year. I'll never forget that: On my twenty-first birthday, Ahmet came down to Chester to see me in that hospital, and he brought me a book on how to sight-read, a pitch pipe and a big tablet to write on, because I had a knack for writing lyrics.
So you hadn't even recorded a note for them, and here they were treating you pretty nicely.
I loved them. I didn't know anything different to do except to love them. I felt like I was part of the family. After I got out of the hospital, Ahmet, Herb Abramson and Miriam Bienstock [Bienstock was Abramson's former wife, as well as a partner in and the comptroller for Atlantic], when they would go somewhere to eat, they would come and take me. We were like family. They took care of me.
Who else was on the label?
Stick McGhee, Tiny Grimes and Ivory Joe Hunter. Ivory Joe used to sit at the piano—in the same room where Miriam had her desk, and cartons were stacked on one wall—and play his material.
The kind of material you were singing in Washington was not exactly the kind of material you became known for on Atlantic.

They really didn't know what I was going to do, what kind of singer I was going to become. They knew I was a good singer, but they didn't know what to do with me. I was recording with the Delta Rhythm Boys; I was recording ballads; they even had me singing some Yiddish songs in English. They really didn't know what to do with me, and my problem was I could sing any of it.

But eventually Rudy Toombs came in with "Teardrops From My Eyes." That was the first one that really turned Ruth Brown in the direction of being an R&B singer.

In 1950, when you recorded it, did you have any idea that this was a change in direction?

I had no idea which way it was going to go; it was just one of the songs. I had come to New York, and I had been playing theaters and working with the big bands. I was working with Count Basie, Charlie Ventura — they didn't know where the hell to put me. I opened for Oscar Peterson; I worked with Charlie Parker; I was down at the Earle Theater with Frankie Laine on his show.

"Teardrops" turned it all around.

"Teardrops" went to the top of the charts and stayed some twenty weeks up there. That song moved Atlantic up as a record company. And with that song, I started to be boxed over there, in R&B. You had Roy Brown, Charles Brown, Larry Darnell, the Dominoes, the Drifters — all of these people were sort of in that.

Rhythm & blues was becoming popular.

Rhythm & blues was a hot item, and that's when I started headlining a lot of package shows. We worked in barns and warehouses in the South.

You had three huge R&B hits in the early Fifties: "Teardrops," "5-10-15 Hours" and "(Mama) He Treats Your Daughter Mean," but I gather that it was still black radio playing them for a predominantly black audience.

Well, it couldn't basically be an all-black audience, because by that time the concerts were integrated, but separately. You had white spectators who had to be listening to the black radio stations. That's why eventually you had to get rock & roll.

Did each tour seem to attract more whites?

Yeah, yeah, and there would be promoters who had sense enough to work together; one would be white and one would be black. And the concerts would be — downstairs where the dancers were — jam-packed black. Upstairs balcony, all the way around: white spectators. Then a lot of times when the building

didn't allow for that — if you had a warehouse or something like that, where there wasn't two layers — they had a dividing line on the floor. That was the rope; sometimes it was just a clothesline with a sign hung on one side to separate them. Or there would be some big, burly white cops standing on one side to make sure that the rope stayed in position, which a lot of times it didn't, because people got to go dancing, and they didn't give a damn about the rope.

Were you making a lot of money at this point?

On my one-nighters, no, but we thought we were.

How about from the records?

I wasn't getting any royalties at the time. You would go in and record singles, either two sides or four, and you'd get $69 or $79 a side, so you're talking maybe $150 for the session. I think the highest was when you got up to about $250.

And there were no royalties at all?

At that time they were charging *you* for everything. You paid for the studio, you paid for the musicians, you paid for the charts, you paid for all the records that were given out for P.R. purposes, you paid for the manuscript paper, you paid for everything. If you needed something, you could always go to the record company and get a couple of hundred bucks.

But you were making money on the road — what you *thought* was money. Like, if I made $750 a night, that's a lot of money. Out of that $750, you had to pay for your hotel bill and everything, but my father made $35 a week on his job, with eight children. That was the danger point for many of us: to have come from an existence where you learned to live on a man's salary of $35 a week. That's a big shift.

At what point did rhythm & blues start becoming rock & roll?

When the white kids started to dance to it. It was the same music, just different people doing it, that's all it was. We went to Cleveland a couple of times and met this guy called Moondog, who later became Alan Freed, but by this time the white kids had took to this music. They loved it. They had bought it; they didn't give a damn who played it — if your face was green — and Alan Freed was smart enough to see that.

Was Alan Freed unique among white DJs?

There started to be quite a few of them; all the cities had somebody in a little corner doing something. He just got the prominence because he was smart enough to start putting shows together. He out-extravaganza'd the extravaganzas. He was smart enough to mix the acts.

jerry wexler and **ahmet ertegun** of Atlantic Records, >
"The House That Ruth Built," with their biggest star
MICHAEL OCHS ARCHIVES/VENICE, CA

And cover versions of black tunes done by white artists started to proliferate. Do you remember some Ruth Brown covers?

Patti Page covered me. Tony Bennett covered me. Georgia Gibbs covered me. Kay Starr covered me.

Was this in any perverse way flattering?

Well, some people might have thought it was flattering, but for me, it didn't do a damn thing except stop me from getting on the top TV shows. I never got to do *The Ed Sullivan Show*. Patti Page did; Georgia Gibbs did.

Your first crossover hit didn't come until 1957, when "Lucky Lips," a pretty silly Leiber and Stoller song, made it to the pop Top Forty.

Leiber and Stoller were coming up with things for the Coasters, and they came up with this song for me. Atlantic was kind of fighting them to see what direction I was going to go in. This was the only song that got me on the Dick Clark show. So I did *American Bandstand*—big deal! Because of "Lucky Lips." What about all the other ones I had? I felt kind of ridiculous singing, "When I was just a little girl, with long and silky curls." Never had no long and silky curls in all my life.

Did you notice any payola going on?

Uh-huh, uh-huh. Yeah, it was obvious that some record companies were taken care of better than others, and that was when you started to notice that the business itself was really a business. You know, there were people collecting tickets and not tearing up the tickets, and taking them back to the people that were selling the tickets, and they would resell the tickets. And you look up sometimes, and the valets and whatnot are looking better than you are.

Did the business begin to turn sour for you?

Well, with the packaging of the big shows, it started to become sort of like a rat race. Performances ceased being experiences and started being like "Here's twenty-one people, each singing one song." I did the Alan Freed show and sang "Lucky Lips" seven times a day, every day. Fiasco is what it started to be. It became so huge, it was like circus time. We'd just meet each other running. I'd bump into the Platters, they'd run up there—[*sings*] "Only yo-o-o-ou"— and before they could get to the chorus, they were off, they're gone; and somebody else, Buddy Knox, is up and does "Party Doll," one song; the Turbans, one song. "Hi, how are you, here we go again." There ceased to be fulfillment.

When did you notice things turning bad for you at Atlantic, the House That Ruth Built?

When I sat in the office one time for four hours before they paid any attention to me. I went over to see them, and by that time the secretaries had secretaries who had secretaries. And I had to stop at the desk and leave my name. "Oh, do they know what this is in reference to?" I said, "I'd like to speak to Mr. Ertegun if possible; if not, his secretary." And I was told to take a seat. And four hours after that, I'm still sitting there.

I was hurt. The receptionist would look at me like I was something that she smelled. And I had gone there to ask for a loan. I was in a little difficulty. But I went rather than called, because I didn't want to be passed from one secretary to the other, and I went hoping to talk to Ahmet on a one-to-one basis.

You were with Atlantic until 1961. Did you have much contact with Ahmet Ertegun in those last couple of years?

No.

You had some difficult years after that.

I got myself a day job, a nine-to-five. Things were just not going well. I was trying to carry on a house out on Long Island with my children, so I became a domestic. And worked in schools—in Head Start, day care, drove school buses. I did that up until 1976. By that time, I had gotten both of my children in college, and I started to climb back up by my fingernails again.

Did you at any point think, "I made an awful lot of money for somebody once; where's all my money?"

That came along in the Seventies. I started seeing records coming out of Europe and different places.

Reissues of your Atlantic albums.

Yeah, and I kept looking in the mailbox and wondering. So I got a lawyer on Long Island to contact Atlantic about my royalties—three lawyers, in fact. And each time there would be a lapse of about a month or so, and then they'd write back and say it was a dead issue: "Well, we wrote to Atlantic, and here is a photostatic copy of the response we got." And each time it would say that Ruth Brown's account is so far in arrears that she owes *us* so many thousands of dollars. Each attorney would come back and say the same thing: "Don't bother with this."

At what point did you make peace with Atlantic?

Through an attorney named Howell Begle. He was a Ruth Brown fan; his mother had taken him to see an

TO
RUTH BROWN
IN HONOR OF HER
FIVE MILLION RECORD

ATLANTIC RECORDS

Alan Freed show. He came to see me perform years later, and he had about eight or nine albums for me to autograph. And I said, "Where did you get all these records?" And he said, "I paid dearly for them, but they're very precious to me."

And I said, "Well, I don't know who got the money that you paid for these, but *I* didn't." And I went on to tell him that I hadn't gotten a royalty statement in over twenty-five years. He couldn't believe it. I said, "Well, not only me. There are a whole lot of us." He said, "Let's have lunch and talk."

When was that?

About ten years ago. He said, "I want to try and help you."

When did you know Howell Begle was getting some results?

When he called me to come to Washington in front of the Senate investigative committee. Then one day I got a statement from Atlantic. *Whoa!* I hadn't seen a statement since I don't know when. They said they didn't know how to find me, that they'd been sending statements to Portsmouth, Virginia, where I hadn't lived in 450 years.

I was doing a little off-Broadway show called *Staggerlee*, and the doorman came and said, "There's a man out here from a record company who wants to see you." I thought perhaps somebody was coming to talk about recording me, because indeed I could use it. And so I said, "Who is it? What record company?"

And a voice said, "It's Ahmet from Atlantic." And there he was. He had seen the show, and he stood in the door—I just looked at him, he looked at me, and I think his eyes got watery, and I got watery. Before I knew it, the tears were running. And he just walked over to me, and I embraced him, and he said in my ear, "Let's don't talk now, but everything's going to be all right. I'd never let anything happen to you."

But he did turn and say, "You know, Ruth, you got a good lawyer."

buddy holly's
texas

By KINKY FRIEDMAN

"I could hardly see across the street. Men had their hats over their faces. Women had their scarves over their mouths with one hand and held down their skirts with another. The dust was like a curtain. It was the middle of the afternoon, and Amarillo was almost dark. Everything was leaning—stoplights, elm trees, my momma and daddy. I was between them at a downtown Pontiac dealership.

"There was a curious crowd gathered around a flatbed trailer. They were listening to a salesman trying to make himself heard over the wind that was popping in a chrome microphone. I remember being fascinated with that strange crackling sound that was coming out of a bent speaker that was propped up between some concrete blocks.

"There was also this wild man pounding the dogshit out of this flimsy piano in a raging dust storm. The wind kept blowing over his mike stand, and I kept wondering if his piano was going to turn to splinters and blow on over to Oklahoma. It terrified me to no end, and I edged around back of my daddy. And this wild man kept pounding, hair in his face, with the wind howling around brand-new dusty automobiles.

"It was more than terrifying; it gave me a direction to follow."

—*JOE ELY on seeing Jerry Lee Lewis*

The past and the present, I've always thought, are very deeply intertwined. History is what happens when one of them gets a little ahead of the other. This is probably why inspiration is often borrowed in the strangest ways from other places and other times.

Before they were moptops, the Beatles cut their hair like Tony Curtis and took their name from the Lubbock, Texas, band the Crickets. One of the Beatles' earliest, funkiest, most primitive-sounding demos reportedly was a cover of "That'll Be the Day," which was never released and remained "lost" over the years like a pearl in the snow. Eventually, the original demo was sold at Sotheby's to an unknown buyer for a price supposedly in the neighborhood of $40,000 possibly a Japanese insurance company or someone with the soul of a Japanese insurance company.

The demo itself may no longer be important, but its reason for existing in the first place tells us something vital about the deep, gnarly, long-reaching roots of rock & roll. And it tells us something about the spirit of a time and a place far away. The song was written by Buddy Holly immediately after seeing a John Wayne movie.

They say Texas is a state of mind, and maybe it is. The Texas tradition of music is so deep and multilayered it would require seven archaeologists with seven brooms seven years just to clear away the dust. When they got to the bottom, after digging through village upon village, they'd probably find King of Western Swing Bob Wills's cigar lying next to blues legend Mance Lipscomb's guitar.

Being the oldest living Jew in Texas who doesn't own any real estate, I recall growing up in the early Fifties as a bastard child of twin cultures. The only thing I could see that Jewboys and cowboys seemed to have in common was that they both wore their hats indoors and attached a certain amount of importance to it. Later I observed other similarities as the two ways of life melded into my own. The songs of both groups, it seemed, were invariably heartfelt, and the music was always of the traveling variety. I realized that cowboys and Jewboys were both wandering—very possibly vanishing—gypsies of the soul, and whether you light campfires or candles as you walk the tortuous trail of this world, nobody really gives a damn whether you make it to the last roundup.

The influence of music on Texas and the music of Texans on the world, be it black, rock & roll or country, is enormous. Not only did Buddy Holly influence the Beatles and T-Bone Walker influence the Rolling Stones, but Texas's early singing cowboys reached higher into the firmament than they might've known. A girl named Anne Frank, with just a fountain pen, touched the conscience of more people than did the entire propaganda machinery of Hitler's Third Reich. After the war, local authorities checked the secret annex in which she and her family had lived. In Anne's little corner of the annex, pictures of American cowboy stars were still fluttering on the walls where she'd left them.

Musically and culturally speaking, the Fifties in Texas were in many ways as insulated as Anne Frank's world. When the decade was dawning, even Willie Nelson, who would become a symbol of Texas and much of its musical legacy by the Seventies, couldn't find anyone willing to give him a tumble.

"In 1950, I was seventeen years old, fresh out of high school," Nelson says. "A quick, miserable eight months in the U.S. Air Force, and then back to Texas to restart my music career. On the way through the Fifties in Texas, I sold cars and books in Fort Worth, where I was fired as a singer in a North Side bar because I wasn't commercial. I guess you could say the Fifties in Texas were noncommercial for me."

Eventually, though, Texas did become a financial pleasure for Nelson, and because of Texas, the rest of the world became one, too. Maybe it's because Texas provided physical and spiritual elbowroom.

Texas's size and fierce independence of spirit often seem to produce an achingly vibrant expanse of time and geography, out of which it is sometimes possible to dream a little bigger. This is not only true for Willie Nelson; it is the only way the Buddy Hollys of this planet are born.

Buddy Holly grew up in the Panhandle of Texas in a simpler time. Cadillacs were getting longer, tail fins were getting higher, dreams were getting as close as they ever do to coming true. It was an era of boom and innocence. As Kent Perkins, an old friend of mine, observed: "Man had not discovered the moon, but he had discovered the moon pie." And nobody remembered where they were the day Kennedy was shot. Buddy Holly was a child of his times.

Sonny Curtis, a member of the Crickets (and possibly the only American to have his songs recorded by both Bing Crosby and the Dead Kennedys), remembers that Holly had a wide appreciation of all musical forms, from bluegrass to early blues stylings by blacks. Curtis first met Holly in Lubbock, Texas, in 1951 and has vivid memories of staying up half the night in Buddy's car, listening to *Stan's Record Rack*, a blues program out of Shreveport, Louisiana. Holly's love of early black music is obvious. He recorded "Rip It Up," by Little Richard, and "Brown Eyed Handsome Man," by Chuck Berry, and often sang Ray Charles's songs, including "I Got a Woman" and "This Little Girl of Mine."

In 1956, Curtis went to Lubbock's Cotton Club to see the blues piano player Charles Brown and remembers being "the only white face in the place." Ironically enough, in early 1957, when Buddy Holly and the Crickets played the Apollo Theatre in Harlem, they were the only white group on the program because of a mix-up by the promoter, who thought they were black. The crowd didn't mind, however. They loved them.

Holly's harmonies also show a clear bluegrass influence. According to Curtis, Holly once tried unsuccessfully to copy Earl Scruggs's stylings with just a flatpick and a four-string banjo.

But two things happened in 1955 that turned Holly's head around: One was meeting Bob Wills at the Clover Club in Amarillo; the other was when Elvis Presley came through Lubbock. Curtis remembers that Elvis wore red pants, an orange jacket and white bucks, and Holly and Curtis—both around seventeen at the time—thought that was about the coolest thing they'd ever seen. The two of them had opened the January 2, 1955, show, so they had backstage privileges, which included talking to Elvis and "getting right up in his face." Elvis had recorded "That's All Right (Mama)" on Sun Records, and Holly was already a big fan. Curtis also recalls that cotton bales were set up all around the stage and police were posted to keep women from attacking Elvis. Presley got paid seventy-five dollars for the show, which he split with Bill Black, his bass player, and Scotty Moore, his guitar player. The day after the show, according to Curtis, he and Holly started "playing Elvis full tilt."

Holly was into leatherwork at the time, and Curtis remembers Buddy making a beautiful wallet trimmed in pink and black with ELVIS in pink letters. A year and a half later, driving through Memphis on the way to Nashville, Holly dropped the wallet off for Elvis at Sun Records. By then, of course, Elvis wasn't using wallets. He was using wheelbarrows.

Sonny Curtis's recollections effectively evoke the pure rock & roll innocence and exuberance of the times. "We used to rehearse in Holly's garage because they had an old, empty butane tank in there, and we'd get a great echo from it," Curtis says of Holly's first band in high school. "We were so excited. It was almost like something was looming in the future."

The Pulitzer Prize–winning writer Larry McMurtry remembers the Fifties in Texas as "a dying twinge of depression; gray, dust blown, intolerant." Ray Benson of Asleep at the Wheel recalls that Texas was "heaven, although hotter than hell the summer of '58 to an eight-year-old Yankee who loved Roy Rogers, Tex Ritter and all singing cowboys." Larry King, the playwright who wrote *The Best Little Whorehouse in Texas*, remembers the times as being "superreactionary, segregationist and mean." I remember taking jitterbug lessons in Houston, Texas, from a girl named Susan Kaufman.

Maybe all of us were right. One thing is for sure, though: At the beginning of the decade, the black music and the white music were almost as completely separate as the segregated communities from which they came. With time, radio, the borrowing of inspiration, stylings and good looks and the help of undaunted early musical pioneers, the cultures grew together in the dusty laboratory of life into a wild, highly contagious new strain of music called rock & roll.

Houston record producer Huey P. Meaux saw no reason for the separation. He remembers blacks and whites crossing the tracks, picking cotton together, singing together in the fields, then going home their separate ways. He recalls sitting in the swamps as a child, getting eaten alive by mosquitoes, listening to black people playing blues. That was as close as the times would let him get.

"Blues and country are the same thing," says Meaux. "Just the moods are different. It all comes from life experiences." The early bluesmen were real, he believes; they bucked the system, they "could care less if the Russians invaded today or tomorrow." This attitude was later adopted by the rockers of the Sixties, who widened the scope a bit: They didn't care if the Martians invaded today or tomorrow.

Along with Alan Freed and Phil Spector, Meaux experimented with what was at the time labeled "mix-breeding music." All three suffered for it, Meaux contends, but he adds that they eventually "broke a hole through the clouds." It didn't make much sense that Jimmy Reed, Chuck Berry, Fats Domino and Little Richard played mostly to white people and that T-Bone Walker, Percy Mayfield, Charles Brown and Big Mama Thornton played mostly for blacks. Why not widen the audience as much as possible?

The Big Bopper, J.P. Richardson, was the first disc jockey in Texas to play a mixed-format show that was so hot nobody could touch his ratings with a barge pole. "The blue-chip white cats hated it," Meaux says of the show on Beaumont's KTRM and the changes it helped produce, "but black and white kids were going to the sock hops together."

Meaux remembers the Big Bopper, who recorded for Mercury, getting ready for a session. In 1958, they were all convinced that "The Purple People Eater Meets the Witch Doctor" was going to be a big hit, but the record needed a backside; forty-eight hours before the session, Richardson wrote "Chantilly Lace." It was one of the first major commercial successes of black vocal stylings performed by a white artist.

Blacks were also beginning to embrace a different kind of music. Just a week before Buddy Holly first saw Elvis Presley, R&B crooner Johnny Ace lost his last game of Russian roulette. It happened backstage on Christmas night at Houston's Civic Auditorium, where the singer was appearing. Ace's death remains a rather mysterious one, and many say that he was murdered. The twenty-five-year-old Ace had a huge hit song at the time, "Pledging My Love."

According to Meaux, "Johnny Ace was the first black guy I know of, way before Ray Charles, who could sing country-tainted songs—blues and country together. He cried a song, and it was a feeling you couldn't forget. He had teardrops in his voice."

The cross-pollination wasn't limited to Texas: Imagine a line stretching from San Antonio to Baton Rouge to Macon, Georgia. Below that line is an area that has consistently turned out artists who appeal to both black and white listeners. The reason, Meaux says, is that every fifty to a hundred miles there was a little enclave of Czechs, Bohemians, Poles, Mexicans or Cajuns who played Polish polkas, Mexican polkas, Cajun two-steps, boleros, waltzes, conjunto and many other unique musical forms.

"In those days," says Meaux, "you had to learn to play different towns with different nationalities and musical stylings." Singer and accordionist Clifton Chenier, whom Meaux produced, helped effect a special kind of musical hybrid, combining black and Cajun-style music to create zydeco.

Black music and the blues have had so much influence upon the world that if you look at the whole cloth of today's music, the black threads almost seem to hold the tapestry together. Those black threads go all the way back to the old bluesmen. Some lacked education and couldn't write down the lyrics, some often forgot them, and some probably liked to give the guys who were following them around with tape recorders a hard time, but one fact Huey P. Meaux knows for sure: "Old blues cats never sang the same song the same way twice."

Back in the Fifties, the hard-shell Southern Baptists used to pull down their window shades when they were hosing, so nobody'd think they were dancing. We had religion in Texas in those days, but as far as I can remember, nobody was born again. Most of us figured it'd been tedious enough the first time around.

But there are many ways of "seeing the light" in this world, and one of them has always been through country music. Hank Williams's death, on January 1, 1953, struck a muted, lingering chord across the South. Williams was only twenty-nine when he died, younger than Jesus and Mozart. He wasn't born in Texas, but his music will always live there. Maybe there's something in the dust and the dreams and the distance of Texas that has helped Williams's music carry across the years. His last hit became a cultural anthem for the people on the lost highway of the Fifties. It was "I'll Never Get Out of This World Alive."

There were other voices of the times, though, other stars in the Texas sky—Bob Wills and the Texas Playboys, Ernest Tubb, Hank Thompson and Charlie Walker, to name a few. In 1958, Walker, a boyhood hero of mine, had the big country hit "Pick Me Up on Your Way Down."

"In the early Fifties," Walker told me, "I had a country-music club, the Old Barn, in San Antonio. Hank Williams played for me there on his last birthday, September 17, 1952. He had the Number One song in the country, 'Jambalaya,' and was paid $500."

The roots of some of our most enduring contemporary country musicians in Texas easily reach back into the Fifties and further. Jerry Jeff Walker and Billy Joe Shaver seem to have an almost karmic linkage with the storytelling singing cowboy. Ray Benson and Asleep at the Wheel have made new generations aware of the great tradition of the Western swing bands that once dominated the Southwestern musical landscape. Keyboardist Augie Meyers, who played with Doug Sahm, derived his style from Spanish country music, which features the accordion and the *bajo sexto*, a Spanish guitar fitted with twelve piano strings.

These distinctive styles nevertheless fall under the heading of country, and the country-music boom in the Fifties enriched them all. If country music truly stems from life experiences, then the Fifties were vividly real, undecaffeinated times. The Fifties in Texas may not have been the Twenties in Paris, but how many different kinds of sauces can you put on a chicken-fried steak?

In the end, all that seems to survive is the music. Where it originated, what its influences were, how it was passed along, we can't always know for sure. But we do know that before the Beatles started listening to the Crickets, and before Huey P. Meaux and a few other brave souls began messing with the music and the minds of so many different kinds of people, still-earlier instances of "mix breeding" had occurred.

One such incident took place around 1935 and involved a twelve-year-old boy who would go further than he dreamed and a man named Tee-tot. Tee-tot was a black blues singer who literally sang for his supper, and on the streets of Greenville, Alabama, he taught Hank Williams how to play the guitar.

If Williams's death brought the Fifties in with a dull, gray morning, Buddy Holly's plane crash over Clear Lake, Iowa, on February 3, 1959, was the other spiritual bookend to the decade. What Buddy Holly, Hank Williams, Johnny Ace or, for that matter, Mozart and Jesus, might've become had they lived is something about which we can only speculate. As Will Rogers once remarked: "Longevity has ruined as many men as it's made."

Some things change, and some things remain the same, and some you always seem to miss the first time around so you're never sure what happened to them. "Hell, in the Forties we were still riding horses to school," says Larry King, "but by the Sixties we'd be riding, stoned, in new cars on new freeways." The DON'T SPIT ON THE FLOOR sign that graced the wall inside the Medina, Texas, post office disappeared sometime in the late Fifties. There are still occasional WE RESERVE THE RIGHT TO REFUSE SERVICE TO ANYONE signs in little, out-of-the-way greasy spoons around Texas, but they hang rather forlornly and mostly just gather cob-webs these days. And the oldest Methodist church in Kerrville had the cross lopped off the top of it and an aluminum drive-through window installed and became a savings and loan. Now *that's* progress.

You'll be pleased to know, however, that according to the Kerrville Bus Company's posted regulations, it is still prohibited to transport bull semen by bus.

my top ten albums of the fifties

By JOHN FOGERTY

I bought many singles, but eventually I wanted to have them in an album, because that artist's world was more completely encapsulated in the album. These records really dominated their time. You'd hear more than just the singles, in much the same way that *Meet the Beatles* was all over the radio in the Sixties. The songs on these records were so great they *had* to play them.

1 ***Elvis Presley*** and ***Elvis*** (RCA). *Goddang!* What a voice! This guy jumped out of those records and took the whole genre along with him. Elvis invented what—because of the success of those records—from then on would be the essential, pivotal rock & roll band: two guitars, bass and drums. I still think a four-piece is the most complete-sounding and most versatile rock & roll band there can be.

2 ***Rock Around the Clock,*** by Bill Haley and His Comets (Decca). I was up in Santa Rosa, visiting my dad, and I was going to buy Elvis's first album. I walked three or four miles to the little shopping center, and the record was sold out. So instead I said, "Well, it's got to be *Rock Around the Clock*, then"—which was every bit as cool. It's a record I listened to thousands and thousands of times. One of my all-time favorite songs, "ABC Boogie," is on this album. The song was about these kids in this mythical classroom somewhere learning the ABC's of rock & roll. I was the right age—eleven.

3 ***Have "Twangy" Guitar Will Travel,*** by Duane Eddy (Jamie). This is one of the ten best records of *all time*. It's influenced me in so many ways. The sound of "Moovin' 'n' Groovin'," the first hit, was just amazing. Duane, of course, was an instrumentalist. When I think of him, I get a picture of this big, fat, tremolo-y guitar in my head, but it's almost like it had words and a voice, too. It's every bit as distinctive as Elvis's voice. I've been hearing people imitate Duane Eddy, and usually it pales by comparison.

The titles, like "Rebel Rouser" and "Ramrod," fit the music and seemed to say so much. I was once asked, "What's the most important thing having to do with a hit record?" I said, "The title."

4 ***Bo Diddley*** (Checker). People sometimes associate me with spooky, almost voodoo imagery. If there's any one place that comes from, it's that Bo Diddley record. Bo Diddley was just the master of that primitive thing. He appealed to things that were—I would say "sexual," except I was too young at the time to know what that was. It opened a door to that primitive thing. I went into that room through Bo Diddley's door.

5 ***Here's Little Richard*** and ***Little Richard*** (Specialty). I'm sitting here visualizing the albums' covers. They captured the essence of Little Richard. This screaming face with sweat running down. This guy with the best scream in all of rock & roll. Little Richard had the essential tools. He had them all. I still believe his voice was more rock & roll than Elvis's. Unrelenting, high-energy rock & roll—and that's even on the slow songs.

6 *Ray Charles in Person* (Atlantic). This is the great live record that had "What'd I Say," "Tell the Truth" and particularly, "The Right Time." As I recall, the liner notes said it was recorded with somebody from the local radio station holding up a single microphone a hundred feet from the stage. I've always considered this the greatest live album of all time. The recording transcended whatever studios sound like. It was a very mysterious sound, almost ghostly. It sounds like night.

7 *The "Chirping" Crickets,* by Buddy Holly and the Crickets (Brunswick). This is one of the pillars of rock & roll. Buddy Holly excelled at pretty melodies and heartfelt songs sung to a rock & roll beat. He had a fragile, vulnerable sound but to a rock & roll beat. He was off all by himself. Believe me, I've tried to sing "Peggy Sue" in the shower with all the hiccups and everything. You can't. No one else could get away with it.

8 *Rock and Rollin',* by Fats Domino (Imperial). That's the one that had "The Fat Man" on it. I don't know why "The Fat Man" isn't a required rock anthem the way "Jailhouse Rock" is—it's certainly the connection between rock & roll and New Orleans. I consider Fats Domino one of the founding fathers of rock & roll, although he doesn't get the play that somebody like Chuck Berry gets.

9 *After School Session,* by Chuck Berry (Chess). The songs seemed to reach right into our world. Because of Chuck's songwriting abilities, he managed to make images out of things that were otherwise ordinary, like the image of the guy rounding third base, headed for home—the Brown Eyed Handsome Man. It would take me three songs to get his images across.

10 *Jerry Lee Lewis* (Sun). I was able to buy this record on sale for two dollars in 1958. It probably had something to do with Jerry Lee's well-publicized scandalous behavior. I was twelve at the time, and I've always considered that the greatest bargain I've ever gotten in rock & roll. I got more pleasure, more use, more satisfaction out of that particular record than anything else I ever bought. It's outstanding.

little richard

By PARKE PUTERBAUGH

The Georgia Peach, the Living Flame, the Southern Child, the King of Rock & Roll: Little Richard is all of these, and he'll be the first to tell you so.

More than any other performer, Little Richard blew the lid off the Fifties. With his mascara-smeared face twisted in a midscream paroxysm of rapture and dementia, hair piled high in a proud pompadour, he was an explosive and charismatic performer who laid the foundation for rock & roll. His outrageous personality captured the music's rebellious spirit, and his frantically charged piano playing and raspy, shouted vocals defined its sound.

Little Richard was born Richard Penniman on December 5, 1932, in Macon, Georgia. His father, Charles "Bud" Penniman, sold moonshine and ran a tavern called the Tip In Inn. His mother, Leva Mae Penniman, raised Richard and eleven brothers and sisters in a small house in the Pleasant Hill section of Macon. As a youngster, Richard soaked up music, which was part of the fabric of life in the black community. He heard acts of all kinds at the Macon City Auditorium—blues, country, vaudeville—where he sold Cokes. He also went to church, not so much for the message as for the music: The fervid, unrestrained style of black gospel singing lit a fire in him.

Little Richard learned to play gospel piano from an equally flamboyant character named Esquerita, combining it with his own love of boogie-woogie in what became a blueprint of rock & roll. By his late teens, he was a veteran of several traveling vaudeville revues, where he was schooled in the theatrical side of performing. He cut his first sides for RCA Camden in 1951, followed by a string of singles for Peacock.

It was at Specialty Records, though, that the wild rock & roller within was turned loose. "One day a reel of tape, wrapped in a piece of paper looking as though someone had eaten off it, came across my desk," Specialty A&R man Robert "Bumps" Blackwell told Charles White, Little Richard's biographer. Richard was scrubbing pots and pans at the Greyhound bus station in Macon while waiting to hear from Specialty about his submission. In 1955 he got the green light, entering J&M Studio in New Orleans with Blackwell and some of the Crescent City's finest musicians. After a slow start, Blackwell grasped the untapped potential of Richard's singing and playing, and they switched gears from conventional urban blues to something that was raw, uptempo and undeniably *new*. The rest was rock & roll history, as Little Richard laid down a stunning succession of sides over the next several years, including "Tutti Frutti," "Slippin' and Slidin'," "Miss Ann," "Long Tall Sally," "Rip It Up," "Good Golly, Miss Molly," "Lucille" and "Keep a Knockin'."

Little Richard scaled the heights of fame as he toured the world with his peerless band the Upsetters, but his success, and the hypersexual lifestyle that went with it, came to an abrupt halt in 1957 when he abandoned rock & roll for religion. He attended Bible college and recorded gospel music until the early Sixties, when he made a triumphant and unexpected return to rock from the stage of a British concert hall. The second chapter of Little Richard's career as a rock & roller saw him recapture his popularity as a live performer and cut some well-received albums for Reprise. By 1975, however, a substance-abuse problem drove him to abandon rock & roll for the Rock of Ages once more.

In the Eighties, Little Richard began testing the waters again, and he has since appeared in films and TV shows, performed and recorded occasionally. His sporadic recordings include a 1992 children's album, *Shake It All About*, for Walt Disney Records. In 1993, he performed at the presidential inaugural.

The following interview was conducted in March 1990 in the mobile environs of a limousine cruising the freeways of Los Angeles, a city he began calling home in 1956. We broke for a lunch of fried chicken, pork chops and collard greens at a favorite soul-food eatery. During the meal, a braided and bespangled entertainer calling herself Afrodyete, the African Goddess of Love, presented him with a signed picture of *herself*, which was inscribed, "Stay Chocolate." With characteristic color-blind wit, Little Richard quipped, "'Stay Chocolate'? Suppose I feel like being pineapple tonight?"

Let's start with a simple question. Did you invent rock & roll?

Well, let me say it this way: When I first came along, I never heard any rock & roll. I only heard Elmore James, Muddy Waters, Sonny Boy Williamson, Ruth Brown and Roy Brown—blues. Fats Domino at the time was playing nothing but lowdown blues. When I started singing [rock & roll], I sang it a long time before I presented it to the public, because I was afraid they wouldn't like it. I had never heard nobody do it, and I was scared.

I was inspired by Mahalia Jackson, Roy Brown, and a gospel group called Clara Ward and the Ward Singers, and a guy by the name of Brother Joe May. I got the holler that you hear me do—"woo-oooh-oooh"—from a lady named Marion Williams. And this thing you hear me do—"Lucille-*uh*"—I got that from Ruth Brown. I used to like the way she'd sing, "Mama-*uh*, he treats your daughter mean." I put it all together.

I really feel from the bottom of my heart that I am the inventor. If there was somebody else, I didn't know them. Not even to this day. So I say I'm the architect.

Where were you hearing music—on records, jukeboxes or the radio?

We didn't have nothing to play records on, 'cause we were real poor. My mother had twelve children, so we didn't have nothing. We would listen to WLAC out of Tennessee. Back in that time boogie-woogie was very popular. I would say that boogie-woogie and rhythm & blues mixed is rock & roll.

Also, back in that time black people were singing a lot of country music. You didn't see this separation of music as you do today. I'm a country-music lover. I think it's a true music. It's from the heart.

Can you remember the first time you sang for people and got a reaction?

Yes. I sung a song called "Strange Things Happening Every Day," by Sister Rosetta Tharpe: [*sings*] "Oh, you hear church people say / We are in this holy way, / There are strange things happening every day...."

And I'd just beat this [*taps rhythm on car seat*] and sing, "There are strange things happening every day." People used to give me quarters and dimes and nickels to sing that song.

How did you choose the stage name Little Richard? Was there a Big Richard?

No [*laughs*]. At the time they had Little Esther, Little Willie John, Little Walter. Everybody was using the title *Little*. And most people used to call me "Penny-man," and nobody would say "Penniman." They couldn't pronounce my name. Another thing: My family did not approve of what I was doing, and I felt if I didn't use my name, people wouldn't know I was a part of them. I didn't want to hurt them. Music was not respected back then. To them, it was down. Everybody was down on it.

As a teenager, you went on the road with several vaudeville revues. What was your role in those shows?

I just wanted to tear up the house. I would pick up tables and chairs in my mouth and dance with them. I would let somebody stand on the table and dance while holding up the table in my mouth.

That sense of competition stayed. You just weren't going to let anyone upstage you.

That's right. I still have that. I think you have to have that in life. I would go onstage, and we didn't have stages like Michael [Jackson] and Prince or Bruce [Springsteen]. We had to go with what they had. If they had spotlights, they had them, but now they carry everything.

You had to do it all with charisma.

Yeah, and that's when I wore the colors, the sequins, the shoes made of stone, so they'd have something to light up.

In the forty-three years you've been playing, has anybody ever upstaged you, taken a show away from you?

Uh, yes: Jimi Hendrix. He was my guitar player, and you know, we didn't know he could play with his mouth. One night I heard this screamin' and hollerin', and they were screamin' and hollerin' for *him!* I thought they were screamin' for me, but he was back there playin' the guitar with his mouth. He didn't do it again, 'cause we made sure the lights didn't come on that area no more. We fixed that! We made *sure* that was a black spot!

How did you end up at Specialty Records?

Lloyd Price came through my hometown. He had this black-and-gold Cadillac, and I wanted a car like that. I said, "How'd you get famous?" He told me about Specialty and gave me the address. I did a tape, and I sent this to Specialty. A year later they got in touch with me.

Did Art Rupe, the owner of Specialty, match you up with Bumps Blackwell?

No. Bumps was the A&R man for Specialty Records. He was in charge of everything. Art Rupe didn't know anything about music. Bumps had been with Quincy Jones and Ray Charles and all those people. Ray Charles did his first tour with us. He didn't have a band. It was my band that played behind him. And he had "I Got a Woman" and sung that on the tour, with my band backing him up. Am I tellin' the truth, Ray? You used to come by my room and tell me, "That's the prettiest suit you got on. I like that suit, that green suit" [*laughs*].

Did you enjoy recording in New Orleans?

Oh, yes. You've got to remember that the same band recorded with me, Fats Domino, Smiley Lewis, Shirley and Lee, Professor Longhair. It was the same band: Lee Allen, Red Tyler, Earl Palmer—all those guys. When they played for me, I played the piano. When they played for Fats, Fats played the piano.

How would you compare recording in the Fifties with recording today?

I enjoyed recording back then better 'cause it was real. You had to play. It wasn't no machines; you couldn't just mash buttons and sound like a band. If you couldn't play, you didn't have no music.

Were your songs based on real characters? Was there a Miss Molly, a Lucille, Miss Ann, Long Tall Sally?

There was a Miss Ann. She was a white lady I used to work for. She had a club in Macon called Ann's Tick Tock. She and her husband, Johnny, were like family to me. They had been good to me when a lot of people hadn't. I really appreciated them, so when I got famous, I made up a song. That's the only real person.

What do you think it was about your music that helped bridge the gap between the races?

"Tutti Frutti" really started the races being together. Because when I was a boy, the white people would sit upstairs. They called it "white spectators," and the blacks was downstairs, and the white kids would jump over the balcony and come down where I was and dance with the blacks. We started that merging all across the country. From the git-go, my music was accepted by whites. Pat Boone covered "Tutti Frutti," made it broader, 'cause they played him more on the white stations.

You could argue it both ways, but overall do you think Pat Boone's cover versions helped or hurt your career?

I believe it was a blessing. I believe it opened the highway that would have taken a little longer for acceptance. So I love Pat for that.

That said, what did you honestly think of his recording of "Tutti Frutti"?

He did the best he could. I think mine was the best, but Pat Boone's version was all right. I think he was forced to record it. He was a balladeer and not a rock singer. I believe his record company saw a chance for him to get bigger.

Is it true you sang "Long Tall Sally" so fast that he'd have difficulty covering it?

Yes, I figured that since he outsold me with "Tutti Frutti," I'd put so many tricks in "Long Tall Sally" he couldn't get it.

How do you think the Beatles did with it?

Fantastic. I think the Beatles did one of the best versions of "Long Tall Sally" I've ever heard.

You toured with them in England before they broke over here, didn't you?

Oh, before they ever recorded, before anybody ever *heard* of a record company.

Did you see potential in them?

I saw it in Paul McCartney. Paul was the one who was so crazy about me. Paul and George. I believe they had it—they were gifted.

They were gifted, but they also did their homework.

They knew who we recorded with; they knew what doorsteps we walked up; they knew what saxophone we played. They knew more about it than me!

Do you see in Prince a younger version of yourself?

Yes, I do.

Do you like his music?

Oh, I really like Prince. I like Prince a lot. I like

Michael Jackson. I like Bon Jovi. I like Bruce Springsteen. I like a lot of them. I get that old thing from them—I think that's the reason I like them.

Have you worked with any producers since Bumps Blackwell who have been able to capture your sound?

It has to be someone who feels that type of music. I think the problem [in 1990] is that a lot of black entertainers don't feel the old music. A lot of white entertainers still use the music, while black people have gone to another type of thing, the synthesized thing that you hear. And you will hear, like, [*sings*] "My, my, my; / Once bitten, twice shy, babe."

"Once Bitten Twice Shy," [a 1989 hit by metal band] Great White.

Now, that's the old way. See, the blacks have gotten so that's not what they want. They like this other thing, with the synthesizer, and the whites are still with the old music. So that's the reason when you play for them, you feel comfortable. They appreciate the type of music, the old music, that you play.

Especially in the Seventies, your audience became really lopsided toward whites over blacks.

With the black audience, if you don't have a hit record, they don't support you. If you've got a hit record, it's all right, but if you don't, you're in trouble.

Do you think the black audience at large will ever get interested in black music from a more historical perspective?

They *should*. I believe that Michael Jackson's generation will be more up on it than my generation. I believe black people love me, and I believe they appreciate me, but I'm not recording the kind of music they want to hear in this generation. I am where I am, so that's it.

You've claimed that your band the Upsetters was the best show band in the country.

Oh, they were. They were choreographed by me and by Grady [Gaines, the tenor saxophonist]. They wore makeup. They wore beautiful colors. It was the only band with a makeup kit. You thought they were showgirls, but they were *showboys*. They were very good. Until this day, I haven't seen another band surpass them.

Would you have preferred to cut your Specialty sides with the Upsetters instead of the New Orleans guys?

I did do one song with them, "Keep a Knockin'." We did that in Washington, D.C. You can't tell the difference, can you?

No, you can't. Led Zeppelin nicked the drum intro on "Rock and Roll." Have you heard that?

No. Did you know Led Zeppelin's manager used to be my chauffeur? Peter Grant was my chauffeur for about three years! I used to argue with him all the time. I saw him in Miami later on, and he said, "Little Richard, I'm wealthy now. I'm a millionaire. You want me to buy you dinner?" I said, "No, Peter."

He said, "I'm gonna buy it, anyway. I have a group called Led Zeppelin. I don't have to take your abuse anymore" [*laughs loudly*]. Old Peter!

And you know, Sonny Bono used to drive me, too. That's before Cher. That was about 1958. He was working for Specialty Records, and they used to send him to ride me around.

As far as your live shows, which are considered to be some of the most incendiary performances in the history of rock & roll, where did the energy come from?

I don't know, and it still comes. We just did Palm Springs, and it was unbelievable. People was crying, screaming. You wouldn't believe I was the age that I am. It was just like a power, and you felt like crying. When I touched the piano, the house just went insane.

In the Fifties, you'd scream, pound the piano and toss clothes into the crowd. How did you rise to that level every night?

I didn't drink or smoke at the time. I didn't take any dope or nothing. The music turned me on. The music still does it! If the music is good, you got me.

Were you ever concerned that you'd taken an audience too far? Has it ever gotten to a point where it became dangerous?

I have seem 'em go a long way. I have seen people worked into frenzies, yeah. I've seen 'em foaming at the mouth; I've seen 'em fall out. I've seen people screamin', cryin', can't stop. I've seen girls who just wanted to touch me, just screamin', lookin' at me, screamin', and fallin' out.

Wasn't there a night when the stage actually caved in?

Collapsed. That was the Olympic Auditorium [in Los Angeles]. The piano fell. The stage fell. One guy broke his leg. It was pandemonium. The crowd was screaming, and they kept screaming. I was on top of the piano, and I was screamin', too, 'cause I was fallin'. Everybody was screamin'. Screamin' and screamin'!

Did you ever get into what the jazz people call cutting contests, where you'd be on the bill with someone, and you'd each be trying to top the other?

Oh, I've been on plenty of those. Me and Chuck Berry, for instance, have done it plenty of times.

He'd say that he's the star, and I'd say that I'm the star. He'd say, "I'm gonna close the show." I'd say, "No, you're not."

I've been on a bill with Jerry Lee Lewis like that, too, and I'd say, "Okay, you can close the show." And I'd go on first and sing for about two hours, and then can't *nobody* come on the stage. We were all of us vain back in that time. It's a shame. The young and crazy often need a spankin' and a plankin'.

What was it like after a show? What would you do to wind down?

I would go to clubs just to hear girls scream. I would go to clubs to have a good time and then bring girls back to the hotel.

We have an impression of the Fifties as being a very staid and conservative era, but to hear you talk, it sounds a lot more sexually liberated than people might imagine.

Oh, it was liberated all right! It was experimental, too, 'cause we were young and hadn't done a lot of things. Being a country boy from the South, I had been held back. My family was religious. Sometimes you couldn't toe-tap or tap a toe or ask for mo', and that's for sho'! And that's the way it go! And we was po'!

I used to like a lot of girls back in that time. But I wasn't into anything out of the ordinary—just regular do's.

Where do you stand on homosexuality now? You made some pretty strong statements against it in your book [*The Life and Times of Little Richard*, by Charles White].

I'm not against it. I believe God gives every man a choice. Every man has a choice to do what he will, bad or good, right or wrong, black or white, rich or poor. I was just saying that from where I stand, a lot of people think different things because of the way you look. Some people will judge you, and they don't even *know* you. I played the piano, I wore the hair, I wore the makeup, and everybody classified me without asking me anything.

But didn't you want to be "the Living Flame," "the Bronze Liberace"?

I *am* the Living Flame. Not so much the Bronze Liberace, but I am the Living Flame. I just wanted to be a musician that spread joy to people. I'm not down on any lifestyle, any shape, form or fashion. Whether God has sanctioned our lifestyle or not, we still have a right to do what we want. So I'm not putting anything down. Neither am I picking anything up! [*Chuckles*] And I'll leave it right there.

When you had your first religious conversion in 1957, what persuaded you to walk away from the phenomenal popularity you'd worked so hard for as a rock & roller?

I wish I knew then what I know today. I was young and didn't have anybody to talk to. I've always been religious, basically. I wanted to do God's will. I've always wanted to do his will. But at the time, I had nobody to really counsel with.

Touring must have taken a toll.

No, I enjoyed touring, but I had a bad dream. I think the dream kind of disturbed me; the thoughts kind of shook my mind. The dream was "Prepare for eternal life." That was it.

And you went to Bible school.

Yes. Let me let down this window and say hello to these people [*rolls down the window of the limousine and greets a couple on the sidewalk*]. I just wanted to make their day. Excuse me. I feel all right [*laughs*]!

When you quit rock & roll for the second time, in 1975, you were coming out of a period of heavy cocaine and alcohol use.

Yes, yes, yes. My nose was big enough to put diesel trucks in. I was payin' almost $10,000 a month for cocaine. I was into it. I was eatin' it. I was snortin' it. I was freezin' everything that could be frozen. I was screamin' and hollerin'. It was a terrible time for me. I've never had this drug they have today, crack. By the grace of God, I don't drink or smoke now, haven't done it in years. I'm just glad to be alive and show the young people that it doesn't pay, that you can live above it and that it don't make you famous: It makes you dead. It steals life from mankind, and we need God in our life. We truly need God in our life, and that's what it is about.

Are you getting more comfortable with the idea of playing rock & roll again?

Well, what I feel about music now is that I love God, I always will love God, and I feel that I'm a messenger for him. To me, rock & roll music is the only way I know how to make a living. I'm making people joyful, and I will still spread my love for God. So I'm still the person that God has placed, but the music is my job.

Did you think Elvis did anything as far as opening the door for the white audience to listen to black singers?

I think the door opened wider, but the door may have already been opened by "Tutti Frutti." I think that Elvis was more acceptable, being white, back in that period. I believe that if Elvis had been black, he wouldn't have been as big as he was. If I was white, do you know how huge I'd be? If I was white, I'd be able to sit on top of the White House! A lot of things they would do for Elvis and Pat Boone, they wouldn't do for me.

It's like they won't even give me a Lifetime Achievement Award, and look at Paul McCartney. I was the first famous person he ever met, the first famous person he ever traveled with. They give him a Lifetime Achievement [Grammy] Award, and they won't give me one. They won't even *mention* me! They give Dick Clark an award, but they don't give me nothing! Don't even mention my existence! It's a shame, but that's what it is. [McCartney was given a Lifetime Achievement Award at the Grammys in February 1990; Little Richard was awarded his own Lifetime Achievement Grammy in 1993.]

Do you think McCartney should have mentioned you in his acceptance speech?

Yes. I just don't understand some things sometimes. I was sitting right there in front of him, and he didn't say *nothing*. It makes you feel like crying, you know?

I was surprised about that myself.

I was shocked. I should have run up on the stage and did one of my outrageous numbers and said, "Listen, Paul, let's face it: Now, you *know* that I'm the one that bought the hamburgers." I should have done that. But I think that when you're in love with God, your reward is what he says it is—eternal life. So I think I'm going to have to settle for that, and I'm not dismayed or disarrayed. I *will* settle for that. In fact, I'd rather have a crown of gold than to lose my soul.

ten great vinyl moments

By ROBBIE ROBERTSON

I grew up in Toronto, and the guy who was probably my most influential teacher was George "Hound Dog" Lorenz, who had a show on a Buffalo radio station. It was the first place I heard Elvis sing "Mystery Train," and his show was the place to go if you wanted to get around listening to Pat Boone. When you heard the Hound playing Clyde McPhatter and the Drifters' "Money Honey," you knew that was *real*.

It's impossible for me to think of just ten records, but what I'm going on are the moments: the time I saw an Alan Freed show with LaVern Baker, Chuck Berry, Fats Domino, Bo Diddley, Buddy Holly and Jackie Wilson; or the time I walked into the little restaurant where everyone hung out, and the jukebox was playing the introduction to "Lucille," by Little Richard. People were talking to me, but all I could see was their mouths moving, and all I could hear was Little Richard. That's what this list is made of—those moments.

1 **"The Fool,"** by Sanford Clark (Dot). This is a guitar-bass-drums record, an early rockabilly type of thing. When rock & roll was born, I was at an age to be completely intrigued—you'd never heard this kind of sound before. I wasn't buying records because they were great songs; you were kind of rebelling against that. I just wanted something that would get under my skin, and this record did.

2 **"All Around the World,"** by Little Willie John (King). The records that James Brown and Little Willie John made for King have an in-your-face quality. Little Willie John opened a door to something for me: It was straight from the heart.

3 **"Riot in Cellblock No. 9"** and **"Young Blood,"** by the Coasters (Atco). I liked "Young Blood" more, but the idea of calling a song "Riot in Cellblock No. 9" really appealed to me. And "Young Blood"—talking about a *girl* that way! That's *bad*.

4 **"Rumble,"** by Link Wray (Cadence). I liked the name of the record and the name of the guy who played it. It was the rawest guitar sound— just dirty and up to no good. "Dirty" to me also meant Bo Diddley and Hubert Sumlin, who was the guitarist on Howlin' Wolf's records. They put me over the top: I had no choice but to play guitar.

5 **"Mystery Train,"** by Elvis Presley (Sun). For me, this was the beginning of the Scotty Moore–Chet Atkins school of guitar, and Elvis sang it just like a train. And again, I liked the title. When I started playing in bands, we always did "Mystery Train" just because I liked saying it.

6 **"Rollin' Stone,"** by Muddy Waters (Chess). Link was raw, Bo was savage, but Muddy was a brilliance of a different sort. I'd never heard slide guitar before, and Muddy's music led me to develop a guitar style that relied heavily on vibrato, because I didn't know what a slide bar was.

7 **"Stagger Lee,"** by Lloyd Price (ABC-Paramount). This is one of the most influential songs in my life. Lloyd's version is a nice record, but it was the *song*. I eventually collected a lot of different versions of it and recorded it— along with Fats Domino's song "The Fat Man"—for the *Carny* soundtrack, although I never used it.

8 **"Susie-Q,"** by Dale Hawkins (Checker). On some records, there were sounds I listened to more than the song itself. Jimmy Reed was like that for me: He had a crying sound that was just baffling, and "Susie-Q" is like that. I wanted to be part of that *sound*. At first I thought these guys like James Burton were really strong to be able to bend strings the way they did. It was only later, when I was in Ronnie Hawkins's band, that I found out that guys would take the heaviest string off, string the other five down, and use a banjo string for the sixth.

9 **"Drown in My Own Tears,"** by Ray Charles (Atlantic). Up until I heard this record, I thought "Pledging My Love," by Johnny Ace, was the most moving vocal I'd ever heard. "Drown in My Own Tears" upped the ante. The way they sang those songs just tore you apart.

10 **"Brown Eyed Handsome Man,"** by Chuck Berry (Chess). The flip side of this record was "Too Much Monkey Business," and I loved them both. Whichever side was the A side, the B side was better. I could say the same about Little Richard's "I'm Just a Lonely Guy," which was the flip side of "Tutti Frutti."

I also don't know how to talk about the great records of the Fifties without bringing up Huey "Piano" Smith and the Clowns' "Don't You Know Yockomo," Jerry Lee Lewis's "You Win Again," Fats Domino's "Blue Monday," Buddy Holly's "Think It Over" and "True Love Ways," and Carl Perkins's "Honey Don't." And that's not to mention "Annie Had a Baby," by Hank Ballard and the Midnighters, and "Love Is Strange," by Mickey and Sylvia.

leiber **and** stoller

By DAVID FRICKE

Mike Stoller noticed two things about Jerry Leiber when the latter knocked at Stoller's door in Los Angeles one afternoon in 1950. The first was Leiber's eyes—one was blue, one was brown. Stoller stared in amazement at Leiber's eyes until Stoller's mother finally asked, "Aren't you going to let him in?"

The other thing Stoller, then seventeen, noticed about his future partner, also seventeen, was the notebook in Leiber's hand. "He had lyrics written in it," says Stoller, a classically schooled pianist and serious blues and jazz buff who had been less than keen when Leiber first phoned him about writing songs together. "I looked at it, and I said, 'These aren't songs, these are blues,' because he would have a line of lyric and ditto marks, then a rhyming line. These were twelve-bar blues progressions. I said, 'I like blues,' and we started writing."

Jerry Leiber and Mike Stoller started writing that very afternoon—and never stopped. Their partnership outlasted most marriages and survived innumerable revolutions in the music they helped create, rock & roll. So have the fruits of that partnership. As hit songwriters and hitmaking record producers, the Baltimore-born Leiber and Long Island native Stoller had few peers and no equals during rock & roll's first golden era. The list of smash sides they wrote or cowrote for their all-star clients throughout the Fifties and early Sixties reads like a history of the music itself: "Love Me," "Jailhouse Rock" and "Loving You" for Elvis Presley; "There Goes My Baby" and "On Broadway" for the Drifters; Ben E. King's solo hits "Spanish Harlem" and "Stand by Me"; "Yakety Yak," "Searchin'," "Poison Ivy" and "Charlie Brown" for those great rock & roll clowns the Coasters; seminal R&B ravers like "Kansas City," "Riot in Cell Block No. 9" and "Hound Dog," a hit for both Elvis and, in its original risqué rendition, Big Mama Thornton.

But it is *living* history. More than any other top writing and production team in the Fifties, Leiber (words) and Stoller (music) initiated mainstream white America into the sensual and spiritual intimacies of urban black culture that fueled the birth of rock & roll. Their songwriting captured the essence and nuances of black music and language with a melodic invention, narrative ingenuity and cool hilarity that were true to the source while transcending it—heavy-duty R&B with a pop sensibility and lyric universality.

"We felt, in some cases, very successful if people thought that what we wrote was traditional," says Stoller, who studied with the great stride pianist James P. Johnson. "We wanted people to hear that we were a part of the tradition, rather than imitating something that wasn't ours."

In 1966, after selling their share of Red Bird Records, where they oversaw the rise of top girl groups like the Dixie Cups and the Shangri-Las, Leiber and Stoller headed for more experimental pastures. They wrote the Brecht-Weill–style hit "Is That All There Is?" for Peggy Lee, produced early-Seventies records for Procol Harum and Stealers Wheel ("Stuck in the Middle With You") and worked extensively in movies and theater. In the late Eighties, their work included an animated movie feature, *Hound Dog*, which includes some of their classic songs, and a film of their life story, aptly titled *Yakety Yak*. In 1995, *Smokey Joe's Cafe*, a Broadway musical written around their songs, began a successful, five-year run.

There has, the two admit, been some flak amid the yak in their fifty years together, although nothing worth splitting up over. "We started fighting the moment we met," Stoller says, laughing. "We fought about words, we fought about music. We fought about everything."

"One thing we never fought about was chicks," Leiber adds with a mischievous grin, "because I got the good-lookin' ones."

At the 1987 Rock and Roll Hall of Fame induction dinner, you said in your acceptance speech, "We were just making R&B records." Were you ever aware of also making rock & roll history?
STOLLER: That may be the case, but that certainly wasn't the intent. What we wanted to do was try and be as good as we could at writing blues, for blues singers, which meant exclusively black performers, writing in the black vernacular.

LEIBER: Our songs did not transcend being R&B hits. They were R&B hits that white kids were attracted to. And if people bought it, it became rock & roll. *That's* marketing. Why couldn't it still be R&B? The bass pattern didn't change. The song didn't change. It was still "Yakety Yak" and "Searchin'." It was just an R&B record that white people bought and loved.

These days, that's called crossing over.
LEIBER: When you talk crossover, you talk about marketing. It's like jingle writing. You're trying to psyche out the public and sell 'em something, rather than something out of your own bones, your own heart, your own soul and insight.

STOLLER: Honestly, when Jerry and I started to write, we were writing to amuse ourselves. It was done out of the love of doing it. And we got very lucky in the sense that at some point, what we wrote also amused a lot of other people.

What were your earliest songwriting sessions like?

LEIBER: We used to go to Mike's house, where the upright piano was. We went there every day and wrote. We worked ten, eleven, twelve hours a day.

STOLLER: When we started working, we'd write five songs at a session. Then we'd go home, and we'd call each other up: "I've written six more songs!" "I've written four more." Our critical faculties, obviously, were not as developed [*laughs*], and we just kept on writing and writing.

LEIBER: "Hound Dog" took, like, twelve minutes. That's not a complicated piece of work, but the rhyme scheme was difficult. Also, the metric structure of the music was not easy. "Kansas City" was maybe eight minutes, if that. Writing the early blues was spontaneous. You can hear the energy in the work.

STOLLER: In the early days, we'd go back and forth note for note, syllable for syllable, word for word in the process of creating.

Like telepathy?

LEIBER: We're a unit. The instincts are very closely aligned. I could write, "Take out the papers and the trash" ["Yakety Yak," by the Coasters], and he'll come up with "Or you don't get no spendin' cash."

STOLLER: That is literally what happened. I think Jerry shouted out that first line, and I started playing that funny shuffle, *oom-paka-oom-paka*, on the piano. He shouted out the first line, and suddenly I shouted out the second line, and we knew we had something.

From the beginning, you were getting your songs cut by top R&B stars like Charles Brown ["Hard Times"] and Jimmy Witherspoon ["Real Ugly Woman"]. Didn't you ever know the pain of rejection, of getting songs thrown back at you?

LEIBER: Almost never. Not so much because they were good or bad. They were almost always *right*. The language was right, the form was right. We knew what we were doing. Then there were mediocre songs that just happened to hit a certain groove and—wham! It happened.

For example?

LEIBER: "Kansas City" surprised me. I had a big fight with Mike about "Kansas City." I originally sang a traditional blues turn on it, like Howlin' Wolf might have sung it. Mike said, "I don't want to write just another blues. There are a thousand numbers out there like it. I got a tune for it." I told him it sounded phony. I gave him all sorts of garbage, and he won out.

When we did it with Little Willie Littlefield, I thought it was all right. It didn't kill me. Then when Wilbert Harrison came out with it, then it sounded right. But it took all that time to convince me that he was right about that melody.

Was "Hound Dog" written specifically for Big Mama Thornton?

LEIBER: Absolutely, the afternoon we saw her. Johnny Otis told us to come down to his garage in the back of his house, where he used to rehearse. He wanted us to listen to his people and see if we could write some tunes for them.

We saw Big Mama, and she knocked me cold. She looked like the biggest, baddest, saltiest chick you would ever see. And she was *mean*, a "lady bear," as they used to call 'em. She must have been 350 pounds, and she had all these scars all over her face. I had to write a song for her that basically said, "Go fuck yourself," but how to do it without actually saying it? And how to do it telling a story? I couldn't just have a song full of expletives.

Hence the "hound dog."

LEIBER: Right: "You ain't nothin' but a motherfucker."

STOLLER: She was a wonderful blues singer, with a great moaning style, but it was as much her appearance as her blues style that influenced the writing of "Hound Dog" and the idea that we wanted her to growl it—which she rejected at first. Her thing was "Don't you tell me how to sing no song!"

Didn't you feel intimidated by the black stars you worked with? These people lived the blues, and here come these two white teenagers telling Big Mama how to growl.

STOLLER: I can remember saying to Jerry, "Tell her this," or "Tell so-and-so." Or Jerry asking me to say something to one of the acts, because he felt funny asking them himself, because we felt such respect and awe for these people, these blues legends that we were working with and actually coaching. But after a while, the results spoke for themselves. In most instances, I felt very comfortable in a black community and a black situation.

LEIBER: I felt black. I *was*, as far as I was concerned, and I wanted to be black for lots of reasons: They were better musicians, they were better athletes, they were not uptight about sex, and they knew how to enjoy life better than most people.

We lived a black lifestyle as young guys. We had black girlfriends for years. In the general sense, it was extreme, but not in the environment that we moved in. They were amused by us, two white kids doing the blues. They thought it was goofy, a lot of fun.

How much money did you originally earn on the early hits?

STOLLER: Some record companies made up their own numbers. I don't think they had to be sophisticated to the degree of keeping two sets of books. When it came to paying royalties, they merely made 'em up.

It first really hit home with "Hound Dog," which was an acknowledged smash. At one point, the late Don Robey [of Duke/Peacock Records, Thornton's label] came to L.A. Our parents got nervous, we got a lawyer and so on. See, we were still minors, so the contracts had to be re-signed with our parents as guardians. So when Robey left L.A., he left a check for twelve hundred dollars, which was an unbelievable sum, even though it was a mere portion of what the record was earning. Then he went back to Texas with the contract and stopped payment on the check.

Was forming Spark Records in 1953 your way of getting artistic and financial control?

STOLLER: Spark was our way of preventing our songs from being misinterpreted. There were things we were incapable of putting on paper. It was a matter of telling somebody it has to be done "like *that*, like *this*." We could do the whole thing from beginning to end.

Spark releases like the Robins' "Framed" and "Riot in Cell Block No. 9" marked the start of the narrative writing style you later perfected with the Coasters at Atlantic. The songs were also striking in their depiction of urban black life. How did that develop?

LEIBER: I think there is a mistake in the view of some of that material now. "Riot in Cell Block No. 9" wasn't a ghetto song. It was inspired by the *Gangbusters* radio drama. Those voices just happened to be black, but they could have been white actors on radio, saying, "Pass the dynamite, because the fuse is lit." People have said, "These are protest songs, early prophecies of the burning of Watts." Bullshit. These are cartoons. We used to write cartoons.

At about the same time, you were also supplying material for Elvis Presley, creating songs like "Jailhouse Rock" and "King Creole" for movies. As R&B boys at heart, was it hard working with Elvis at a time when Colonel Parker was grooming him for Hollywood?

LEIBER: Elvis was incredibly cooperative. He would try anything. He wasn't a diva, no prima donna. When it came to work, he was a workhorse.

STOLLER: If he didn't like something—his own performance, primarily—he would say, "Let's do another one." And this would go on and on—take thirty-eight, take thirty-nine—until he felt he had it. We thought we already had it! We'd got it twice!

LEIBER: In writing the songs for those scripts, it did get rather stultifying. In fact, we quit. That was a great avenue, to be working with the automatic hitmaker of all time, but we were repeating ourselves, and the films were getting too dumb for words.

But we did make an attempt at one point to do something that we thought would be much more interesting. We cooked up this idea for *A Walk on the Wild Side*; it would be an incredible property for Elia Kazan to direct and for Presley to play the lead as Dove. We got this notion to Parker, and the word we got back was, "If you two jerks don't mind your own business and stay away from the business of Elvis Presley, I'm going to put you both out of business."

Did Elvis ever ask you to come up with some bluesy tunes?

STOLLER: He came to me one day, and this was the only time he ever expressed anything specific about something. "Mike, I'd like you guys to write me a real pretty ballad." Not for a movie. He just wanted one. It was the only time he ever asked *for* something. The rest of the time he was just doing material that had been submitted, selected and approved in advance.

Did you write him one?

STOLLER: Yeah, "Don't" [in 1958]. The next weekend, Jerry and I went into the studio and cut a demo with Young Jessie [a Spark act]. I brought Elvis the demo, and he loved it. He recorded it, but it caused a lot of friction, because it didn't go through channels. He asked us for a song, and we gave it to him.

At Atlantic Records, did you have the freedom to pick the acts you wanted to produce or write for, like the Drifters, or were they assigned to you by Ahmet Ertegun and Jerry Wexler?

LEIBER: It wasn't that formal. "You want to cut Ruth Brown? Go ahead. Joe Turner? Fine. You want the Drifters? They're cold now; we don't know what to do with them." They'd been dead for two years; that's why they gave 'em to us [*laughs*].

Once we took them over and had a string of hits, we were running the Drifters. Mostly production. We would give songwriting assignments to everybody—Burt Bacharach and Hal David, Barry Mann and Cynthia Weil, Doc Pomus and Mort Shuman— because we couldn't fill that demand.

The Drifters' "There Goes My Baby" [from 1959] is considered to be the first rock & roll record with strings. How was it made?

STOLLER: The rhythm was *baion*, a Brazilian rhythm which we really loved. Then we started to orchestrate what was really done on a tom-tom in Brazilian bands with all kinds of percussion sounds. We learned later that people would call a music-instrumental rental place and ask for the "Leiber-Stoller kit."

Was it an expensive session?

STOLLER: No, it was five violins and a cello.

It sounds a lot richer.

LEIBER: That's because it's a noisy studio.

STOLLER: And the out-of-tune percussion was because the *baion* was played on a timpani that happened to be in the studio. We asked the drummer to play it. He was a good drummer, but he didn't know anything about tuning timpani, so he played just one note.

LEIBER: It made for this weird, charismatic sound, so we played it for Jerry Wexler. We call this the tuna fish story. Jerry's got his tuna fish sandwich on his desk. He put this tape on, the song started, and the timpani came on. He had a mouthful of tuna fish, and all of a sudden he goes, "What the fuck is this?" Tuna fish goes all over the wall. "What is this shit? You're burning my money up! What the fuck are you playing me?" Jerry's screaming all these obscenities, says it's never coming out, how much money did it cost, it's out of tune.

STOLLER: Ahmet was nice. Ahmet said, [*affects Turkish accent*] "Fellas, you boys cut beautiful records. You've made many hits. But you can't hit a home run every time." We finally convinced them that there were some problems with the studio we used, so they gave us two hours of studio time to play with it.

LEIBER: But it didn't need fixing. Later, we tried to get the same sound with the timpani in tune on "She Cried," with Jay and the Americans.

STOLLER: Except that time, the only thing out of tune was the singer [*laughs*].

Ben E. King's "Stand by Me" went Top Ten in 1986, fifteen years after it first became a hit. How do you account for its continuing appeal?

LEIBER: The bass pattern.

Can you elaborate?

LEIBER: I don't have to. It's the bass pattern. There are lots of great songs, but that is an insidious piece of work. It can put a hole through your head.

It's not a great song. It's a nice song, but it's a great record. And there's always one special element. In "There Goes My Baby," it's the out-of-tune timpani. "Stand by Me," it's the bass pattern. Of course, all the elements come together to make a great record, but there's always one standout.

In 1964, you started Red Bird Records, ushering in the girl-group era with the Shangri-Las and the Dixie Cups. Meanwhile, the Beatles were transforming the record business by doing their own songs and calling their own shots in the studio. How did those changes affect you?

LEIBER: It influenced us to some degree, but there were other forces at work. With George Goldner [who cofounded Red Bird] came his point of view, which was very much like Don Kirshner's, which was a twelve-year-old girl's point of view. The stuff that Mike and I liked to produce, which in comparison was real macho stuff, was considered vulgar and out of date—which meant not salable.

Is that why you walked away from Red Bird in 1966?

LEIBER: We lost interest in the process. It became too predictable. Too samey. We started to get interested in other forms, hoping to be able to write things that were of more interest to us. We've been looking around, playing around with the theater. I'm not sure where our slot is now, but there are things we want to say and ways we want to say them. And we haven't found the medium yet.

Do you miss writing rock & roll and R&B songs?

LEIBER: I still write them from time to time. I've had no place to put them, frankly. I wrote a little lyric a while ago; it was going to be a kind of straight-on blues. Then Mike took the lyric and set it to a sweet, tuneful kind of dance [*laughs*].

STOLLER: I think, in a way, that for me to try to write what I wrote then...I could do it as an exercise, and I'm technically capable of writing in that style, but I don't know if it would be an honest expression. It would be a conscious effort to write in a particular genre, as if I was trying to write a Viennese waltz. R&B was something I used to write, but I don't live there anymore.

carl perkins

By DAVID McGEE

When Carl Perkins died from the effects of multiple strokes on January 19, 1998, rock & roll at once lost a founding father, an archetypal guitarist, a prolific songwriter and a philosopher king. By the time of his death, Perkins's place in history was long secure. Far more important to Perkins himself, though, was the satisfaction of having had a full life that had seen him face misfortune head-on and then battle it, time and again; one that had seen him keep as a rock-solid unit the people he loved most—his wife of 45 years, Valda; three sons (two of whom, Stan and Greg, played in his band from 1975 on); a daughter; their spouses and children, who were a fount of strength for each other and for him.

He learned of family strength early on, as one of three sons of Tiptonville, Tennessee, sharecroppers. At age six, he was working the cotton fields, trying to help the family out of its desperate straits. By the time he was thirteen, he and his older brother, Jay, billed as the Perkins Brothers Band (later joined by the youngest Perkins brother, Clayton, on bass and W.S. Holland on drums), were working the honky-tonks in and around Jackson, Tennessee (where Carl would make his home for the rest of his life), still trying to elevate the family to the next economic rung. Their efforts began to bear fruit in 1954, when they were signed to Sam Phillips's Sun label in Memphis, shortly after the release of another new Sun artist's first single, Elvis Presley's "That's All Right (Mama)" / "Blue Moon of Kentucky."

The struggle paid off in January 1956, when Carl's song "Blue Suede Shoes" spoke to the language and values of an emerging teen culture and became one of rock & roll's defining treatises. Then, as quickly as his break had arrived, it fled. Injuries sustained in an auto accident in March 1956, when he was on his way to a national TV appearance in New York, took him out of action at a time when he was, as he said, "toe to toe with that pretty Elvis." Commercially, he never recovered, but he remained undeterred, even as tragedy continued to stalk him, including Jay's death from a brain tumor in 1958 and Clayton's death from a self-inflicted gunshot wound in 1973. Perkins's long bout with alcoholism threatened to undermine everything he had worked so hard to attain since first setting foot in Jackson's Cotton Boll honky-tonk in 1946.

Down but never out, Carl produced some of his finest work in the years after "Blue Suede Shoes" put him on the map. Solo success proved elusive, but his voice as a songwriter remained resonant through the ensuing decades. Johnny Cash and the Judds both took Perkins songs to the top of the country charts: "Daddy Sang Bass" and "Let Me Tell You About Love," respectively. In 1991 alone, Dolly Parton scored a hit with a moving interpretation of Perkins's revealing "Silver and Gold," Mark O'Connor's New Nashville Cats earned a CMA Award with their brisk rendering of Perkins's 1968 wanderlust classic "Restless," and George Strait chalked up another in his endless string of hits on a bit of Perkins philosophy-in-song entitled "When You're a Man on Your Own."

When death came that morning in January 1998, Carl was still looking ahead to new challenges, optimistic as always that there was an audience for his point of view. His passing cannot diminish the truth of his life: It was one of triumph, in the end, not tragedy. Rock & roll too often celebrates those who succumb to their demons. Carl stared into the abyss more than once himself but stepped back and chose to fight. His monuments are the body of work he produced in a forty-three-year recording career and the people in Jackson, who called him husband, father and friend. Those are monuments for the ages.

The following interview was conducted at Carl's home in Jackson in February 1990.

You've had more than your share of problems in life, yet nothing about the way you carry yourself suggests a defeated man.
I have been, and am to this day, a very happy man. That may have stemmed from being brought up so very poor, having absolutely nothing, longing for a bicycle or a guitar or just clothes and shoes I didn't have. My daddy would take hog ringers [steel rings that were placed in the noses of pigs] to hold my shoe soles on.

I felt out of place when "Blue Suede Shoes" was Number One. I stood on the Steel Pier in 1956 in Atlantic City, followed Frank Sinatra there. And the Goodyear blimp flew over with my name in big lights: APPEARING TONIGHT AT THE STEEL PIER, CARL PERKINS. And I stood there and shook and actually cried. That should have been something that would elevate a guy to say, "Well, I've made it," but it put fear in me.

When guys like Eric Clapton or George Harrison say that I influenced 'em, it knocks me kind of way down, because I don't understand how I ever influenced anybody. I'm not a good guitar player in no sense of the word. I may have had a little different way of playing it, but how it ever influenced great players like Clapton—and I've said to him, "Hey, man, I don't hear no Carl Perkins licks." No, man. *Mmm-mmm.*

What kind of music did you hear as a boy?
I grew up in the cotton fields of Tennessee, and I listened to them singing—I'm talking about blacks. My mom and dad and my two brothers and I were the only white people who lived and worked on this Wilbur Walker farm. Back then you chopped and picked by hand and plowed it with mules.

But I heard this black music. They sang because there was not a lot to look forward to in a cotton field, and I sang along with 'em. It was that gospel feel that bled into my country music. And in talking to Elvis, Jerry Lee—all these cats loved black gospel music.

I'd listen to the *Grand Ole Opry*, and I loved Bill Monroe's music because it was uptempo from the other country dudes. There's a lot of kinship to bluegrass and early rockabilly—I mean a lot.

When did you start playing music?

I got an old beat-up guitar. A black man sold it to my dad, and the old black dude taught me two or three blues licks. His name was John Westbrook, and I was no older than seven, eight years old.

I'd be so tired, chopping or picking cotton, whatever we was doin', and I'd take off for Uncle John's after we'd work hard all day. Looking back on it now, there's that old black man who was tired, much tireder than I was as a young boy, but yet he took time and sat on his porch and showed me licks that he knew. I was dealing with a black angel. He didn't have to take time to show me anything. And under the circumstances of segregation back in those years, when he couldn't go get him a drink of water at the courthouse, he could have hated a little white boy like me, but he didn't. He loved me.

What moved you to start writing your own songs?

I don't know. The first song I wrote was the first one I ever recorded. I was about thirteen years old, and the song was called "Movie Magg." It was about the way things were in Lake County. You took your girl to the picture show on the back of a mule. Stupid, little ol' song—was ashamed to even sing it to Sam Phillips.

You were playing around Lake County with your brothers and sending off demos to Nashville and New York City, all of which were turned down. You didn't go to Memphis until you heard Elvis's version of the Arthur Crudup song "That's All Right (Mama)." Why did that get you to Sun Records?

We'd make these tapes, send them off, and I'd sometimes get 'em back, sometimes not. If one had been opened, that thrilled me. I don't know what label it was, but they said, "It's not bad, but we don't know what it is." I said, "God, that's what I *want* them to say! Someday somebody will know what it is." And then I heard Elvis's first Sun record; I knew that this man in Memphis knew what it was.

Getting into Sun wasn't easy.

You better believe it. I walked in the office, and Marion Keisker [Phillips's assistant] was sitting there. She said, "We're not takin' any auditions." I said,

"Well, ma'am, we sure did drive a pretty long ways to get down here. . . ." And she said, "Well, he's not here. I can save you some time: We got this new boy, Elvis." I said, "Yes, ma'am, I've heard some of his records. I kinda play the kind of stuff he does." She said, "He's not gonna listen to you."

So I went back and sat down in the car, and Sam pulled up in a new, '54 Cadillac, dark blue with a light blue top. And he was dressed just like his car: He had on a light blue sport coat with dark pants. He was mad 'cause we had his parking place. We were drivin' a '41 Plymouth—had the bass fiddle in a nine-foot, tar-bottom cotton sack tied up on top of it. And I jumped out of the car and beat him to the front door. I said, "I know you won't listen to us, but I sure do wish you would." After that, he said, "I couldn't turn you away. Your world looked like it would have ended."

What kind of man did you find Sam Phillips to be?

No doubt about it, he had to be genius. Any man who recognized that talent—Elvis, Johnny Cash, Jerry Lee Lewis, Charlie Rich, Roy Orbison. Such a string.

Did you ever ask him how he decided who to sign?

Yeah. His answer was, "Just raw bone, man. The way they walked in the door." He said, "You take Jerry, for instance. He walked in here and said, 'I come here to make a record.' That's *strong*. You got to give a guy a shot that comes in like that."

Was he difficult for you to approach?

Yes, and he was for all of us. We held him in such high esteem. We didn't have nothing, and he was the man who had given us the chance to make a record, and didn't none of us think he really would. Elvis couldn't believe what was happening to him. If he'd told any of us to do anything, we'd have done it. And we did. Sam told us, "Listen, it isn't going to be easy to get this music played. You boys see a radio tower, go and talk to them disc jockeys. Go to them country stations, 'cause that's what you are. You're country boys. Just go in there and let 'em know what kind of guys you are, and they'll play this music." And they *were* the ones that played it.

Was everybody aware that Elvis was in his own class?

No question about it. Let's face it: Elvis had sex appeal there that Carl Perkins didn't have. He was young, single, handsome; I was married and looked like Mister Ed. But he wasn't a smart aleck. Elvis wasn't that at all.

I knew early—and I'm talking about when I first started working flatbed trailers with him over in Marianna, Arkansas, and all around within a hundred-mile radius of Memphis—I knew there was something very magic about this boy. Girls were screaming and didn't realize until the next morning that they had bitten their fingernails off, tore it off to the quick.

You spent a lot of time alone with him. Did he confide in you what his real dreams were?

I'll tell you something that really gave him a lot of push. Things for Elvis really started happening after he signed with Colonel Tom Parker. There's a picture called "Million Dollar Quartet." The day that that picture was made was the day "Matchbox" was cut. And Elvis walked in. And we had been talking about it, said, "Man, he's out in Las Vegas. Man, that's as high as you gonna get." He played a place called the Last Frontier. Played a week. Then he walked in during this session, and it just killed the whole thing.

I remember I said to him, "Boy, what are you doin' back here? You're supposed to be—"

He said, "Aw, they didn't like me."

"They didn't *like* you?"

"Kids can't get in—gambling and all that stuff—and the old people didn't like me. They paid me for three weeks, though. [*Slaps thigh*] Got it here in my pocket."

But then there was a seriousness came over his face. He said, "Someday I'll go back, and I'll be the highest-priced act they've ever had." That might've flown by. I remember I brought it up to Cash, and I brought it up to Jerry Lee. I said, "Remember what he said sittin' at the piano?" And John said, "Yeah, I sure do. I remember what he said." He did it. When he went to the Hilton, he was the highest paid. Being rejected out there really hurt him and built a fire under him, too.

What was it like hanging around the Sun Studio then?

It wasn't unusual for the guys to come around when the others would be recording at Sun. There wasn't a dude down there that wasn't thrilled for the other one. Everybody couldn't wait until he got him a record and got him a Cadillac. That street was lined with Cadillacs, and everybody was thrilled to death for each other.

You take that superstar, and he can pull energy out of people around him. That's why rock & roll music owes so very much to Elvis. And it wasn't so much talent; it was the way he looked, and yet he was such a common guy. He didn't act like he was no movie star, but he looked better than anything you'd ever see on the screen, even when his britches cost $2.98 off a table down at Lansky's in Memphis.

Jerry Lee Lewis has always made a lot of noise about being the true king of rock & roll.

That's the old wildfire Louisiana boy that was that way the first time I ever met him. Bless his heart, he's fooled around and probably damaged more than just his stomach. I think Jerry has hurt his mentality by abusing himself so much, but he was always cocky. He knew the Bible quite well and would call your hand if you made a statement about it: "No, that ain't what it says," and he'd quote it. He knew it. Grew up around those preachers [one of Lewis's cousins is Jimmy Swaggart]. Now, he is a super-talented dude. He's just his worst enemy.

Apparently, Jerry Lee was shy about performing. You and Cash pulled him aside and talked to him about his show.

He would not turn his piano where they could see him. He'd sit sideways. Still sets it up a little to the side. We was in the dressing room; he was down *and* drinkin'. And I said, "Whatsa matter, Killer?"

He said, "It ain't *fair*. Y'all got them damn guitars on, and y'all can jump around and move. Piano player's just gotta sit there."

I said, "Well, can you play it standin' up?"

He said, "I can play it layin' on top of it!"

As a joke, I said, "Well, you oughta crawl up on top of it and play it. That'd be unusual."

I remember John laughing about it and saying, "That'd be something. You mean you can play it down like this, Lewis?" [*He mimes playing the piano while lying on top of it.*]

Jerry Lee said, "I can play the son of a bitch with my *feet* better than anyone else!"

But up to that point he was sittin' down with almost his back to the crowd. That second show he was doing "Crazy Arms"—that was his first record. He opened the show. I said, "John, he's fixin' to stand up." I could tell he was scootin' his stool and singin', [*sings*] "Cra-a-a-azy arms," and when he got up, he accidentally turned that stool over. He didn't know what the hell he was gonna do then, so he kicked it back. Well, they started screamin'. And I don't know whether that was the right thing to tell him or not, 'cause I had to follow him.

It was kinda like with Elvis. Elvis was so nervous, instead of his legs shakin', he'd try to stop, he'd kick it out, and they'd scream. He'd turn to [his guitarist] Scotty [Moore], and he'd say, "What'd I do?" Scotty would say, "I don't know, but do it again." Elvis was so scared that his legs were shaking.

Johnny Cash was your best friend at Sun.

When I first saw him, I liked him. Big ol' tall, quiet type of guy, you know. We got talkin' about where we was raised. He was very poor. John and I got to talkin' pickin' that ol' cotton—it was a real close thing set in between Johnny and I, and it remains to this day. I stayed with him for ten years; I stood behind him and watched a drug addict, as he's openly admitted, and I saw a man build himself. He's uplifting. He's that dream that we were taught: that you could take that guitar, go out there, throw them shoulders back, and you can do it. Elvis was, too.

At Sun, Roy Orbison was about as obscure as Johnny Cash was famous. Sun's engineer, Jack Clement, said Roy never quite got what Sun was after.

That's right. I remember Sam playing me a song called "Ooby Dooby," and it was a tape Roy had sent him from out in Wink, Texas. And he had a little picture of him and his band. And he said, "He don't look like much, but there's something in his voice, Carl."

Roy was real sweet, real humble, but he was not exciting onstage in his Sun days. He was very intimidated with all the pretty boys that were coming out. But down under there, Roy, he always seemed to have a knowledge that he could write something. He'd sing some of these slow songs a lot of times in the car. We worked a lot together, and he'd say, "What do you think about this? I think I'll go up another octave."

I'd say, "How high can you go? You're just about through the car roof right now."

You also knew Chuck Berry. What do you remember of him from the early days, and how did he change?

When I first met him, Chuck was a joy to be around. In '56, after the wreck, I started back on the road with a tour. They were all blacks, and I really was nervous about it, being the only white boy on the tour. I told my brother, "We could get killed," 'cause about that time in Birmingham, Alabama, Nat "King" Cole was onstage, and two guys jumped up and hit him hard. They was gonna kill him. Two red-dogs. He was singing to a white audience or a mixed

audience. And I just said, "We're gonna be the Nat 'King' Coles. Somebody's gonna git us."

But I remember very well: It was the Coasters, the Drifters, Al Hibbler, Frankie Lymon and the Teenagers, Chuck Berry, Little Richard and myself. Two Greyhound busloads, and I pull up in this new Cadillac. Chuck didn't want to ride with them. He said, "Can I ride with you?" I said, "Shoot, yeah, man."

On that tour, he said, "I started me one last night, Carl." I mean, this is the kind of guy he was—he was jolly; he was welcome to ride with me in my car. I venture to say that at least four or five of the big hits that he had, he started either in that car or the night before, and I would hear 'em. He'd say, "Is it worth finishing?" He'd say, "Is that 'Memphis' junk any good?" And I'd say, "Oooh, it's awesome, Chuck! Finish it!" It was great to be around him.

Then I didn't work with him [for several years] and read about his problems with prison and the young girl [Berry was arrested and imprisoned for violating the Mann Act in 1962]. He iced up. The next time I worked with him was 1964 in England. I went over there and found Chuck to be very different: steely eyed, very quiet. I wanted to talk to him, but he didn't act like he wanted to talk.

One time, we're sittin' behind a stage, and I ask him, "Chuck, what's happened, man? Why don't you write us some more songs? Why?"

He'd look at you with them beady eyes: "Whaddya tryin' to say to me?"

I'd say, "What happened? 'Two men in the bottom of the third; / It was a high fly into the stands; / Round third base he was struttin' for home, / That was a brown eyed handsome man; / And you know somethin'? That won the game; / The brown eyed handsome man.' Where is the man that wrote those songs? Why did you quit?"

He said, "Would it be all right if I *never* answered that? Can I be your friend and reserve the right?"

How did the sudden success of "Blue Suede Shoes" affect your life?

Well, the first thing was I had to move out of the projects. They called me up to the office and said, "You can't live here making this kind of money." My rent was thirty-two dollars a month, with a stove and refrigerator and my utilities furnished. The change was really a dramatic thing.

At Christmas in 1955, I bought my little boy a wagon. Back then they stacked 'em at John A. Parker

Seed Company: big wagon, smaller, smaller, smaller. And up at the top, the little one cost $2.98. That lady in there [Valda] ironed for her mama and her sister, and we had ten dollars to spend. We didn't get each other nothing. We bought for our two kids, my oldest son and my daughter. The wagon cost $2.98, Debbie's little doll cost about three dollars, 'nother little thing or two.

I knew the wagon was too little. On Christmas morning, he sat down on it, and it flipped over on him. I walked out the back door as the boy was crying; his mama was rockin' him. I stood on the back stoop of that project, and I was serious as I could be about anything. My mama raised me to go to church—I wasn't living as good as I should have, but I wasn't a mean boy. I never robbed, I never stole nothing; I was taught better than that. And I walked out on that stoop and said, "Lord, this is it. Next Christmas, if I can't get that big wagon, you're gonna have a thief on your hands to deal with. I need your help."

They didn't have a wagon big enough at John A. Parker's in 1956. I had him to order 'em. By that time, I had another kid, and I pulled all three of 'em around the yard. God heard me, and God answered my prayers.

But you didn't have long to enjoy it, because of the car accident in March 1956.

Uh-huh. You know, I was on top of the world, so to speak, with a big record—standing toe to toe with that good-lookin' Elvis. We was swapping Number One positions on the charts. In some cities, "Heartbreak Hotel" was Number One, "Blue Suede Shoes" another. And all of a sudden I woke up in a hospital; three days had passed that I didn't know about.

It was just outside of Dover, Delaware. I was eighty-five miles from New York.

You were on your way to *The Perry Como Show*?

Right. I'd worked in Norfolk, Virginia, the night before. Me and my brother Jay went to sleep. It was a Chrysler limousine that we'd borrowed. Another guy was driving it, a disc jockey in Memphis. He was hangin' around Sun Records some, and Sam had him to drive us up there, and he went to sleep and hit the back of a pickup truck—killed the guy he hit, and it hurt me real bad. Busted my skull, broke my right shoulder. I was cut all to pieces. It fractured my neck in three places. It totally broke Jay's neck.

You wound up in about three feet of water?

Oh, yeah. They were lookin' for me, just at daylight. They heard the gurgling sounds. I was in the grass and water, mud, and they just grabbed me by the hair and pulled me out. I was layin' facedown. I would've drowned, I'm sure.

Jay lived about six months after that, but he was never right. He went back; he played a few shows with me with a neck brace and all this on.

Was touring the same for you after that?

No. Lookin' back at it, I used it as a reason to drink. I missed Jay so much, and I just couldn't get it together. I drank every day. I'd drive off to places around here. I had a favorite lake place I'd go to, and I'd park there, and I'd set. I knew when I went that I was just gonna get drunk. I had a fifth bottle, and it got to the point when dark came, Valda knew where to tell somebody to find me, and they'd get me and bring me home.

Your career wasn't important anymore?

No, and I couldn't write. I just got to the point where I was an alcoholic, that's all. It was a terrible time for me. I gradually did get a boy to play in Jay's place, and we started back playing, but it was a good year before I could do that.

At the end of the Fifties, early Sixties, did you sense that the vitality wasn't there in rock & roll anymore?

Exactly. Looks entered into it too heavy. Rock has got some good shots in the arm through the years, a great one with the Beatles in 1964, 'cause when they first came out, these boys were hittin' hard at the old Sun Records sound.

When I first met 'em, it was at the end of the tour that Chuck and I did over there in 1964. They gave a party for me, and I didn't know them. I'd heard "I Want to Hold Your Hand." My kids were coming home from school, [*sings in a mocking tone*] "I wanna hold your hand." And I'd say, "Them damn boys look like *girls*. They ain't no good." But Stan, my oldest boy, said, "George Harrison said you was his favorite guitar player." I said, "I don't care what he said. They're sissies." I was joking but down inside kind of meant it a little bit. But I did hear some raw Sun Records sounds with these guys.

That night they were sittin' on the couch, and I'm sitting on the floor, and John Lennon said, "How did you kick off 'Right String Baby (Wrong Yo-yo)'?"

I said, "Where did you hear that stupid song, man?"

"We've got all your records! We slowed 'em down from 45 to 33⅓." George was telling me that was how he learned to play.

And then I said, "Well, I don't guess you're trying to, but it sounds like the old Sun Records."

John Lennon jumped up off the couch. Well, I'm kinda gettin' set, if he kicks at me or somethin'; I didn't know what he was gonna do. He said, "Guys, you heard it." And he reached down—like I say, I'm sittin' on the floor—he puts both arms around me and kissed me on the jaw. They asked me to go to Abbey Road and sit there as they cut three of my songs that night.

What happened?

Paul and John was finishing a song, "Slow Down." I was sittin' in a chair kinda against the wall in the studio, and Ringo was sittin' beside me, and he called me Mr. Perkins. I said, "I wish you'd call me Carl, son. Mr. Perkins is my daddy."

He said, "This sure is hard for me to do." I knew something was on his mind, and I said, "Shoot, spit it out, man. What is it?" He said, "Would you care if I sang some of your songs?"

"You mean you want me to write you some songs?"

He said, "Well, yes, sir, that would be fine, but I love 'Honey Don't' and 'Matchbox.'"

I said, "Do I *care?* Shoot, no, man. I'd *love* it."

And he jumped up, and he said, "Guys, he said it was all right!" Then he sat down on the drums, and "Matchbox" was the first thing they cut. They got that thing in two or three cuts.

When I got on the airplane next day, I knew I had a place that loved me and my music. I had begun to feel in America that it was over. I was a big cause of that with alcohol. In fact, I'd got me a farm, and that's what I was gonna do.

But I came back, and I was more determined. Right after then is when I joined with Johnny Cash. England was alive for me; they never forgot me.

53

dick clark

By HENRY SCHIPPER

There's something ambiguous and slightly out of focus about Dick Clark. As host of *American Bandstand*, he brought rock & roll—*the* cultural controversy of the Fifties—into America's living rooms, which was no small accomplishment, considering the hysterical opposition the new music provoked. Clark succeeded, however, largely by doing everything he could to take the controversy out of rock & roll.

The boyish, edgeless and well-groomed Clark was reassuring to adults. Though one could sense he genuinely liked the music, it was hard to tell how deep the feeling ran. An easygoing pitchman, he brought the same sunny attitude to Little Richard and Chuck Berry that he did to Clearasil and Beech-Nut gum.

The man whose tombstone will probably read AMERICA'S OLDEST TEENAGER never really was a teen—at least not in the rock & roll sense of the word. Clark became host of *American Bandstand* in 1956 at the age of twenty-six, and he was in many ways older than his years. A product of the Eisenhower era, he was driven, ambitious and savvy enough to turn a Philadelphia dance show into a national obsession.

In Clark's hands, *American Bandstand* was a phenomenal success. Five days a week in the late afternoon, the show held teenage America in its thrall, launching careers, breaking hits, sparking dance fads and drawing the highest ratings of any daytime program in the land. *American Bandstand* featured two live performances a day—more than ten thousand overall— including national debuts by Chuck Berry, James Brown, Johnny Cash, Sam Cooke, Fats Domino, Buddy Holly, Jerry Lee Lewis and many others who couldn't get a booking on the antirock TV variety shows of the day.

Clark's own success paralleled the show's. By the time he was thirty, he was a millionaire, not from his *Bandstand* salary but from spinoff investments. His light and smiling persona aside, Clark was a hungry entrepreneur, working every angle to build a small empire of music concerns, including record labels, music publishers and pressing plants.

In 1960, Clark's publishing interests drew the attention of congressional payola investigators, who accused him of trading *Bandstand* airtime for copyrights to songs. Clark denied the charge, though he did hold the copyrights to more than 150 tunes, some of which were assigned to him gratis and were played on the show.

Clark's grilling on Capitol Hill was the crisis and crucible of his life. The man who groomed himself so carefully, whose career depended on a clean, trustworthy image, was having his clock cleaned on the front pages of America's newspapers. Ultimately, the pols couldn't nail him on anything, and Clark, one of the era's great survivors, walked away with his reputation and his image more or less intact. His empire, however, fell apart. ABC ordered him to choose between *American Bandstand* and his other holdings, and Clark decided to stay with the show. He then set about building a less vulnerable portfolio.

He has since branched out to become one of the busiest producers in the world, handling everything from TV specials (*Bloopers, Live Aid, American Music Awards*), feature films and game shows to beauty pageants (*The Most Beautiful Girl in the World*), sitcoms and an

< **dick clark** questions **don** and **phil everly** [ca. **1957**]

55

annual New Year's Eve broadcast. In the 1990s, Clark remained an active music entrepreneur, as well, with the formation of Click Records in 1995. It all added up to a spot on the Forbes 400 list and an estimated wealth of $180 million.

Through the Eighties, Clark continued to host *American Bandstand* as it danced into the record books as the longest continuous-running variety show in television history. *Bandstand* was still an important industry showcase in the 1980s, reflecting and surviving every trend—folk, acid rock, punk, disco—until MTV came along and suddenly made it seem quaint and obsolete.

After thirty years, ABC dropped *Bandstand* in 1987. Clark hung on, syndicating the show. It ran on the USA Network until 1989, when he finally passed the hosting job to a younger hand. Six months later, *Bandstand* died; in the late 1990s, MTV's sister channel VH1 aired old segments from *American Bandstand.*

The world's oldest teenager, now in his seventies, is still going strong and still something of an enigma. Although he will always be identified with rock & roll, a form of music that celebrates abandon, Clark has played it very close to the vest—"Protect your ass at all times" has been his motto since the payola trauma. Rock's most famous DJ is so cautious that during the following 1990 interview, he wouldn't divulge to ROLLING STONE the name of even one record on the 100-title jukebox in his Malibu home—for fear of offending artists who weren't represented.

Yet there is something frank and genuine about Clark. Though many of his anecdotes are canned, his overall manner is not. Clark will even vent himself in raw language that cuts sharply against his image: When asked about the censorship campaign spearheaded by the Parents' Music Resource Center and Tipper Gore, he lashed out with scathing and impressive invective. Alas, the outburst came only after his insisting that those remarks not be quoted. This happened on quite a number of occasions.

"But Dick, why won't you go on the record with this? This is interesting."

"'Protect your ass at all times.'"

You became host of *American Bandstand* in 1956, at the age of twenty-six. What did you know about rock & roll?

Very little. I'm not sure anybody knew a lot about it.

The man you replaced, Bob Horn, was fired for getting arrested for drunk driving. He was charged with statutory rape [and later acquitted]. Was your clean-cut image a factor in getting the job?

I don't think there's any doubt about it. *American Bandstand* was a very valuable property, and I'm sure that somebody at the TV station decided that they'd better get somebody in there who had a chance to save it.

They said, "Do you want to?" and I said, "Hoo, yeah!" It was my dream. That show was successful beyond anyone's imagination. It drew 60 percent of the audience. It was gigantic.

Alan Freed was the best-known and most successful DJ of the time. He had a wild, almost missionary rock & roll style that seemed to complement the music and made him a hero to his fans. Why didn't you emulate Freed?

Alan was the man who made it happen—we owe a great deal to him. I had my own way of doing things. I wore a coat and tie. Everybody in that *Bandstand* studio who was a male wore a coat and tie. The thinking behind that was, if we looked presentable, *normal*, the way *they* think we oughta look, *they'll* leave us alone. It sorta worked.

The show was very influential, and to keep it going was a hell of a lot more important than whether people liked what I was doing. I've taken a lot of lumps over the years from people who say I've homogenized the music and only presented people from Philadelphia, and that's all bullshit.

The rap against you and *American Bandstand* is that you watered down rock & roll, tamed it for mainstream America.

I haven't watered down anything. All I've done is stock the store. Stocking the store with roots music and white-bread music and everything in between doesn't necessarily mean I've interfered with it.

It's a lot more fun to write about whitewashing rock & roll than looking at the truth. The truth is that over two-thirds of the people who've been initiated into the Rock and Roll Hall of Fame had their television debuts on *American Bandstand*, and the rest of them probably debuted on other shows we produced.

But rock & roll—especially in contrast with the rest of pop in the Fifties—was defiant, unruly, loud. You offered a well-groomed, inoffensive version.

Yeah, but in that mix you had Little Richard and Jerry Lee Lewis, and later on Jefferson Airplane and the Doors. That's not whitewashing music. To write that the music we presented was all white bread is a fallacious premise. It's an easy angle. It happens to be wrong.

Let me put it to you this way: Because of your image, a lot of people doubt that you're really, at heart, a rock & roller.

Who has the right to determine what kind of music I personally like? I happen to like rhythm & blues, but it's nobody's damn business. What I *play* is what's asked for. At one time it was disco music. Right now it's rock and heavy metal and dance music again. We stock the store with what the public wants.

We're dealing with the image here, and yours is very square.

Hey, if I had a beard and during one time in my life wore earrings and love beads, they probably woulda liked me better. The easiest thing in the world is to write an unattractive critique of Dick Clark—it doesn't take the brains to pound salt down a rat hole to do that, because I've been around a long time, I've made money, I'm white. They would've liked me to have looked differently or acted differently or been wilder. I am what I am. I'm the perfect target, but that doesn't demean what I've been doing all these years, which I'm not unproud of.

Is there a wild side to Dick Clark?

No.

A rebellious side?

No.

Not to wear you out on this point, but because of your image, some people think you have more in common with someone like Pat Boone than—

But that was an obvious ploy to protect the music.

You created your image to protect the music?

It was 150-percent deliberate and well thought out.

In order to do what?

In order to perpetuate my own career, first and foremost, and secondly the music. I'm not gonna sit here

and tell you I did this solely to keep the music alive. I was keeping myself alive, and in so doing, helped keep the music alive. And it's in one-and-two order: self-survival and taking care of the music, and it worked. You go back and look at the old television shows: You see the decorum in the way they're presented; you know it's not gonna upset station management, make the parents go crazy. Had it been a snake pit of writhing bodies, it woulda been on and off the air in a week.

Okay, Dick, what IS the basis of your connection to rock & roll, on a personal, emotional level?

I don't know what the question means.

Has there ever been a screaming rock & roller inside Dick Clark wanting to come out?

No...no. I'm not that kind of person.

You had a front-row view of just about every rock legend in his or her prime. Who was or is the most charismatic?

The guy I really loved a great deal and miss is Bobby Darin, who upon his recent induction into the Hall of Fame it was fashionable to criticize—"Why him?" And I wanted to throw up. The man was one of the most multitalented individuals I ever met.

The man who had the most charisma in the world was Elvis Presley. That goes without saying. There are no competitors.

Some quick impressions, Dick. What's the first thing that comes to mind when I say... Chuck Berry?

The father of rock & roll. A lot of people claim the title, but he's probably the one. The king of rock & roll was Elvis, the father was Chuck Berry. He was an extraordinarily influential man.

Sam Cooke.

Too angry and bright for the moment in which he lived.

That's a surprise. He was so smooth.

Sam was an angry man and rightly so—angry about integration, the problems facing blacks in the world. It was new; it wasn't talked about.

Fabian.

Fabian was a sign of the times. He looked the part. He walked into a record hop and looked like a rock & roller, and the girls went crazy. They did not critique his music—they critiqued his look. The same is true in the Nineties. If you want some good examples, you can figure it out yourself by looking at the bestseller charts.

^ Dancing teens on the original set of **American Bandstand**, with **clark** in the background
MICHAEL OCHS ARCHIVES/VENICE, CA

Little Richard.
Back in the Fifties, when he was on *Bandstand* with the processed hair, sometimes it was sprayed silver. He was probably the most bizarre performer presented in that time, and you can imagine the reaction in Middle America, but the audience loved him.

Do you miss the Fifties?
Yeah, 'cause it was an exhilarating period—the pioneer days. "The Fifties" is a misnomer, by the way. What they really mean is somewhere between 1955 and 1964. *Those* are the Fifties. Prior to '55 was almost the Forties. The music I listened to was the last vestige of the big-band era. Then it changed. Then it radically changed after 1964.

The reason everybody loves the Fifties is nothing ever happened. It was a bit of fluff, the last time I can think of in American history that we thought we were the good guys. It was a make-believe period. We didn't have a lot of substance.

On the surface, the Fifties seemed to be placid. Wasn't there a dark side?
I don't recall one, other than in normal life. Girls got pregnant; they had illegal abortions. Nobody did drugs; a lot of people drank.

Those things aside, you felt you were living in the best of all possible worlds?
Yeah. I was a white, middle-class kid. I'm talking about my personal experience. I wasn't black. There wasn't a thing in the world that I could conjure up that wasn't going well.

The music establishment, and adults in general, really hated rock & roll. Politicians, ministers,

older songwriters and musicians foamed at the mouth. Frank Sinatra reportedly called Elvis Presley a "rancid-smelling aphrodisiac." Why do you think they had such a violent reaction?

All you had to do was listen to the old records. Put one on next to the music they were listening to prior to that. The change was shocking. It was alien music. It was heathen. It was against all the rules.

I can tell you the reaction I saw. It was loud, and the adults said, "Turn it down." They didn't understand the lyrics—"We're gonna ball all night." We would explain that meant we were going to dance all night. The term *rock & roll* was a sexual term when it first started. I don't think they knew any of that. I just think they didn't like the sound and the loudness.

I remember when we were touring, we had to use the house sound system, and I would turn to some ancient stagehand and say, "Turn it up." He'd get to a point, and I'd say, "Crank it up four more notches and *leave* it there." They couldn't understand that we wanted an ear-blasting sound, and that was like chamber music compared to what we're listening to today.

In 1960, you appeared before the House Legislative Oversight Subcommittee, which was looking into allegations of payola in the record business and on *American Bandstand*. To what extent was the payola issue an excuse to try and kill rock & roll?

You wanna get right down to the core of what that was all about? It was an election year. The politicians had finished with show scandals, and they needed another headline grabber. They did their damnedest to respond to the pressures they were getting from parents and publishing companies and people who were being driven out of business [by rock] and said, "Aha! People are being paid to play records!"

They knew little or nothing and cared less about what the music was. They knew it hit a responsive chord with the electorate, the older people. If they said, "This music is rotten, it's bad for your kids, it's gonna rot their teeth and their hair will fall out . . . or . . . they'll all turn into maniacs by listening to it," they had a chord they could play very loudly.

The miracle of all this is that despite the opposition of old-line music publishers, songwriters, politicians, a lot of vociferous parents, schoolteachers, religious leaders—that was a pretty tough set of adversaries, and they full-out *hated* the music—it stayed alive. It could've been nipped in the bud, because they could've stopped it from being on television, radio.

You mention song publishing. Another rap against you was that you used your position as host of *American Bandstand* to rip off artists, that you traded airtime on the show for publishing rights to songs. While host of *Bandstand*, you acquired over 150 copyrights and branched out to own or partly own thirty-three businesses. That's part of what the congressional subcommittee was investigating.

I was probably the most prominent disc jockey, and they assumed that because I was successful, I was taking money to play records. To a congressman, someone in their twenties making half a million dollars a year was obviously a thief. It proved not to be true. I did have publishing interests, because in all honesty, I wasn't being paid to do television. Our budget in those days was $1,500 a week to do *Bandstand*, so I went into the music business to make a living. I had ABC's permission to be in the record business. Nothing I did was illegal. It may not have been without a conflict of interest, and that was when ABC came to me and said, "What do you want to be in: the broadcasting business or the record business?" I said, "I want to be in the broadcasting business." It probably cost me a few million dollars.

How did you get those song-publishing rights? Was there a quid pro quo? Airtime for publishing credit?

No. That was the one thing the congressmen discovered was not true. Try as they could, they couldn't prove it.

That there had been any payoff in airtime for— I woulda been in jail. Actually, I *wouldn't* have been in jail, 'cause it wasn't illegal. But they tried real hard to make that point, and failing that, they let me go with a pat on the back, saying, "You are obviously a bright young man. You didn't invent the system; go on about your business."

Why'd they go after you?

Headlines. These guys would sit in a hearing room and leave early to go make a statement to the press for the afternoon and evening newspapers and television. They tapped my phone and broke into my house. It was the first time I ever realized that our governmental system wasn't all pure.

The contrast is often drawn between you and Alan Freed. He came out of the payola scandals a broken man. You survived and prospered, seemingly unscathed. Did the experience leave scars?

Yeah. The guy that chased me for months, the interrogating attorney, said *awful* things about me. At one point, he characterized me as the Baby Face Nelson of the music business. Yet when they took a luncheon dismissal, he allowed his kid to skip school, and took me into the anteroom to say, Would I please take pictures with him and give him [an] autograph. It was all an *act*. It was very upsetting. One of the congressmen was a drunkard, and he would show up and barely be able to speak. These assistants would hand him notes, and he'd interrogate me having no idea what he was saying. Another man was—you wouldn't hire him to work for you if you had a company—he was a borderline moron. I don't know if I'll ever get over it.

What did you learn?

Protect your ass at all times. I think that's good advice for anybody growing up.

What do you think about the album-stickering movement that's springing up from state to state, making it a prisonable offense to sell so-called obscene records to minors?

Anyone who believes in any form of censorship in this country has to be misinformed or have some other reason for doing it. If you object to lyrical content or what the words of a song say or the tempo or the beat or whatever else [because] you have young children in the house, well, that's your job. You're supposed to watch over your kids. You don't want the government doing it.

Why don't you take a strong public stand against people like Tipper Gore and the anti-rock crusaders?

Because the minute they get Frank Zappa [who appeared before Congress to oppose the PMRC's censorship campaign], God bless him, they've got headlines.

One thing you did take a stand on was integration. You integrated American Bandstand on your own long before the other network shows had the courage to do so.

When I got the show in 1956, a few blacks were allowed in the audience, just a smattering. When we went on the network in 1957, I sat down with producer Tony Mammarella and said, "We gotta do something." We weren't integrationists or pioneers; we could see it was gonna happen, and there was no sense not doing it.

I recall the very first day I ever spoke to a black kid on the air. I was terrified, because I didn't know what the reaction was going to be. I ran backstage to see if there was any reaction, and the wonderful irony was, nobody called. From that day forward, nobody ever called, and it just happened.

You integrated a five-day-a-week, nationally televised show, and no one noticed?

There wasn't one letter, and we had fifteen thousand letters a week.

From 1959 through the early Sixties, you put together some pretty amazing Caravan of Stars tours, barnstorming the country with the Drifters, the Crystals, Chubby Checker, the Shirelles, Duane Eddy, Dion. The country was still segregated in many areas. What kind of problems did you encounter?

The Caravan of Stars was a group of people that came together on a Tuesday for rehearsal and on Wednesday were put on a bus and sent on the road for sixty to ninety days. Blacks and whites. The proportion in the early days might've been sixty-forty black to white. Whites and blacks got along fine. The shocking part was to walk outside the bus and go into a theater where the blacks sat downstairs or upstairs or on one side or in separate shows. To have to eat in a Greyhound bus terminal, live in different hotels. For most of us from the semi-integrated world of the North, it was scary.

You can't live and eat and sleep next to people in a bus for that long and not begin to feel these are my people, we are together. Some redneck was giving the Drifters a bad time somewhere in North or South Carolina, and a white group, I think it was the Dovells, came out and kicked the shit out of the white guys.

The bus broke down once, and Dick and Deedee, two white performers, had to go into a restaurant and cook the food to bring it out to the others, because they wouldn't let the blacks inside.

One of your rules of the road was that artists were not allowed to incite the crowd. That's not a very rock & roll attitude.

Yeah, that was for insurance, practical purposes. They'd had riots, stabbings, incidents where people from the stage incited people to run to the front of the stage. That's sheer stupidity. You don't want to see people hurt, killed. You don't want to get sued. If it happens, you've added another nail to the coffin.

You ended every show with a white ballad. Why?

The star of the tour was usually a white teen idol. That was the performer who'd get the most screams and probably the highest pay. In those days they got $2,500 a week.

While you were touring, you'd have a party every few weeks to relieve tension. For entertainment, the artists would impersonate one another.

People would change costumes. Three white guys would do the Supremes, and the Supremes individually would do Gene Pitney. I've got 8mm film that a friend took of one of the caravans. I've got great pictures of Tom Jones in drag doing one of the acts on the show.

You've worked and palled around with the most talented people in the business since 1955. What's your talent, Dick?

My talent is bringing out the best in other talent, organizing people to showcase them, and being able to survive the ordeal. I hope someday that somebody will say that in the beginning stages of the birth of the music of the Fifties, though I didn't contribute in terms of creativity, I helped keep it alive.

You've probably played a million requests through the years. Are there any songs that tell your story?

My favorite all-time song is Jesse Belvin's "Goodnight My Love." It was the last song we would play at the record dance [in Philadelphia]. I did seven a week; that's how I made money, seventy-five cents a head, and I ground those things out—sometimes two a night. The last record I would play was "Goodnight My Love." That meant I could go home.

my favorite childhood 45s

By PETER WOLF

My older sister was a dancer on Alan Freed's TV show *The Big Beat*. We lived in a small, three-room apartment in the Bronx, and it was almost impossible to get away from the music she and her friends were always dancing to.

I've been an insomniac all my life, and I've always listened to radio at night. Back then, you could turn the dial and find such unique music; each DJ had a personalized style and programmed his own show. Alan Freed was the most popular, and Jocko Henderson did a lot of jivin' fast patter on *Jocko's Rocketship Show*. In the wee, wee hours, the Magnificent Montague had a program for lovers, and on weekends, there was *Slim's Radio Show*, which was broadcast from a record store in the Times Square subway station. They featured doo-wop groups from all over the city. Groups could be on the street corner singing a cappella one day, go in the studio, and by the end of the week, their record would be on the streets. There weren't any demographics or ratings; it was a simpler process from street corner to airwaves.

1 **"Heartbreak Hotel,"** by Elvis Presley (RCA). I remember sitting on the stoop of my building and hearing this song coming from a neighbor's window. The sound of the voice, the echo, the slap-back, was like nothing else. It was a record I had to own immediately.

2 **"Long Tall Sally,"** by Little Richard (Specialty). There was a place called the Bronx Community Center, which my sister's friends used as a clubhouse. They had an old jukebox with "Long Tall Sally" on it. The aggressiveness of the track and the voice made me a Little Richard fan instantly.

3 **"Why Do Fools Fall in Love,"** by Frankie Lymon and the Teenagers (Gee). Being a kid growing up in New York in the Fifties, there was no way the power and high emotion of Frankie Lymon couldn't touch you. He was the first great child star of rock & roll.

4 **"Whole Lotta Shakin' Going On,"** by Jerry Lee Lewis (Sun). I was in a record store the first time I heard this. In those days people would buy a label—they'd say, "Got anything on Sun?" The owners worked one-on-one with the customers, and I remember the guy saying, "If you like that Little Richard record, you'll love this."

5 **"School Day,"** by Chuck Berry (Chess). This was one of the first great theme songs of getting up early in the morning—school, school, school.

6 **"Maybe,"** by the Chantels (End). I was at an Alan Freed show at the Bronx Paradise Theater. Ed Townsend was singing "For Your Love," when there was a commotion in the theater: The Chantels had arrived to go backstage; they came down the theater aisle in pastel crinoline dresses, and the audience went nuts. Ed Townsend had to stop singing. It was, unfortunately, the first example I saw of one-upmanship. Yet when the Chantels sang "Maybe," it was a holy moment.

7 **"Dream Lover,"** by Bobby Darin (Atco). Along with Dion, Bobby Darin was a "must" for a guy growing up in an Italian-Jewish section of the Bronx. Bobby was a particular favorite of mine because he wrote his own material and was one of the first artists to produce himself.

8 **"Bye Bye Love,"** by the Everly Brothers (Cadence). The first time I ever performed was in the Bronx Park Community Talent Show. The group's name was the Three Imps—it was myself, Steve Schwartz, and Steve Salerno with Richie Gold, who played clarinet. Minutes before we were to perform, Richie's mother wanted him to go solo; he nearly lost his life in the boys' bathroom. We did "Bye Bye Love" but lost the talent show to Steve Schwartz's little sister, who sang "This Old Man." So much for following kids.

9 **"Bo Diddley,"** by Bo Diddley (Checker). It's got a great beat, and you can dance to it.

10 **"The Wind,"** by Nolan Strong and the Diablos (Fortune), and **"Deserie,"** by the Charts (Everlast). My sister and her friends did a dance to these records called the grind, and it was pretty much as the name implies: It was impossible to dance any closer. Even today these records make me stop, and I get lost in two truly great ballads of the period. The idea that records like these were created by such young guys off the street makes me believe that youthful innocence will make rock & roll go on forever.

the sixties

By MIKAL GILMORE

For a long and unforgettable season, rock was a voice of unity and liberty. In the 1950s, rock & roll meant disruption: It was the clamor of young people kicking hard against the Eisenhower era's ethos of vapid repression. By the onset of the 1960s, that spirit had been largely tamed or simply impeded by numerous misfortunes, including the film and army careers of Elvis Presley, the death of Buddy Holly, the blacklisting of Jerry Lee Lewis and Chuck Berry and the persecution of DJ Alan Freed, who had been stigmatized by payola charges by Tin Pan Alley interests and politicians angered with his championing of R&B and rock & roll. In 1960, the music of Frankie Avalon, Paul Anka, Connie Francis and Mitch Miller (an avowed enemy of rock & roll) ruled the airwaves and the record charts, giving some observers the notion that decency and order had returned to the popular mainstream.

But within a few years, rock would regain its disruptive power with a joyful vengeance, until by the decade's end, it would be seen as a genuine force of cultural and political consequence. For a long and unforgettable season, it was a truism—or threat, depending on your point of view—that rock & roll could (and *should*) make a difference: that it was eloquent and inspiring and principled enough to change the world, maybe even save it.

How did such a dramatic development take place? How did rock & roll come to be seen as such a potent voice for cultural revolution?

In part, of course, it was simply a confluence of auspicious conditions and ambitious prodigies that broke things open. Or, if you prefer a more romantic and mythic view, you could say that rock & roll set something loose in the 1950s—a spirit of cultural abandon— that could not be stopped or refused, and you might even be right. Certainly, rock & roll had demonstrated that it was capable of inspiring massive generational and social ferment and that its rise could even have far-reaching political consequences. This isn't to say that enjoying Presley or rock & roll was the same as subscribing to liberal politics, nor is it to suggest that the heroism of R&B and rock musicians was equal to that of civil rights campaigners like Martin Luther King, Jr., Medgar Evers and Rosa Parks, who paid through pain, humiliation and blood for their courage. Rock & roll *did* present black musical forms—and consequently, black sensibilities and black causes—to a wider (and whiter) audience than ever before, however, and as a result, it drove a fierce, threatening wedge into the heart of the American musical mainstream.

By the 1960s—as the sapless Eisenhower years were ending and the brief, lusty Kennedy era was forming—a new generation was coming of age. The parents of this generation had worked and fought for ideals of peace, security and affluence, and they expected their children not only to appreciate and benefit from the bequest but also to affirm and extend their prosperous new world. But the older generation was also passing on legacies of fear and some unpaid debts—anxieties about nuclear obliteration and leftist ideologies and sins of racial violence—and in the push to stability, priceless ideals of equality and justice had been compromised, even lost.

Consequently, the children of this age—who would forever be dubbed the Baby Boom Generation—were beginning to question the morality and politics of postwar America, and some of their musical tastes began to reflect this unrest. In particular, folk music (which had been driven underground in the 1950s by conservative forces) was now enjoying a popular resurgence. Under the influence of Joan Baez and Peter, Paul and Mary, folk was turning more politically explicit, becoming increasingly identified with civil rights and pacifism, among other causes.

But it was in the nasal-toned, rail-thin young Bob Dylan—who had moved from Minnesota to New York to assume the legacy of Woody Guthrie—that folk found its greatest hope: a remarkably prolific songwriter who was giving a forceful and articulate voice to the apprehensions and ideals of the emerging restless generation. With "Blowin' in the Wind" and "A Hard Rain's a-Gonna Fall" in 1963, Dylan penned songs about racial suffering and the threat of nuclear apocalypse that immediately acquired the status of anthems, and with "The Times They Are a-Changin'" in early 1964, he wrote an apt and chilling decree of the rising tensions of the coming era. "Come, mothers and fathers / Throughout the land," he sang in a voice young with anger and old with knowledge. "And don't criticize / What you can't understand; / Your sons and your daughters are beyond your command; / Your old road is / Rapidly agin'; / Please get out of the new one / If you can't lend your hand, / For the times they are a-changin'."

For all its egalitarian ideals, though, folk was a music of past and largely spent traditions. As such, it was also the medium for an alliance of politicos and intelligentsia that

bob dylan in New York City, **1964** >
MICHAEL OCHS ARCHIVES/VENICE, CA

viewed a teen-rooted mass entertainment form like rock & roll with derision. The new generation had not yet found a style or a standard-bearer that could tap the temper of the times in the same way that Presley and rockabilly had in the 1950s.

When rock & roll rejuvenation came, it was from a place small, unlikely and far away. Indeed, in the early 1960s, Liverpool, England, was a fading port town that had slid from grandeur to dilapidation during the postwar era, and it was viewed by snobbish Londoners as a demeaned place of outsiders. But one thing Liverpool had was a brimming pop scene, made

The Fab Four storm London, **1963** >

MICHAEL OCHS ARCHIVES/VENICE, CA

up of bands playing tough and exuberant blues—and R&B-informed rock & roll—and in December 1962, the city's most popular group, a four-piece ensemble called the Beatles, broke into Britain's Top Forty with a folkish rock song, "Love Me Do." There was little about the single that heralded greatness—the group's leaders, John Lennon and Paul McCartney, weren't yet distinguished songwriters. Nonetheless, the song began a momentum that would forever shatter the American grip on the U.K. pop charts.

In many ways, Britain was as ripe for a pop cataclysm as America had been for Presley during the ennui after World War II. In England—catching the reverberations not just of Presley but of the jazz milieu of Miles Davis and Jack Kerouac—the youth scene had acquired the status of a mammoth subcultural class, which was the by-product of a postwar population top-heavy with people under the age of eighteen. For those people, pop music denoted more than preferred entertainment or even stylistic rebellion: It signified the idea of autonomous society. British teenagers weren't just rejecting their parents' values: They were superseding them, though they were also acting out their eminence in American terms— in the music of Presley and rockabilly, in blues and the jazz tradition.

When Brian Epstein—a Liverpool record store manager who was aspiring to a more eventful life—first saw the Beatles at one of the city's cellar jazz clubs, the Cavern, he saw a band that not only delivered its American obsessions with infectious verve but also reflected British youths' joyful sense of being cultural outsiders, ready to seize everything that they had been refused. What's more, Epstein figured that the British pop scene would recognize and seize on this kinship. As the group's manager, Epstein cleaned up the Beatles' punkness considerably, but he didn't deny the group its spirit or its musical instincts, and in a markedly short time, his faith paid off. A year after "Love Me Do" peaked at Number Seventeen in the *New Musical Express* charts, the Beatles had six singles active in the Top Twenty in the same week, including the three top positions—an unprecedented feat. In the process, Lennon and McCartney had grown enormously as writers—in fact, they were already one of the best composing teams in pop history—and the group itself had upended the local pop scene, establishing a hierarchy of longhaired male ensembles playing a popwise but hard-bashing update of 1950s-style rock & roll. But there was more to it than mere pop success. In less than a year, the Beatles had transformed British pop culture, redefining not just its intensities and possibilities but turning it into a matter of nationalistic impetus.

On February 9, 1964, following close on the frenzied breakthrough of "I Want to Hold Your Hand" and "She Loves You," the TV variety show kingpin Ed Sullivan presented the Beatles for the first time to a mass American audience, and it proved to be an epochal moment. The Sullivan appearance drew more than 70 million viewers—the largest TV audience ever, at that time—an event that cut across divisions of style and region and drew new divisions of era and age; an event that, like Presley's TV appearances, made rock & roll seem an irrefutable opportunity. Within days it was apparent that a genuine upheaval was under way, offering a frenetic distraction to the dread that had set into America after the assassination of President John F. Kennedy, and summoning a renewal of the brutally wounded ideal that youthfulness carried our national hope. Elvis Presley had shown us how rebellion could be fashioned in eye-opening style; the Beatles were showing us how style could have the impact of cultural revelation—or at least how a pop vision might be forged into an unimpeachable consensus. Virtually overnight, the Beatles' arrival in the American consciousness announced not only that the music and times were changing but also that *we* were changing. Everything about the band—its look, sound, style and abandon—made it plain that we were entering a different age, that young people were free to redefine themselves in completely new terms.

All of this raises an interesting question: Would the decade's pop and youth scenes have been substantially different without the Beatles? Or were the conditions such that, given the right catalyst, an ongoing pop explosion was inevitable? Certainly other bands (including the Dave Clark Five, the Searchers, Gerry and the Pacemakers, the Zombies and Manfred Mann) contributed to the sense of an emerging scene, and still others (among them the Kinks, the Who, the Animals and the Rolling Stones) would make music just as vital and more aggressive (and sometimes smarter and more revealing). Yet the Beatles had a singular gift that transcended even their malleable sense of style, or John Lennon's and Paul McCartney's genius as songwriters and arrangers, or Brian Epstein's and producer George Martin's unerring stewardship as devoted mentors. Namely, the Beatles possessed an almost impeccable flair for rising to the occasion of their own moment in history, for honoring the promise of their own talents, and this knack turned out to be the essence of their artistry. The thrill and momentum wouldn't fade for several years. The music remained a constant surprise and delight; it continually transfixed and influenced us, as the Beatles' work and presence intensified our lives.

In short, the Beatles were a rupture—they changed modern history, and no less a craftsman than Bob Dylan understood the meaning of their advent. "They were doing things nobody else was doing," he later told his biographer Anthony Scaduto, "but I just kept it to myself that I really dug them. Everybody else thought they were just for the teenyboppers, that they were gonna pass right away, but it was obvious to me that they had staying power. I knew they were pointing the direction that music had to go. . . . It seemed to me a definite line was being drawn. This was something that never happened before."

Coming from Dylan, this was considerable praise. In his stint as a folk eminence, he had been writing vastly influential songs that held a brave and glaring mirror up to the face of cultural corruption, and he did it all with unequaled poetic grace. But Dylan—who, like the Beatles, had grown up on the music of Presley, Jerry Lee Lewis and Buddy Holly—was feeling confined by the limited interests of the folk audience and by the narrow stylistic range of folk music itself. After witnessing the breakthrough of the Beatles and after hearing the rawer blues-based rock being made by the Animals and the Rolling Stones, Dylan realized it was possible to transform and enliven his music, connecting with a broader and more vital audience in the process. (When the Byrds scored a June 1965 Number One hit with their chiming folk-rock cover of "Mr. Tambourine Man," it only further convinced him.)

On July 25, 1965, Dylan took the stage with the Paul Butterfield Blues Band at the Newport Folk Festival and played a brief, howling set of the new electric music he had been recording. The shocked folk purists howled back at him in rage, and for fair reason: The music that Dylan began making on albums like *Bringing It All Back Home* and *Highway 61 Revisited* would effectively kill off any remaining notions that folk was the imperative new art form of American youth and confer on rock a greater sense of consequence and a deeper expressiveness. Clearly, it was music worth the killing of old conceits and older ways. In particular, with "Like a Rolling Stone" (the singer's biggest hit and the decade's most liberating, form-stretching single), Dylan framed perfectly the spirit of an emerging generation that was trying to live by its own rules and integrity and that was feeling increasingly cut off from the conventions and privileges of the mainstream culture. In the same manner that he had once given voice to rising political consciousness, Dylan seemed to be voicing our deepest-felt fears and hopes, to be speaking for *us*. "How does it *fee-eel*," he brayed at his brave new audience, "To be without a *home*, / Like a complete *unknown*, / Like a *RO-olling STONE?*"

How *did* it feel? It felt scary, it felt exhilarating, and suddenly it felt *exactly* like rock & roll.

Combined, the Beatles and Dylan had a seismic effect on popular music and youth culture. They changed the soundscape and ambition of rock & roll in thorough and irrevocable ways that still carry tremendous influence. They also had a sizable impact on each other. The Beatles opened up new possibilities in style and consensus; without their headway, Dylan probably would never have conceived "Like a Rolling Stone," much less enjoyed a smash hit with it. If the Beatles opened up a new audience, though, Dylan determined what could be done with that consensus, what could be *said* to that audience. His mid-1960s work single-handedly reinvented pop's known rules of language and meaning and revealed that rock & roll's familiar structures could accommodate new, unfamiliar themes, that a pop song could be about *any* subject a writer was smart enough or daring enough to tackle. Without this crucial assertion, it is inconceivable that the Beatles would have gone on to write "Nowhere Man," "Eleanor Rigby," "Paperback Writer," "Strawberry Fields Forever" or "A Day in the Life" or even that the Rolling Stones would have written the decade's toughest riff and most taunting and libidinous declaration: "(I Can't Get No) Satisfaction."

Dylan also influenced the Beatles in two other important respects. For one thing, he was reportedly the person who introduced them to drugs (marijuana, specifically), during his 1964 tour of England. This brand of experimentation would gradually affect not only the

< THE ROLLING STONES, FROM LEFT TO RIGHT:
brian jones, mick jagger, keith richards (seated), **charlie watts** and **bill wyman**
MICHAEL OCHS ARCHIVES/VENICE, CA

^ THE SUPREMES, FROM LEFT TO RIGHT:

diana ross, mary wilson and **florence ballard**

MICHAEL OCHS ARCHIVES/VENICE, CA

Beatles' musical and lyrical perspectives but also the perspectives of an entire generation. Indeed, in the mid-1960s, drug use became increasingly identified with rock culture, though it certainly wasn't the first time drugs had been extolled as recreation or sacrament or exploited for artistic inspiration. Many jazz and blues musicians (and truth be known, numerous country & western artists) had been using marijuana and narcotics to enhance their improvisational bent for several decades, and in the 1950s, the Beats had brandished dope as another badge of nonconformism.

But with 1960s rock, as drugs crossed over from the hip underground (and from research laboratories), stony references became more overt and more mainstream than ever before. Getting high started being seen as a way of understanding deeper truths and sometimes as a way of deciphering coded pop songs (or simply enjoying the palpable aural sensations of the music). Just as important, getting stoned was a way of participating in private, forbidden experiences, as a means of staking out a consciousness apart from that of the "straight world." Along with music and politics, drugs were seen as an agency for a better world, or at least a shortcut to enlightenment or transcendence. Though the Beatles would stay demure on the subject for another year or two, by 1965, hip kids and angry authorities were already citing various Dylan and Rolling Stones songs for what were perceived as their "druggy" meanings. "Satisfaction," "Get Off of My Cloud," "Mr. Tambourine Man" and "Rainy Day Women #12 and 35" were among the singles targeted by conservative critics.

The other thing Dylan did for the Beatles was help politicize them (in fact, he helped politicize a vast segment of rock culture), inspiring the group to accept its popularity as an opportunity to define and speak to a vital youth constituency. More and more, Lennon and McCartney's music—and rock at large—became a medium for addressing the issues and events that affected that generation.

This interplay between Dylan and the Beatles was one of the central dynamics of mid-1960s rock, but it didn't make for the bulk of the action. Some of the most pleasurable and enduring music of the period was being made by the monumental, black-run Detroit label Motown, which by 1965 had scored over two dozen Top Ten hits by such artists as Smokey Robinson and the Miracles, the Supremes, the Four Tops, Marvin Gaye, Stevie Wonder, the Temptations, Martha and the Vandellas and Mary Wells. By contrast, a grittier brand of the new soul sensibility was being defined by Memphis-based artists on the Volt, Stax and Atlantic labels, like Sam and Dave, Booker T. and the MG's, Wilson Pickett, Carla and Rufus Thomas, Johnnie Taylor, Eddie Floyd, William Bell and, most memorably, Otis Redding. In other words, black forms remained vital to rock's and pop's growth (in fact, R&B's codes, styles and spirit had long served as models for white pop and teen rebellion).

As racial struggles continued through the decade, soul—as well as the best jazz from artists like Miles Davis, John Coltrane, Charles Mingus, Eric Dolphy, Ornette Coleman, Archie Shepp, Cecil Taylor and Sonny Rollins—increasingly expressed black culture's developing views of pride, identity, history and power. By 1967, when Aretha Franklin scored a massive hit with a cover of Otis Redding's "Respect," black pop signified ideals of racial pride and feminist valor that would have been unthinkable a decade earlier.

Yet perhaps the greatest triumph of the time was simply that all these riches—white invention and black genius—played alongside one another in a radio marketplace that was more open than it had ever been before (or would ever be again) for a shared audience that revered it all. Just how heady and diverse the scene was came across powerfully in the 1965 film *The T.A.M.I. Show*, a greatest hits pop revue, which in its remarkable stylistic and racial broad-mindedness anticipated the would-be catholic spirit that later characterized the Monterey Pop and Woodstock Festivals. For those few hours of *The T.A.M.I. Show*, as artists like the Supremes, the Beach Boys, Chuck Berry, Smokey Robinson and the Miracles, Marvin Gaye, Jan and Dean, James Brown and the Rolling Stones stood alongside one another onstage at the Santa Monica Civic Auditorium, rock & roll looked and felt like a dizzying, rich, complex and joyous community in which any celebration or redemption was possible.

In many ways, this longing for community—the dream of self-willed equity and harmony, or at least tolerant pluralism, in a world where familiar notions of family and accord were breaking down—would haunt rock's most meaningful moments for the remainder of the decade. Unfortunately, the same forces that deepened and expanded music's social-mindedness were also the forces that would contribute to the dissolution of the dream. In 1965, after waging the most successful "peace" campaign in America's electoral history, President Lyndon B. Johnson began actively committing American troops to a highly controversial military action in Vietnam, and it quickly became apparent that it was the young who would pay the bloodiest costs for this lamentable war effort. Sixties rock had given young people a sense that they possessed not just a new identity but a new empowerment. Now Vietnam began to teach that same audience that it was at risk, that its government and parents would willingly sacrifice young lives for old fears and distant threats—and would even use war as a means of diffusing youth's sovereignty. The contrast between those two realizations—between power and peril, between joy and fear—became the central tension that defined the late-1960s youth culture, and as rock increasingly reflected that tension, it also began forming opposition to the jeopardy.

Consequently, the music started losing its "innocence." The Beatles still managed to maintain a façade of effervescence in the sounds of records like *Beatles for Sale, Help* and even *Rubber Soul,* but the content of the songs had turned more troubled. It was as if the group had lost a certain mooring—Lennon was singing more frequently about alienation and apprehension, McCartney about the unreliability of love—and whereas their earlier music had fit into the familiar structures of 1950s rock, their newer music was moving into unaccustomed areas and incorporating strange textures. Primarily, though, the band was growing fatigued from a relentless schedule of touring, writing and recording. Following the imbroglio surrounding Lennon's assertion that the Beatles were more popular than Jesus Christ and after one last dispirited swing through America (in which they were unable to play their more adventurous new material), the Beatles called a formal quits to live performances.

Meantime, Dylan was changing the language and aspirations of popular culture with his every work and gesture. In fact, he was the clearest shot at an individual cultural hero that rock & roll had produced since Presley, but he had also been pushing himself in intense personal and creative ways. In July 1966, following a triumphant but strenuous tour of England with his storming backing band the Hawks, Dylan suffered a motorcycle accident that broke his neck and would remove him from the recording scene for over a year.

The bad news continued: Mick Jagger, Keith Richards and Brian Jones of the Rolling Stones were arrested for drug possession in a series of 1967 busts in London and pilloried by the British press and legal system. "I'm not concerned with your petty morals, which are illegitimate," Richards bravely (or perhaps foolishly) told a court official at his trial. Plainly, generational tensions were heating up into full-fledged cultural war.

Maybe these developments should have been perceived as harbingers of dissolution, but the vision of rock as a unifying and liberating force had become too exciting, too deep-seated, to be denied. By this time, rock & roll was plainly youth style, and youth was forming alternative communities and political movements throughout Europe and America. In the Haight-Ashbury district of San Francisco, something approaching utopia seemed to be happening. Bands like the Jefferson Airplane, the Grateful Dead, the Quicksilver Messenger Service, Big Brother and the Holding Company and the Charlatans were forming social bonds with their audiences and trying to build communal ethos out of a swirling mix of music, drugs, sex, metaphysics and idealistic love.

In mid-1967, after a yearlong hiatus, the Beatles helped raise this marginal worldview to worldwide possibility with the release of *Sgt. Pepper's Lonely Hearts Club Band*, a cohesive, arty and brilliant work that perfectly tapped the collective generational mood of the time and reestablished the foursome's centrality in rock's power structure. It wasn't that the Beatles invented the psychedelic or avant-garde aesthetics that their new music epitomized—in fact, the spacey codes and florid textures and arrangements clearly had been derived from the music of numerous innovative San Francisco and British bands. With *Sgt. Pepper*, though, the Beatles refined what these other groups had been groping for, and they did so in a way that unerringly manifested the sense of independence and iconoclasm that now seized youth culture. At the album's end, John Lennon sang "A Day in the Life"—the loveliest-sounding song about alienation that pop had ever yielded—and then all four Beatles hit the same loud, portentous chord on four separate pianos. As the chord lingered and then faded, it bound an entire culture in its mysteries, its implications, its sense of power and hope. In some ways, it was the most magical moment that this culture would ever share, and it was the last gesture of genuine unity that we would ever hear from the Beatles.

Sgt. Pepper was an era-defining and form-bursting work. To many, it certified that rock was now art and that art was, more than ever, a mass medium. It also established the primacy of the album as pop's main format, as a vehicle for fully formed concepts and as the main means by which rock artists communicated with their audience. Rock was now saturated not only with ideals of defiance but also with dreams of love, community and spirituality. Even the Rolling Stones, who had always sung about much darker concerns, would start recording

songs about love and altruism (that is, for a week or two). "For a brief while," wrote critic Langdon Winner of the *Sgt. Pepper era*, "the irreparably fragmented consciousness of the West was unified, at least in the minds of the young."

That blithe center couldn't forever hold. By the time *Sgt. Pepper* was on the streets, the Haight-Ashbury was already turning into an ugly place riddled with hard drugs like cocaine, heroin and speed and overpopulated with runaways, bikers, rapists, thieves and foolish shamans. In addition, a public backlash was forming. Many Americans were afraid they had lost their young to irredeemable allures and ideologies, and in California, Ronald Reagan had already won a gubernatorial campaign that was largely predicated on antiyouth sentiment. It was a time for media panic, for generational recrimination and political separatism, for opposing views of America's worth and future. It was an intoxicating time but also a frightening one. More and more, it looked as if there was no turning back and as if *everything* was at stake.

Then, within a few months, a pop counterrevolution (or at least a redefinition) was under way—headed by none other than Bob Dylan. In some ways, it was Dylan who had made psychedelia possible; more than anybody else, he had announced that all rules of form, length and content were subject to new visions and ambitions. But as works like *Sgt. Pepper* were finding their way into Dylan's remote Woodstock, New York, home (where he was recuperating from his accident), rumor had it that he was put off by the stylistic baroqueness, facile rhetoric and relentless drugginess of much of the new pop—or perhaps he was simply concerned about whether rock had outdistanced him.

In any event, at heart, Dylan was (and remains) a die-hard American formalist and Jeffersonian moralist, and the rock & roll that he had been making in seclusion with the Hawks (now simply called the Band) was music that explored the idea of what could be salvaged from the American value system. In January 1968, Dylan took this fixation one step further with his formal return to the public arena, the release of *John Wesley Harding*, a record that on one level was about a nation coming apart from within (but then, Dylan's best work had always been about America's forsworn potentials). On another level, with its sparse, almost stoical three-piece, Sun Studio—derived acoustic rock & roll sound, *John Wesley Harding* was also the boldest musical critique or challenge that Dylan ever offered. If nothing else, its simplicity made the current music of the Beatles *(Magical Mystery Tour)* and the Rolling Stones *(Their Satanic Majesties Request)*—which is to say the entire mainstream and avant-garde realm of rock—seem frivolous, if not irresponsible. It was as if Dylan thought there might be direction home after all.

John Wesley Harding helped set in motion a reevaluation—and a reaffirmation—of rock & roll root values. In a short time, old and new blues guitarists were enjoying fresh currency, gospel singers were scoring pop hits, Everly Brothers—style groups like Crosby, Stills and Nash were finding a mass audience, and even country & western was meeting with a new reception. This last trend, in particular, disturbed some critics a year later, when Dylan recorded an LP of lovely and pure country songs, *Nashville Skyline*, which included a raggedy duet with C&W star Johnny Cash. Since country was widely viewed as the music of a working-class sensibility and since it represented a conservative audience that was seen as giving stalwart support to the war in Vietnam, did this mean that Dylan had now switched political sides, or had he simply lost faith in political solutions altogether?

The truth was, folks like Dylan and his cohorts in the Band—who had emerged in their own meaningful right with *Music From Big Pink* and *The Band*—were simply trying to offer a saner, more embracing alternative to the rancorous spirit that had alienated many everyday Americans from the rock revolution. Dylan and the Band understood that there was still much to love about America and its people, despite their grand failings; in addition, there was no way the young could alienate the working- and middle-class masses and still win a genuine revolution. In late 1969, the Band's leader, guitarist Robbie Robertson, described his and Dylan's new music as a refutation of "the punky attitude that had nothing to do with music—hate your mother and stab your father. . . . So what if your parents did do you wrong?" Roberston asked. "Maybe they did, but so what? I'm tired of hearing. . . Jim Morrison and those people. I just think they're a drag. Even if that is their situation, who cares? That's got nothing to do with music."

Plenty of other artists, of course, had fewer reservations about offering music as a force of division or rebellion. Among them were the Doors (who indeed had sung gleefully about the prospect of offing dad and fucking mom), the Velvet Underground (who had popularized songs about S&M and heroin addiction), Iggy Pop and the Stooges (who acted out impulses of self-destruction), the Mothers of Invention (who looked like bikers and played like prodigies) and MC5 (a white Detroit band that was openly dedicated to the ideal of violent black revolution). In part, perhaps, these bands were simply trading on the increasingly commercial value of shock. They were also making plain, however, that underneath the veneer of altruism and idealism, the 1960s youth scene was riddled with some considerably darker truths—namely, that drugs had quickly become as much a means to obliterate as to enlighten, and that in a truly free or anarchistic society, bloodshed was as likely to be encountered as lasting peace or equality. It is a testament to the merit of such bands as the Velvets, the Doors and the Stooges that their ability to face and address these realities has helped make their music among the more enduring and oddly affirming legacies of the era.

Increasingly, the best late-1960s music was about fear, doubt and the possibility of apocalypse, and no band addressed these concerns more forthrightly or valuably than the Rolling Stones, who were quickly establishing themselves as perhaps rock's smartest and greatest band. Throughout their history, from the time they were arrested for pissing in public to the brouhaha over their drug busts, the Stones epitomized rebellion and disrespect to both fans and detractors, and they had long been the band that many parents and authority figures

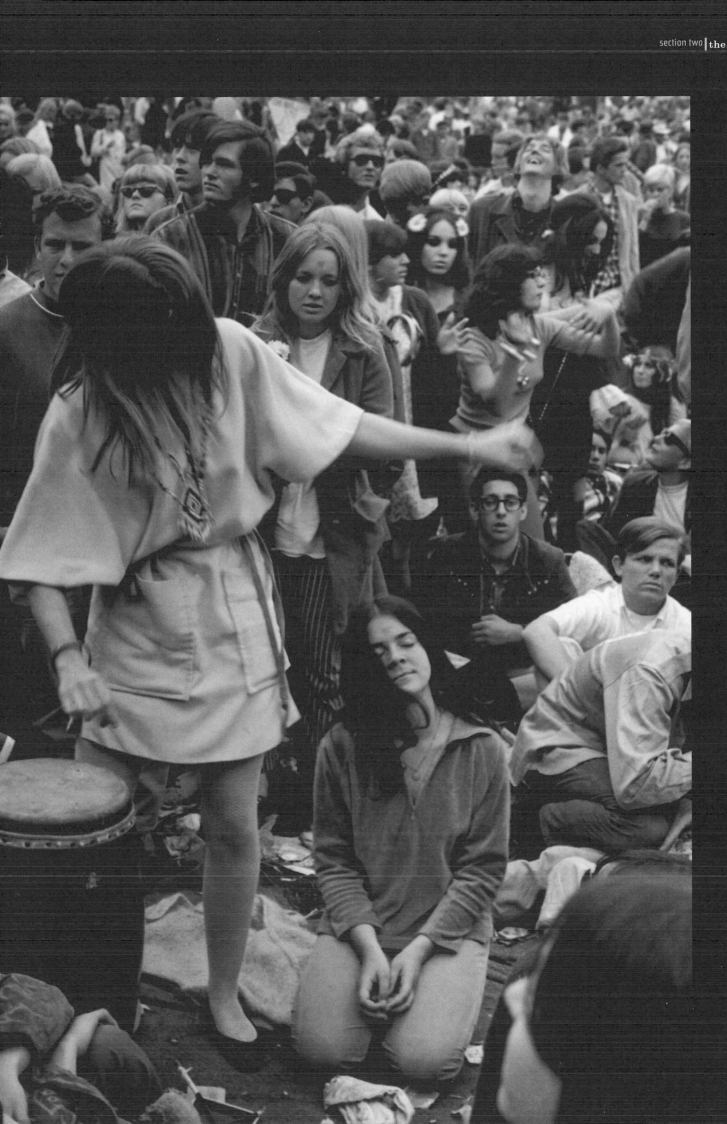

hated the most. Now, like Dylan and the Band, Mick Jagger and Keith Richards had started reasserting primal blues and country forms, and they were also asking some of the toughest questions around ("I shouted out, 'Who killed the Kennedys?'" sang Jagger in "Sympathy for the Devil," then answering unabashedly, "When, after all, it was you and me"). Whereas Dylan would, more and more, make music of withdrawal and abdication, the Stones flirted openly with questions about evil and violence that aimed to reveal both themselves and their fans as accomplices in all the modern terror and chaos.

In the year 1968, Robert Kennedy was murdered in Los Angeles, Dr. Martin Luther King, Jr., was shot to death in Memphis, and the broken hopes of millions of people erupted in costly, long-term violence (perhaps most famously at the Chicago Democratic National Convention, at which police brutally bludgeoned American youth). By now, rock & roll had become a field of hard options and opposing arguments. The Beatles seemed dazed and wearied by their role as youth leaders. On the one hand, they had recorded two versions of "Revolution," in which they opted in, and then out, of the notion of violent revolt; then, on the other, they issued "Hey Jude," their greatest anthem of community and forbearance.

The Stones, though, faced the contradictions of their positions more directly. In "Salt of the Earth" (from *Beggar's Banquet*), Jagger extolled the working-class masses, only to admit his hopeless distance from any real involvement with such people ("When I search a faceless crowd, / A swirling mass of gray and black and white, / They don't look real to me; / In fact, they look so strange"). In "Street Fighting Man" (banned in several U.S. cities for fear that it might incite more political riots), the Stones admitted to both a desire for violent confrontation and a longing for equivocation ("Hey! Think the time is right for a palace revolution, / But where I live, the game to play is compromise solution").

This meant that rock's consensus of joy and opportunity was finished, and its most significant components came apart quickly. The Beatles made more great music, but they shortly disintegrated into a tense, mutually distrusting partnership. In many ways, their deterioration was a metaphor for a larger dissolution: the failed hope for a social community we had longed for but never really achieved. Dylan withdrew for a time into writing domestic bromides, and though he would go on to make some of his most resourceful music in the 1970s (*Blood on the Tracks* and *Desire*), he would never again affect rock music and American culture as sweepingly as he had with "Like a Rolling Stone" and *John Wesley Harding*.

In the meantime, the Rolling Stones capped their grandest triumph with a tragic debacle. At the end of 1969, following the dismissal and then death of founding member Brian Jones, the Stones recouped with their strongest album, *Let It Bleed*, and with an American tour that amounted to rock's most successful large-scale concert series to date. At the end of the tour, though, eager to deflect charges of greed, the Stones staged a free concert outside San Francisco at Altamont Speedway, and following the example of the Grateful Dead, they hired the Hell's Angels as a security force. It was a day of legendary violence: The Angels pummeled scores of people, usually with little or no provocation, and in the evening, as the Stones performed "Under My Thumb," the bikers beat and stabbed a young black man to death in front of the stage, in full view of the band, the audience members and a camera crew.

Altamont was rock's ugliest moment. For years, it deflated the culture's sense of its own idealism. It also brought the Stones face to face with the violence that had been implicit in their work for years, scaring Jagger and Richards away from the themes they had been pursuing, and helped contribute to a long bout of artistic decline from which the band never fully recovered.

The dream, as one of rock's most honest voices would shortly announce, was over.

Did this series of disintegrations and bad ends negate the joy or worth of 1960s pop music? Hardly. Though it's easy to overromanticize the period, rock in the 1960s achieved some sizable victories, and the best of them have enjoyed an enduring legacy. For one thing, rock established itself as a remarkably protean form: It was now a field with a sense of its own history and traditions, as well as a field that was willing to stretch and disrupt its own aesthetics by incorporating ideas and textures from numerous other disciplines. Today we can see the perpetuation of that spirit of adventure and openness as more and more pop artists fuse African, Jamaican, Brazilian and other musical forms with familiar American and British pop sounds.

Sixties rock also showed that it was capable of more than disruption—that it could unite masses for worthy causes and could actually bring about social and humanitarian change. That assertion helped pave the way for later philanthropic and political ventures like Rock Against Racism, No Nukes, Live Aid, Farm Aid and the antiapartheid efforts. More importantly, in the 1990s when countless conservative strategists claimed credit for the rise of freedom and democracy movements throughout the world, it was imperative to declare that the protests of the 1960s youth culture—and the spirit of courage and defiance that those protests shared with rock music—probably served as an even greater impetus for many of the recent revolutionists.

Finally, 1960s music not only deepened rock & roll's ability to work as a music of rebellion, disobedience and disrespect—often worthy and noble impulses that were reenacted in 1970s punk and are still acted out in much of today's best (and worst) rap and metal music—but also made plain that pop music had become capable of expressing emotional and thematic truths that were as rich and consequential as anything contemporary film or literature had to offer. In other words, the 1960s proved that rock is anything but a trivial music; it *does* have impact, and at its worthiest, it still aims to threaten, to draw boundaries, to defy, and to win young people over to its view and its ethos.

Yet, it is also true that rock has lost much of its political and social conviction in recent years, that it is now a music that can accommodate ugly views of sexism and racism, and that perhaps too much of it has helped spread an unthinking affection for alcohol and drugs. To put it differently, 1960s rock *didn't* save the world—maybe didn't even change the world enough—but it fought good battles, and it enriched a progressive struggle that is far from finished, and far from lost. In the end, rock and youth culture met with considerable and determined opposition—and that opposition is still formidable—but for a moment, in the middle of a momentous decade, rock & roll was heroic enough to tell us the essential fact of our time: that we were finally on our own, "with no direction home." In some ways, the most important music since that time has struggled either to deny that bold truth or to follow its chilling and liberating implications to their bravest and most surprising ends.

steven tyler's
dirty dozen stones songs

I love the fucking Rolling Stones. Mick and Keith were the baddest boys on the block. Theirs was the hole I crawled out of.

1 **"Jumpin' Jack Flash."** Went without sodas for months because the jukebox took all my quarters.

2 **"Down the Road Apiece."** Mama's cookin' chicken, fried in bacon grease; a little bit of R&B, a lotta bit of sleaze.

3 **"Not Fade Away."** Buddy Holly would have loved that version—with just a touch of Bo that makes it rock.

4 **"Time Is on My Side."** It was then for the Stones and still is.

5 **"19th Nervous Breakdown."** What the early Stones gave everybody.

6 **"All Down the Line."** I used this song instead of heroin—it's a real shot in the arm. I've got a ten-minute outtake that smokes the album version. I used to keep time to it when I made love to my girlfriend.

7 **"Brown Sugar."** Pure Stones classic.

8 **"She Said Yeah."** Captured the total pandemonium of the Stones in concert.

9 **"My Obsession."** Reminds me of meeting mine in my room with a record player and the Stones' new album.

10 **"It's Only Rock 'n Roll (but I Like It)."** This capsulizes the whole Stones thing for me.

11 **"Rip This Joint."** A barn burner. It's how the Stones used to leave their concerts.

12 **"Ruby Tuesday."** Someone told me that it wasn't Brian on the recorder, so I pushed him out of the window. Spent the weekend in jail and wrote my first blues song—ah, sweet revenge.

bob dylan

By KURT LODER

Did you start out wanting to be a star?
Not really, because I always needed a song to get by.
There's a lot of singers who don't need songs to get
by. A lot of 'em are tall, good-lookin', you know?
They don't *need* to say anything to grab people. Me, I
had to make it on something other than my looks or
my voice.

**What was it that made you decide to become a
rock & roll songwriter?**
Well, now, Chuck Berry was a rock & roll songwriter,
so I never tried to write rock & roll songs, 'cause I
figured he had just done it. When I started writing
songs, they had to be in a different mold, because
who wants to be a second-rate anybody? A new generation had come along, of which I was a part—the
second generation of rock & roll people. To me, and

to others like me, it was a way of life. It was an all-
consuming way of life.

**What was the rock scene like when you arrived
in New York in the early Sixties?**
What was happening was Joey Dee and the Starliters,
which was, like, a twisting scene. There was a big
twist craze. There were little pockets, I guess, all across
the country where people were playin' rock & roll
music. But it was awfully difficult. I knew some guys
that played in the Village, and to make some extra
money, they would play in midtown clubs like the
Metropole, which used to be a burlesque house on
Seventh Avenue. Those were pretty funky places. You
could play for six hours and make ten dollars, and
there'd be some girl stripping all that time. Pretty
degrading gig, but economics being what they are,

you got to make *some* kinda money to exist with electric instruments. That's what got me out of it, actually. It was just too hard.

So you opted for folk music.

Folk music creates its own audience, because you can take a guitar anywhere, anytime. Most of the places we played in the early days were all parties—house parties, rent parties. Any kind of reason to go play someplace, and we'd be there.

Were you surprised by the public reaction to your early songs or by your eventual mass acceptance?

Not really, 'cause I paid my dues. It didn't happen overnight, you know. I came up one step at a time, and I knew when I'd come up with somethin' good. For instance, "Song to Woody," on my first record: I knew that no one had ever written anything like that before.

Still, given your unique style of writing and singing, you did seem an unlikely candidate for stardom on the pop scene in the mid-Sixties.

Well, I wasn't tryin' to get onto the radio. I wasn't singin' for Tin Pan Alley. I'd given up on all that stuff. I was downtown, you know? I wanted to make records, but I thought the furthest I could go was to make a folk-music record. It surprised the hell out of me when I was signed at Columbia Records. I was more surprised than anybody. But I never let that stop me [*laughs*].

Did you ever feel that you had tapped into the Zeitgeist in some special sort of way?

With the songs that I came up with?

Yeah.

As I look back on it now, I am surprised that I came up with so many of them. At the time, it seemed like a natural thing to do. Now I can look back and see that I must have written those songs "in the spirit," you know? Like "Desolation Row"—I was just thinkin' about that the other night. There's no logical way that you can arrive at lyrics like that. I don't know how it was done.

It just came to you?

It just came out *through* me.

By the time of "Desolation Row," in 1965, you had gone electric and had been more or less drummed out of the purist folk movement. Was that a painful experience?

No. I looked at that as an opportunity to get back into what I had been into a long time ago and to take it someplace further. Folk-music circles were very cold, anyway. Everybody was pretty strict and severe in their attitudes; it was kind of a stuffy scene. It

didn't bother me that people didn't understand what I was doing, because I had been doing it long before they were around. And I knew, when I was doin' that stuff, that *that* hadn't been done before, either, because I'd known all the stuff that had gone down before. I knew what the Beatles were doin', and that seemed to be real pop stuff. The Stones were doing blues things—just hard, city blues. The Beach Boys, of course, were doin' stuff that I didn't think had ever been done before, either. But I also knew that *I* was doing stuff that hadn't ever been done before.

Did you have more of a drive to write back then? More of a drive to make it?

Well, yeah, you had all those feelings that had been bottled up for twenty-some years, and then you got 'em all out. And once they're out, then you gotta start up again.

Do you still get inspired the same way these days?

I don't know. It's been a while since, uh...What moves you to write is something that you care about deeply. You also have to have the time to write. You have to have the isolation to write, and the more demands that are put on you, the harder it is. I mean, it seems like everybody wants a piece of your time at a certain point. There was a time when nobody cared, and that was one of the most productive times, when nobody gave a shit who I was.

Life gets complex as the years go by.

Yeah. You get older; you start having to get more family oriented. You start having hopes for other people rather than for yourself. But I don't have nothin' to complain about. I *did* it, you know? I did what I wanted to do, and I'm still doing it.

A lot of fans would say that the Band, which was backing you up in the mid-Sixties, was the greatest group you ever had. Would you agree?

Well, there were different things I liked about every band I had. I liked the *Street Legal* band a lot. I thought it was a real tight sound. Usually, it's the drummer and the bass player that make the band.

The Band had their own sound, that's for sure. When they were playin' behind me, they weren't the "Band"; they were called Levon and the Hawks. What came out on record as the Band—it was like night and day. Robbie [Robertson] started playing that real pinched, squeezed guitar sound; he had never played like that before in his life. They could cover songs great. They used to do Motown songs, and that, to me, is when I think of them as being at their best—even more so than "King Harvest" and "The Weight" and all of that. When I think of them, I think of them singin' somethin' like "Baby, Don't You Do It," covering Marvin Gaye and that kind of thing. Those were the golden days of the Band, even more so than when they played behind me.

What were some of the most memorable shows you guys did together?

Oh, man, I don't know. Just about every single one. Every night was like goin' for broke, like the end of the world.

It's funny: The music business was small back then, primitive, but the music that came out of it was really affecting. Now the business is enormous, yet it seems to have no real effect on anything. What do you think was lost back there along the way?

The *truth* of it all was covered up, buried, under the onslaught of money and that wolfish attitude— exploitation. Now it seems like the thing to do is exploit everything, you know?

A lot of people are happy to be exploited.

Yeah.

They stand in line.

Yeah, exactly.

Have you ever been approached to do a shoe ad or anything?

Oh, *yeah!* They'd like to use my tunes for different beer companies and perfumes and automobiles. I get approached on all that stuff, but shit, I didn't write them for that reason. That's never been my scene.

Do you still listen to the artists you started out with?

The stuff that I grew up on never grows old. I was just fortunate enough to get it and understand it at that early age, and it still rings true for me. I'd still rather listen to Bill and Charlie Monroe than any current record. That's what America's all about to me. I mean, they don't have to make any more new records—there's enough old ones, you know?

Who are some of the greatest live performers you've ever seen?

I like Charles Aznavour a lot. I saw him in sixty-something, at Carnegie Hall, and he just blew my brains out. I went there with somebody who was French, not knowing what I was getting myself into.

Howlin' Wolf, to me, was the greatest live act, because he did not have to move a finger when he performed—if that's what you'd call it, "performing." I don't like people that jump around. When

people think about Elvis moving around, he didn't jump around: He moved with *grace.*

Mick Jagger seems to jump around onstage a bit too much, don't you think?

I love Mick Jagger. I mean, I go back a long ways with him, and I always wish him the best. But to see him jumping around like he does—I don't give a shit what age, from Altamont to RFK Stadium—you don't have to *do* that, man. It's still hipper and cooler to be Ray Charles, sittin' at the piano, not movin' shit. And still getting across, you know? Pushing rhythm and soul across. It's got nothin' to do with jumping around. I mean, what could it possibly have to *do* with jumping around?

Do you think there's any point today in people getting together—the way they did in the Sixties— to try to change things?

Well, people are still strivin' to do good, but they have to overcome the evil impulse, and as long as they're tryin' to do that, things can keep lookin' up. But there's so much evil. It spreads wider and wider, and it causes more and more confusion. In every area. It takes your breath away.

Because so many of the things that were scorned in the Sixties, like living your life just to make money, are accepted now?

Yeah, but it isn't really accepted. Maybe in America it is, but that's why America's gonna go down, you know? It's gonna go *down.* It just can't exist. You can't just keep rippin' things off. Like, there's just a *law* that says you cannot keep rippin' things off.

Have you ever considered moving to another country? Where would you feel more at home?

I'm comfortable wherever people don't remind me of who I am. Anytime somebody reminds me of who I am, that kills it for me. If I wanted to wonder about who I am, I could start dissecting my own stuff. I don't have to go on other people's trips of who *they* think I am. A person doesn't like to feel self-conscious, you know? Now, Little Richard says if you don't want your picture taken, you got no business being a star, and he's right, he's absolutely right. But I don't like my picture being taken by people I don't know.

But you are a star—

Yeah, well, I guess so. But, uh . . . I feel like I'm a star, but I can shine for who I want to shine for. You know what I mean?

roger mcguinn's
top ten bob dylan songs

1 **"Mr. Tambourine Man."** I love the poetry in it and the melody. The way I interpreted it, it was like a prayer, although I didn't know what Bob had in mind. I never asked him. I think he sort of meant what I meant by it, too, which is kind of "Take me, God, and use me in this life for something."

He was doing a 2/4 thing, a folk arrangement of it. I changed it around to make it more radio oriented, more rock & roll, with a 4/4 beat to it. I put the chorus first—he put the chorus first, too, but I cut it down to one verse for time. We picked the verse with the "boot heels" because it seemed cool.

2 **"Positively 4th Street."** The Byrds did this on *Untitled*, and I think it's just an amazing song. It's got a beautiful, flowing melody, like a lot of his best songs. And it doesn't have a chorus as such, just this melody that carries you along, this gentle flow that has so much subtle power to it.

The words are interesting, too, because I have had personal experiences that relate to what I think he's talking about. He was surrounded by a lot of these sycophants at the time, which he couldn't stand, people he could not trust: "Oh, you like me now, but where were you back then?" Or people who used to act like his friends but who turned the other way because he wasn't doing what *they* wanted him to do, like when he went electric. And I know how he felt, because I went through a lot of the same things with the Byrds.

3 **"My Back Pages."** Our manager, Jim Dickson, who was no longer working with us, and I were both coming up Laurel Canyon in our Porsches, and he happened to be next to me at a stoplight. He rolled the window down and said, "Hey, I've got a song you should do." I said, "What?" And he said, "'My Back Pages.'" I went home,

got the Dylan record out and learned it. Again, we did change the arrangement a bit. The original was in a 3/4 beat, and we changed it to 4/4.

This is a song about the wisdom that comes with experience. Another great melody—it's another one of those great Anglo folk melodies. It makes you wonder how a kid from Hibbing, Minnesota, came up with these melodies. Where did he hear these things?

4 **"It's All Over Now, Baby Blue."** Another one of *those* melodies. You wouldn't think of Dylan as someone who was much of a singer, but he came up with these melodies that were unbelievable. When he did them, a song like "Baby Blue" would have that lonesome Ramblin' Jack Elliott kind of sound. Our version, though, didn't work out, because of poor execution. We were not very well disciplined in the studio. Also, John [Lennon] and Paul [McCartney] were in the studio watching [Bob Dylan was reportedly also there], and that put a lot of pressure on us [*laughs*].

5 **"Up to Me."** It's on the *Biograph* album. It wasn't released for a long time [the song is a 1974 outtake from *Blood on the Tracks*], but I did it on my *Cardiff Rose* album. It was time to record, and I called up Dylan's publishing people. They sent over a couple of songs, and that was one of them. And I loved it when I heard it. I liked the melody, the lyrics, the whole atmosphere it produced. It's very autobiographical, and I identified with that: "The old Rounder in the iron mask / Slipped me the master key; / Somebody had to unlock your heart; / He said it was up to me . . . So I waited all night 'til the break of day, / Hopin' one of us could get free; / When the dawn came over the river bridge, / I knew it was up to me." You can hear him going through this labyrinth of different rooms, with all these mysterious, clandestine things going

on in each one. My version came off pretty well. Mick Ronson produced it, and Howie Wyeth, Rob Stoner and David Mansfield from the Rolling Thunder Revue were all on it. It's pretty up.

6 **"Blowin' in the Wind."** You can't talk about Dylan songs without talking about "Blowin' in the Wind." I was over at the White Horse Tavern, in the West Village, one night—I used to hang out there quite a bit in the early Sixties—and Theodore Bikel came in and pulled out his guitar, as he frequently did for the regulars there, and he played "Blowin' in the Wind." He'd just been over to Folk City, where he'd just heard Dylan play it for the first time that night, and Bikel was sort of the town crier, going around to the different pubs, playing it for people. He was totally blown away, as we were, too. It's the ultimate civil rights song, and the civil rights movement was really starting to take root at that point. It's an anthem of that, a new "We Shall Overcome."

The Byrds didn't do it, I think, because Peter, Paul and Mary had already done it so completely. It wasn't something that was fair game or open territory anymore. I never played it as a solo. I never even played it for fun. It was kind of sacrosanct.

7 **"Knockin' on Heaven's Door."** Oh, I love this one. I was on the session with Bob on this one. He was at my house in Malibu, California, with Harry Dean Stanton right after they got back from Durango, New Mexico, where they shot *Pat Garrett & Billy the Kid.* We were hanging out, and he said, "I'm going to be cutting a song for the movie. You want to come down?" So, I drove him down to the studio, and I was on the session, playing twelve-string on "Knockin' on Heaven's Door" and singing backgrounds on a couple of other things. I played banjo on "Turkey Chase" and did some *la-la-la*'s.

But I love that scene when Slim Pickens gets shot and his wife comes out. She's with him, and he's dying out there, and this song comes up on the soundtrack. It gives me goose bumps every time.

Dylan's always been a spiritual person. He's always been searching. He was always reading

the Bible, and a lot of his stuff is right out of the Bible—"For the loser now / Will be later to win" [from "The Times They Are a-Changin'"]. It's all in the Bible.

8 **"You Ain't Goin' Nowhere."** That was a single from our *Sweetheart of the Rodeo* album. That was also one of Dylan's first ventures into country music that I can remember. It was also one that he hadn't recorded at that point. We got this one before he did it. It was more of a skiffle thing when he did it with the Band, with a steel guitar and all that.

I figure he wrote it after his motorcycle accident, when he was laid up and wasn't going anywhere. Living up in Woodstock, New York, looking out at the fence: "Clouds so swift, / Rain won't lift." And maybe Sara was gonna come up and see him: "Tomorrow's the day / My bride's gonna come." I don't know if that's what was really happening, but it's a very vivid picture. Of course, some people still say he never had a motorcycle accident [*laughs*].

9 **"Just Like a Woman."** I love this one just because of the melody [*hums the verse*]. It's just a soaring melody, an anthem. It sounds like the British national anthem or something. And the words—"With her fog, her amphetamine and her pearls." He paints this picture that is amazing. I did record this one once, but it never came out.

10 **"Sara."** I really like this one from *Desire.* I love almost all of the things on *Desire.* He cowrote those with Jacques Levy, who had been my songwriting partner. The songs on that album were so autobiographical. And "Sara"—"Stayin' up for days in the Chelsea Hotel, / Writin' 'Sad-Eyed Lady of the Lowlands' for you." There's this whole picture of him and Sara being there. I'd seen them there at one point, and the song gives such a great feeling of what it must have been like for them then. He has a gift for summing things up in just a few words.

I think his whole songwriting technique is spiritual. I read things where he's said that he just plugs into something out *there*, tunes into it like a radio, and it comes out of him. He doesn't know where it comes from—he just gets it.

8
3

roger mcguinn

By DAVID FRICKE

Roger McGuinn never particularly liked Los Angeles. He lived there for the better part of two decades, 1963 through 1980. As the principal singer, lead guitarist and de facto leader of the Byrds, McGuinn was also one of the city's most distinguished rock & roll citizens—an early champion of Bob Dylan's songs, a confidant of the Beatles and a major instigator of the folk-, acid- and country-rock movements that transformed pop music during the Sixties.

But he never really *liked* Los Angeles. "I always looked down on L.A., like it wasn't the real world," McGuinn says with a chuckle. "Just the whole attitude here, where people are superficial and so caught up in material things—I couldn't deal with that."

It was, however, the very surreal quality of life there—the singular collision of great wealth, high commerce and deviant art in the film, television and music communities, heightened by the rising tide of teenage discontent and the impact of the British Invasion—that made Los Angeles the ideal playground-workshop for the mid-Sixties hip rock elite. And while the twang 'n' harmony magic of Brian Wilson and the Beach Boys embodied the SoCal myth of wild surf and sweet beach romance, the real sound of swinging Sixties L.A. was that of the original Byrds—McGuinn, David Crosby, Gene Clark, Chris Hillman and Michael Clarke. The distinctive chime of McGuinn's twelve-string Rickenbacker guitar and the metallic resonance of the group's choirboy vocals on "Turn! Turn! Turn!" "So You Want to Be a Rock 'n' Roll Star," "Eight Miles High" and on covers of Bob Dylan's "Mr. Tambourine Man" and "My Back Pages" vividly captured not only the city's sunny allure but also its restive, and hopeful, adolescent spirit.

Ironically, James Joseph McGuinn III (he changed his name to Roger in 1967, during a flirtation with Eastern religion) thought Los Angeles was "a sleepy little town" when he first passed through in 1960 while touring as a backup musician with the Limeliters. "Pop radio was people like Steve Lawrence and Eydie Gorme," says McGuinn, then seventeen and already a veteran of the folk scene in his native Chicago. "There wasn't much going on on the street, either. I don't think the Beach Boys had even started yet." There was more action in New York; during 1962 and 1963, McGuinn was in the Brill Building writing tunes for Bobby Darin, doing session work and playing folk gigs in Greenwich Village.

By mid-1965, however, Los Angeles was alive with the crisp sound of electric guitars and the cumulative roar of expensive Porsches driven by the city's new mod gods. These included McGuinn and the Byrds, who were a vital force in L.A.'s metamorphosis from Snoozeville to America's new capital city of pop. With the Number One success of "Mr. Tambourine Man," Los Angeles became the main spawning ground for folk rock; the Mamas and the Papas, Sonny and Cher, the Grass Roots and the Turtles quickly followed in the Byrds' wake. The band's legendary residency at a Sunset Strip discotheque called Ciro's started a live-music scene that included historic clubs like the Trip, the Whisky a Go Go and the Cheetah and gave birth to future legends like Buffalo Springfield, the Doors, Love and Frank Zappa's Mothers of Invention. The Byrds were also central figures in pop schmooze circles, enjoying friendships with Dylan and the Beatles, helping newcomers like Joni Mitchell and Jackson Browne and partying with Papa John Phillips, Phil Spector and young movie outlaws like Peter Fonda and Jack Nicholson.

The Byrds themselves were a fractious bunch; by 1969, McGuinn was the only original member left, and the hit singles had dried up. (He finally put the Byrds to rest in 1973.) Throughout his career, though, Roger McGuinn—who now lives on the west coast of Florida—has been a keen observer, and often a strong critic, of life and music in Los Angeles. But, if McGuinn never really liked Los Angeles, why did he stay for seventeen years? "I guess I liked the weather."

In the early Sixties, you were making a name for yourself on the New York folk circuit. Why did you chuck it all to go to Los Angeles?
I got a job offer to play as an opening act at the Troubadour. I did feel that the real folk scene was in the Village, but the Beatles came out and changed the whole game for me. I saw a definite niche, a place where the two of them blended together. If you took Lennon and Dylan and mixed them together . . . that was something that hadn't been done.

So I got an offer to play the Troubadour as an opening act for Hoyt Axton and Roger Miller. I came out and started blending Beatles stuff with the folk stuff, and the audience hated it. I used to get mad at 'em because I thought it was good. Roger Miller took me aside one night and said, "I know what you're trying to do up there. It would go a lot

better if you didn't get mad at the audience. Just try to smile and be nice to 'em."

Later on, I ran into Gene Clark at the Troubadour. He was one of the few people who understood it. He asked if I wanted to write some songs with him. Then David Crosby came in and started singing harmony. I'd already met David back in 1960, when I was with the Limeliters. I knew what kind of guy David was, and I wasn't sure I wanted to get into that [*laughs*], but it worked out okay because his harmony was real good.

Los Angeles was caught up in the clean-cut hedonism of the Beach Boys and Jan and Dean then. Did you feel out of place?
It was changing, slowly. There was a copycat mentality here that is still going on. People will follow what's cool, and if it isn't cool, they won't get into it. If it

suddenly becomes cool, they've *always* been into it. And it suddenly got cool to do what I was doing. It was the British influence. It was the Beatles and the Rolling Stones. Suddenly, it became cool to be like *that*.

How did you go about selling this folk-rock concept before it was "cool"?

We got some good breaks. One of our managers, Jim Dickson, knew this agent named Benny Shapiro. We went over to Benny's house with a tape of background tracks and sang live over it. Benny had a fourteen-year-old daughter at the time. She came running down the stairs because she thought it was the Beatles in her living room. Benny was impressed by that, to the point that when Miles Davis, who was a friend or client of his, came over, he told Miles about it, and Miles said, "Well, I'll just pick up the phone and call Columbia Records, tell 'em to sign these guys"—and he did. And that was how we got a record deal.

What did you live on before the royalties from "Mr. Tambourine Man" started rolling in?

Jim Dickson bought us a hamburger a day. That was our ration. We were starving artists. I could always go to the Troubadour and get a hamburger or something. We could always bum things off of them. I used to play there at hootenannies. The Troubadour was the only mecca for people to hang out at, where you could exchange ideas. The front room was kind of a coffeehouse where you could buy strings and picks and stuff; I think McCabe's Guitar Shop was originally there.

Did you have a car?

I did for a while, but then I blew it up. I didn't know about oil. I'd grown up in a city where you don't have a car. I was on the freeway one day, and the car started to make this really great sound, like a jet, and I love jets. And then it just stopped; the engine just froze up. I was still paying for it, and they repossessed it.

How did you manage in Los Angeles without wheels?

It wasn't easy. I had to catch a bus to rehearsals, and sitting on a bench for the bus was a really grueling experience. I had long hair at the time; nobody else did. These greasers would go by and go, "Hey, Ringo, did your barber die?"

But long hair had its advantages, right?

The Rolling Stones were playing at the Santa Monica Civic Auditorium. This was '64, before the Byrds broke. I got my guitar case, and I walked right in

backstage. The guards let me through because they figured nobody had long hair except musicians. And while I was in there, these girls went, "Ooooh!" And then they said, "Oh, he's nobody."

I didn't get close to the Stones, but I saw the show from backstage. I wanted to be in on it. I'd seen *A Hard Day's Night* and wanted to be *there*, and within a year, the Byrds were opening for the Stones, and the girls were screaming for us.

How did you get the residency at Ciro's?

Jim and Eddie [Tickner, comanager] got us the job somehow. As far as the club was concerned, we were another club band. We'd work five forty-minute sets a night, and they didn't care what we played. You can still go and see the place. It's called the Comedy Store now.

Did people dance to the Byrds?

Oh, yeah. Carl Franzoni [a charter member of the local freak scene] used to dance with his arms out, bouncing up and down, sort of like Big Bird. Other people would do jitterbuggy things. No air guitars, though.

You actually took some of the Ciro's dancers on the road.

Yeah, that was our manager's idea. It was a crazy thing. They were really wild, wilder than we were. They had hair down to their shoulders, they were painted up in psychedelic colors—before psychedelia was even happening—and we took them to the Midwest, where they scared people to death.

There were a couple of girls and some guys. They weren't professional dancers. They were part of Vito's gang; Vito was this mad sculptor who hung out with Zappa a lot. We used to rehearse at Vito's and take acid there, and all his friends would come down to Ciro's when we played. We still run into some of them. They're out there.

Metaphorically or literally?

Both.

There's a famous photo of the Byrds playing with Bob Dylan onstage at the Trip. Did you hang out a lot together when he was in Los Angeles?

He came out here on and off to write. I remember one time he stayed at the Thunderbird Motel, on the Strip, for about three weeks. He had a typewriter on the balcony. He'd sit there and write a song a day. We were real impressed by that. We never did it, though. It was too hard.

He was miles above us. He'd kind of humor us a little bit. He was Dylan, and we were this band who did one of his songs and happened to have a hit with it. That was his attitude. We weren't really close.

But he did perform that night. He got up and played harmonica. We did "All I Really Want to Do," but he didn't recognize it when he heard it. He said, "What's that song?" because he did it in 3/4 time, and we changed it to 4/4.

You also spent a lot of time with the Beatles when they passed through Los Angeles on tour.
They came to our concert at Blazes, in London, in '65. It was really a disaster for us. Chris broke a string on the bass, and when you break one, it just knocks the whole band out of tune. There's no way to recover from that. After the show, we met George and John, and they said, "Great show, guys." We went, "Oh, man, how can you say that?"

We hung with them when they came out here later, and they were really nice. This was also '65; they were playing the Hollywood Bowl. They were up in the hills here, in one of the houses, a place with a gate and guards and the little girls camped up on the hillside. They sent a limo down for us, and we came winding up the road, through this gate. It was like a movie.

We went into this house, and there were all these guards walking around, and we were all trying to get high. We didn't have any place to do it, so we locked ourselves in the bathroom; we closed all the windows and blinds and sat in this huge, square shower.

We sat on the floor exchanging guitar licks. Crosby showed Harrison some Ravi Shankar stuff he'd just been into, and Harrison had never heard this stuff before. Indian music was a new thing to him. John and I were talking about "Be-Bop-a-Lula," our first favorite song. *Barbarella* was playing out in the other room, and everybody hated it. Joan Baez was out at the pool. Then Peter Fonda came over and showed John his scar, and he said, "I know what it's like to be dead." We were on acid, and it freaked John out so much that he later wrote that song with the line "I know what it's like to be dead" ["She Said She Said"]. It was really some afternoon.

The Beatles also attended some Byrds recording sessions.
George and Paul came down one afternoon while we were recording "She Don't Care About Time." I remember George was really into the Bach thing in the middle that I did on that. It was "Jesu, Joy of Man's Desiring." And Paul was looking at all the machines and taking notes on all the recording levels.

It's ironic that you were first inspired by the Beatles, and here they were, picking up tips from you.
That was really a kick. The Dylan thing, you could never really tell whether that connected or not. The Beatles, you could, because George was very open about it, and John said the Byrds were his favorite group. George wrote "If I Needed Someone" off the lick from "The Bells of Rhymney," and he sent it to us in advance and said, "This is for Jim" because of that lick.

One of the Byrds' contributions to Sixties fashion was your colored granny glasses. Where did you get them?
I'd known John Sebastian [of the Lovin' Spoonful] in the Village. He had these little, round, cobalt blue glasses on. I said, "Wow, those are great." And he said, "Yeah, look through 'em. Look up at the streetlights. It's really groovy." (He liked that word *groovy* a lot.) I did, and it was. I wear glasses, and I'd worn contact lenses, but they were expensive. So when we finally got a little money, I bought these little frames, took 'em to the eye doctor and had him put some dark cobalt blue prescription lenses in them.

Within a month or so of "Mr. Tambourine Man" and the publicity with the cover shot, the Japanese had cornered the market on them. They were in all these drugstores for a buck a pair. I tried to get the trademark on them, but it was too late.

What about your threads? There are some early photos of the Byrds wearing suits and ties!
They had velvet collars. We'd found a place in Watts that had these suits—real soul stuff. But our suits got ripped off at Ciro's when we were playing there with Little Richard. Jimi Hendrix was his guitar player. And somehow during that gig, our suits disappeared. We started wearing jeans after that. I remember when we were comparing notes with the Beatles, they said, "Boy, we wish someone had stolen our suits."

On the cover of the first Byrds album, you were all decked out in pointy boots, turtlenecks, striped T-shirts and tight Levis.
That was California style. We used to go to a shop called DeVoss; it was on Sunset. In fact, that's where I got the glasses. It was a little boutique, a Carnaby Street kind of thing. There was a section of the Strip

that had some pretty hip stuff. It was just a couple of blocks, between Sunset Plaza Drive and Doheny. Now it's all record stores and Thai and Japanese restaurants.

Did local hipsters socialize at these boutiques as well?

You'd go in, you'd shop, you'd buy and you'd split. There was really no culture here. The only places you would see people would be at parties at night or on the set of some TV show. We used to do a lot of these lip-sync shows: *Shindig, Shivaree, Hollywood a Go Go, Hullabaloo, Where the Action Is.* One of the first ones was *The Lloyd Thaxton Show.* It was almost like a kiddie show. He had these little puppets that would sing along between cuts, and there would be all these twelve- and thirteen-year-old girls in the audience. It was like a pajama party.

Casey Kasem had a show. In fact, I got in trouble with him one day. He was asking me all these square questions, and I was giving him cool answers like, "Man, I don't know." We went to a commercial break, and he went, "I don't know; these people— I'm walkin' out!" He didn't like that attitude.

Were you friendly with other local folk rockers like Barry McGuire or Sonny and Cher?

No, we weren't connected. I'd known Barry before, when we were in the folk thing, but once Barry got "Eve of Destruction" and we were the Byrds, I didn't see him anymore. And I never saw Sonny and Cher. We were in separate camps completely. It was highly competitive. We did a cover of "All I Really Want to Do," and they did one, too, and they got a hit with it. Dylan got mad at us. He said, "You let me down, man."

What about Buffalo Springfield? In the 1981 Byrds biography *Timeless Flight*, Chris Hillman says he was interested in managing the band and that he tried to get you to go in on it.

Stephen [Stills] asked Chris if he wanted to manage Buffalo Springfield, and Chris said to me, "Let's go down to the Whisky and see this group." I watched them, and I said, "Nah, you don't want to be a manager. It's a pain in the neck. We don't need that." That was a bad piece of advice.

In the book, Crosby claims he was asked to join Springfield.

I know that Stephen was grooming David. He wanted to do something with him. In fact, that led to the breakup of the Byrds, because Stephen was really pulling at David to get him out of the Byrds, and David was going for it. Stephen was sort of a home breaker in that way.

Buffalo Springfield's first hit, "For What It's Worth," was inspired by the teenage riots on Sunset Strip in the summer of 1966. What started the ruckus?

There was a big generation gap and sort of a sloppy revolution going on, where the young people wanted to just wear funny clothes and hang out on the Strip, and all the proprietors in the shops wanted to get rid of them because they were slowing business down. So the police were called in, and that's when the riots started.

It was hardly a serious political action, though— more like a lot of teenage energy with no place to go.

It was political. It was the leftist kids against the right-wing proprietors, and there was a real polarity here between people under and over thirty. It was amazing. It doesn't exist today, but you could feel it everywhere then. If you were young, you were discriminated against. I remember not being able to get into Disneyland with long hair.

Was there much organized political activity in the rock community on issues like civil rights or the Vietnam War?

Not that I can remember. I was political in that I didn't like inhumanity to man, but I really didn't get involved. I didn't vote, either. I didn't do anything. I was tied up in my own little world.

Yet the Byrds were writing and recording songs that fueled the civil rights and antiwar movements.

We figured that was our contribution. Actually, we were just doing songs. We really meant them when we did them, but that was the end of it. When I was off the road, I was at my house, playing with my gadgets—and staying stoned a lot. That was my life. I mean, we were hedonists.

Who were some of the movie people in your circle of celebrity hedonists?

I hung out with Peter Fonda and Brandon DeWilde, who was a child actor. Nicholson was around. Dean Stockwell, too. The B-movie motorcycle crowd.

How involved were you in the making of *Easy Rider*, besides writing the title song?

I didn't know much about it until it was already in production. Peter came to me. He wanted one or two songs that would be custom-made for the movie, and he asked me to write one. Actually, he went to Dylan first, and Dylan turned him down, but Dylan scribbled something on a napkin and gave it to Fonda to give to me. Peter gave me the napkin, and it said, "The river flows; / It flows to the sea; / Wherever that river goes, / That's where I want to be; / Flow, river, flow." I came up with the second verse and a melody for it. I gave credit to Dylan on the record, and he called me up and said, "What is this? I don't need the money. I don't want that credit. Take it off," so I did. He was just doing me a favor.

Another interesting thing is that Peter said, at the time, that he was drawing his character partially from me and that [Dennis] Hopper was drawing his character from David Crosby. He was paranoid, uptight and everything, and I was always going around saying, "I trust everything will work out all right; it's gonna be okay." So that's kind of in the movie.

For a time, you subscribed to an obscure Eastern faith called Subud. Of all the Eastern religions that were big in the Sixties, how did you pick that one?

It was a small organization out of Indonesia, and frankly, I don't know much about it myself. It was a "surrender" kind of thing, where you just release yourself to God, and it cleans you up. I thought it was cool, a religion without any responsibilities. You didn't have to learn a whole lot or use any props. Brian Wilson got into it, but he didn't want to go to the place where they had the meetings, so he sort of developed his own brand of it with his friends. That's when he got really weird. He incorporated acid into it and a few other strange things, and drugs were not part of it at all.

Speaking of strange, you changed your first name from Jim to Roger because of Subud.

They had this name-change option. The sound of your name is supposed to vibrate with your spirit. So I thought I'd see what my Subud name was, and Roger was one of them. I was into gadgets and space, and Roger was from two-way radio airplane talk: "Roger that." I wish I hadn't done that now. I'd still be Jim.

How did you convince people to start calling you Roger?

People would say, "Hi, Jim," and I'd say, "Call me Roger." Most people were cool about it. Hey, it was the Sixties: "Whatever feels good, whatever's your groove" [laughs]. Some people still call me Jim. George Harrison still does.

Were drugs a big part of your daily diet?

I used to wake up and smoke a joint, stay high all day and maybe take some speed. Quaaludes, I got into those later, and coke. I just did a lot of drugs—acid, mescaline, peyote.

LSD was an experimental thing that was part of this spiritual search when I started doing it. We thought that we could improve ourselves mentally and spiritually by opening up these other levels of consciousness. I can't say it did me any harm. I don't know that I'm a better person for having done it, but it didn't make me a worse person. I didn't have any nasty flashbacks or panic attacks.

Was heroin prevalent in L.A. rock circles?

The people I knew were afraid of it. They didn't like needles. They wouldn't even snort it. But Cass [Elliot, of the Mamas and Papas] did heroin, and she got David [Crosby] into it.

Cocaine, though, later became the rock & roll drug in Los Angeles.

But we didn't think of it as a hard drug at the time. We didn't think it was addictive, and socially, it was fun, like pot. It was a status symbol. If you could afford to turn everybody on to coke, you were really rich.

Cass got me into coke. She gave me a big pill bottle with a couple of thousand dollars' worth of coke in it—I didn't know how much it was worth— and I was scared of it. I put it on a shelf and didn't touch it for a long time, and Crosby would come over with all his friends and chip away at it. So I thought I'd give it a try, and after a week or so, I liked it a lot. That was a bad thing to do.

In the late Sixties, San Francisco eclipsed Los Angeles as the happening city on the West Coast. Why do you think psychedelic pop culture flourished upstate instead of here?

San Francisco was a better breeding ground for that. It's too sterile here, too much chlorine in the pools and sunshine. It was a fungus that really grew well in San Francisco. I lived in San Francisco for a few months around the time I was working with Bobby Darin. I took my first acid up there. It was '61 or '62. I wasn't sure what would happen to me, but I thought it would be fun to test myself, to see if I'd go crazy or not. So I got in the shower with all my clothes on. I said to myself, "If I'm gonna be irrational, I'll turn the shower on and get myself wet," and I never turned the water on. So I figured I had it under control [laughs]. Foolproof test.

Eventually, Los Angeles had its own be-ins and psychedelic clubs, like the Kaleidoscope and the Cheetah, but did the peace-love-and-music aesthetic ever really take root here?

Not in the same way. L.A. always had that tension, that competitive thing. I always felt when I was onstage that guitar players were watching my hands to see what I was doing. There was still that feeling here, that it was serious business.

The interesting thing about the 1967 Monterey Pop Festival was that although it was associated with the San Francisco scene, it was actually organized by L.A. big shots like Lou Adler and John Phillips (of the Mamas and Papas).

The event was actually a good blending of the two styles, the Northern and Southern California things. There was a lot of genuine feeling for that kind of thinking down here, but it probably needed the administration from down here, to make it more organized. Up north, they were mostly interested in getting high. The Los Angeles people gave it form; the San Franciscans made it flourish.

Younger acts like Tom Petty and R.E.M. have been instrumental in reviving the Byrds' jangly guitar style. How do you relate to its renewed popularity and the Sixties nostalgia that comes with it?

I relate to it probably the same way Chuck Berry related to the Beatles doing his songs. It doesn't bring back memories. It's just good to hear those sounds again, because they were sounds that I liked, or I wouldn't have made them.

But it's hard not to feel a little sentimental about the town's mid-Sixties salad days whenever that opening twelve-string Rickenbacker riff from "Mr. Tambourine Man" comes over the radio.

It's a fantasy thing people have. I remember that kind of thing from when I lived in Chicago and James Dean was out here, *Rebel Without a Cause* and all that. I saw that movie and thought, "Wow, I really want to get out to California; that's where it's happening," and when I got out here, it wasn't quite like that. I went up to the Griffith Park Observatory, and nothing was going on—no gangs, no nothing. It was a great fantasy, but that's all it was.

< Motown mogul **berry gordy**
MICHAEL OCHS ARCHIVES/VENICE, CA

berry gordy

By MICHAEL GOLDBERG

On a bright Los Angeles day, Berry Gordy, Jr., the man who founded Motown Records and made stars of Michael Jackson, Marvin Gaye, the Temptations, Stevie Wonder, the Four Tops, Diana Ross and the Supremes, Martha and the Vandellas, Smokey Robinson and many others, removes his shirt.

"We'll do the *Playboy* shots now," jokes photographer Norman Seeff, who is shooting a portrait at the wealthy record man's Bel Air estate. Gordy, bearded and looking quite fit at age sixty, demurs: "I've rejected *Playgirl* so many times."

"Actually," asks Seeff gently, "could I take some without the shirt?"

"I'd better not," says Gordy, with a grin. "That could start a sexual revolution."

It was a *musical* revolution that Gordy launched in Detroit in the late Fifties, when, at age twenty-nine, he borrowed eight hundred dollars from his family to make "Come to Me," a simple R&B record that reached Number Six on the black-music chart. Five years later, Motown was one of the hottest record companies in the world. Looking back, Gordy would say, "I earned $367 million in sixteen years. I must be doing something right."

Gordy's impact on popular music cannot be overstated. Motown's artists, songwriters and producers have influenced everyone from the Beatles and the Rolling Stones to Eighties chart-toppers like Janet Jackson, Paula Abdul and Madonna. Motown artists were usually black, but the music they made—dubbed the Sound of Young America by Gordy—was indeed loved by nearly everyone who was young, or young at heart. Motown crossed over before anyone thought to use that term to describe black records bought by whites. "We were a general-market company," is the way Gordy puts it. "Whether you were black, white, green or blue, you could relate to our music."

Although there were other important record companies during the Sixties, Motown was the greatest, producing an unprecedented body of work. The street poetry of Smokey Robinson, the inventive productions of Holland-Dozier-Holland and the striking vocal performances of the Motown artists themselves were key elements in dozens upon dozens of classic records. Consider that Smokey Robinson and the Miracles scored twenty-five Top Forty hits during the Sixties; Diana Ross and the Supremes had twenty-three.

It is doubtful that anyone would have gambled much on the likelihood that Gordy, previously unsuccessful as a professional boxer, record-store owner and Ford auto worker, would succeed in the record business. Before starting Motown, Gordy had moderate success as a songwriter, cowriting hits like "Reet Petite" and "Lonely Teardrops" for his former boxing buddy Jackie Wilson. Gordy says he just wanted to be a songwriter—but that he couldn't get adequately paid for his efforts. "I didn't want to be a big record mogul and all that stuff," he says. "I just wanted to write songs and make people laugh."

But when the royalties trickled in, eighteen-year-old Smokey Robinson encouraged Gordy to start his own company. "Why work for the man?" Robinson put it to Gordy. "Why not *you* be the man?"

"I didn't know any better," says Gordy. "If somebody told me today, 'Okay, you're gonna go into business, and you've gotta make a profit every year for the first five years, or you'll be out of business,' I'd say that's not a good gamble. But that's what we did. Motown was a freak."

In 1988, Gordy sold his company to MCA and the investment group Boston Ventures for $61 million, but he still owns Jobete Music Publishing, the gold mine of a publishing company that holds the copyrights for nearly all the Motown hits. As head of the Gordy Company, furthermore, he remains involved in the production of records, movies and other entertainment projects. Gordy lives in a multimillion-dollar Tudor-style mansion set amid a ten-acre estate in the hills of Bel Air.

It's been more than two decades since Gordy has spoken at length about the Motown sound. While Gordy has been silent, others—ranging from Gordy lieutenant Smokey Robinson to disillusioned artists like former Supreme Mary Wilson—have offered their memoirs of life inside Hitsville, U.S.A. Gordy dismisses most of the books that have been written about Motown, however. "These books are all erroneous," he says brusquely. What follows is his version of the Motown story, a version that at times diverges from those of the people who worked for him. "For thirty years, I've just been so goal oriented," he says at the onset of the first of two interview sessions held in his dark, wood-paneled study. "You know, it's like a football player running on the field: If he stops to try to bother with one of his attackers, somebody's gonna say, 'Let's get him.' He's gotta keep running as fast as he can straight forward. So we had the various stories coming out about us, and I would never comment, because I didn't have time. Consequently, after thirty years, people think that the things that were said were actually true. But now I realize that I *do* have time."

During the Sixties, did you understand how popular and influential Motown was?
No. At the time, I had no sense of how big this thing was. All these different factions were fighting each other: the police and the radical groups, the government and the Black Panthers, and the black organization groups and the bigots. All these people were fighting each other, but they were all listening to Motown music. I read about this one Black Panther leader in Chicago who was shot down in bed, and his

favorite song was "Someday We'll Be Together" [which went to Number One in November 1969]. And there was this big, big funeral, and all the blacks from all over came, and "Someday We'll Be Together" was constantly playing.

And in Vietnam. In *Platoon*, you see the soldiers going to their deaths dancing to Smokey's music—"The Tracks of My Tears" [Number Sixteen, August 1965]. It gave them confidence; it gave them hope. You know, you've got to get a feeling when you look at that. The music pierced the Iron Curtain. And you know that on *The Beatles' Second Album*, there were three Motown tunes. The influence that the music had—when the Motown Revue went to England, I went with my father and my kids to meet the Beatles. And we had pictures taken of us with them, and they were so respectful and grateful to me. I'm looking at the Beatles, and I'm saying, "This is *so* incredible." I mean, one of the songs they did *I wrote*.

Smokey Robinson was one of your first and most important discoveries. You first met him in 1957.

He had some songs for Jackie Wilson's manager, and he was turned down, and I happened to be there that day. He was leaving the office dejected, and I went and caught up with him, 'cause I thought those songs were not that bad; I mean, they were pretty good songs. I went up to him, and he said, "Who are you?" I said, "I'm Berry Gordy." And he said, "Berry Gordy! You write for Jackie Wilson." He was like a fan.

So I said, "Yeah, I heard some of your songs, and you have one there called 'My Mamma Done Told Me.' That's not a bad song, nice little rhythm." He said, "Well, I got a book of a hundred songs." He was so excited, he sang every song, and each one either missed the point or had something wrong with it, and I started telling him, with each one, what was wrong. He kept me there for, like, an hour, and he went from song to song to song, and I rejected every single one of them—a hundred songs. But instead of taking this as a rejection, he was very excited that someone understood his songs and talked to him about them. So anyway, we became friends.

He started writing songs for you.

I gave him advice. I told him to go out and listen to the radio, and at the time the Silhouettes had a Number One record called "Get a Job." So he came to the office one day so excited. He had this song he'd written called "Got a Job." He started singing the song to me, and I liked it right away. I stopped

him for a moment right after he got through the first part and told him it was great. He said, "Wait 'til I finish," and he sang the whole song—all eight minutes of it—and I said, "It's much too long. We got to edit it, but it's a hit." So we worked on it, we put it out, and it was a hit ["Got a Job" went to Number One on the R&B charts in 1958].

But the thing I liked about Smokey was bigger than a song. He had a purity about him, and he had a feeling of great thankfulness. Even as I rejected every song, he got stronger, and that's hard. That's the mark of a real kind of winner.

You called Motown "Hitsville, U.S.A." You hung a big sign up on the outside of the offices. You were pretty confident.

Oh, yes. I also did an ad for *Billboard* or *Cashbox* in '59 or '60, when I was just starting my company. It's even a little more cocky than that. It started off with little letters, and it got bigger and bigger, and it said: "From out of the West comes a young man who's gonna revolutionize the record business and" do whatever—I forget what I said, exactly. And people said, "That is so arrogant." I said, "No, that's what I'm gonna do."

It's been said that when you were developing Motown, you modeled it after the Ford auto plant where you had worked.

Yes, yes. I worked in the Ford factory before I came in the [record] business, and I saw how each person did a different thing, and I said, "Why can't we do that with the creative process?" It was just an idea of coming in one door one day and going out another door and having all these things done. You know: the writing, the producing, the artist development—that's the grooming of the act, how to talk, how to speak, how to walk, choreography, all that stuff. And when you got through and you came out the door, you were like a star, a potential star. It was just that assembly line approach to things.

Tell me about the legendary Motown studio.

It was a very small studio. We would record everything there at first. We had a two-track machine that I had bought from a local disc jockey. I was doing the engineering. We didn't know anything about having an engineer and an arranger. We just went down and did everything, and we all knew how to work the machines.

And everybody came and played at everybody's session. Marvin would play drums on certain people's sessions. The secretaries would sing on the sessions.

9
3

That's how Martha [Reeves] was discovered, singing on a Marvin Gaye session. When someone didn't show up, she ended up singing the lead on something, and the next thing you know, there's Martha and the Vandellas.

Some of your biggest stars started out as secretaries.

The way that people could get into Motown was to get a job there and do something meaningful, and then they could come every day. I'm not even sure Martha was getting paid at the time she was a secretary. Diana Ross worked for me for a summer. They [the Supremes] had come to us, and they were rejected 'cause they were in the twelfth grade, and I had a responsibility not to have them quit school. Later they came back, and they sang background on some Marvin Gaye recordings. And then Diana wanted to get a job at Motown so she could be there, but there was not really a job she could do, but I needed a secretary at the time, so I let her try that out. She worked for me for a summer, but she was so bad as a secretary that I had to let her go. You know, my messages were mixed up and everything.

There were some very unusual sounds on Motown records.

Oh yeah. There was a sound we got on "Reach Out I'll Be There," with Holland-Dozier-Holland. There's a point near the beginning of the song where the music breaks, and there's this little drumbeat— [*he imitates it*] da-da-da-da-da-da-da—and everybody around the world was trying to figure out how that was done, and it was so simple. It was just on a chair, and that was it, you know [*demonstrates drumming on coffee table with his hands*]. And everyone said, "What instrument was that?" And we were doing things with tin cans, we were doing things with cardboard. On the Supremes song "Where Did Our Love Go" [Number One, July 1964], we'd get a piece of cardboard, and that was our drumbeat: [*demonstrates beat by slapping hands together and singing*] "Baby, baby." We weren't concerned about whether it was right or wrong; we just wanted to know if it sounded good.

Since you were using a two-track machine for the early records, there were no overdubs—you had to record the music and the vocals at the same time.

Oh, yes—on two tracks, and we would never be happy with the sound. I remember when we cut "Way Over There" with the Miracles [in 1959]. It was a great record with feeling and soul, so we put the record out, and it started selling, but I was unhappy with it. There was a great studio in Chicago, so I put the Miracles into that studio, and we recut the tune. I got the exact same tracks, the exact same everything, only I had strings on it. We had a beautiful recording. I was so happy and proud of that recording! Now, when we first put it out, without strings—our original version—it sold sixty thousand copies, which was incredible for us because we were new. Sixty thousand copies! Then I went and recut it, 'cause I wanted to get a real home run. We switched records and started shipping the one with the strings, and the record stopped selling. It did not sell another copy.

And that was such a lesson to me, 'cause the first version had a certain honesty about it. It wasn't slick. So after that, we continued to produce songs in our own little studio, but we just didn't have respect for the studio. It was a little studio that had real wonderful acoustics and magical sound, but we just never fully recognized that at the time. We took it for granted.

Every week you would hold a meeting with key executives at Motown to listen to the recordings made that week and to decide what you would release.

We had meetings each Friday, and we would evaluate all the records—five, six, seven records, you know. A lot of stuff was being cut all week, and the one that would get released was the one that we liked best for the week. We would debate and fight over which ones to release.

What were those meetings like?

Those meetings were taped. I have the tapes. I listened to one the other day; I've got it here [*Gordy has an aide locate the tape and a machine to play it on*]. This is maybe twenty-six years ago.

[*The tape begins just prior to the start of a weekly creative meeting. Gordy is talking*] "I definitely want my A&R to be here. That's $100 [fine] for Mickey [Stevenson, director of A&R]."

[*Unidentified voice on the tape*] "He's got five minutes."

[*Gordy responds*] "Four minutes. Lock the door." [As it turned out, Stevenson showed up and was docked only $50 dollars.]

So we used to lock the door [*Gordy laughs*]. There was never a question in my mind—the minute you were late, you were fined. The heads of the office had to be there five minutes before the meeting started.

Even though Mickey came in, he was supposed to be there five minutes early. He was three minutes early, so he got a $50 fine instead. See, at Motown, no one had any questions about the direction we were going in, because I was the leader. I was very firm and very strict.

I remember the day Smokey was knocking on the door. He would be a little late, and he couldn't get in. He'd be locked out: "Let me in, let me in! This is Smokey; I'll never be late again!"

You earned a reputation for sending records you were unhappy with back to be reworked, re-recorded.

Yeah. Like "Baby Love" was a sad song. When Holland-Dozier-Holland finished it the first time, I said, "It's great, but it has no life; there's no gimmick here; there's nothing here that makes it sound really good. There's nothing really different about the record." And they looked at me, and of course they disagreed with me, because they always did, but they went back in the studio and recut it. And at the beginning, they put in the little thing, "Ooh-ooh-ooh"—that little bit. And I said, "That's perfect. It gives it something different, yet it's not crazy." And they cut it fast, so it was brighter, and then we put it out that way ["Baby Love" went to Number One in October 1964]. I was known for recutting things that were almost there.

As a songwriter, your best-known composition is "Money (That's What I Want)." Your original version, featuring singer Barrett Strong, reached Number Twenty-three in March 1960. It became known to millions of people around the world when it was recorded by the Beatles a few years later.

Many psychologists have studied that song and studied me and tried to figure out why I wrote it. People have had all kinds of different reasons to explain why I wrote the song. The truth of the matter is that I was broke at the time, and I had a couple of girlfriends who said they loved me and so forth. I thought to myself, "I'm gonna write a song about this. I really don't want to write about love, because everybody else is writing about love, and I don't remember anyone writing about 'I need money.'" I thought that would be kind of funny. Later, a lot of people said, "Oh, that's the way you feel: You just wanted money," but I thought other people would find the song funny and amusing.

In 1961, Motown scored its first million seller with "Shop Around."

When Smokey came to me with the song, he actually wanted Barrett Strong to sing it. I had just done "Money" with Barrett Strong. So Smokey sang the song for me, and I said, "No, Smokey, this is perfect for you." But he said, "No. I didn't write it for myself. It's not for me." Finally he agreed, so he did the song, and we released it, but it didn't quite have the life that I thought it should have. I listened to it and listened to it. You go through these changes where you think that your mind is playing tricks on you. You loved it at one time, and now you don't love it, and you just feel that maybe it's just your mind, so maybe you should put it out anyway, and we did.

But I couldn't sleep, and finally, I made up my mind to recut it. It was two o'clock in the morning when I called Smokey. Of course, he was very sleepy. I wanted him to come down to the studio with the group to recut the song. He was very, very surprised and very confused, but he did get himself together and got the rest of the Miracles, and they were all grumbling like mad. They came into the studio at three o'clock in the morning. The piano player, he didn't get up, so I played piano, and we recorded it again. So we put the new record out, and it went straight to Number Two pop and Number One R&B.

What was your reaction to "Please Mr. Postman," "Money" and "You've Really Got a Hold on Me" appearing on *The Beatles' Second Album*?

[*Long pause*] Well, it was a very strange reaction. Brian Epstein's office called for a [discount] rate on the publishing royalty. They wanted to pay a cent and a half instead of two cents per song [for each album sold]. I had mixed emotions. I was honored that they wanted to do the songs, but to ask for a lesser rate...We didn't do that unless a person would do a lot of our tunes—but three tunes! We were very arrogant about it. Maybe not arrogant but firm, because I thought that quality songs were quality songs. At that time, we felt the songs would help to make their second album a success. We said no until the last minute, so it wasn't until later that I really enjoyed them doing it.

Marvin Gaye was not only one of your biggest stars, he was also your brother-in-law for a time. Tell me about the first time you met him.

We were having a party at Hitsville. Marvin Gaye came with Harvey Fuqua [formerly of the Moonglows] and my two sisters, and I noticed him sitting in the studio, just messing around at the piano. It was a big party going on, but there was this guy at the piano. One of my sisters said, "That's Marvin Gaye. He wants to be a singer. He's a great singer. He used to sing with the Moonglows." They were building him up, and I had no idea that my sister [Anna Gordy] liked him, but anyway, they brought him to my attention.

He played some jazzy-type Broadway things, and I could hear the mellowness in his voice, and it was really good. He really wanted to do ballad-type things, and after hearing his voice—the velvetness of his voice—I really wanted to do that kind of an album with him. I thought Motown could branch out into this kind of music. Unfortunately, I was wrong on that one, because his first album, *The Soulful Moods of Marvin Gaye*, didn't sell. Marvin did a rendition of "Mr. Sandman" that was so great. It's still one of my favorite songs.

How did you get him to do pop music?
He was a very stubborn man, and he was determined to stick with the semijazz stuff he was doing. But one day he needed money or something, and they ended up coming up with a thing, "Stubborn Kind of Fellow" [Number Eight on the R&B charts in August 1962]. And it was a really nice, little hit.

So then we started really watching him. We said, "Okay, where should this guy be?" And I realized that he was a very handsome man and had sex appeal, and I thought that we should have him work directly to the women. So I said, "Let's write songs with 'you'—'You Are a Wonderful One,' you are my 'Pride and Joy.'" We wanted him to be direct. We right away hit with that, and he became the sex symbol—he became everything we wanted and more.

And later, of course, he would get tired of this and go on to his protest things, which turned out to be bigger than everything, even though I personally wasn't for it. I tried to convince him that talking about war and police brutality and all that stuff would hardly make him more popular than the romantic stuff.

What was it about Stevie Wonder that impressed you?
When I first saw Stevie, I did not think he was a great singer.

So why did you sign him?
Because he had other talents. He was ten or eleven years old, and he was not anything that special with his voice, but his talent was great. His harmonica playing was phenomenal, but I was worried that when he got to thirteen or fourteen, his voice would change, and we wouldn't even have that, but lucky for us, it changed for the better.

You told me a few years ago that Stevie Wonder played a lot of practical jokes on you.
Oh, yes, he played tricks. His biggest trick was imitating my voice. He used to call my secretary and say, "Give Stevie Wonder $50,000," you know, and "Hurry up! This is me, this is me!" And they would say, "Mr. Gordy?" And he would say, "Don't ask me questions. Give Stevie Wonder a check for $50,000."

They'd be very confused, and they might come back to me and say, "You still want me to do that?" And I'd say, "Do what?" "Give Stevie $50,000."

And I'd say, "Are you crazy? That was Stevie calling you. Can't you tell the difference between my voice and Stevie's voice? Didn't he laugh?" She said, "No, he laughed a little bit but just hung the phone up." I said, "I never thought you'd fall for that. Call him back and tell him his fifty thousand's on the way." And then when they did, he'd bust out laughing.

Marvin would also imitate me, and they would have imitating-me contests. One day Stevie and Marvin were imitating me, and I walked up behind both of them.

What happened when they saw you?
Well, well, they both looked at me, and of course, they both just bust out laughing. They were saying all the stuff I'd say. Like when I didn't like a record, I'd always say it was ridiculous and garbage: "It's garbage, it's garbage, it's garbage!" They were a comical version of everything in me. I never thought I talked like that, but everyone in the office said, "They're imitating you perfectly." I said, "Okay, fine."

The Temptations were with you for four years before they had a real hit. Why did you stick with them for so long?
Because they had talent, and I was always a believer that talent will win out in the long run. It's not about who gets hits and who doesn't get hits. These guys—the Temptations—could sing a cappella and had the greatest barbershop harmony that you've ever heard. They had this warmth. There was so much love coming from Melvin and artistry from David, who was a superstar in his own right. You had, like, five stars there, and each one could sing lead. So the public was getting tremendous benefits for their money.

The Temptations' "Cloud Nine," cowritten and produced by Norman Whitfield, was probably the most controversial record Motown released.

"Cloud Nine" was an interesting situation, 'cause I hated that record—not because it was bad. I loved the record's sound, but I felt that it was talking about drugs. That was our biggest argument. I felt that Norman was promoting drugs with that record, and I said, "Norman, we have this company, Motown, that stands for something. We can't say, 'I'm doing fine on cloud nine,' referring to drugs." He said, "This is art, and it's not about drugs. It's talking about something else."

But it was about drugs, wasn't it?

I know, but Norman convinced me that it was something other than that.

He convinced you it wasn't about drugs?

Well, you want to believe it, especially since I thought it was such a great record. That record was very painful for me—until it went Top Ten [*laughs; "Cloud Nine" reached Number Six, December 1968*].

The Supremes were with Motown for at least four years before they had a major hit.

I cut stuff with them, but it wasn't until Mary Wells left that we had a chance to really devote ourselves to the Supremes.

Why did Mary Wells leave?

I made a major mistake with Mary. I made a lot of mistakes, and one of them was that shortly before her twenty-first birthday, I put out a smash-hit record on her, "My Guy" [Number One, April 1964], not even thinking or knowing that at twenty-one, she would be able to disaffirm all contracts—which she did. I mean, the record was Number One, you understand, and all of a sudden she's out of the pocket—she's not talking to anybody, and I'm going, "What is this?"

That's when you really pushed the Supremes?

I had talked to Mary's attorney and convinced him that I was the best place for her, and then I understood that she fired him and got another attorney and left anyway. I was trying to cover up any hurt that I might have had and said, "To hell with her. Let's deal with these new girls here who I like anyway." I'd always wanted a female star, and Mary was, like, the first one, and when she left, we were down, but we weren't out. I always had this desire to have an artist who I could really mold, and Diana happened to be that. And it wasn't until Michael Jackson came on later that I had that same kind of thing again.

Why did the Supremes break up?

It had gotten to the point, as it does in many groups, when there's total miscommunication between the two factions. The ones in the background were having conflicts with the one in the front. Diana never wanted to leave the girls, particularly. She was more or less pushed out, but that's what happens when a person is up front and people are telling the background singers that she's stealing the show. They would complain to me, and I would say, "Wait a minute. She does roll her eyes, and she does have a flirty look, but that's helping the group, not hurting the group."

It was always a problem for me having to take the responsibility for the choices. I made the choices of who sang lead, and my opinion was that Diana had the magic and Mary [Wilson] didn't. But Mary felt that she should be the one, and I said no, and then, of course, favoritism was charged. And it was perhaps favoritism, because Diana was a favorite of mine, but she had the talent to justify that favoritism. But it wasn't favoritism in terms of their personalities as much as it was the fact that we had a commercial venture here, and the lead singer had to be a person that would best move the group forward.

Now, the breakup of that group was very sad for all of us, but we tried very hard to make the group remain successful. We brought in Jean Terrell to replace Diana, and the group had a couple of big hits. As Mike [Roshkind, a former Motown vice-chairman now employed as a consultant to Berry Gordy] put it, we had a two-for-one split. And actually, the Supremes had a better shot than Diana. That's right, because the Supremes were a much, much bigger name than Diana Ross.

Over the years, people have written some nasty things about Motown.

It used to hurt me a lot when those kinds of things were written—stuff that was totally without foundation. Some people who used to be at Motown would be unhappy about a decision I had made. All the major decisions, I made them personally, and so unfortunately for me, Motown was synonymous with Berry Gordy. At other record companies, when an artist would leave, or they wouldn't make money, or they weren't a success, there was no individual singled out, but when one of our artists didn't make it, it was Berry Gordy's fault. I'd say, "Wait a minute. It's the company, it's the business. Everybody's not going to be successful."

I've had people come to me and say, "I would love to sign with you, but I heard you ripped off several artists." And I'd say, "Well, what artists did I rip off?" And they'd say, "Well, you ripped off Diana Ross, Marvin Gaye, Stevie Wonder, Michael Jackson and Smokey Robinson." And I'd say, "Well, every artist you named is a superstar. Wouldn't you like to be ripped off like that?" And they'd say, "You know, I never thought of that."

Let's talk about Michael Jackson and the first time you saw him.

Michael was a born star. He was nine years old when the Jacksons auditioned for me. He was a classic example of understanding everything. He watched me like a hawk. I recognized that he had a depth that was so vast, it was just incredible. And these songs sung with a certain amount of pain—he was a kid, so where did he get that pain from? The first time I saw him, I saw this little kid as something real special. He reminded me of a kid I used to see earlier, Frankie Lymon. I decided that I would pattern his style after Frankie Lymon, and that's what I did. I came up with the melody for the first song we released on the Jackson 5 myself.

You came up with the melody for "I Want You Back"?

The kid inspired me so much, I walked around, and I came up with this melody: [*starts to sing*] "Da-da-da-da." Because I was thinking of Frankie Lymon and picturing the kid: [*sings*] "Oh, baby, give me one more chance / To tell you I love you; / Won't you let me back in your heart? / I want you back, yes I do." That was it ["I Want You Back" went to Number One, December 1969].

We had a very close relationship. When I was moving to California, I decided to move him out with me. People said, "You're crazy—he's a kid, and there will be expenses." We moved him out to California anyway.

So you moved the entire group to California. Did they stay with you?

They stayed with me after they were kicked out of several houses. You see, they would make too much noise. They had their band, and we would put them in a house, and then they would get kicked out. Finally I said, "Okay, you move into my house," because I wanted them to rehearse.

You've stayed in contact with Michael Jackson. Recently Michael came to Detroit to do a benefit for the Motown Museum. One of his requests was to go to my house in Detroit where they stayed when they were first with Motown. It has a swimming pool and an underground tunnel and a bowling alley and some other stuff, and when they would come to Detroit, that's where they would stay, on the third floor. So Michael said he wanted to have dinner with me there. Just he and I, and we'd take off our shoes, and we would run around like we sort of did years and years before. Michael has never lost that childlike quality. We had fun. We had dinner alone, and we talked. He wanted to do some of the childlike things that he did before, and it was so much fun for me, too.

What effect did the civil rights movement have on Motown?

I was always very conscious of human suffering and freedom. I don't like bigotry in any sense of the word, and so I was indebted to the civil rights leaders at that time, as everyone was, black or white. I was a very, very close friend of Dr. King's. To have a hero, your hero, as your friend was incredible. [*He gets up and brings over a photo*] That's Dr. King and Lena Horne and myself. I was so inspired by the "I Have a Dream" speech that we released it on an album. We started the Black Forum label, where I put out various albums of people like Elaine Brown and Stokely Carmichael.

But as far as the civil rights movement, I was not so much affected by it as I was appreciative that they were moving in that direction, and I liked Dr. King's approach, the nonviolent approach. I admired his courage. When you say, "The civil rights movement: What did it do?"—it did a lot for me as a human being, to know that other people were fighting and dying, black and white, who just believed in people having equal rights. It was a great part of my life. I mean, it's a great part of the lives of all of us who lived through that. You know, the Sixties is an era

not to be believed in terms of what was happening in our culture and society.

Do you think you could have had the success you had with Motown if there hadn't been a civil rights movement?

It's hard for me to say. I don't see the connection to success and failure based on any one thing. It was not a visible factor as to whether a person had a hit record or didn't have a hit record. When we went on tours to the South, we were attacked in our motorcades like everybody else.

But both sides were playing Motown music. So, you know, the whites and the blacks, the liberals and the conservatives were playing Motown music. People are people. That was the whole basis for our whole kind of musical thing. To realize that white people are people, too [*laughs*]. That's a joke. That's a joke. That all people have the same wants and likes and dislikes. That's always been my thing—trying to get the thread between all people. We were just trying to create the type of music that would move us into a wider audience.

If rap had been happening in the Sixties, would Motown have been a rap label?

I like rap, but if rap was in when I was in, I wouldn't be where I am today, because I would have done all my records myself. Because I had no voice quality, so if rap had been in, I would have been doing all my own songs because I wouldn't have needed the voice quality. I would have been talking many of my songs. There wouldn't have been any need for me to have artists.

[*Michael Roshkind, who arranged this interview, interrupts*] "Uh, Berry, I think we've got to cut this off now."

[*Gordy to Roshkind*] "You've already gone over [the time allotted]. It's your responsibility, so that's a fine for you!" [*laughs*]

⑨
⑨

southern soul

By ROBERT PALMER

"Our orientation was strictly R&B," says Norbert Putnam, once a session bassist in Muscle Shoals, Alabama, who went on to become a successful Nashville producer. "We were young Alabama kids who loved soul music." There, in a nutshell, is the motivation for a group of young, white musicians, record producers and independent-label owners who worked with black musicians, songwriters and singers to create the most racially harmonious music scene of the Sixties—in the heart of the Deep South. In a time of rapid social change and unprecedented racial turmoil, blacks and whites quietly worked together in Memphis and in nearby Muscle Shoals to create one of the most popular and lastingly influential sounds of the Sixties—soul music, Southern style.

The Memphis and Muscle Shoals scenes—completely separate at first but increasingly interrelated as the Sixties progressed—took off with the beginning of the new decade. Their beginnings seem remarkably similar. In Florence, one of four Alabama towns clustered together along the Tennessee River (the others were Muscle Shoals, Sheffield and Tuscumbia), a group of young, white musicians who had honed their chops playing R&B covers at Southern frat parties got together with tyro producer Rick Hall to record a string of early Sixties hits with a local black gospel singer, Arthur Alexander. Leased to a major label and distributed internationally, Alexander's hits—"You Better Move On," "Anna," "Go Home Girl," "A Shot of Rhythm and Blues"—were a decisive influence on a generation of young performers, including John Lennon, who covered several of them with the Beatles and kept the originals permanently installed on his home jukebox at the Dakota, in New York.

In Memphis, the young, white R&B band was the Royal Spades, later renamed the Mar-Keys, and the studio and homegrown record label were first called Satellite, then Stax. With the help of engineer-producer Chips Moman, the Stax crew cut two instrumental hits, "Last Night," by the Mar-Keys, and "Green Onions," by Booker T. and the MG's, and classic early soul vocals by Carla Thomas ("Gee Whiz") and William Bell ("You Don't Miss Your Water"). Jim Stewart, a former country fiddler, and his sister, Estelle Axton, owned and operated Stax. Not being well informed about black music, they wisely let their musicians and Moman run the sessions.

Having proved themselves, the Stax operation in Memphis and Rick Hall's Fame studio and label, which he'd set up in Muscle Shoals, attracted the attention of Jerry Wexler of Atlantic Records, who made distribution agreements and helped out both fledgling operations in other ways. By the mid-Sixties, with America's top black-music label distributing their product, Stax and Fame—and smaller labels and studios that grew up around them (like Goldwax, in Memphis)—had hit their stride. There was no shortage of local talent to record. From Muscle Shoals came the transcendent "When a Man Loves a Woman," by Percy Sledge, the Sixties' definitive soul ballad. The Stax rhythm section, with former Royal Spades Steve Cropper and Duck Dunn on guitar and bass and two black musicians, Booker T. Jones on organ and Al Jackson, Jr., on drums, became a hitmaking machine on its own.

‹ **otis redding** live [ca. **1967**]
MICHAEL OCHS ARCHIVES/VENICE, CA

< The **bar-kays** in front of the Memphis
headquarters of Stax/Volt
MICHAEL OCHS ARCHIVES/VENICE, CA

Atlantic sent vocalists down South to get "the treatment." The one who benefited most spectacularly was Wilson Pickett, who recorded "In the Midnight Hour" (cowritten with Cropper) at Stax and both "Mustang Sally" and "Land of 1000 Dances" in Muscle Shoals. Sam and Dave, a vocal duo from Florida, also struck gold at Stax, with "Hold On, I'm Comin'," "Soul Man" and other classics. And when Georgia performer Johnny Jenkins showed up at Stax to audition, he brought a vocalist named Otis Redding, who rapidly became the king of Southern soul, cinching his reputation with a triumphant appearance at the Monterey Pop Festival before his tragic death, along with all but two of his band members, in a plane crash.

Both Memphis and Muscle Shoals continued to turn out hits through the Seventies, but with black music changing from soul to funk, the records were likely to be straight AM pop. Still, the sound created in those years never died. To this day, the quickest way to get a crowd out onto the dance floor is to spin "In the Midnight Hour" or "Soul Man." The excitement is still in the grooves.

the wall of sound:
phil spector

By PARKE PUTERBAUGH

"Just about every rock & roll record of the last twenty-five years has been influenced by Phil Spector's sound, by the noise he made," says producer Jimmy Iovine, who's worked with Tom Petty, Patti Smith, Stevie Nicks and others. "He added a drama to music that I don't think existed before him. Making dark records and pop records are separate things. When you can

combine the two worlds, you've achieved greatness. He not only achieved it, he basically invented it."

From the spectacular success of the Crystals' "He's a Rebel" in 1962 to the spectacular failure of Ike and Tina Turner's "River Deep—Mountain High" in 1966, Spector elevated the seven-inch, monaural 45 record to an art form. He captured the high anxiety of adolescence with grandiose, gripping performances. "Little symphonies for the kiddies," he called them—but he wasn't kidding. *Control* was the operative word in Spector's universe when he set up shop at Gold Star Studios, in Los Angeles. He viewed himself as the artist, while he regarded his artists as sidemen, his sidemen as a rock & roll orchestra, his orchestra as a Wall of Sound and his Wall of Sound as Wagnerian-scale music blaring over Top Forty radio.

For four years, Spector's label, Philles Records—whose yellow-and-red labels bore the motto "Tomorrow's Sound Today"—was unstoppable: Nineteen singles sailed into the Top Forty. Though Spector enjoyed success before and after that reign, the Wall of Sound towers above all, intriguing disciples of rock & roll nearly forty years later.

The secret behind the Wall of Sound has a lot to do with some cement boxes. They were the echo chambers at Gold Star: concrete rectangles barely large enough for a human being to crawl into. When music was piped through them, they provided a natural reverberation that gave texture and depth to a recording. The studio had the best echo chambers in the country, and echo was a prime component of Spector's sound. His arranger, Jack Nitzsche, likened echo to garlic: You can't get enough of it.

Spector began working in earnest at Gold Star in 1961. "What made Gold Star was the personality of the place," says engineer Larry Levine. "We were having fun. It wasn't like a big studio where nobody gave a shit about the product." Founded in 1950, Gold Star was a popular place where songwriters could inexpensively record demos of their tunes to peddle around Hollywood. Levine worked the board for such seminal rock & roll sessions as "Summertime Blues," by Eddie Cochran, and "Tequila," by the Champs. Though he was not initially enamored of Spector as a person—"I thought he was a stuck-up little prick," Levine says, chuckling—he admits he was awed by Spector's talent.

The first Spector-produced Philles sides—"There's No Other (Like My Baby)" and "Uptown"—were actually recorded back east with the Crystals. The sessions were marked by tension and resistance from old-guard musicians who couldn't comprehend Spector's offbeat ways. Consequently, he beat a path to L.A. to cut the Crystals' next single, "He's a Rebel," *without* the Crystals, with whom he was feuding. Vocalist Darlene Love sang lead, and session singers added backup. The song hit Number One in November 1962. Spector was twenty-one years old.

The elements of the Wall of Sound came together with "He's a Rebel." It was Spector's first session with Levine and Nitzsche. It was also Spector's first summit meeting with the new breed of West Coast session musicians, a collective of schooled jazz, pop and country virtuosos whose hearts beat for rock & roll. Within the industry, they came to be known as the Wrecking Crew, because the older musicians they displaced grumbled that they were wrecking the industry.

Spector further refined his Wall of Sound on his next single, "Zip-a-Dee-Doo-Dah," a song lifted from a Walt Disney movie, *Song of the South*. Working again with Darlene Love, he contrived a group around the name Bob B. Soxx and the Blue Jeans. In his hands, the children's song became a sultry, seductive number with a dense blur of instruments grinding out funky rhythms behind the singers.

The recording of "Zip-a-Dee-Doo-Dah" started out with an argument but ended with a revolution in sound. Following Spector's repeated calls for loudness, engineer Levine found the needles of his soundboard meters pinned far into the red zone. In frustration, he turned everything off. Then Levine carefully began bringing instruments in one at a time, trying to get volume without distortion. "That's the sound right there!" shouted Spector.

Innovations came fast and furious with each new record. Singles were lavished with days and even weeks of rehearsals and unheard-of budgets. (Albums, on the other hand, were dismissed by Spector as "two hits and ten pieces of junk.") He worked his orchestra like a drill sergeant, tinkering with arrangements and textures until he heard exactly what he wanted. The guitarists' hands bled, and the other musicians slumped from fatigue in the heat of the cramped, airless studio. "I have a theory that he wanted to get all the musicians so tired that they weren't individuals, so that they blended in more to this wall of what he wanted to hear," Levine says.

"It was hard work," says drummer Hal Blaine. "But it was fun; we were always laughing." The lengthy rehearsals often yielded impromptu riffs or bits that found their way into songs. Musicians would play absentmindedly while tuning or restringing instruments. Roaming the floor while running over parts and setting up mikes, Spector would hear something he liked and say, "I want that—remember that."

On any given session, twenty to twenty-five musicians would crowd into Studio A, which was intended to accommodate half that number. Even those who dropped by to watch—from fellow producers and disciples such as Brian Wilson and Mick Jagger to chance acquaintances—were often handed percussion instruments and pointed toward the studio. Therein lies another acoustical principle of the Wall of Sound: lots of warm bodies. "They provided baffling," explains Levine, "so the room worked better."

Each new Spector production was greeted as a special event, like "Be My Baby," Spector's first single with a teenage trio from Harlem called the Ronettes. Released in September 1963, it was the apex of girl-group rock and a sublime expression of romantic desire. (Later, Spector would marry lead singer Veronica "Ronnie" Bennett.) For all his mastery of studio craft, Spector ultimately judged a recording on its emotional impact, and he had an unerring sense of the teen market. "If we did a take and it felt wonderful, there may have been a couple of glitches, but nobody cared," says drummer Blaine. "They loved what they were hearing. It made you move."

His magnum opus was "You've Lost That Lovin' Feelin'," nearly four minutes of exquisitely tempered blue-eyed soul. Righteous Brothers Bill Medley and Bobby Hatfield spent two intensive eight-hour days laying down vocals. "It didn't bother us to keep doing it over and over, because we heard it getting better and better," says Medley. Too slow for rock & roll, too long for AM radio and too adult for the teenage audience, "Lovin' Feelin'" was a special track—but would it fly? The Righteous Brothers had their doubts, but "Phil knew from the git-go," says Medley. "He said, 'This is a Number One record.'" It topped the charts in February 1965.

Spector attempted to top "Lovin' Feelin'" a year later with "River Deep—Mountain High," wherein the full fury of Tina Turner's voice was cast into a raging musical vortex. The single's failure to break the Top Forty remains a hotly debated controversy. Was the record too far ahead of its time or too far behind the times? Was it too busy, too intense for the Top Forty? A paranoid Spector believed, perhaps correctly, that the industry had conspired to blackball him for his unconventional ways and seeming arrogance.

One thing is certain: An era had ended. Although he would emerge from semiretirement to work with John Lennon and George Harrison at Apple, "River Deep—Mountain High" marked the spot where Philles Records, the Wall of Sound and the tightly bonded team at Gold Star played out their final chapter. "I think it really broke his spirit when 'River Deep' didn't make it," Medley says. "I don't blame Phil for feeling real bad, because that is one amazing record."

THE JEFFERSON AIRPLANE, FROM LEFT TO RIGHT: >
marty balin, paul kantner, jorma kaukonen, grace slick, jack casady, spencer dryden [ca. **1967**]

MICHAEL OCHS ARCHIVES/VENICE, CA

Today, Gold Star exists no longer, having been sold in the mid-Eighties to developers and razed to make way for a shopping center. Those involved with Spector in his heyday scattered to various corners of the music industry. Tales of tormented and reclusive behavior dogged Spector throughout the Seventies. Levine continued to work with him until suffering a heart attack during a particularly trying session for a Ramones album; eight years passed before they spoke again.

In time, Spector began circulating again, at least socially. An informal reunion took place on April 19, 1991, to celebrate the publication of Hal Blaine's musical memoir, *Hal Blaine and the Wrecking Crew*. The party was held at the Baked Potato, a North Hollywood nightclub owned by pianist and Wrecking Crew alumnus Don Randi. The cream of the L.A. Sixties pop scene turned out: Brian Wilson and members of the Beach Boys, the Association, Jan and Dean and the Fifth Dimension; Gold Star founders Stan Ross and Dave Gold; Jack Nitzsche, Larry Levine and various producers; many members of the Wrecking Crew; and, to everyone's surprise, Phil Spector. A button was pinned to the lapel of his suit coat. Presaging the title of his four-CD retrospective, it read BACK TO MONO. This box set of Spector master-works, *Back to Mono (1958–1969)*, was released to critical acclaim in 1991.

Spector turned sixty in 2000. Those who remain close to Spector are just pleased to see him healthy and in good spirits. "Phil lived by the image that was created around him," says Levine. "Now he seems to be his own man, and he's in better shape than at any time I've known him."

the san francisco sound

By MICHAEL GOLDBERG

No one can quite put a finger on it, but in 1964 (or was it '65?), something began to change in San Francisco. People were growing their hair and dressing like they were on their way to a costume ball, wearing purple velvet capes and fringed leather Wild West jackets. They were living together in funky old houses and experimenting with psychedelic drugs. Young folk musicians were trading acoustic guitars for electric instruments and playing a new kind of music that mirrored the life they were inventing for themselves.

Some of these maverick bohemians lived in a big rooming house at 1090 Page Street, Haight-Ashbury. In the spring of 1965, a long-haired Texan named Chet Helms started holding dance parties in the basement there; for fifty cents, you could dance to a band that later became Big Brother and the Holding Company. Others headed up to the old Nevada mining town of Virginia City that summer, commandeering the Red Dog Saloon and turning it into the prototype for the trippy dance concerts that would soon be held in old ballrooms and auditoriums throughout the Bay Area. Down in Palo Alto, Ken Kesey and his Merry Pranksters went public with their "acid tests," free-form parties at which Kool-Aid was spiked with LSD and the house band was the Grateful Dead.

Out of this came the San Francisco Sound, an elusive blend of electric folk, blues, jazz, country and rock & roll. During the next two years, hundreds of bands formed in the Bay Area. Some of the best were the Charlatans, the Quicksilver Messenger Service, the Jefferson Airplane, the Grateful Dead, the Steve Miller Blues Band, Country Joe and the Fish, Big

Brother and the Holding Company, Santana, Creedence Clearwater Revival and Moby Grape. Though not all of these bands went on to achieve fame or even to record many memorable albums, they all created new and original music. "There was a community in need of music, and music in need of a community," says Mickey Hart of the Grateful Dead. "I think the Grateful Dead made the most of those times of experimentation. And we graduated: We didn't stay in the Sixties any longer than the Sixties lasted. But it's good to know that a place like that existed once."

To get a sense of what that period of time was like, ROLLING STONE spoke with some of the key on-the-scene figures: Country Joe McDonald, whose group Country Joe and the Fish wedded barbed political and social commentary to an acid-rock sound; Howard Hesseman, then a member of the satirical theatrical troupe the Committee, as well as a DJ at the first underground rock radio station in the U.S., KMPX; Boz Scaggs, who came to San Francisco in 1967 to join the Steve Miller Blues Band; Alton Kelley, one of the great San Francisco poster artists, who helped organize the first psychedelic dance concert in the city; Grace Slick, lead singer for the Great Society and the Jefferson Airplane; Bill Graham, who promoted the dance concerts at the Fillmore Auditorium and managed the Jefferson Airplane; Peter Albin, bass player and cofounder of Big Brother and the Holding Company; Bill Ham, the first light-show artist; Mickey Hart, percussionist for the Grateful Dead; Chet Helms, who promoted dance concerts at the Avalon Ballroom and managed Big Brother and the Holding Company; and Tony Pigg, a DJ who hung out and worked at San Francisco's revolutionary underground radio stations, KMPX and KSAN. Their memories offer a vivid look back at what was clearly a most remarkable atmosphere.

country joe (center) surrounded by his fish [ca. **1967**]
MICHAEL OCHS ARCHIVES/VENICE, CA

birth of a scene

The San Francisco music scene seemed to develop naturally as musicians, excited by the records of English bands like the Beatles and the Rolling Stones and the folk rock of Bob Dylan, formed their own groups and started seeking an audience.

ALTON KELLEY: We didn't really have anything to do, so we thought about putting on some dances. And the first dance event really made the scene jell. We called it A Tribute to Dr. Strange, and it took place at Longshoremen's Hall, in the city [on October 16, 1965]. The Charlatans played, and the Great Society and the Jefferson Airplane and the Marbles. We had a light show by Bill Ham, who projected lights through colored liquids onto the wall. I guess about 600 people showed up, and they all had long hair and were dressed hip, and it was a shocker. Everyone went, "Where the hell did all these people come from?" We had no idea there were that many freaks in the city. And then it just started to roll.

PETER ALBIN: We invented freak rock. It was after Jim Gurley joined Big Brother [in late 1965]. His playing was extremely fast and also kind of bizarre. Sometimes he didn't sound like he was playing

^ GRATEFUL DEAD ON THE STREETS OF SAN FRANCISCO, FROM LEFT TO RIGHT: **bob weir, mickey hart, jerry garcia** and **phil lesh**

MICHAEL OCHS ARCHIVES/VENICE, CA

in the same key you were in. We were a lot freakier than the Grateful Dead. We were looser. We'd bump the amplifiers and crash the reverb—early sound effects. We wanted to be kind of wild and crazy.

BILL GRAHAM: I saw it and felt it on a specific night: the first San Francisco Mime Troupe benefit, November 6, 1965 [which Graham organized and held in the Mime Troupe's loft, on Howard Street]. The Jefferson Airplane and John Handy and Allen Ginsberg and Lawrence Ferlinghetti and others performed. We expected a few hundred people; thousands showed up. There were people with huge hats and loud colors and baggy pants and costume jewelry and army coats. A sea of visual expression. Cinema people put up bedsheets and projected their 8-millimeter films on the walls. We had these big barrels filled with vodka and grapefruit juice. People were dancing around the loft in groups of five and ten. And the response we got: "My eyes were opened. There's a new world and a new society and a new spirit."

MICKEY HART: There was music everywhere. The first time I saw Janis was probably one of the most revealing moments. I saw her at the Matrix, a tiny, little club in North Beach. May have held fifty people; it was like a hallway. It was an amazing scene.

Big Brother was going crazy feeding back, and Janis stepped to the mike, and it split your head open. It was so out of hand. It was music that was springing from a community. It was a certain kind of soul-spirit music. It was bordering on religious experience. These people were obviously moving into altered states.

BOZ SCAGGS: I was kind of amazed at the situation in San Francisco when I arrived in 1967. I was already aware of it. I remember sitting in Bombay looking at *Time* magazine, at color pictures of kids dressed up like cowboys and Indians, and thinking there was something kind of silly about what was going on. My impression upon arriving in San Francisco was somewhat the same. There were a lot of people dressed up like cowboys and Indians playing a new game, a new American game.

the red dog saloon, the trips festival, multimedia events and the acid tests

It was these events—parties at the Red Dog Saloon, in Virginia City; the Trips Festival, a multimedia event held at San Francisco's Longshoremen's Hall; and Ken Kesey's Acid Tests, held at various locations around the Bay Area—that set the stage for the San Francisco music scene.

ALTON KELLEY: The Red Dog Saloon [which opened June 21, 1965] was an old, abandoned bar in Virginia City. A whole mess of people came up from San Francisco, including myself and the Charlatans and Bill Ham. We all painted the place, fixed it up, made it a workable building. We wore Western-style clothes, and we all had guns and the long hair. We actually carried guns in the street. There was no such word as *hippie* yet; we were all young mods. The Red Dog was the Charlatans' first booking. They had a light show, too. Bill Ham built a light box that was responsive to music playing on the jukebox. The Red Dog Saloon was like this twenty-first-century figure thing in the middle of this ghost town. They would jam the place full of cowboys, tourists and college kids. The cowboys were tough guys—shooting guns through the ceiling. They shot right up into [Charlatan] Dan Hicks's room while people were in the room.

The Red Dog sparked the whole thing, 'cause after the gigs at the Red Dog Saloon, we all came back to the city, and there was nothing to do. So myself and Luria Castell and Ellen Harmon and Jack Towle [calling themselves the Family Dog] got together and said, "Let's see if we can throw some dances down here."

PETER ALBIN: What the Trips Festival [January 21–23, 1966] did that was different was combine rock & roll music with all the different kinds of hip things that were going on at the time. Like Stewart Brand's *America Needs Indians* multimedia show. There was a tepee set up, and slides and films showing Indian life were projected. The Psychedelic Shop [a Haight Street store] had an exhibit over in one corner. The Grateful Dead were there; Ken Kesey and the Merry Pranksters were involved. I remember Kesey going around with this jumpsuit on, directing people here and there. It was one of Bill Graham's first productions. He was very uptight.

We sounded real rough and raw. I remember after playing a disjointed set, we got off, and some girl started taking off her clothes, and some guy started passing around a bucket of ice cream laced with acid, and the place just started vibrating.

BILL HAM: And shortly thereafter Bill Graham produced *Sights and Sounds of the Trips Festival* at the Fillmore. And one thing led to another, and all of a sudden it was every weekend.

GRACE SLICK: I remember an acid test held out at somebody's ranch in Marin. Neal Cassady [Kerouac sidekick and a member of Kesey's Merry Pranksters] was high on acid and holding forth. Twelve or so people were in a sloppy circle listening to Neal's acid rap. Someone was painting the side of a bus. Another person was reading somebody's aura. Other people were upstairs making love. I'm sure there are parties that go on now that are similar to that—the outfits are different.

the dance concerts

Although dance concerts were held all over the Bay Area, the Avalon Ballroom on Sutter Street and the Fillmore Auditorium on Geary Boulevard were the key places to go in San Francisco during 1966 and 1967.

ALTON KELLEY: For maybe the first year, there weren't people sitting down at the dance concerts. The dances were really dances. People came there to party, and they really *did* party. I can remember going between the Avalon and Fillmore so I wouldn't miss any shows—there were shows Friday, Saturday and Sunday. It was great, 'cause nobody knew who the bands were; it was before the bands were anybody. So it was a different kind of experience. Now the bands are famous people, and it's a totally different thing.

^ janis joplin
MICHAEL OCHS ARCHIVES/VENICE, CA

GRACE SLICK: We didn't have Broadway dressing rooms at the Fillmore and the Avalon. We just came in whatever we were wearing, so nobody got dressed [at the concert site]. We were already in costumes; we lived in costumes. It wasn't like you'd come in a suit and tie and then change into something wacko—we were already in something wacko. So we didn't really need dressing rooms. The only thing we needed dressing rooms for was to tune the guitars.

MICKEY HART: Every week the Avalon and Fillmore would print up these posters, and they would get them out to the community, and that's how the word was spread. We didn't do ads in the newspaper. It was just posters—magnificent posters. Every one of them surprised me. It was like a mystery tour. You could look at them twenty ways and see twenty different things in them. The artists tried for that kind of illusion. I thought they were great works of art—even back then.

BILL HAM: I walked into the Avalon and made up what was the light show. We had to work some things out: how to relate to the music, how to relate to the time, how to relate to 360 degrees or whatever [of wall space]. I had this rare opportunity to start from scratch. There was no stage lighting at the Avalon. Had there been, it would have been much harder to take these projections and fit them all in, partly because the equipment we had was so limited. We were using classroom overhead projectors and army-surplus things. I was doing purely liquids. I would work spontaneously for an hour, making an abstract image to the music....

The Dead painted all of their speakers white for their second night at the Avalon, 'cause the first night, I'd spent the whole day putting up some white material on the walls to project on, and when I came back for that night's performance, the Dead's road gang had stacked up all these black boxes [amps and speakers] over the white screens. It hadn't occurred to anyone to wonder about it. So the only thing they could offer to do was paint it white for the next night.

COUNTRY JOE McDONALD: Everyone was experimenting with how to play the instruments. We were always discussing feedback and what to do about it and how to stop it. I remember one New Year's, with Chet Helms up onstage at the Avalon completely going nuts with a fog machine. He was obviously so into the fog machine that he had forgotten what the program was, and we couldn't even see each other onstage. We were all yelling at him to turn it off.

On the other side of town, Bill Graham would get up onstage at the Fillmore and beat on a cowbell. There were times where he was just pulled like a magnet to the stage and would just appear there banging on a cowbell, which was quite unprofessional of him, and we used to tease him about it. Back then he was always there, picking up trash on the floor after the show, talking to people, yelling at people, kicking people, pushing them around and schmoozing, which was always very nice. He'd appear in your dressing room and just shoot the shit. But there wasn't any star treatment, which was understandable, because no one was a star.

CHET HELMS: For one of the yearly Tribal Stomp dances at the Avalon, we gave everybody a little leather thong with a little Indian bell and a long, white turkey feather tied to it. I can't tell you how effective that thematic favor was. It made everybody

a member of the tribe, and at the end of that evening, the energy was such that no one wanted to stop the party, but it was two o'clock in the morning, and we had to stop the party there.

So we stood up onstage and said, "We're going to the beach. Anyone who wants to go to the beach, come with us." So we went to Ocean Beach. And things were so tribalized that without anyone dictating it from the top, those people who perceived themselves as sentries sat along the ridge overlooking the beach and kept an eye out for the cops. Others gathered wood and built fires. Others sang and danced. It went until sunrise, with big bonfires. Maybe 400 people. I remember watching this Hell's Angel who had this big, fat wallet. He was so stoned on acid, he started out pulling out unessential pieces of paper and feeding the fire, but then it got to his draft card and his I.D. and his driver's license. We were all pretty stoned, watching him burn up his biography, one piece at a time.

free in the park

For a few years, bands performed for free at parks in San Francisco and Berkeley. First hundreds, later thousands of people came to hear the new music performed outdoors on a sunny Saturday or Sunday afternoon.

MICKEY HART: I loved playing for free. It made you play real good. You were relaxed. People weren't paying money to hear you play, so you could do anything you wanted. And it felt good to be able to give the music away and let people would couldn't afford the music hear it. We used to like to play one free and one for pay. We thought we could manage that. It didn't cost that much to live then. We all lived together pretty much in two houses.

I remember when we blocked Haight Street off. We just took Haight Street, put two flatbed trucks across and closed the street off. And it filled up, eventually—we played to ten, fifteen, twenty thousand people. That was really guerrilla theater. We got up in the morning, looked around and said, "Hey, what are we gonna do today?" Somebody said, "Let's play on Haight Street." "Okay." The thought was always there—this was just the day to do it.

the bands

MICKEY HART: All of the bands were very close— the Quicksilver and the Grateful Dead and Big Brother and the Airplane. We were like sister bands. We'd be over at each other's houses, see each other all day long, party at night. There were no hassles about who was going to open the show or close the show. It seemed like when we played with one of our sister bands, our *compadres*, we always played better for each other. Maybe we just assumed it, but it felt like that. It felt like we were validating each other's sound.

PETER ALBIN: You have to give credit to George Hunter [who led the Charlatans] for being a spearhead on the San Francisco scene. Here's a guy who would probably admit himself he was no musical genius. The only instruments I remember him playing were autoharp and tambourine. But he was a very definite kind of charismatic hipster who got things going. He was an innovator. He was one of the first guys I saw with long hair, hair past his shoulders. Wearing funny Edwardian clothes. The Charlatans had all these fantastic clothes. From college stuff with block letters to old cowboy chaps, straw boaters and cowboy hats. The music they played was okay, but it was their visual style that was important. I think they influenced people in the other bands to be different in their dress and in their style. They allowed people not to be afraid to wear different kinds of clothes.

MICKEY HART: Quicksilver was one of my favorite live bands, when they were just a four-piece outfit with David Freiberg and Gary Duncan and Greg Elmore and John Cipollina. Those four guys, Jesus, they were magic. There was one gig they played so well that if they weren't good friends, it would have been really intimidating. We were closing for them. Freiberg's bass just turned into a thunderous wave of sound. Cipollina just cut the air with his guitar. They were playing possessed. We'd been known to do that from time to time, but to be able to do it on cue is not the thing. We went out there and played the best that we could, but they certainly had the evening. I remember Phil and I just looked at each other: These guys are the best band in the world tonight.

GRACE SLICK: When we first started, Great Society played five sets a night at a former strip joint on Broadway called Mothers. We played to about five drunken sailors. They had no idea what we were doing. I mean, they're like in the military, they've got a day off, they want to get laid, they're getting drunk, they haven't found a woman yet, and they're sitting in the bar looking at these insane-looking people onstage playing this weird-ass music. I was never a dedicated musician. I was just enjoying myself. Getting paid to hang out and play music.

ALTON KELLEY: Stanley [Mouse, who was Kelley's poster-making partner at the time] and I had a studio in an old barn in San Francisco that had been used as a horse stable for a fire station. We had our studio upstairs, and Big Brother and Janis would come in and practice downstairs. When Janis sang, it would give you chills. This was when she was really young and before she was too far gone with the drugs and drinking. I mean, she would shatter glass, practically.

One day they came, they practiced and they left, and then the police show up and pound on the door. We go down and open the door, and they say, "We've got a report of a woman screaming," and we had to explain to them that that was the band practicing; there wasn't anybody being murdered.

underground radio

Underground, or alternative, rock & roll radio began in San Francisco, in the spring of 1967, at KMPX, an FM station that until then broadcast mostly foreign-language programming. Although Larry Miller pioneered a new, radical approach to radio at the station, it was the late Tom Donahue, a former Top Forty DJ who had dropped out and taken LSD for over a year, who popularized this new format in San Francisco. Following a dispute with KMPX's owner and a strike, Donahue took most of his staff to KSAN, until then a classical-music station, and made it the hippest radio station in the country.

TONY PIGG: I was the first DJ in the country to play "Viola Lee Blues," by the Grateful Dead. Someone gave me the record and told me to play it. It was unheard-of in those days to play something that long. "Viola Lee Blues" is at least six minutes long. All I know is when I saw the Dead, that was the song that made me understand what their appeal was. It all came together in that song.

PETER ALBIN: Larry Miller started this real hip format at KMPX. His style was one of the most important a DJ could have at that particular time. He always seemed to have Indian raga music behind his talking. And he'd talk in a low voice. He played a variety of music that was extremely eclectic, really incredible: odd things like Louis Jordan, Screamin' Jay Hawkins, Arthur Crudup, early Elvis and then Rolling Stones and the Beatles. And not just music: maybe a Lenny Bruce routine or Lord Buckley. Marches, heavy-duty rock & roll, a classical piece, then some local rock music. He set the style. A lot of other DJs sounded like Larry Miller copies.

HOWARD HESSEMAN: I was an old friend and neighbor of Tom [Donahue]. For years we talked about a radio station that would sound like you were sitting in the living room of somebody who had an incredible collection of records and really good taste and imagination. The way Tom and those of us who came with him sort of infiltrated the station [KMPX] was to just take over slots as previous time-buys were exhausted. Kind of freak fungus slowly spreading across the clock face until pretty soon it was a twenty-four-hour operation.

ALTON KELLEY: It was like *the* radical radio station. KMPX is what everybody listened to. Who else were you going to listen to? We knew every single person on the station. It was like our radio station. We got a piece of the sky. I'd be sitting there working on a poster at night, and we'd call up and talk to someone we knew: "Hi, this is Kelley; we're working over here. Could you play us some Rolling Stones songs or 'Trouble Coming Every Day,' by Frank Zappa?" They'd say, "Oh, yeah, no problem." The music would inspire us.

BOZ SCAGGS: One of the first things we [the Steve Miller Blues Band] did after we completed recording our first album in London was go to KSAN. That was like the first stop when you had the vinyl or the test pressing in your hand. You'd go down to KSAN and give it to Donahue, and you wanted them to play it on the radio and talk about it. It was sort of a community drum.

COUNTRY JOE McDONALD: When I got into electric music, it seemed natural that I would be listening to a radio station that would be playing my music. I remember being with Janis, and we'd be listening to see if KMPX would play one of our songs—and they would. I didn't turn the radio on to hear what they were doing; I turned the radio on to hear what we were doing.

psychedelics and the music

BOZ SCAGGS: My mind is reeling with clichés: "Tripping out on notes." I think cannabis had more of that kind of effect than psychedelics. Psychedelics tend to really distort things into other impressions, whereas cannabis tends to allow people to relax and expand on more specifically musical elements. I would say cannabis had more to do with the sound of things.

GRACE SLICK: "White Rabbit" was directed not to the kids but to the parents. People think I was exhorting all young people to take drugs. We already were taking drugs. I didn't have to exhort young people. I was telling the older people, "This is what we're doing and why we're doing it. You tell us not to take drugs, and yet you read us books—when we're very young—like *Peter Pan*, which says sprinkle something on your head and you can fly, books like *Alice in Wonderland*, where she takes at least five different drugs and has a wonderful time. What do you think you told us? That a chemical is going to get you where you want to go?"

COUNTRY JOE McDONALD: As far as the first Country Joe and the Fish album [*Electric Music for the Mind and Body*] is concerned, there are some songs on there written on drugs. There are some songs written not on drugs. There are some songs written before I'd ever had illegal drugs, and there are some songs written after I had illegal drugs. And no one can tell—including myself.

MICKEY HART: Psychedelic drugs had an incredible effect. It opened you up to a whole new set of musical values. It altered your time perception, your auditory perception, and allowed you to get together as a group without being competitive. I think you'd have to attribute a jam like "Dark Star" [on *Live Dead*] to the psychedelic experience. Nobody played like that before, know what I mean? Make your own deductions. I think it's pretty obvious.

paul mccartney's
top sixties songs

It's impossible for me to choose ten records from the Sixties, because it was just too rich a period, in my estimation. So here are some of my all-time favorites.

1 **"A Whiter Shade of Pale,"** by Procol Harum

2 **"God Only Knows"** or **"Pet Sounds,"** by the Beach Boys

3 **"Mr. Tambourine Man,"** by Bob Dylan

4 **"Hey Jude,"** by the Beatles

5 **"Strawberry Fields Forever,"** by the Beatles

6 **"(Sittin' on) The Dock of the Bay,"** by Otis Redding

7 **"Sunny Goodge Street,"** by Donovan

8 **"You Really Got Me,"** by the Kinks

9 **"What'd I Say,"** by Ray Charles

10 **"Papa's Got a Brand New Bag,"** by James Brown

11 **"In the Midnight Hour,"** by Wilson Pickett

12 **"Hold On, I'm Comin',"** by Sam and Dave

And so many more! Like the Who's "My Generation," for instance!

keith richards's
top ten rolling stones songs

I don't fucking know why these are my favorites.

1 "Jumpin' Jack Flash"

2 "Street Fighting Man"

3 "(I Can't Get No) Satisfaction"

4 "Honky Tonk Women"

5 "Gimme Shelter"

6 "Sympathy for the Devil"

7 "Midnight Rambler"

8 "Brown Sugar"

9 "Ruby Tuesday"

10 "I Got the Blues"

the seventies

By STEVE POND

Somehow, it's hard to remember the Seventies fondly without feeling guilty. Nostalgia for the rock & roll of the Fifties, the decade in which the music was born, is easy; for the Sixties, when rock & roll changed pop culture and did its damnedest to change the rest of the world as well, it's *de rigueur*. But the Seventies? Wasn't that the decade that came along after we figured out that the starry-eyed optimism of the Sixties didn't work? The decade when cynicism and self-interest were the prevailing impulses? The decade when rock & roll found that fervent idealism didn't sell nearly as much product as calculated professionalism?

In the Nineties it became okay to like the Seventies, but it still felt a little campy. Sure, go ahead, pull out that old Barry White album—but to be safe, do it when nobody's around. Or, at the very least, give a knowing wink when you cue up *Frampton Comes Alive!* and mutter, "Ah, those were the days."

Of course, even in the Seventies, the Seventies had a serious image problem. The problem was, rock & roll simply wasn't dangerous anymore. Maybe it never was; maybe all that fuss about Elvis Presley's hips and the Beatles' hair and Jim Morrison's penis was overblown; maybe none of it was ever really a threat to the established social order. At the dawn of the Seventies, though, nobody had to think much about those maybes, because rock music wasn't scaring anybody—apart, perhaps, from a few businessmen who were worried that they weren't getting their market share.

The other problem was that rock had no center. At first, Elvis *was* rock & roll; later, as the Beatles and the Stones and Dylan went, so went rock. As the Seventies began, though, the icons that had unified rock were cracking apart. The Beatles were breaking up. The Rolling Stones were reeling from what many saw as the logical outcome of their self-conscious air of danger: Altamont. And Bob Dylan celebrated 1970 by releasing the ineffectual *Self-Portrait*.

As a result, there was no unifying presence in rock, no sense that its audience was party to something subversive or threatening, and no artist whose latest record *had* to be heard by every fan and musician. By the time the decade began, rock was entertainment; in fact, it was well on its way to being *the entertainment industry*.

So rock in the Seventies quickly became diffuse, scattered and unfocused, fragmenting into little genres whose fans paid less and less attention to the other little genres. In the Seventies, rock had a hundred different focal points: Elton John for popsters; Led Zeppelin for hard rockers; Joni Mitchell for the singer/songwriter contingent; David Bowie in the glam-rock corner; Stevie Wonder for soul aficionados. Instead of a center, rock had a batch of radio formats.

Hell, it's even hard to figure out just when the Seventies began and ended. The Seventies, you could say, began when the Rolling Stones played Altamont Speedway and the Hell's Angels security guards killed a member of the audience, and ended when Mick and Bianca Jagger got divorced. You could just as easily posit that the decade began with the breakup of the Beatles and ended with the breakup of the Eagles.

Or it began when Bob Dylan accepted an honorary doctorate in music from Princeton University and ended when Dylan won his first Grammy Award for "Gotta Serve Somebody."

Or it began with the deaths of Jimi Hendrix and Janis Joplin and ended with the deaths of Sid Vicious and Joy Division's Ian Curtis.

Or it began when Sly and the Family Stone released the classic single "Thank You (Falettinme Be Mice Elf Agin)"/ "Everybody Is a Star" and ended when Prince released *Dirty Mind*.

Or you might be as literal as possible and mark the Seventies by what was on the *Billboard* charts in the first week of January 1970 and the last week of December 1979. That way, the decade sounds pretty dismal: Its first Number One single was "Raindrops Keep Fallin' on My Head," by B. J. Thomas, and its last was "Escape (The Piña Colada Song)," by Rupert Holmes.

If you keep track this way, the conclusion is inescapable: The Seventies sucked. Certainly, wimpiness attained a commercial clout during those years, which brought Bread and the Carpenters and Tony Orlando and Dawn; saw "Seasons in the Sun," "The Night the Lights Went Out in Georgia" and "Billy, Don't Be a Hero" hit Number One; made stars of John Denver, Barry Manilow and Olivia Newton-John, who shed a decade-defining tear on *The Tonight Show* as she reached the final verse of "I Honestly Love You." It was a time when Anne Murray headlined over Bruce Springsteen in New York City, a time when sales records were broken by the wimp-pop national anthem, Debby Boone's "You Light Up My Life."

All of this commercially successful dreck was, however, simply one small part of the sprawling mess that was Seventies popular music. Yeah, the Seventies was the decade of "You Light Up My Life," but it was also the decade of "Stairway to Heaven." It was the decade of Al Green and David Bowie and George Clinton and Neil Young and Rod Stewart and Led Zeppelin. It was the decade that shattered when Johnny Rotten screamed, "I am the Antichrist!" and also the decade in which mainstream rock & roll reached its peak with Bruce

‹ **joni mitchell**

© STEPHANIE CHERNIKOWSKI/
MICHAEL OCHS ARCHIVES/VENICE, CA

Springsteen's *Born to Run*, Bob Seger's *Night Moves* and Tom Petty's *Damn the Torpedos*. It was the decade in which unsung pop heroes like Big Star, the Raspberries and the Shoes recorded small masterpieces that few people ever heard, and the decade in which Captain Beefheart and Can and Pere Ubu convincingly argued that corrosive industrial noise is rock & roll, too. It was the decade for which Sly Stone set the tone, in which Stevie Wonder blossomed into pop music's studio genius, in which black dance music helped turn the recording industry into a billion-dollar business.

And it was a decade in music that was powered, in many ways, by two contradictory means of making the best of a splintered scene. On the one hand, musicians in the Seventies embraced competence with a vengeance: From Blood, Sweat and Tears and Steely Dan to the Eagles, REO Speedwagon and Journey, music of the decade is known for being slick, sleek and, as often as not, soulless. On the other hand, it was a decade that saw the release of *Blood on the Tracks, John Lennon/Plastic Ono Band, Layla, New York Dolls, There's a Riot Goin' On* and *Tonight's the Night:* untidy records, messy records that couldn't be bothered with anything as mundane as competence. It was this impulse—the embrace of ugliness, if you will—that kept the Seventies from turning into a bland expanse of professionalism. And it was this uneasy combination—the embrace of competence and the embrace of ugliness—that in the end made it a surprisingly good decade for rock & roll.

But at the dawn of the Seventies, none of this was apparent. Without a center, musicians went in every direction at once. Rock got louder and heavier. By 1970, blues rock had reached two distinct apotheoses. The first was *Layla*, the monumentally anguished album by Derek and the Dominos that contained the most electrifying guitar work Eric Clapton had ever done (assisted by Duane Allman, who before his death in 1971 would virtually invent Southern rock with the Allman Brothers Band). The other modern blues-rock archetype was created by Led Zeppelin, which gave the music its most thunderous reworking. The band started the new decade with the acoustic experimentation of *Led Zeppelin III*, then brought hard rock to an early peak with "Black Dog," "Rock and Roll" and, of course, "Stairway to Heaven." In Led Zeppelin's wake came all manner of thrash and thunder, from Aerosmith— which was at the top of the heap around the middle of the decade—to Deep Purple, Black Sabbath and Grand Funk Railroad.

While those guys vied to see whose blues riffs could be the most ponderous, a posse of quieter performers took up the slack left by Bob Dylan, strumming acoustic guitars and singing of romance. The singer/songwriter crop included onetime rock & rollers like Neil

Young, veterans like Paul Simon and neophytes like Carly Simon, whose privileged upbringing didn't stop her from writing the splendid pop guessing game "You're So Vain." While James Taylor set his disturbing tales of emotional dependency to placid folk rock and Joni Mitchell gave confessional songwriting a new intelligence and grace with works like the stunning *Blue*, a former Brill Building writer for hire, Carole King, captured the commercial prize. After its release in 1971, the lilting *Tapestry* became the biggest-selling album to that point in history.

You could say that Lou Reed was a singer/songwriter, too, but he inspired something else altogether. The brutally realistic New York cityscape and alternately abrasive and alluring music of Reed's Velvet Underground proved to be enormously influential as the Seventies began; it inspired the likes of David Bowie, who'd begun his career by trying to be Anthony Newley, switched his allegiance to Bob Dylan and then began to affect a fashionable androgyny. Singer/songwriter restraint soon gave way to the studied outrage that became glam rock: the theatrical hard rock of Bowie's *Ziggy Stardust* and *Aladdin Sane;* the unstoppable riff that powered T. Rex's "Bang a Gong"; and the haughty delirium of Roxy Music, led by the stylish lounge lizard Bryan Ferry.

After the Velvet's touching swan song, *Loaded*, Reed himself trafficked in more deliberate decadence on "Walk on the Wild Side" and *Berlin*. The former was produced by Bowie, who also talked the struggling hard rockers in Mott the Hoople out of breaking up and into sticking around long enough to provide the genre's high-water marks, the albums *All the Young Dudes* and *Mott*. Subsequently, Alice Cooper and Kiss would pick up on glam's flash; Bowie would change direction every few years, leaving his glittery roots behind as he made his most convincing music in the second half of the decade; and Reed would take a willful, often destructive, but in the end triumphant path of his own.

At its most outrageous, glam was perhaps the early Seventies' chief way to assert rock's rebellious nature; art rock, on the other hand, was the chief way in which musicians tried to be taken seriously. The Beatles, of course, had already achieved respectability; art rockers like Yes and Emerson, Lake & Palmer wanted to go further, to flaunt their classically trained chops and show that not only could rock be respectable, it could be downright highbrow. So they crafted rock arrangements of Bach (Procol Harum), Stravinsky (Yes) and Mussorgsky (ELP) and played interminable solos whose whole point was to showcase virtuosity. Once in a while, as on Pink Floyd's *Dark Side of the Moon*, the solos took a backseat to a cohesive whole.

All of these genres produced works of distinction, and the leaders of the prior decade also came through on occasion: witness Paul McCartney's *Band on the Run*, the Rolling Stones' *Exile on Main Street* and Bob Dylan's soundtrack to *Pat Garrett & Billy the Kid*.

The best, truest music of the early Seventies, however, probably came as black singers and songwriters responded to the oppressive atmosphere that hung over the inner cities in the wake of the assassination of Martin Luther King. Motown, the company that brought black music to white America throughout the Sixties, was too cautious to reflect the times fully; it fell to the troubled, mercurial Sly Stone to show how bad things had gotten, following a few years of joyous, groundbreaking funk with the defiantly listless sound of *There's a Riot Goin' On*, in 1971. Sly shoved black America's plight in the face of rock radio, and others followed suit: Curtis Mayfield with "Freddie's Dead," the O'Jays with "Back Stabbers," the Staples with "Respect Yourself," War with "Slippin' Into Darkness," and the Temptations—for by then, even Motown was getting into the act—with "Papa Was a Rollin' Stone."

Sly Stone's career would shortly self-destruct, but other inescapable black voices survived. Marvin Gaye and Stevie Wonder began the decade asserting their independence from Motown's production line mentality, and both produced works of genius: Gaye with *What's Going On* and *Let's Get It On;* Wonder with *Talking Book, Innervisions* and *Songs in the Key of Life*. The voice that remained the truest, however, belonged to Al Green, who began the

<elton john decked out in his Nudie suit
© HARRY GOODWIN/MICHAEL OCHS ARCHIVES/VENICE, CA

decade singing impossibly beautiful love songs and ended it singing gospel. And the record company that occupied center stage was Philadelphia International, whose leaders, Kenny Gamble and Leon Huff, whipped up a lush and sinuous but tensile sound that resulted in a string of hits for the O'Jays, Billy Paul and Harold Melvin and the Blue Notes. For a while, Philly soul was as dominant as any one sound could be in the early Seventies—that is to say, the songs got played a lot but didn't really dominate radio at all.

Nearly everyone, it seemed, was working on one fringe or another; the closest thing to a center was the multiplatinum pop album, a new phenomenon made possible by the clout of FM radio—which sold LPs, not singles—and by the increasing marketing savvy of the record industry. *Tapestry* was the first such record, selling 5 million copies within a year of its release. *Dark Side of the Moon* soon settled in for a decade-long run on the *Billboard* charts. Then Elton John appeared, cranking out a seemingly endless series of tuneful singles, putting them across with unself-conscious flash and racking up seven consecutive Number One albums in the United States.

Sometimes John was great; more often you could say he was competent, and competence was something the record industry knew how to sell. Before long, the Seventies were swamped by skilled craftsmen: rock bands like Bad Company and pop groups like Chicago. Some of the most competent knew enough to leaven the professionalism with enough odd touches—Steely Dan, for instance, balanced slickness with an off-kilter but largely impenetrable worldview, and Randy Newman wrote lovely songs about the most repellent characters—but this clearly wasn't the way out of the statis that was affecting Seventies rock.

Yet, in the middle of what seemed to be shaping up as a lamentable decade were a string of undeniable, uncompromising works. In 1975, Bob Dylan released *Blood on the Tracks*, an astonishingly moving chronicle of romantic desperation; Bruce Springsteen threw off his cult stardom with *Born to Run*, a bravura statement of purpose; Neil Young shouted down his personal demons in the scarifying *Tonight's the Night*; Bob Marley broke through with angry *Natty Dread*; Patti Smith mixed Jesus and sex on *Horses*; Pete Townshend ignored the orchestrated hard rock of his FM staple *Who's Next* in favor of the fatalistic, understated *Who by Numbers*; Gary Stewart took country music to emotional extremes with *Out of Hand*; and even Elton John ditched his competent band and made the unexpectedly gritty *Rock of the Westies*. Individually, they were remarkable albums; collectively, they made it clear that something was happening.

‹ **peter frampton** coming alive
MICHAEL OCHS ARCHIVES/VENICE, CA

Then, of course, what happened was that Peter Frampton sold more than 10 million copies of *Frampton Comes Alive!* This was *not* what all those other albums had been portending; this was simply another reminder that the business was getting better and better at selling mere proficiency. Frampton, a likeable but basically uninteresting journeyman rocker, wasn't the only mid-Seventies success story: In 1976, records that sold more than 3 million copies were also released by Boston, Linda Ronstadt, Boz Scaggs and Stevie Wonder. The two most important bestsellers of 1976, though, were Fleetwood Mac, a onetime British blues band that became state of the art with the addition of two California singer/songwriters, Lindsey Buckingham and Stevie Nicks; and the Eagles, who epitomized the carefully considered, seamless world of Southern California rock. *Hotel California*, released in 1976, was the Eagles' finest moment artistically, though the best fruits of the L.A. music scene were more often than not the products of musicians like Jackson Browne, Tom Waits and Warren Zevon.

Fleetwood Mac and *Frampton Comes Alive!* defined the mid-Seventies mainstream, but on the fringes, outside the corporate machinery and the confines of increasingly strict playlists, intriguing musical subcultures were springing up. The task was either to find ways to coexist with the conservative record industry or to struggle to undermine it. Disco and funk and reggae did the former; punk the latter.

Disco emerged from urban dance clubs, from an underground network of DJs, producers, independent labels and performers that made their own brand of dance music, using the sleek sound of the Chi-Lites and Philadelphia International, the make-out epics of Isaac Hayes and the even lusher pillow talk of Barry White and the newfound accessibility of synthesizers. It was music designed for the club audience, not for the radio, but slowly, beginning with the likes of the Hues Corporation's "Rock the Boat" and KC and the Sunshine Band's "Get Down Tonight," it made inroads on the radio. There disco was both praised and damned; if the mindless good times promised by records like Van McCoy's "The Hustle," Donna Summer's "Love to Love You Baby" and the Trammps' "Disco Inferno" filled dance floors and caught the ears of musicians like the Bee Gees, it also aroused the elitism and even racism of the mainstream white audience.

So disco's rise was accompanied by backlash: *Saturday Night Fever* sold 30 million copies worldwide, while nonbelievers burned records at DISCO SUCKS rallies. Artists like Summer and Chic, who should have been heard by all open-minded rock fans, weren't the only ones who had to settle for narrower audiences than they deserved. In the grittier, weirder terrain of funk music, for example, George Clinton was waging virtually a one-man campaign to fuse the rough-and-ready dance beats of James Brown and Sly Stone with hard rock, cosmic sci-fi and general strangeness. Clinton expanded the musical vocabulary of the time as much as anyone, but only the black audience was listening; white radio wouldn't hear it, just as it

< FLEETWOOD MAC, CLOCKWISE FROM LEFT:

**lindsey buckingham,
mick fleetwood,
christine mcvie, john
mcvie** and **stevie nicks**

MICHAEL OCHS ARCHIVES/VENICE, CA

ignored the polyrhythmic gumbo served up by the New Orleans funk masters the Meters. Reggae had a tremendous influence on white and black musicians on the charts in Britain; in America, however, Bob Marley became the sole reggae superstar, while deserving acts like Burning Spear, Culture, the Mighty Diamonds, and Toots and the Maytals had to make do with small cults.

Emerging at the same time was another movement that was dominated by outsiders who saw no place for themselves in the record industry, but unlike disco artists and producers— who came to prominence by finding alternative approaches to the mainstream—the punks wanted to make the mainstream obsolete. Punk started quietly, in ways that were easy for the businessmen to ignore: some early-Seventies thrash from Iggy and the Stooges; two records by the New York Dolls, who fell somewhere between glam and hard rock but were newer and fresher; and, in the middle of the decade, the music that began to surface at the New York Bowery bar CBGB. Its habitués included the poet turned musical primitivist Patti Smith, the art school students turned Talking Heads, the deliberately trashy pop band Blondie and, most arrestingly, a group of four grungy New Yorkers who called themselves the Ramones and played songs that were so fast, short, loud and harsh that those who weren't mesmerized took them for a joke.

"Blank Generation," by Richard Hell and the Voidoids, was the first punk anthem, but it fell to the Brits to live it out in ways that the artier New York punks couldn't quite manage. In the United States, after all, we were muddling through a post-Nixon malaise; things could have been better, but young Americans weren't facing the type of high unemployment and decaying social institutions that crippled Great Britain. Whatever their initial impetus— whether they were the results of the calculations of a management Svengali, as the Sex Pistols were, or simply London street musicians whose idealism had been shattered, as the Clash was—the early British punks played and sang as if they meant to bring about the downfall not only of the British record industry but of the empire, as well. The contrast with main-stream rock couldn't have been clearer: Both the Bee Gees and the punks sang about stayin' alive, but only one of them sounded like they meant it.

The punks aimed to show that anybody, anywhere, could play rock & roll, that the music belonged not to the multinational corporations and big-money producers but to any kid with the guts to steal a guitar and stand on a stage. Naturally, the record industry ignored the punks for a while—especially in the United States, where the threat posed by a record like "Anarchy in the U.K." was diluted by distance—and then found ways to sell them. In the late Sixties, Columbia Records had tried to market "the revolution" with the ad line "The Man can't bust our music"; ten years later, Warner Bros. sent out pretorn promotional T-shirts to herald *Never Mind the Bollocks, Here's the Sex Pistols.*

Still, parts of the message got across, in the process clearing a space that could accommodate the thousands of kids who'd been inspired by punk's do-it-yourself ethos. Punk mutated into postpunk and grew to include everything from Talking Heads to Pere Ubu; from PiL, the band formed by Johnny Rotten after the Sex Pistols predictably self-destructed, to the Specials and the Beat, which looked back to the Jamaican pre-reggae beat ska but added a bit of punk-inspired frenzy; from Elvis Costello, a ferociously literate songwriter who said his favorite topics were "revenge and guilt," to Joy Division, which launched a thousand doom-rock bands with its icy, haunted evocation of England's industrial North.

Even though disco fans ignored punk, and punks scoffed at the mainstream, and the mainstreamers turned a deaf ear to everything else, seepage began. Slowly, some of the folks who were embracing competence began a dialogue with those who were embracing ugliness. After the enormous success of *Rumours*, Fleetwood Mac went to work on *Tusk*, a sprawling, unkempt and determinedly unpretty record masterminded by Lindsey Buckingham, whose appreciation of punk was clear in his jagged songs. Blondie leavened its pop diet with "Heart of Glass," a true disco song. In Great Britain, bands like Gang of Four and A Certain Ratio emerged from the postpunk movement playing funk. A teenager who went by the name of Prince came out of Minneapolis and quickly began adding rock to his R&B. Neil Young

‹ bob marley live, **1979**
MICHAEL OCHS ARCHIVES/VENICE, CA

recorded an album called *Rust Never Sleeps:* One side was gorgeous and folkie, one side was harsh and abrasive, and both sides saluted Johnny Rotten by name. Patti Smith had a Top Twenty hit with a Springsteen song, "Because the Night," and it sounded right. And when the decade ended, it was with more hope for the future of rock than had seemed possible in years.

But it was a far different future than had been envisioned in 1970, when a good many pop fans hunkered down to wait for the Next Big Thing. The theory was simple: We had Elvis in 1955 and the Beatles in 1964, so shouldn't something similar come along around

ANARCHY IN THE U.K.: >
The Sex Pistols' **sid vicious** and
johnny rotten
MICHAEL OCHS ARCHIVES/VENICE, CA

1974, '75, '76? It turned out that Elton John was too lightweight, Stevie Wonder became too self-indulgent, David Bowie changed directions too often. Bruce Springsteen was derailed by legal troubles and his painstaking pace. Bob Marley sounded too foreign to American ears— and anyway, nobody could have caught us off guard the way Elvis and the Beatles had done, because too many professional would-be John the Baptists were scouring the underbrush for the first signs of a messiah.

So, by the middle of the decade, most sensible listeners had stopped waiting for the revolution; that's when they got two revolutions. The record business didn't take either of them all that seriously, because "disco sucks" and because punk had a negligible commercial impact. By the end of the decade, though, rock was undergoing a renaissance, spurred on by the unlikely rapprochement, maybe the true legacy of the decade; certainly, it's a better legacy than the cheesy songs for which the Seventies are damned or the by-now-tiresome standards that form the backbone of the classic-rock radio format.

It was a decade in which two new genres—whose fans, in true Seventies form, wouldn't be caught dead listening to one another's music—began to coexist, mingle and create the music that would dominate the Eighties. That didn't give rock & roll a new center, but it might have put a small touch of danger back into the music. And if nothing else, it means we ought to stop feeling guilty.

led zeppelin

By J. D. CONSIDINE

At the time, nobody thought it would work. Keith Moon, after hearing the Yardbirds' Jimmy Page explain his idea for a new blues-based band, simply laughed. The band, the Who's drummer predicted, would go over not like a lead balloon but like a lead zeppelin.

Needless to say, Moon was wrong. Led Zeppelin was a smash virtually from the moment its first album, *Led Zeppelin*, was released in 1969, and the band would dominate rock & roll for the next decade. Yet it was an entirely new kind of success. Unlike the rock titans of the Sixties, Led Zeppelin had little use for singles; albums were the band's currency, generating a whole new canon, including tracks like "No Quarter," "Immigrant Song," "Communication Breakdown" and the eternally popular "Stairway to Heaven."

Classics, every one of them, but classics of a new sort. Other bands had done their best to make rock seem bigger, louder, tougher and more ambitious, but it was Led Zeppelin that made the music *heavy*. From the galloping rumble of "Whole Lotta Love" and the blues-spiked growl of "Black Dog" to the exoticisms of "Kashmir," Led Zeppelin's sound was invariably larger than life. The band's music rarely conveyed the brutality of proto-metal acts like Black Sabbath or Deep Purple, though; its impact was more a matter of intensity than jackhammer insistence.

Live, Led Zeppelin was without peer. Constantly reinventing itself onstage, the band made improvisational forays through songs like "Dazed and Confused" that were the stuff of legend. As the fans flocked to its concerts, Led Zeppelin seemed to tower over its competition; by 1975, the band was unquestionably the most popular group in rock. It might also have been the most powerful, thanks to the band's manager, Peter Grant, who changed the way business was done on the concert circuit, shifting the power—and the money— from the pockets of the promoters to the hands of the artists.

Such success, of course, was not without its costs. Before long, Led Zeppelin's very preeminence assumed the status of myth, and all sorts of stories sprang up. Some were sinister, some salacious, some downright silly. The band was alleged to have indulged in everything from secret devil messages (ostensibly on "Stairway to Heaven") to seafood orgies (in which willing groupies took in the catch of the day). There were also tragedies along the way, among them a car accident in Greece that put singer Robert Plant in a wheelchair (and nearly killed his wife) and an altercation in Oakland, California, with promoter Bill Graham that landed drummer John "Bonzo" Bonham in jail. It was Bonham's death in 1980 that finally grounded Led Zeppelin. Apart from *Coda*, an album of previously unreleased material that emerged in 1982, there was no new music from Led Zeppelin in the 1980s.

Since Bonham's death, the three surviving members of the band—Page, Plant and bassist John Paul Jones—have performed in public only four times: at Live Aid, with drummers Phil Collins and Tony Thompson; at Atlantic Records' fortieth-anniversary concert, with Bonham's son Jason on drums; at Jason Bonham's wedding; and at the band's 1995 induction into the Rock and Roll Hall of Fame.

At the time of this 1989 interview, all three were busy with post-Zeppelin pursuits. Page had returned to London after remastering tracks for the 1990 four-CD *Led Zeppelin* retrospective. Plant was touring behind *Manic Nirvana*, his sixth solo album. Jones had been in Barcelona, Spain, recording an "industrial flamenco" group call La Sura Dels Baus.

During the fall of 1994, Page and Plant released *No Quarter*, the pair's collaboration featuring musicians from Marrakech, India and Egypt. They also taped an MTV *Unplugged* special, *Unledded*, and toured together in 1995. In 2000, Led Zeppelin songs were performed live on a Jimmy Page–Black Crowes tour, tracks from which were released on an album, *Live at the Greek*, available on the Internet.

It's been almost a whole decade since Led Zeppelin broke up, and yet for a lot of fans, it's like it never ended.

PLANT: Well, it hasn't ended for anybody, really. I mean, Bing Crosby hasn't ended, either, you know? Elvis certainly hasn't.

Do you worry about that?

PAGE: Oh, good Lord, no. Why should I? I thought I was in the greatest band in the world. But musically, around that point in time, things were so healthy in so many areas.

Did you, as you were remastering tracks for the box set, find yourself thinking about where Led Zeppelin stands right now in rock history?

PAGE: Yes, and I realized what an absolutely brilliant textbook it was, and obviously still is. Because of the different areas of music we touched on and the different pathways that we were prepared to tread down— sometimes really mosey down, steamroller down— that gave such a wide variety of styles. And you know, pretty much, it was all done really very well. There was a lot of soul and depth in it.

These days, though, radio—particularly classic-rock radio—seems to be a major factor in preserving the Zeppelin legacy. Do you think that's a healthy perspective?

PLANT: It depends. If that had happened in 1968, I don't think we'd ever have been heard at all. If we'd been on the receiving end of this conservatism, maybe we'd have never been exposed, because we didn't sound like Tommy James, and we didn't sound like Gary Puckett or whatever.

But Led Zeppelin did meet a lot of resistance early on, from press and radio.

PLANT: Not from radio; just from the press. And that was because we just didn't play whatever game the game was. We figured the best thing to do was shut the fuck up and play, you know? It's no good trying to be prophetic when you're twenty years old. So the thing was, if you don't know what you're talking about, keep quiet.

JONES: The first review we got from ROLLING STONE [RS 29] was . . . the total subject matter was all about the *hype* of Led Zeppelin. You know: "It's just another band of do-nothings, and here they are hyped up by everybody, and it's a bunch of shit, anyway." And that was really hurtful at the time, because we knew we'd done a good record. It helped foster my general hatred of the press.

But audiences had no difficulty responding to what you were doing.

JONES: Yeah, well, they came to the gigs. That was the difference. It was the same thing in England. We packed our gigs everywhere we went. There were lines right way round the block where the clubs or pubs were. Purely people there by word of mouth. You know: "This is a good band, this will be a good gig; go to it"—and they did. And the press, I feel, were a little bit miffed at the fact that they weren't really there at the making of the band. So they chose then to ignore it, and we chose to ignore them. It was actually quite nice, not having to answer an enormous amount of stupid questions. I'm not saying that this is the case at this very moment [*laughs*], but you know what I mean.

PLANT: It's funny, really, because the acclaim always came from the street, never from the written critique. And really, in a much more basic manner, the same thing is happening to me now, because people are comparing me, or not comparing me, or trying to screw me down, or complaining about my constant changes as a solo artist. All I'm doing is

what I was always part of doing anyway—I'm having a great time and weaving around like a fucking lunatic. But it's the same kind of situation, two generations on—journalists who were sucking their mother's breast when the first querulous Led Zeppelin reviews came in are now doing the same thing to me.

You know, Led Zeppelin's sledgehammer attitude or reputation, if you like, was only just one part of the whole spectrum of what it was. Sometimes it was gross and very indecent, and sometimes it was delicate and beautiful, you know?

JONES: Certain people just don't get it at all. There was a lot of humor in the group, a lot of humor in the music—not all this glowering, satanic crap [*laughs*].

What about the way Led Zeppelin has begun to be seen in almost mythic terms?

PAGE: It's only a myth to people who never heard us live, I suppose. I mean, if you heard us live, you'd know exactly where it was at.

Obviously, though, there are quite a few bands out there whose only point of reference is Zeppelin's recorded word and that make almost slavish attempts to recapture the power of those recordings. Isn't that a sort of mythification?

PAGE: They miss the point. They miss the whole spirit that was behind it and the passion—*passion*'s the word. They just get caught up in imitating the riffs without going for what was underneath. It was a very passionate band, and that's what really comes through the whole thing.

What about the fans? Do you think they understand what the band was about? Or do they have their own vision of what made Led Zeppelin great?

PLANT: Well, I don't know, because nobody ever tells me anything about what they feel. They just go "Yeah, man—Zeppelin," and that's it! They don't say, "Did you really fuck somebody with a snake on your head?" [*Laughs*] You don't get the dreamscapes.

Well, did you ever fuck somebody with a snake on your head?

PLANT: Ahhh, no, that must have been Jimmy [*laughs*].

But there's a devotion, and I don't think the contributing factor is the hedonistic lifestyle or anything like that. I think the fact is that some songs do actually have a timeless appeal. I don't know whether it would have been better that they didn't, so that I could get on with my life without constantly having to cross t's and dot i's that belong in sentences way back, you know? But it doesn't matter, really. One should always be proud of any good piece of work, and there are whole bunches of good pieces of work going back there.

Did you have a concept for the group?

PAGE: Well, certainly on the first album, I had a very good idea of what I wanted to try and get with the band, because at that stage, I was extremely instrumental in the total direction of it. Obviously, there was a definite concept of what one was trying to do and achieve there, and it was done. But we were definitely right out there on a limb, weren't we? Doing what we believed in, and it didn't really follow any sort of trend that was going on at all—or certainly nothing relative to any other band.

Did you ever look at other bands as competition—the way, for instance, the Beatles looked at the Stones?

PLANT: We were more concerned with diversity, self-satisfaction, creativity. So, really, there was nobody to compete with, because we were trying to entertain ourselves first and foremost, with no intentional stab at a pretty song for a pretty song's sake.

From the beginning, really, it was a group policy that singles were not to be considered, that the whole game would be that if you wanted to find out about Led Zeppelin, you had to get into the whole thing. We would not put out singles as calling cards. So, really, there was nobody to compete with. It would be nice to think that we could walk alongside Kaleidoscope or Buffalo Springfield for diversity. I don't think Jimmy'd agree with that [*laughs*], because I don't think he thought much of Buffalo Springfield.

But I think the way the music moved around—in its Englishness and its blues roots—the inspiration didn't allow it to compete with anybody, really, because it wasn't a pop band. I mean, it's popular, but it certainly was not pop.

There's probably no better example of that than "Stairway to Heaven," which may be the most popular radio song of all time yet has never been available as a single.

PLANT: Yeah, but the fact that it caught people's imaginations is interesting, really, because it's kind of the legend that created "Stairway to Heaven."

How do you mean?

PLANT: Well, because when we played it at the beginning, before the album came out, you could often see people settling down to have forty winks.

Really?

PLANT: Yeah! Because people hadn't heard it. They didn't know what it was.

PAGE: Oh, that's not true. No, I remember playing that at the L.A. Forum, and . . . I'm not saying the whole audience gave us a standing ovation, but there was this sizable standing ovation there. And I thought, "This is incredible, because no one's heard this number yet. This is the first time they're hearing it!" It obviously touched them, you know, and that was at the L.A. Forum, so I knew we were onto something with that one, because it's always difficult to hear a number, especially something that long, which you've never heard before.

JONES: "Stairway" embodies a lot of what Led Zeppelin was about. It actually had a sort of precedent in a song on the first album called "Babe, I'm Gonna Leave You," which had many of the same elements: the acoustic start, the build and the sort of "heavy" end.

It's a good tune, for a start. Jimmy came up with the original guitar phrases and the original idea, and I think Robert might have had a short lyric, a first verse or something, a couple lines. And then Jimmy and I basically sat down—just the two of us sat down and worked out the entire arrangement; we plotted it through. It came together, basically, through quite a lot of hard work.

What strikes me about "Stairway to Heaven" is that there are folk-oriented songs like "The Battle of Evermore" and "Going to California," and there are hard-rock songs like "Black Dog" and "When the Levee Breaks," and "Stairway" seems to be where the two sides meet.

PLANT: Yeah, I think you're right. I mean, it wasn't particularly unique, that approach, because some of the West Coast bands were doing it, combining that sort of stuff. It's just that it's ambiguous to such a degree that the only thing you know about it is that it's affirmative, and it's going the right way.

Obviously, Led Zeppelin drew from a wide range of musical styles. How did the band find its common ground?

JONES: It wasn't a purist band, as you get nowadays, where the entire band listens to the same type of music. Between the blues influences of Robert and the rock & roll influences of Jimmy—who also had strong blues influences—the soul influences of Bonzo, and my soul and jazz influences, there seemed to be a common area, which was Led Zeppelin: the fusion of all different types of music and interests.

1
2
9

There was also quite a difference in experience, too, between the four members. Robert, what was it like for you and Bonham—who were essentially unknown before joining Led Zeppelin—to be thrown in with established, successful players like Page and Jones?

PLANT: Everything is in the eye of the beholder. Jimmy was a member of the Yardbirds, and he was a session musician, so he was successful. Jonesy was much more the back room boy—I didn't care, really, whether he'd produced "Mellow Yellow" or not, because it was a pop song, and it just started and stopped; pretty song, but somebody had to write the song, never mind organize it. So their sort of positions and previous roles weren't really that daunting.

But how they handled themselves with us was important. Jonesy was a bit . . . not withdrawn, but he stands back a little and shoots the odd bit of dialogue into the air. It's good stuff but an acquired taste, really. And Jimmy's personality, initially, was . . . I don't think I'd ever come across a personality like it before. He had a demeanor which you had to adjust to; it certainly wasn't very casual to start with. But then again, the music was so intense that everything was intense. The ambition was intense, and the delivery was intense, and where we were going was intense. Nobody knew what the fuck it was, but we all knew that this power was ridiculous from the beginning. So it was very hard to relax, sit down, have a beer and be the guys from the Black Country. Bonzo and I were much more basic in every respect in how to deal with everything—including Jimmy, because he had to be dealt with.

It must not have been all that difficult, though. Didn't the lineup click from the first time the four of you got together?

PAGE: Yeah. We got together in this small rehearsal room and just played "Train Kept a-Rollin'," which was a number I used to do with the Yardbirds, and I think Robert knew it. And at the end of it, we knew that it was really happening, really electrifying—*exciting* is the word. We went on from there to start rehearsing for the album.

What was it about the way you four played together that made the music so exciting?

JONES: In a band like that, everybody's got their ears open. That's what it is. It is a chemistry, I suppose, that nonmusicians might not understand, but you follow the music, really, all sorts of ways, in all sorts of combinations—which was very important for us. There's no way I could have been in a band where you'd have to do the records note for note every night and the only person who got to play any different was the lead guitarist—you know what I mean? And at the time we really didn't think about how anything would go down. We weren't worried about making a record that would sell. The records were primarily for us, I think. So it wasn't a case of analyzing the first album to work out what was successful, like they do these days. It was like, "That's done—now it's ever onward."

Zeppelin had an ability to skip from style to style. Where did that come from?

PLANT: Personalities.

There must be more to it than that.

PLANT: Yeah, but you didn't see the Band of Joy, before Zeppelin, and that was the same.

Really?

PLANT: Yeah! Me and Bonzo: In the Band of Joy, we used to do versions of "White Rabbit," the Airplane thing, with "March of the Siamese Children," from *The King and I*, in the middle—in half time. We did all sorts of strange stuff. . . . "Hey, Grandma," from Moby Grape, which turned into something else most peculiar. There was always that looking around and getting goose bumps. When I first heard Om Kalsoum, it was a very important day for me, because it opened, it just enriched my life so much. Even though I hardly understand a word she's singing, because it's in Arabic, I had to take some of the effect it had on me and put it into the music. As with *Manic Nirvana* right now, you stimulate yourself through your own excitement.

Don't you still need a certain amount of ability to pull that off?

PLANT: But if nobody else is doing it, you've got nothing to be measured against. We got it right, at times. Tracks like "Friends" and "Four Sticks"— Jimmy and I went to India, and we recorded versions of these two tracks with the Bombay Symphony. We'd got a sort of disheveled gang of musicians together in Bombay, and we recorded two Led Zeppelin tracks. The session went very well until I got a bottle of brandy out, and . . . There's nothing like a good Indian, and there were no good Indians in that room at the end of the bottle. It's a shame, really, that they won't include it on this box set.

Why not?

PLANT: I don't know. Maybe Pagey didn't think about it [*laughs*]. I didn't think about it until just a second ago.

PAGE: Well, the only things that were left over that had complete vocals came out on *Coda*. Those tracks were something that we were going to work on, probably at some later point in time. The actual master plan after having done that was to maybe do a tour through the Far East, going through Egypt and Bombay, then on to Thailand and all the rest of it, and then recording in those places. And that was like a first taste, to see how it would go. Of course, we never got that far, but that's one of the game plans we had at the time.

PLANT: We liked to travel and explore. I mean, we can't be considered anthropologists or anything like that, but we knew of a few good brothels in the Far East. . . .

"Knew a few good brothels"—now, that's more typical of the Led Zeppelin myth than imagining you guys with the Bombay Symphony.

PLANT: You can do a lot of things in one day.

Indeed. Of course, back then there was what now seems an almost legendary groupie scene—the likes of which may never be seen again. That seems to leave a lot of younger fans feeling as if they've been gypped.

PAGE: You mean the whole scene, in the younger fans' minds, has changed from sex, drugs and rock & roll to contraceptives, no drugs and rock & roll? [*Laughs*] That's what you mean, is it?

Exactly. Was it as wonderful back then as kids today imagine?

PAGE: You'd better ask Robert [*laughs*].

PLANT: Yeah. That era, the whole thing of the G.T.O.'s and—what was that thing of the G.T.O.'s and, what was that Zappa album? *10,000 Hotels*? "I've Been to Bed with Robert Planet.". . . Yeah, shoving the Plaster Casters' cast of Jimi Hendrix's penis up one of the girl's assholes at some hotel in Detroit was . . . quite fun, actually. I don't remember who did it, but I remember I was in the hotel at the time.

It was . . . free love.

And it's pretty much gone now, isn't it?

PLANT: Well, I think you now have to adapt a totally different attitude to the whole thing. Just when my stamina is really getting good, too [*laughs*]!

But it was great, and that whole preposterous thing of the vocalist being larger than life—the way I was viewed in the mid-1970s—was hysterical. Actually, I couldn't take myself seriously for very long, because I would be constantly hacked to pieces by my fellow band members, who'd be giggling at me.

Didn't they call you Percy?

PLANT: Mmmm.

After Percival the hero?

PLANT: It was something to do with my anatomy, at the time. Maybe they wouldn't call me that now; I dunno [*laughs*].

While we're on the subject of Led Zeppelin legends, fundamentalist groups have claimed for years that there are satanic messages backward-masked onto "Stairway to Heaven." Is there any truth to the charges?

PAGE: Well, I don't pass any comment on them [*sighs*].

PLANT: I mean, who on earth would have ever thought of doing that in the first place? You've got to have a lot of time on your hands to even consider that people would do that. Especially with "Stairway." I mean, we were so proud of that thing, and its intentions are so positive, that the last thing one would do would be . . . I found it foul, the whole idea, you know? But . . . it's very American. Nowhere else in the world has anybody ever considered it or been concerned or bothered at all about that. I figure if backward masking really worked, every record in the store would have "Buy this album!" hidden on it.

PAGE: You've got it; you've hit the nail on the head. And that's all there is to say about it.

JONES: Of course, it's fatal, you know, because you tend to wind these people up after a while. If you go around saying, "Oh, yes, if you play track 8 at 36 rpms, you'll definitely hear a message," they'll say, "All right," and go right home and try it. English bands tend to be more ironic and sarcastic, and once they discover the average American's lack of irony and humor, it's just sitting ducks, really. You just sort of have to go for it.

That cuts both ways, though. I mean, just look at all the fans who think Stephen Davis's *Hammer of the Gods* is actually some sort of tribute to Led Zeppelin. I would imagine you three were a little less enthusiastic about it.

PAGE: I think I opened it up in the middle somewhere and started to read, and I just threw it out the window. I was living by a river then, so it actually found its way to the bottom of the sea [*laughs*]. That's a fact.

I mean, I couldn't bother to wade through that sort of stuff. I mean, that's true masochism. The whole humor of the band disappeared in the parts that I read, and it was just a sensationalist book. I can understand, obviously, what you're saying—that fans read it just purely out of interest. And there's no smoke without fire, but it wasn't a very factual account. **Thinking about the way Led Zeppelin is perceived now, I wonder: Would people even recognize Led Zeppelin if it were around today?** PLANT: Of course not. It couldn't possibly be anything like where it was when it stopped. We'd probably be a lounge act now in San Antonio—who knows? I mean, it wouldn't be recognizable, I wouldn't think. Could we play "Black Dog" for a further ten years? I don't think so—only if it turned out like Dread Zeppelin, and then you could enjoy yourself. I mean, we were doing reggae versions of "Stairway to Heaven" when [Dread Zeppelin lead singer] Tortelvis was thin—just doing sound checks and stuff like that. I mean, it wasn't sending the thing up; it was just like "Here's another way of doing it."

PAGE: Our trademark, so to speak—I suppose you could tell it anywhere. Like Robert's voice is his trademark, and hopefully, the same can be said of my guitar [*laughs*]. So even though we obviously would have gone through a lot of changes and tried all different musical approaches, nevertheless, that would have been the telltale clue that it was Zeppelin. It would be immediately recognizable by the audible qualities of the four players.

What was that quality, though? What was it that gave Led Zeppelin and its music such distinctive spirit? PLANT: Muddy Waters said—when, fifteen years ago?—that nobody's got the deep blues anymore. Maybe now, in this second—or third—generation of Zeppelinisms, people are losing the plot. Maybe people . . . they don't feel it the way it was felt originally. But we had it—and that's a hell of a sweeping statement. But we did have something up there, which was not just token cloning or token theft or whatever it was. We had a weave of . . . I don't know. It was conspiratorial elegance, if you like. In the middle of it all, occasionally, it really did work. And it was wholehearted, and we gave it all a new personality.

ann and nancy wilson
of heart on their favorite led zep songs

nancy

1 **"The Rain Song."** This achieves a perfect balance between lyrics and music and between acoustic and electric. It has always struck a deep chord in me concerning the cyclical nature of life: Upon us all, a little rain must fall.

2 **"Kashmir."** So hypnotic is this groove, that it could keep on going forever. You can picture the sun setting there on rock & roll Shangri-la.

3 **"No Quarter."** This one comes to us through the misty, ancient, mysterious annals of rock & roll lore. I am a complete sucker for this groove.

4 **"Trampled Underfoot."** Perhaps the *funkiest* them darn Zepsters ever got (except maybe "The Crunge").

5 **"You Shook Me."** The heaviest blues tribute ever accomplished. Back in the acid daze, I would sit cross-legged and stare at the record player like a charmed snake.

ann

1 **"Black Dog."** When I first heard the vocal on this, it completely melted me—especially "Gonna make you burn, gonna make you *stang. . . .*" Unbelievably hot.

2 **"The Battle of Evermore."** Plant, the androgynous. The imagery is pretty thick Tolkien, but it really is beautiful, organic and powerful, especially combined with that wild mandolin part. I love the big scream on the end. I always think it can be heard down the ages.

3 **"Going to California."** Nancy and I have probably sat around playing this song together hundreds of times over the years. This song is like a good, old friend.

4 **"The Crunge."** I always thought this was one of Jimmy Page's and Robert Plant's big laughs on amateur musicians who would try to work out Zep tunes with turnarounds. James Brown on acid, with that androgynous twinkle.

5 **"When the Levee Breaks."** Relentless. That's why I've always thought this one was so sexy. Relentless. The distorted harp is great, and I always twitch when Plant comes in with "Cryin' won't help ya, / Prayin' won't do ya no good."

the allman brothers band

By GAVIN EDWARDS

The Allman Brothers don't talk to each other much these days. It's not that they're nursing grudges from decades ago or that they're in imminent danger of a fistfight over a backhanded remark. It's just that after thirty long years together, they've learned that the secret of surviving as a band is to keep a safe distance.

So when the Allman Brothers Band arrives at the Riverbend Amphitheater in Cincinnati to play another show in the fading light of a long summer evening in 1999, seven musicians pull up in three separate buses. Organist Gregg Allman's allows dogs but no smoking, guitarist Dickey Betts's allows dogs and smoking, and the third carries the group's three drummers.

∧ ORIGINAL MEMBERS OF THE ALLMAN BROTHERS BAND AT HOME IN GEORGIA, FROM LEFT TO RIGHT:
jai johanny johanson (a.k.a. Jaimoe), **berry oakley, duane allman, butch trucks, gregg allman** and **dickey betts**

They amble around the stage, displaying no effort to make a dramatic entrance for this crowd of six thousand; about five thousand of them have been alive for less than the three decades that the Allman Brothers have been a band. Drummer Jaimoe, wearing an ABB T-shirt, sandals and a ludicrous pair of yellow-and-black-striped socks, does a few rolls on his kit. His young daughter scampers around the side of the stage. Allman drinks tea to prepare his throat for singing and cocks an ear disapprovingly to the music coming out of the PA. "What is this bullshit they're playing?" he grumbles. "Sounds like country. There needs to be six-foot fucking blues, to get the audience in the fucking groove."

At 8:15 P.M. on the nose, they start playing "Don't Want You No More," and it becomes immediately clear that although they may not speak much offstage, their conversation onstage is eloquent and profound.

Allman spends most of the show behind his vintage Hammond organ, singing the blues with the husky abandon of somebody who's lived them. After he finishes a chorus, he often grabs the microphone with his left hand and pushes it away. This gesture signals that we are about to witness some extended improvisational guitar. Mind-expanding guitar solos are what the crowd has come to hear, and it gets plenty of them as the fifty-six-year-old Betts and the twenty-year-old Derek Trucks (Butch's nephew) trade licks, tell stories and write epic poems in the key of A, while a hallucinogenic light show flashes behind them. It's all anchored by the steady, flowing groove of the band's three percussionists (Butch Trucks, Jaimoe and Marc Quiñones) and Allman's subtle work on the organ.

The encore, like the set list, is ever-changing, but tonight it is simple: The Allman Brothers play their two most famous songs. First Betts sings "Ramblin' Man," the country song from 1973 that was the ABB's biggest chart single. The melody is as joyful as ever, and Betts's weather-beaten voice underlines the song's advocacy of the road. Then bassist Oteil Burbridge plays an ominous, thunderous riff that turns back on itself like a staircase to nowhere, and the band throws itself into the concert favorite "Whipping Post." It is pure no-way-out bluesman doom; Allman moans, "Oh Lord, I feel like I'm dying."

If you were looking for a band from central casting to embody the story of American rock & roll, you'd want to call the Allman Brothers. They're from the South, where the music was born, and have always been an interracial band. They combined country and blues—just as the music's inventors did—and then added some jazz. They embraced the community aesthetic that hippie rock aspired to, and later they were also full-fledged participants in the excesses of cocaine, limousines and, in the body of Cher, showbiz. Naturally, they got screwed financially. Despite having long ago lost their resident genius to an early death—another essential component of the rock myth—they persisted and celebrated their thirtieth anniversary by making some of the best music of their career.

Like many American musical stories, the Allman Brothers' tale begins in Nashville. Willis Allman fought in World War II—storming Normandy—and returned to his young bride, Geraldine, after the war. He got a job as an Army recruiter, and they quickly produced two sons: Duane, born November 20, 1946, and Gregg, born December 8, 1947. In 1949, the day after Christmas, Willis was robbed and killed by another veteran. They had just met that day over a game of shuffleboard.

Geraldine, known to the band as Mama A, needed to support her family, so she went to school to become a CPA. She remembers that Duane's drive emerged early: "You might say he was born to lead. Some people are. Gregg is a lover, and laid-back—he'd rather have a leader. One summer, when they were preschoolers, they had a lemonade stand, Duane and Gregg and one little neighborhood boy. So when I got home, they were telling me about it. Gregg says he got to pour the lemonade, and the other little boy says he could hand it to the customer. So I said, 'Duane, what did you do?' And he says, 'Oh, I'm the appetizing manager.'"

When Gregg and Duane got a little older, Mama A sent them to the Castle Heights Military Academy in Lebanon, Tennessee. The brothers hated it, but it did provide them with their first musical training: They both took lessons in piano and then trumpet and joined the academy's marching band. In 1957, Mama A graduated from accounting school, pulled her sons out of the academy and moved the family to Daytona Beach, Florida; the brothers felt like they had ascended from purgatory into the heavenly kingdom.

In the summer of 1960, when Duane was thirteen, he got a Harley-Davidson motorcycle, and he was soon speeding all over Daytona Beach. That same summer, Gregg got a paper route for one reason: He wanted enough money to buy a guitar. Come fall, he had twenty-one dollars; with a ninety-five-cent donation from Mama A, he had his very own Sears Silvertone. Gregg played the guitar nonstop; Duane was busy riding his bike around town, but pretty soon Duane started skipping school, staying home to play his baby brother's guitar. They started fighting over it, and both got better guitars as birthday presents that year. Gregg found that the music was a comfort he would need to turn to many times in the years ahead.

Duane dropped out of school after ninth grade and had plenty of time for guitar practice. The brothers played with local bands like the Untils, the House Rockers and the Nightcrawlers, crossing Daytona Beach's color line; they would invite friends over when Mama A was at work and play guitar and drink beer all day.

In an effort to keep Gregg on the straight and narrow, Mama A sent him back to military school, but the summer before his senior year, he and Duane formed the band that would be known as the Allman Joys. Gregg couldn't bear thinking about the good times his brother was having without him in Daytona Beach, so after twelve days of school he headed home. That year's buzz cut was the last time Gregg has ever worn his hair short.

Gregg was considering going to college to become a dental surgeon. "I let them run free with their choices of what they would do with their lives," says Mama A. "But I told them they would either go to school or they would work. So they chose the music."

"Hell, I had some adventure in my soul," Gregg chortles. "I figured I'd go out and play the chitlin circuit for a year—the places that had the chicken wire up so the beer bottles wouldn't hit you. I knew we weren't going to make any money, but perhaps we'd meet some fine-looking women."

It was 1965. As the eldest son in a fatherless family, Duane was exempt from the Vietnam draft; Gregg was not. So Duane came up with a plan: The night before Gregg's physical, they would have a "foot-shootin' party." Girls were invited; whiskey was drunk; a bull's-eye was painted on Gregg's moccasin. Gregg called for an ambulance and then went outside. Guests said later that you could hear the sirens before you could hear the report of the pistol. The bullet grazed his foot; the next day, Gregg showed up at the induction center on crutches. He was classified 4-F.

In the summer of 1967, a young drummer named Butch Trucks met the Allman Joys. Trucks had gone to college to become a minister but left after three months to be a hippie. He played in a band called the 31st of February; they headed up to Daytona, which is where he met the Allmans. "Duane was a ball of fire," he remembers. "He walked into a room, everybody stopped and looked. If you're lucky, you meet one guy like him in your lifetime. Gregg was just a pretty boy. He had blond hair, and the girls were hanging all over him."

The Allman Joys hit the road; Gregg switched from guitar to Hammond organ so that they could better replicate the Top Forty hits of the day. The band evolved into the Hour Glass and headed to L.A., where they signed a record deal. They released two mediocre albums and broke up in 1968. The brothers argued about where they should go next and angrily parted ways. Gregg stayed in California, but Duane went back East.

"He knew right where he was going," Gregg says. "He was going to Muscle Shoals, and he wasn't going to call before he came. He was like that. He was gonna go and get the damn job. Why call?"

Duane showed up at the Muscle Shoals Sound Studio in Alabama; by 1968, it was already famous for the records it had made with Percy Sledge, Wilson Pickett and Aretha Franklin, among others. With his solos on the Hour Glass records as his calling card, Duane played on a Wilson Pickett session and suggested that they cover "Hey Jude." Pickett snapped that he wouldn't be recording a song about "no Jew." Duane prevailed and contributed a majestic solo on the fade-out; the resulting single went to Number Twenty-three. Duane left the session with a steady job at Muscle Shoals and the approval of Pickett, who dubbed him Skyman.

Jaimoe, born July 8, 1944, is the Allman Brothers Band's most eccentric figure and its greatest philosopher. "He's like Yoda," says Burbridge. "The Force is strong in him."

When I meet the Jedi drummer in his Cincinnati hotel room, he is wearing only a pair of green athletic shorts. His large potbelly protrudes over the waistband. "We've got three drummers up there," he says. "That's so much power, it can be overbearing." Jaimoe says that sometimes he won't play his bass drum for an entire show, just to change the band's chemistry, or he'll step away from the drums for a song and go listen in the audience. He takes the same nonlinear approach to conversation—a story about his childhood might be prefaced with a ten-minute discourse on water aerobics—but it's well worth the effort to hear what he has to say.

Originally known as Jai Johanny Johanson, he grew up in Gulfport, Mississippi, where he spent his adolescence trying to decide between his dreams of being a pro athlete and being a jazz drummer. He saw Louis Armstrong play in New Orleans, and that settled it: He hit the road in 1965 with R&B singer Ted Taylor.

A year later, he remembers, he was playing in Otis Redding's road band: "I couldn't play in that Otis band—it was way too loud—and I couldn't play rock & roll like I can now, but Otis was a great cat. He was funny, he was serious. If you see Muhammad Ali, you see Otis—he was a riot, man.

"I played with Otis from December of '66 to April of '67. When that tour was over, I was getting ready to go to Europe with him, but I didn't have any identification, because I had lost my wallet. So I didn't go to Europe. When Otis died [five months later, in a plane crash], so many people called me, because they thought I was on that plane."

Jaimoe played with Percy Sledge for a while, and then Joe Tex. He decided to move to New York and really pursue jazz. Then a friend called to tell him about Skyman: "He's a skinny white boy with red hair, and Jai, I ain't never heard nobody play the guitar like that." Late one night soon after that, Jaimoe got out of bed to go to the bathroom; as he was falling back to sleep, he heard Wilson Pickett's "Hey Jude" on the radio and knew it had to be Skyman. When Jaimoe also heard that Jerry Wexler of Atlantic Records was a supporter of Duane's, "the dollar signs went off in my head, and I got on the bus."

One very long Trailways ride later, Jaimoe was in Alabama shaking hands with Skyman. He moved into Duane's place by the river, where they would hang out and listen to records. Jaimoe turned Duane on to John Coltrane; Duane exposed him to Buffalo Springfield and Dylan's *John Wesley Harding*. After Jaimoe had been in Alabama for six weeks, Duane decided that his sideman days were over. Jaimoe relates, "Duane said, 'Man, I'm tired of doing this shit. Pack up your drums. We're leaving.'" They went down to Jacksonville, Florida, to steal away a bassist Duane knew, Berry Oakley, who'd been touring with bubblegum singer Tommy Roe but had been born in Chicago and was steeped in the blues. While in Jacksonville, they stayed with old Allman friend Butch Trucks. There were rock jams in the local park every Sunday afternoon, so Duane and Jaimoe joined in.

On Sunday, March 23, 1969, they stayed home to jam instead of going into the sunshine, and a group was born. Duane and Jaimoe were there, and Trucks, and Oakley, and guitarist Dickey Betts from Oakley's band, the Second Coming. They played for three hours straight, seamlessly flowing from slow blues to uptempo shuffles, reading each other's cues perfectly. When it ended, everyone in the room had chills; Duane stood in front of the door and told the others, "Anybody in this room who's not going to play in my band, you've got to fight your way out."

The quintet moved up to Macon, Georgia, because that was where their manager, Phil Walden (previously the manager of Otis Redding), was based. He signed them to management contracts and to recording contracts with his new label, Capricorn Records, a conflict of interest that would cause many gallstones later on.

"We rehearsed for a month," Betts says, "and Oakley keeps coming to me. He says, 'Dickey, our band is ten times better than our singing. We need Gregg. Duane won't call him.' So I'd go talk to Duane, Berry'd go talk to Duane, Butch'd go talk to Duane. Everyone's pulling on Duane's coat. Finally, Duane says, 'All right, damn it.'" Betts cackles at the memory.

While Gregg was living in L.A., he wrote a bunch of songs that would enter the Brothers' repertoire, among them "Dreams" and "It's Not My Cross to Bear." When Duane called him, he followed his big brother's lead and went back East—with his soulful vocals, the tentatively named Allman Band was now the Allman Brothers Band.

Butch Trucks greets me at the door of his hotel room. His hair is white; his voice is a soft Southern drawl. He invites me in and offers me some superb white wine. On the coffee table is a copy of Bertrand Russell's *History of Western Philosophy*, which Trucks has been reading as part of his continual program for self-improvement; when he drives around Florida in the winter, he listens to college lectures on audiotape in his car. There's also a laptop, which he uses mostly for playing EverQuest, the online swords-and-sorcery game. He's been known to show up late for the bus to a show because he's busy whacking orcs. He demonstrates the game's 3-D graphics and his fifteenth-level ranger character, then tells me about the band's early days in Macon.

"Our roadies, Twiggs and Red Dog, were both Vietnam vets, and our only real source of income was from their VA checks. They pooled the money, and it came to three bucks a day apiece. And that was to buy cigarettes, drugs, food—you name it. So a buck thirty-five at the H and H Restaurant, that was the meal for the day. And then there would be enough left for a pack of cigarettes, and we could pool some money and get a bottle of wine. Mama Louise at the H and H ran a tab on us for a long time.

"We wrote 'Elizabeth Reed.' We'd learned a few songs in Jacksonville: 'Whipping Post,' 'Trouble No More,' 'Don't Want You No More.' And we'd played one gig at the College Discotheque and made thirty-two dollars. Sent our roadies out and bought two cases of Ripple. I remember before the night was over, one of the roadies was out of his mind, chasing this girl around the club with his dick in his hand. She's screaming, and he's saying, 'C'mere, honey!'

"After about four weeks, we said, 'We gotta go play for somebody.' So we piled into this Ford Econoline van, drove up to Atlanta and drove around Piedmont Park until we found a nice spot, with some flat concrete and some power not far from it. We didn't say shit to anybody. We just set up the gear, plugged in and started playing. Within the hour, there's a couple of thousand people.

"The next week in this underground newspaper, *The Great Speckled Bird*, there's this article about the Allman Brothers, and all of a sudden, we became the band of the revolution, you know? So we started going back every Sunday. Within a month, we'd have five or six bands show up, and ten thousand people every Sunday. All for free. The cops never did a thing. They were really trying to get along with the hippies, and I think they said, 'Well, as long as they're playing music, let's leave them alone.'"

Duane went back to Muscle Shoals for one last session when he was invited to play on Boz Scaggs's debut album (produced by ROLLING STONE editor and publisher Jann S. Wenner). The album's highlight was the thirteen-minute blues "Loan Me a Dime." It was recorded at the last minute, to make use of the horn players who had come down from Memphis for some overdubs. This spontaneous move had some problems, since the horns needed to be kept separate from the other instruments so that sound wouldn't bleed into their microphones. Says Scaggs, "We arrived at the solution of putting Duane in this bathroom that was barely big enough to turn around in. He sat up on top of the toilet contraption, and he let at it." The resulting solo was one of his best.

The band was living in one house in Macon, at 309 College Street, dubbed the Hippie Crash Pad. Sometimes they would have a "dead-bird feast," when they would clean up the backyard, barbecue chicken, ingest some hallucinogens and watch the backyard pond, which was full of fornicating frogs.

In the fall of 1969, they recorded and released *The Allman Brothers Band*. It contained such staples of their repertoire as "Whipping Post," but it didn't stand up to the band's live show. The various players' love for rock, blues, country and jazz resulted in a potent brew, allowing for lots of improvisation. Duane got the most attention, for his molten-gold solos, but the heart of the band was its two drummers. Trucks provided a steady, locked-in backbeat, which let Jaimoe handle accents and texture. The band toured constantly, slowly building a following.

Duane, whose nickname had mutated to Skydog, was the leader, bolstering the confidence of Trucks or Betts when they seemed hesitant and hectoring his little brother when he got out of line. Oakley was the one most in love with the idea of the band as a hippie commune or a family, and he always tried to take care of everybody. Gregg was the band's lady-killer, nicknamed P.B. for "pretty boy." He was also the member with the most anxiety about performing and would sometimes vomit before a show.

In 1970, producer Tom Dowd was walking down the street in Macon, on his way to visit Phil Walden, when he heard a band rehearsing that made him late for his appointment. At Walden's office, he asked who was making that joyful noise. On discovering that it was the Allmans, he exclaimed, "Get them out of there! They're hot as a pistol! Get them in the studio!" Two days later, he began recording them and continued in short sessions between live dates. The excellent resulting album, *Idlewild South*, was named after the ranch where Betts lived and the band sometimes rehearsed. It contained the love-is-everywhere anthem "Revival," Gregg's acoustic-based blues "Midnight Rider" and "In Memory of Elizabeth Reed," an elegant Betts instrumental.

The Allmans kept touring and kept consuming whatever drugs they could get their hands on. They referred to cocaine as vitamin C. They ingested such vast quantities of psychedelic mushrooms that the mushroom became a band logo: Each member got one tattooed on his upper calf. (Jaimoe found the tattoo so painful, he stopped after the outline was done.) Sometimes a few of them would take speed and have a "fuckathon" with six or eight groupies.

After *Idlewild South* was completed, Dowd's next sessions were in Miami with Eric Clapton, working on Derek and the Dominoes' *Layla*. Clapton was an admirer of Duane's, largely on the strength of his work on "Hey Jude" and other sessions as sideman; Duane considered Clapton one of his heroes. And so when the Allman Brothers played Miami, Dowd escorted Clapton to the concert. Dowd remembers, "As we snuck into this place to be seated, Duane was playing a solo. He opened his eyes and stopped dead in his tracks. Dickey looks at Duane, who's looking down with his mouth open, so Dickey starts playing a solo to cover for Duane, not knowing what his problem is."

After the show, both bands repaired to the studio, where they hung out and jammed. Clapton and Duane quickly achieved a rapport, playing each other licks, comparing strings, trading instruments. Duane showed Clapton how he played slide: with an empty bottle of Coricidin (a cold medication) on his ring finger. That weekend, Clapton invited Duane to the studio to play on a couple of tracks. After they cut "Tell the Truth" and "Key to the Highway," Clapton asked him to play on the whole record; they completed the double album in five and a half weeks.

"Duane walked in and set those guys on fire," says Trucks. "They were all so fucked up: They were all snorting coke, doing smack, drunk. They had all these great musicians, but nothing, no fire." Trucks was watching on the day "Layla" was recorded and says Allman transformed the tune, speeding it up and adding its famous introductory riff. "He set fire to whoever he was working with," says Trucks, "and that's what he did to us. I mean, he was very much a messiah type."

In October 1970, while the band was visiting Nashville, everybody ate some opium. Duane had a second helping. The next morning, they couldn't wake him up; when they took him to the hospital, the doctors told them there was little hope. Oakley started crying and praying: "Please, just give him one more year." About an hour later, Duane started to get better.

Idlewild South sold respectably, but the Allman Brothers knew that their greatest strength was onstage. They took the logical step: They booked the Fillmore East in New York for two nights—March 12 and 13, 1971—to cut a live album. The double album from that weekend, *At Fillmore East,* was the Allman Brothers' first gold record and remains their best work. It's a demonstration of how tight they had become after two years of touring and how loose they were willing to unwind. They were playing jazz music for rock fans; they were also creating a blueprint for all the Southern-rock bands that would follow. Duane's solos made a strong case that he was America's finest living lead guitarist. Dowd says that for all the relaxed-fit atmosphere of the music, the album was highly organized and premeditated. After completing a night's work around 2 A.M., they would head up to the Atlantic studios with Dowd and listen to the playback for hours, thinking about which songs they needed to do again and which ones they had nailed.

Ten days after the Fillmore shows, while touring the South, the band paused to refresh itself at a truck stop in Jackson, Alabama. A cop there made the keen-eyed observation that they were a bunch of longhaired hippies and searched them: They were charged with possession of heroin, marijuana and PCP, and all spent the night in jail. "I can remember it like it was an hour ago," says Gregg. "Incarceration—I just couldn't do it. If I had to go to jail for three years, I'd probably come out of there crazy." They plea-bargained the charges down to disturbing the peace. That October, Phil Walden set up visits for the band at a heroin-detox center in New York. Some of the members flew up, including Duane and Gregg; none found it useful.

On October 28, 1971, Duane returned to Macon from New York; the following day there was a birthday party for Berry Oakley's wife, Big Linda. After the party, around 5:30 P.M., Duane got on his Harley for the trip home. Candace Oakley, Berry's sister, trailed behind in her car, going down Hillcrest Avenue. She watched as Duane passed slow cars and zipped through the yellow light at Inverness. At Bartlett Avenue, there was an approaching Chevy flatbed truck making a wide turn through the intersection. Duane tried to veer left around it—but the truck unexpectedly stopped in midturn. Candace saw Duane clip the truck, saw his helmet fly off, saw him fall off the Harley, saw the Harley fly into the air and land on top of him. Candace had to go to three houses before she could find someone who would let her use the phone. An ambulance took Duane to the hospital, but he had sustained massive internal injuries; at 8:40 P.M., he was pronounced dead. He was twenty-four years old.

"Duane always used to say, 'I'll be the first one to go in this band,'" swears Jaimoe. "I remember this shit coming up three or four times." At the funeral, the remaining members of the band did a somber set for 300 mourners, starting with "The Sky Is Crying." Duane's tombstone was inscribed with the guitar tablature for "Little Martha," a wistful instrumental he had written shortly before his death.

The band had lost its brightest light and its messianic leader; the apostles tried to figure out what he would have wanted them to do. The consensus was that he would have wanted them to keep going. They hit the road as a five-piece band, still playing 300 gigs a year, with Betts forced into the uncomfortable position of playing Duane's solos. Gregg had lost his brother and his rudder, but perhaps Oakley took the loss hardest. "He was just too fragile a character," says Trucks. "It was a big hole in his heart. The rest of us did a better job of moving on, but Berry was never able to fill that in."

In February 1972, the Allmans released *Eat a Peach*. It was their second double album in a row, with two-thirds of the material drawn from the Fillmore shows. It did include some lovely new material, such as Gregg's ballad "Melissa" and Betts's love song "Blue Sky," which featured his first vocals on an ABB album.

Morbid rumor had it that the record's title was a reference to Duane's crash; the truck he crashed into, the story went, had been carrying peaches. The truth was much more interesting. Walden's original nomination for the title was *The Kind We Grow in Dixie*; Trucks saw the mocked-up cover and told him it sucked, but he remembered something Duane had said in an interview just before he died: "Every time I'm in Georgia, I eat a peach for peace."

A few years ago, Trucks was reading T.S. Eliot's poem "The Love Song of J. Alfred Prufrock" for the first time. Toward the end of this poem about a man afraid to embrace life was a line that pinned Trucks's ears back: "Do I dare to eat a peach?" Trucks asked Gregg whether Duane had read Eliot; the answer was yes. Trucks mulls and states, "Duane never finished high school, but he was one of the more educated people I knew. He said, 'Damn, I'm smarter than these people,' so he went and got the books."

The Allman Brothers needed another musician to fill out their sound. Many of their songs are built around twin melody lines, but asking another guitarist to step into Duane's shoes seemed morbid and unfair, so they recruited pianist Chuck Leavell from Tuscaloosa, Alabama, and began work on a new album, *Brothers and Sisters*.

On November 11, 1972, Berry Oakley was driving around town on his Triumph motorcycle, recruiting musicians to jam with him that night at a local club, under the name the Berry Oakley Jive-Ass Revue, Featuring the Rowdy Roadies and the Shady Ladies. Oakley was slightly intoxicated and not very smooth on a bike; he took a turn too wide and plowed into the middle of the side of an oncoming bus. He was three blocks from the site of Duane's accident, which had happened a year and two weeks earlier.

Then something remarkable happened: Oakley stood up. Perhaps death and misfortune would not dog every single step of the Allman Brothers Band. Oakley had a nosebleed, but it soon stopped, so he caught a ride home. When he got there, however, he became incoherent and was taken to the hospital. It turned out he had fractured his skull and was hemorrhaging violently. He died forty-five minutes later.

"He just was not a happy man that last year," says Trucks. "When he died, it was almost a relief." Oakley was buried right next to Duane. At his funeral, the Allman Brothers trudged out to play another memorial set, gob-smacked by grief, unable to believe they were watching a rerun of the same horrific TV show.

After a concert in Seattle, Dickey Betts invites me onto his tour bus. Beneath his cowboy hat and above his American Indian T-shirt, there is a lined face with careful eyes. As a general rule, he is happy to let others do the talking. We chat about his hobbies of fishing and golf; sometimes he partners with retired baseball star Carlton Fisk.

Asked about his shirt, he unwraps a pack of Marlboro reds and talks about how there's some Cherokee on his father's side of the family. Betts's father played fiddle, guitar and mandolin on weekends; during the week, he was a carpenter. Dad taught his son Forrest Richard Betts (born December 12, 1943, in West Palm Beach, Florida) to play mandolin but wouldn't show him his woodworking secrets. "You got too much talent," he said. "If you don't want to play music, I want you to be a doctor or an attorney."

Dickey Betts graduated from weekend country-music jams with his family to the electric guitar, striving to copy Chuck Berry licks. At seventeen, he got his first professional gig: touring with the Swinging Saints, who played on the midway of a circus twelve times a day. Betts learned carny talk and then came home and falsified his birth certificate so he could play in nightclubs—which he did for the next eight years.

Asked about Berry Oakley, Betts leans forward, and his drawl accelerates as he eulogizes his friend:

> He was so original with his bass playing. I mean, there's never been a bass player, before or since, who wants to sound like him—because his sound is god-awful. He would play a Fender bass, with a giant amp on full treble: It was rattly-ass sounding. If you're not Berry Oakley, it sounds like shit. If you asked him who his influence was, he would jokingly say, "James Burton." You know who James Burton is? Ricky Nelson's lead guitar player, remember, who had that really rattly string sound.
>
> But from that perspective on bass, he did things. When he first heard "Whipping Post," for instance, he said, "Let me sleep on this tonight." And I lived with him at the time—he stayed in his room all night, and I could hear him working on it. That whole growly-ass 11/4 intro, that was Oakley.
>
> I'm a dumb-ass guitar player, you know? But I was smart enough to listen to people who had ideas, like Berry, and he organized all of our free concerts. And he argued and argued and argued to keep ticket prices down: "Our people can't afford these horrendous ticket prices." He kept us calm. He was the guy who would say, "Now, you know, let's be cool." He was a great, great influence on the band.

The Allmans replaced Oakley with Lamar Williams, a childhood pal of Jaimoe's. They completed the very fine *Brothers and Sisters*, which brought Betts even further to the forefront of the group with another ecstatic instrumental, "Jessica," and his song "Ramblin' Man." Betts says he writes most of his instrumentals driving around in his truck; when passengers ask him why he doesn't play the radio, he tells them that he has a radio in his head.

"Ramblin' Man," though, was written at 3 A.M. while sitting at the kitchen table in the Oakleys' house. It was inspired by a hillbilly friend of his who built barbed wire fences down in Florida. Whenever he saw Betts, he would greet him, "Hey, Dickey? How you been doing? Playing your music and doing the best you can?" The single became the band's biggest hit, going to Number Two (kept from the top by Cher's "Half-Breed"). "Ramblin' Man" was the last song Oakley ever recorded.

Contrary to popular belief, Woodstock wasn't the largest concert of its time; it wasn't even the largest in upstate New York. The biggest crowd to see a rock show in the Seventies was the 600,000 at the Watkins Glen Summer Jam on July 28, 1973, lodging it in the *Guinness Book of World Records*.

According to Trucks, the day was remarkably peaceful, without even a fistfight. The Grateful Dead played for five hours, the Band played for three and the Allman Brothers for another three. Then, at 2 A.M., just in case any of the audience members hadn't quite gotten their fill, the three bands jammed for another ninety minutes. Says Trucks, "It's one of the only times I can remember where the jam didn't work because the drugs didn't mix. The Band were all drunk, the Dead were all tripping, and we were all full of coke. So we tried to jam, but there was just no common ground."

The Allmans' consumption of drugs, including heroin, only increased. They kept touring; by now, they were playing stadiums. Trucks complains, "We got further and further away from the music. We got more and more into the limousines and the cocaine and the booze and chicks—and all that other stupid shit. It reached a point where we were the number one band in the country, and we didn't work for a year. We just sat on our asses getting fucked up."

The Allmans began 1975 in Macon, embarking on their first album in two years, *Win, Lose or Draw*. They recorded a crisp cover of Muddy Waters's "Can't Lose What You Never Had," and then the sessions fell apart. They argued about whether to pursue a jazzier sound. Betts's marriage was on the rocks. Trucks kept driving drunk and was eventually put on probation. Jaimoe was in a car crash, had a serious back injury and needed heavy painkillers.

Allman gave up and skipped town for L.A. His first night there, he went to see blues belter Etta James and ended up sitting in. He agreed to come back the following night; that time, the audience included David Geffen and his girlfriend, Cher. The next night, Cher showed up without Geffen. A smitten Allman asked her out.

They had a disastrous first date; Allman sucked on her fingers and tried to kiss her, and Cher fled. Against her better judgment, she agreed to a second date. Allman took her dancing, and they started to connect. "Pulling words out of Gregg Allman is like . . . forget it," she told *Playboy* that year. "Things started to mellow when he found out that I was a person—that a chick was not just a dummy. For him up till then, they'd had only two uses: make the bed and make it in the bed."

On June 30, 1975, five days after Cher's divorce from Sonny Bono was finalized, Cher and Allman went to Las Vegas and got married at Caesar's Palace. It was her second marriage and his third. They went to Jamaica for the honeymoon, but after a few days, Allman picked a fight with Cher, pulling a knife so that she would leave and he could score some heroin. After nine days of marriage, Cher filed for divorce. Allman entered rehab, and a week after Cher had filed, they reconciled.

Somehow, the band managed to finish the soggy, pasted-together *Win, Lose or Draw* and went on tour, performing some fund-raisers for Jimmy Carter along the way, each member arriving at each show in his own limousine. Allman's marriage wasn't stopping his drug abuse and womanizing; realizing the relationship wasn't working, he filed for divorce in November 1975. When Cher discovered she was pregnant a month later, they reconciled once more.

By 1976, Allman was waking up with a morning snort of cocaine, some of it pure pharmaceutical cocaine obtained by his sidekick and valet, Scooter Herring. He was scoring it from Joe Fuchs, a Macon pharmacist who staged a robbery of his drugstore and made some extra money selling off what had been "stolen."

What Allman didn't know was that both Fuchs and Herring were involved with the Dixie mafia, the Southern version of organized crime. The Macon ringleader was one J.C. Hawkins. In 1976, a federal investigation into corruption at the Macon Police Department led to the drug trade and the Hawkins gang. It also inevitably led to Allman as one of the main consumers of drugs in Macon.

Fuchs turned state's witness and wore a wire to gather more evidence against Hawkins. Allman was targeted by the grand jury and cut an immunity deal from prosecution in return for what he knew about Fuchs and Herring. The government was leaning on Herring, trying to build a case against Hawkins, but Herring resisted: Not only was he worried about further exposing Allman and his circle of drug buddies, he was afraid that Hawkins might kill him. So Herring volunteered to take the heat; in the odd vicissitudes of our legal system, this meant standing trial for dealing drugs to Gregg Allman. What's more, because of his immunity agreement, Allman would be testifying against his friend.

The trial began on June 22, 1976, and took only three days; Herring was sentenced to seventy-five years in prison (later reduced to thirty months on appeal). The other members of the band were livid: From where they stood, Allman had betrayed the brotherhood of the band. "There is no way we can work with Gregg again. Ever," Betts told ROLLING STONE at the time. "[Scooter's] the patsy," said Trucks.

The rest of the band made their loathing of Allman abundantly clear at the time, but years later, they sympathized with the untenable position he was in. "Gregg was made out to be a fink in the papers," says Trucks, "and we reacted accordingly." That they read about their band mate's legal travails in the newspaper instead of calling him on the phone is a good indication of how far apart they had all grown.

The trial was the final straw for the Allman Brothers Band, or maybe even an excuse to end something that had stopped being fun a long time before. They broke up. Says Jaimoe, "Gregg became a whipping boy for everything that had mounted up from the time of Duane's death."

The Allman Brothers might have parted ways with a sense of relief and a determination to enjoy their respective retirements, except for an unpleasant discovery: They were broke. Trucks says, "We were a young band in love with our music, and we had a guy [manager Phil Walden] who was going to take care of the business. That's what he did: He took care of all the business." Trucks laughs hollowly.

Trucks says, "We were the number one band in the country through the Seventies. We sold thirty million records. I think the biggest year I ever had, I made three hundred thousand dollars. And when we split up, not only did I not have anything, I was in debt up to my ass. I was living in a trailer." Phil Walden, acting as both manager and record company, had kept the royalty rates artificially low. When the Allmans started doing audits, they found they were still owed money. (Walden declines to comment on any aspect of his history with the band.) Betts filed the first lawsuit, which freed him to record a solo album on Arista. With its flagship band broken up, Capricorn was having financial problems of its own. In 1976, the label released another live double ABB album, *Wipe the Windows, Check the Oil, Dollar Gas*, this one a grab bag of recent performances.

Allman and Cher made a 1977 album, *Two the Hard Way*, under the name Allman and Woman; in an act of kindness and good taste, the American record-buying public completely ignored it. When Allman passed out at an awards banquet, his face landing in a plate of spaghetti, Cher decided enough was enough. She filed for divorce in 1977; this time there was no reconciliation.

Allman packed up and went back to Macon, where he tried to reassemble the Allman Brothers Band. It took a full year for the group members to overcome their doubts and their commitments to solo projects; Chuck Leavell and Lamar Williams stayed with their band, Sea Level. The ABB recorded an uneven album, *Enlightened Rogues*; released in March 1979, it took its name from one of Duane's old descriptions of the band.

In the summer of 1979, with creditors closing in on all sides, Capricorn finally melted in the heat. It was done in by a combination of mismanagement and its reliance on a steady diet of Southern rock when the public taste had switched to disco. On October 21, the label filed for bankruptcy. Walden would eventually emerge with a net worth of $7 million, but the Allmans' royalties to that point were lost forever.

The Brothers struggled on, making two more albums for Arista, in 1980 and 1981, that they would just as soon forget, *Reach for the Sky* and *Brothers of the Road*. They complain that the label kept trying to turn them into Led Zeppelin. Southern rock had become a cliché, so the band was instructed not to wear cowboy hats onstage. In January 1982, the Allmans broke up, a move that met with shrugs of apathy both inside and outside the group.

The story could end there; it does for many bands. Those who were once Brothers went their separate ways in the Eighties. Trucks built a recording studio. Lamar Williams died of lung cancer in 1983, maybe caused by exposure to Agent Orange during his time in Vietnam. Allman recorded a couple of solo albums, toured clubs and had a Top Forty hit with "I'm No Angel" in 1987. Allman and Betts lived five miles away from each other in Florida but would go years without seeing each other.

By 1988, Southern blues rock had rehabilitated its reputation somewhat, through the efforts of performers like Robert Cray, Stevie Ray Vaughan and even the Georgia Satellites. Epic Records called Betts and asked him to put together a twin-guitar band; if he really wanted, he could even wear his cowboy hat. Betts released *Pattern Disruptive*, and then the label asked him what he would think about the Allman Brothers Band getting back together.

The exceptional four-CD box *Dreams*, released in 1989, had reminded the world of the heights of the Allmans' triumphs before they collapsed. And everyone in the band had bills to pay and no money saved for retirement. Surely they were mature enough to collaborate again. So they cautiously reunited, uncertain of whether they could count on Allman to show up in any condition to work. They couldn't, it turned out, but they proceeded anyway, recording *Seven Turns* in 1990 and *Shades of Two Worlds* in 1991. They added young salsa drummer Marc Quiñones on percussion, Warren Haynes on second guitar and Allen Woody on bass; Chuck Leavell was invited to return but opted to play piano with the Rolling Stones instead.

The Allmans discovered a remarkable thing: People still wanted to hear them play. They took a one-year-at-a-time attitude and for ten years kept deciding that it would be fun to do one more year. The crowds kept growing, and the ABB kept collecting accolades: induction into the Rock and Roll Hall of Fame in 1995, a Grammy for a live version of "Jessica" in 1996.

A month after the 1999 Cincinnati show, Gregg Allman speculates about how his brother would have probably ended up spending the Eighties playing in small clubs, just like he did. "It made me really remember who I was. I had to tote that organ a few times. It weighs the same as a heartache, but if you want to play badly enough, you'll carry the damn thing."

The same as a heartache?

Allman cracks a smile. "No, the same as a Harley—406 pounds. Nothing weighs as much as a heartache."

If you could go back thirty years, and you knew everything that was going to happen with this band, both the good things and the tragedies, would you go down that road again?

Allman snorts. "Well, at that age, it would be pretty overwhelming to receive all that information at once." Then he pauses and weighs the balance of his life, the festivals and the funerals, and decides on the path he's already taken. "But yeah. Once music gets you, you'll go wherever it takes to play. Yeah." He walks off into the night, heading for his dogs-but-no-smoking bus.

disco

By MIKAL GILMORE

At the outset of the 1970s, rock & roll still prided itself on its aspirations to revolution. From rockabilly to glitter rock, it was music that not only articulated and vented the frustrations of cultural outsiders but also won those upstarts a station and voice that they might otherwise have been denied.

But in the mid-1970s, a genuine revolution took place within the bounds of pop culture—and rock & roll hated it. The upheaval was called disco, and it subverted not just rock's familiar notions of fun and form but also its pretended ideals of community and meaning. It was a music that, without rhetoric or stridor, seized and transformed the pop mainstream and its long-unchallenged star systems, and it empowered cultural outlanders that rock & roll had snubbed or simply abandoned. In the process, disco became the biggest commercial pop genre of the 1970s—actually, the biggest pop-music movement of all time—and in the end, its single-minded, booming beat proved to be the most resilient and enduring stylistic breakthrough of the last twenty-five years. In short, disco—the pop revolution that was quickly overthrown by an ungrateful pop world—figured out a way to outlast its own demise, a way to remain dominant, while feigning an ignoble death.

So how did this cultural rupture happen? How did disco become both the most popular and reviled milepost in pop music's history?

To answer these questions, one has to look at the confluence of musical history and social longing that produced the disco explosion. Musically, disco was a logical outgrowth of how soul music had developed in the 1960s and how it had adapted in order to survive in the early 1970s. From the terse protofunk of James Brown and the spare but accentuated dynamics of the Stax-Volt sound, disco derived its obsession with a simple but relentlessly driving beat; and from the pop savvy of Motown, as well as from the suave romanticism of such Philadelphia-based producers and writers as Thom Bell (who had defined the Spinners' sound) and the team of Kenny Gamble and Leon Huff (who worked with the O'Jays, the Intruders, Harold Melvin and the Blue Notes and Teddy Pendergrass, among others), disco gained its undying passion for elegant, swooning, sexy surfaces that were their own irrefutable rewards. But disco was more than music as sound, or sound as style or artifice. It also aimed to reaffirm one of music's most time-worn purposes: namely, its power as a social unifier, as a means of bringing together an audience that shared a certain social perspective and that found meaning and pleasure in the ritual of public dancing. In this sense, disco had roots in traditions as urbane as big-band and swing music, as rowdy as blues-style juke joints and country-western honky-tonks, and as sexually irrepressible as early rock & roll and its cleaned-up public exposition, *American Bandstand*.

More immediately, though, disco extended—in fact, *revived*—some of the most joyful ambitions of 1960s pop. In the early 1960s—before Motown or the Beatles—the media largely perceived pop music as little more than a medium of transient dance styles, like the Twist, Mashed Potato and Hully Gully, that lived out their heady but brief vogues in crowded and intoxicating public venues, such as New York's Peppermint Lounge and numerous other discotheques scattered across America and Europe. When the 1960s exploded with the British Invasion and soul, it became apparent that rock was more than an agency for dancing—though clearly, dancing was now more fun, more an assertion of generational identity and power, than ever before. But as rock became more ambitious, more "significant," it gradually abdicated the dance floor. Though it isn't often acknowledged, the San Francisco hippie community grew out of a dance movement: young people coming together in the city's ballrooms and clubs to dance exhaustingly to the colorful psychedelia that was being invented by such community bands as the Jefferson Airplane and the Grateful Dead. Indeed, dancing, even more than drugs or sex, was how that scene first publicly realized its ideals of communal ecstasy.

Within a season or two, however, the scene's followers were no longer dancing. Instead, they were paying serious attention to the new music, to its lyrical pronouncements and aural constructions, and as often as not, they did so from a sitting posture. By the early 1970s, rock was something you *listened* to, and for whatever the numerous and undeniable virtues of such artists as the Eagles, Pink Floyd, the Allman Brothers or even early David Bowie, there was little about their music that inspired a mass terpsichore. Dancing was something practiced by established stars like Mick Jagger—it was not something that an audience did. The star was empowered to *move*, while the audience was obliged to pay, to watch and listen, to revere.

Still, there were audiences for whom dancing was a vital social bond and an essential sensual act, though they were largely audiences that had been shut out by rock & roll's developing styles and pretensions. Certainly, for the black audience—which had enjoyed something of an alliance with the rock mainstream in the mid-1960s—pop no longer offered much embrace or much satisfaction in the early 1970s. For the various Hispanic audiences and for numerous other ethnic minorities, the reality was even more exclusionary: Pop accommodated ethnic styles in only the most vague or diluted sense, as in the pyrotechnic Latin rock of Santana. In addition, there was one other large audience that had been shut out of rock's concerns, and that was the gay underground, an audience for whom dancing proved an important assertion of identity and community.

In 1973 and 1974, these audiences gradually (and perhaps a bit unwittingly) began to form an ever-expanding network—or at least they began influencing each other's musical preferences—as dance clubs sprang up around the East Coast and Europe and as the DJs at these clubs began searching out some of the hippest dance-oriented black, Hispanic and European pop to play for these audiences. As the trend grew, the DJs refined their style of programming: Usually cutting back and forth between two turntables, the DJs aimed to play a sequence of songs in such a manner that beats between the songs were consistent, each track blending into the following track, making for a steady, seamless flow and for a mounting mood of physical frenzy among the dancers. Like the music of the 1960s, disco was supposed to be a celebration of community and ecstasy—only this time, the revelers who were celebrating these ideals were the same ones who had been forgotten or expatriated by the established rock world.

This emerging dance movement turned out to be one of the most pivotal and radical developments in 1970s rock. In fact, it upended pop's common values and its known hierarchy. Whereas for the vast majority of the post-Beatles audience it was the artists and their statements that constituted rock's main pleasures and main worth, disco's partisans agreed on some new values. What mattered in disco's ethos wasn't the apotheosis of the artist but the experience and involvement of the audience itself. Consequently, disco elected a new system of pop heroes. On the romantic side, the heroes were the dancers, who were acting out this new egalitarianism on the dance floor. On the practical side, the heroes were the people who knew how to shape and manipulate sound in order to construct moods and motivate an audience— the DJs and producers and arrangers, who were the *real* auteurs of disco style and meaning.

In other words, in disco, the artists—the singers and instrumentalists—were an essential backdrop, but they weren't the focus of the action; disco fans didn't go to disco shows to watch disco stars. Indeed, what disco declared was that our pop stars *weren't* our representatives but that we could (and should) be the stars in our own scenarios of pleasure and empowerment. To some pop fans and critics, this assertion—namely, that "Everybody is a star"—seemed a bit trivial, even pathetic. To the emerging disco audience, though, it amounted to nothing less than a vision of empowerment: It said that whatever the reality of your existence, you could refuse to be defined by menial conditions; you could put on your best clothes, go out in public and act out your worthiness, as if you were entitled to all the acts and trappings of luxury that were flaunted by the dominant culture. In other words, you could appropriate those trappings. In *other* other words, strike a pose; there's nothing to it.

In time, disco's obsessions with dressiness would become elitist and defeating—especially once the scene's clubs began enforcing dress codes that simply affirmed the very ideals of affluence and privilege that the original disco audience had meant to usurp, rather than simply emulate. But in the early 1970s, disco's "Everybody is a star" mentality was genuinely liberating: It had the effect of empowering (and even briefly unifying) an audience of gays, blacks and ethnics that had, for too long, been disdained or displaced by a rock world that had become overwhelmingly white. This rising coalition of outsiders—pop's equivalent of a silent majority—was about to become the biggest audience in pop's history, though in a thoroughly unprecedented way. In fact, disco became a mass revolution at pretty much the same time that it remained an underground phenomenon. Because disco was a music played in clubs, a music without clearly identifiable central stars, a music that radio and pop media largely ignored at first, its massive popularity was initially almost invisible. Indeed, for a year or two, the disco world was a network of clubs, dancers and music makers that didn't so much enter the pop mainstream as simply form an equally viable alternative to that mainstream, that could launch massive-selling hits without benefit of radio or media exposure. Without intending to, the disco world had seized and exercised its own power by the most effective means possible—by means of pure commerce—and this development would have a galvanic effect on the business and culture of popular music.

Of course, this meant that disco's genuine mainstream assimilation was inevitable and that the music itself would be co-opted and marketed as a formula. Indeed, by 1974, disco had been codified. The beat ruled—it was a tightly uniform, booming 4/4 pulse, without patience for rhythmic shifts or improvisation. Within its rigid limitations, however, the structure allowed for a surprising amount of nuance and variation. It could be elegant, coy and tuneful, as in Van McCoy's "The Hustle"; it could be taut and sweetly funky, as in Shirley and Company's "Shame, Shame, Shame"; it could be sexy and evocative, as in the Hues Corporation's "Rock the Boat" and George McCrae's "Rock Your Baby"; it could be propulsive and soulful, as in the Average White Band's "Pick Up the Pieces." The following year, disco even launched its first certified star, a former church and theatrical singer named Donna Summer, who began as merely another pop singer (with the mock-orgasmic "Love to Love You Baby") but would shortly become the form's most ambitious and enduring artist.

In the mid-1970s, disco fused with the public imagination in an incendiary mass moment. By this time, numerous artists—including Donna Summer, Labelle, KC and the Sunshine Band, Wild Cherry and Silver Convention—had already scored Top Ten disco hits. But the genre's biggest milestone, of course, was *Saturday Night Fever*, a 1977 film that gave a sympathetic and fairly accurate portrayal of how disco nightlife provided a transcendent identity for certain East Coast working-class, ethnic youths. More significant than the film, though, was its soundtrack album. Featuring the music of the Bee Gees and the Trammps, among others, it rapidly sold over 25 million copies and set a record as the biggest-selling record in pop history at that time.

Disco's triumph was complete, which of course only signaled the movement's end. Actually, disco had been taken out of the hands of both its creators and its audience. *Saturday Night Fever*'s (and disco's) biggest stars were the Bee Gees, a group of British pop stars who had created a glossy adaptation of the form's style and popularity as a way of reviving their flagging careers. In addition, in the rush to exploit disco's hitmaking abilities, several other established pop stars—including the Rolling Stones, Paul McCartney, Elton John, the Eagles and Rod Stewart—had also started accommodating their music to the disco style and its audience. Suddenly, disco's pulse was omnipresent: It dominated film scores, TV commercials, Top 40 radio, and almost every lounge and club where recorded music was played for a dancing audience. It wasn't just that the music was now pervasive but that it even seemed bent on revising all known music history. Indeed, everything—from the hits of the Beatles to the dark beauty of Beethoven—became fair game for disco's pounding 4/4 formula, and the sameness of it all began to rub many people the wrong way.

1
4
9

As disco became the pop norm, a counterreaction set in—in swift and fierce terms. By 1978, rock fans were beginning to sport T-shirts emblazoned with hostile decrees—DISCO SUCKS and DEATH TO DISCO. And then, in July 1979, a hard-rock radio DJ from Chicago's WLUP turned a baseball doubleheader at Comiskey Park into an anti-disco rally. Between games, as he incited the audience to chant "Disco sucks," the DJ piled disco LPs into a wooden crate in center field—and exploded the crate. It was a supremely ugly moment, and its message was plain: The mainstream pop audience wasn't about to allow a coalition of blacks and gays to usurp rock's primacy. Indeed, it seemed hardly coincidental that at a time when America was about to elect Ronald Reagan as president and enter its most savage period of cultural denial, disco's dream of an all-embracing audience would invite rabid antipathy. Instead of opening up the pop world to a new consensus, disco had made it plain that rock was fast becoming a field of diverse, often mutually antagonistic factions.

So disco was ended. Even as the Village People—a gay goof that became tiring quickly—became, for a short time, the biggest-selling band in America, the pop industry and media were already in retreat from disco. By 1980, *disco* was clearly a dirty word. Record sales plummeted almost overnight, and numerous artists, producers and executives—even entire record labels and radio stations—fell into an irreclaimable oblivion. Disco had been overthrown, in part by its own excesses and in part by a rising ugly racist and anti-gay sensibility.

But in many ways, disco transmuted its style and survived ingeniously—or at the very least, it has had a considerable legacy. In fact, in the 1980s, its rhythmic principles were adopted by two divergent audiences: the new wave crowd, who—from the Tom Tom Club to Billy Idol to Depeche Mode—enjoyed their biggest commercial successes by adapting disco's dance structures to their own conceits; also, hip-hop and rap music have based much of their linguistic and textural innovation on disco's foursquare rhythmic pulse. In addition, the success of many of the 1980s biggest stars—including Michael Jackson, Prince and Madonna—would have been unthinkable without the breakthroughs that disco made in both style and audience appeal. It's also true, of course, that disco didn't necessarily make the pop world more tolerant. Too much of the best black dance music is now anti-gay and misogynist, and given the hatred and fear that many rap artists have experienced firsthand, it is lamentable that music that people now dance and celebrate to can be seen as a tacit advocacy of sexual hatred and violence of all sorts.

In general, though, disco managed to restore to rock the principle of dancing as one of music's primary purposes and pleasures—and if anything, that truth is more dominant in today's hip-hop, house and postpunk pop scene than it was twenty-five years ago, at disco's height. It also reasserted a vital truth: that dancing could be an act of affirmation—that it could unite people, could redeem (or at least vent) their pains and longings, and could even empower those who had been too long denied or forgotten. In the end, the question isn't why disco enjoyed such phenomenal success. The real question is, Why didn't *more* of 1970s rock & roll stand for these same worthy values?

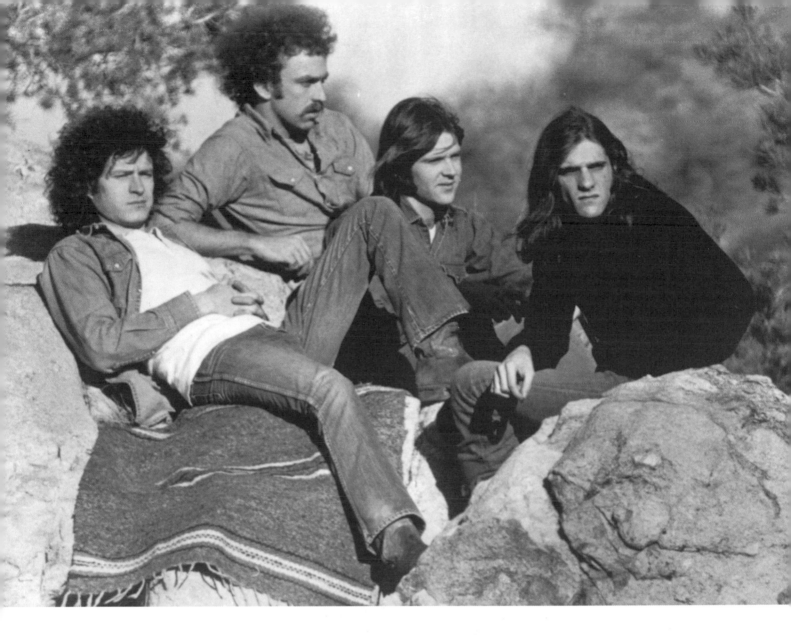

the eagles

By ANTHONY DeCURTIS

"I don't know why fortune smiles on some / And lets the rest go free," sings Don Henley on "The Sad Café," the concluding song on the Eagles' last studio album, *The Long Run*. Those lines capture eloquently the degree to which the Eagles had come to see the superstardom they enjoyed in the Seventies as a kind of curse that generated dissension between the band's members, critical controversy, creative paralysis and a nearly metaphysical discomfort with the hedonistic delights—however fully indulged—that were the reward and price of their success.

Things started out innocently enough. When the Eagles were formed in Los Angeles in 1971, the group—guitarists Glenn Frey and Bernie Leadon, bassist Randy Meisner and drummer Don Henley—set out on an exuberant exploration of the country-rock synthesis that had been a hallmark of earlier California bands like the Byrds and the Flying Burrito Brothers. The Eagles' first three albums—*Eagles* (1972), which yielded the hits "Take It Easy," "Witchy Woman" and "Peaceful Easy Feeling"; *Desperado* (1973); and, as guitarist Don Felder was joining the band, *On the Border* (1975)—were distinguished by catchy melodies, reassuring harmonies and a fascination with outlaw imagery.

On *One of These Nights* (1975), the Eagles began to examine the dark side of the California dream, a concern that grew into an obsession on *Hotel California* (1976), the band's greatest album. *Hotel California* is a clear-eyed, wistful examination of California as the last stop on the American journey westward, the country's destiny made manifest and then foreclosed. Novelist Joseph Conrad used the term "fascination of the abomination" to describe the hypnotic power that self-destruction can exert on the soul, and that phrase well suits *Hotel California*'s depiction of a gorgeous paradise—the geographical end point of American aspiration—transformed into a sunny hell of unsatisfying pleasure.

With *Hotel California*'s massive success, Henley and Frey clearly emerged as the main voices of the Eagles, not only because their songwriting and singing had come to define the band's vision but because—with the departure of Leadon and Meisner and the addition of guitarist Joe Walsh and bassist Timothy B. Schmit—they were the last remaining members of the original lineup.

Battles over the direction of the group, anxiety over crafting a worthy followup to *Hotel California*, legal struggles with the band's management and a growing perception by critics of California rockers as spoiled, narcissistic sybarites stalled the band's productivity. One million dollars and two years later, *The Long Run* appeared. By then the Eagles were exhausted and disaffected, and when Glenn Frey announced in 1981 that he had begun work on a solo album, their breakup became official.

The Eagles sang in the perfect voice of the Seventies, in soaring harmonies aching with a Sixties hangover. It was a voice of desperate pleasures sought in the wake of a failed dream, a messenger of damaged ideals and disappointed longing. Their voices still carry those meanings. The band has been inducted in the Rock and Roll Hall of Fame, and *Eagles: Their Greatest Hits 1971–1975* has become the best-selling album of all time, surpassing even Michael Jackson's *Thriller*—convincing proof that while the Eagles' music is an essential expression of the Seventies, it far transcends nostalgia.

On a bright day in August 1989, Henley and Frey met at Henley's home in Beverly Hills to do their first interview together since the Eagles' split. (At the time, rumors were flying about a possible reunion, though that would not happen for another five years.) They looked back on providing the soundtrack to a time, a movement from youthful exuberance to a depleted cynicism and the transition from the Sixties to the Eighties.

Do you think of the Seventies as a distinct era, or does it blur around the edges?

FREY: Well, it can sort of be defined by the life of our band, because the band started in the fall of '71 and broke up probably sometime in 1980, so we were working together for the whole decade.

HENLEY: The decade has some definite parameters for me because I came to L.A. in the summer of 1970 from Texas. And then the band. I think of the *Desperado* period, which was '73, and then '75, which was *One of These Nights*. I think '75 was around the point when the Seventies changed—'74, '75, '76. And then late '76 started another period, the *Hotel California* period. That's when disco and punk were starting to come in, and I guess that was the beginning of the Eighties.

FREY: We changed, too. I think we got a little more serious; maybe we were a little more politically active. You know, something happened around the time of the Bicentennial. We got *Hotel California* out by Thanksgiving 1976—we wanted badly to have an album out in that year.

I remember interviews in which you'd say that the record was about more than California. It was really about America.

HENLEY: America, in general, California being the microcosm. That didn't seem to take. I mean, it just went in one ear and out the other.

FREY: There was a time, somewhere in 1976, when I thought things were going to get better. We had gotten rid of Nixon. We had a Democrat in the White House. Jimmy Carter and the boys were going to have barbecue on the hill.

The president was quoting Bob Dylan.

HENLEY: It seemed like the Sixties were back for a second.

FREY: And then Khomeini—

HENLEY: And the helicopter mechanics. Events conspired against ol' Jimmy.

Let's go back a bit. The two of you come from very different parts of the country. What brought you to California?

FREY: Well, I grew up in Detroit, so I never really had any desire to go East. Being from the Great Lakes and watching the sun set in the west, that's where I wanted to go. I played in one of the only bands in Detroit that did surfer music!

What was your sense about it when you got here? Did it meet your expectations?

FREY: Oh, I think I was a little bit intimidated, a little awed, but you get over that. I came here once and went back to Michigan and *really* decided I hated Michigan. Then I figured I better just go and try to make something out of my life in California.

What were your first impressions when you got here, Don?

HENLEY: Kind of "Gaw-lee!" I mean, I used to read a lot of the fan magazines, the music magazines of that day, and everything musically that excited me seemed to be emanating from here. It was all happening here. There were the Byrds; Crosby, Stills, Nash and Young; Linda Ronstadt and Joni Mitchell; Steppenwolf and Spirit. The thing that definitely pushed me in this direction was that Kenny Rogers had discovered my little group [Shiloh] in Texas, and he lived here. He was the only person we knew here, and we didn't know *anybody* in New York. So he was instrumental in our decision to come out this way, with the promise of an album, a record deal.

We came here for first time, I believe it was February of 1970. We came out to cut a single, not really to move here. I remember driving into town; we came up on the Hollywood Freeway. It was a nice, clear February night, one of those nights when the town looks really pretty. I had never seen the Capitol Records Tower—I was freaking out. It was, like, there was this big metal and concrete symbol of the record industry. I had so many Capitol records when I was a kid—45s, you know, when they had that purple label with the Capitol dome. I believe the writing was in silver. It was a manifestation of all my childhood records. I was awestruck. I had never seen any terrain like this. Where I come from, there are rolling, gentle hills but no vistas like this. And, of course, I had never seen a grid of lights like that in my life. It just went on forever.

What about when you got the Eagles together? What were your ambitions?

FREY: I think we had a lot of optimism. You don't know any better than to think that you can do really well. I mean, every time you put together a band, you think, "This is going to be the one."

HENLEY: "The best band in the world"—until you really get to know everybody. We were young, and the times were exciting, and the world lay stretched out before us. The beginning is when it's great. Money and girls were the two big motivations— that's what it was for everybody. Then you become a serious artist and set out to change the world.

FREY: There was a time during 1976, 1977, where the record business went crazy. That was when *Hotel California* came out, and *Saturday Night Fever* and also *Rumours* by Fleetwood Mac, and—

HENLEY: *Frampton Comes Alive!*—for a minute.

FREY: That was the music business at its decadent zenith. I remember Don had a birthday in Cincinnati, and they flew in cases of Château Lafite Rothschild. I seem to remember that the wine was the best and the drugs were good and the women were beautiful and, man, we seemed to have an endless amount of energy. *Endless* stores of energy. Hangovers were conquered with Bloody Marys and aspirin, you know what I mean? There were no two-day purges or hiding in your bed. It seemed that you bounced back, you were resilient.

HENLEY: There was much merrymaking. Those kind of record sales were unprecedented. I guess everybody thought it was going to continue like that. Lots of money was spent on parties and champagne and limos and drugs. And then, of course, the bottom fell out.

FREY: I know we were pissed off, but the music business seemed a little friendlier to me.

HENLEY: It was friendlier to the young man or woman starting out. It wasn't quite the claw-your-way-into-the-business that it is now. It was much more organic, as was the world. The whole country-rock movement—I hate that label, but for lack of a better term—was even connected to environmentalism, because it was a music that had grown, in part, out of country music. It was very much connected to the earth, and everybody was wearing earthy clothes and celebrating the outdoors.

The term *country rock* suggests a rural origin.

HENLEY: It was a very natural time, and it all made sense with the music. Then in the late Seventies, there was a backlash against that. Music started to become very urban oriented, a reflection of the concrete and steel and the pace. So we didn't, to paraphrase Joni Mitchell, "get back to the garden." If we did, we didn't stay there. The country, the natural sound that is connected with nature, has gone out of music

1
5
3

pretty much. I lament that. I lament that loss, that contact we had with nature.

FREY: I think when the Seventies started, music wasn't giving much hope. There was almost no way that, musically, the Seventies were going to be on a par with the Sixties. The only people that even got remotely close were Crosby, Stills, Nash and Young, but all their problems—they sort of blew it. But they had that myth going for a while. Looking back on things, the music of the Seventies doesn't sound that fucking bad to me at all. You can name the great albums of the Seventies. I don't know if you can name the great albums of the Eighties, but if you do, how great are they compared with, for example, *Layla*?

What other records do you think really stand out?

FREY: I might forget some things, but I'm thinking of a string of Elton John hits. We had the Spinners, we had the Philadelphia Sound—I liked those records. It's kind of funny even to have resented disco compared with where that kind of music has gone. Some of the older disco songs—shit, if it's Harold Melvin and the Blue Notes, those are pretty good fucking records. Some of the Donna Summer records I like a lot better than things that I've heard recently. There's a lot more craft and a lot less programming involved, that's for sure.

HENLEY: Some great R&B records were being made in the early Seventies—that wasn't only in the Sixties.

How do you feel about your own stuff?

HENLEY: I pretty much like the same things and hate the same things now that I did then. I mean, we knew when we were making those albums that some of the songs weren't very good. We were trying to run a democracy, and there wasn't a hell of a lot we could do about it. We just had to swallow it, just to keep the group happy and together. As time progressed, there would be another album; Glenn and I would put up more of a fight to try to get the quality of each song to rise. But, I mean, shit—we were what? Twenty-five, twenty-six, twenty-seven years old? We weren't exactly mature. We were growing up in public, you know? I look back at some of the lyrical content and cringe sometimes, but we were just as mature as anybody else that age, I guess.

A few moments ago you both were describing what a great time you were having as the Seventies kicked into high gear. But as the decade went on, your records got darker and darker. Why was that?

HENLEY: I think we knew intuitively that it would pass. I think we could sense the future. It *was* kind of idyllic. It was very exciting. It was a time of discovery, and people were just friendlier in general. But I think intuitively we were aware of the end of the boom, not exclusively for ourselves but the nation.

Was there a sense that the tensions within the band or that the tensions between the two of you were getting channeled in your work?

HENLEY: We did use the tension a lot to be creative. We would divide up into factions. It was me and him against them, in general, and we would use that. We were very much for quality music and growth and mature subject matter. At the same time, we wanted to be successful. We wanted to get a big audience. We felt that that was the whole purpose of being in the record business in the first place. There were some people in the band who didn't, for one reason or another. Guilt. And I understand that, you know, but the tension took its toll after a while. It finally got the better of us.

FREY: The band just got bigger and bigger, and it became unmanageable. I think the underbelly of success is the burden of having to follow things up. We started to run out of gas. Don sort of blew his literary nut on *Hotel California*. I mean, we covered it, from love to sex to drugs to the future of the planet to—

HENLEY: Religion.

FREY: We weren't thinking about selling fifteen million records at the time. It's one thing if you have a couple of hit singles and get a gold record. That's different from selling fifteen million albums. There's only a few artists who have had the education of having to continue working on stuff after some sort of blockbuster success. So it wore on us. We spent a lot more time in the studio toward the end of the decade, and we got a lot more critical of our own work, because we wanted it to be better than the last thing we did. We probably should have just given up and written a couple more love songs and put out *The Long Run* a couple of years earlier. Now I realize that.

HENLEY: So much momentum built up that instead of controlling the momentum, we started getting pushed along by it. Instead of having maybe six months or a year after *Hotel California* to sit back and take a deep breath and assess the situation and figure out what direction we should go in, we plunged into another album. The beast wanted to be fed. We tried to feed it, and we were pretty much paralyzed. Like Glenn said, I didn't have much left to say at that point. I don't think any of us did. We were pretty tired.

Obviously, the two of you went through a real bad patch. Do you have any regrets?

FREY: So much time has passed now that I'm not even mad at the guys I was *really* mad at. We just sort of drifted. The Eagles were like an ongoing nightmare for us toward the end.

HENLEY: It was also responsible for the failure of several relationships with the opposite sex.

FREY: Yeah, we weren't doing really well with that.

You once called your relationship with Don "my longest successful romance."

FREY: Well, here we are. We're still laughing.

HENLEY: Yeah, the women came and . . . It was funny: He and I would live together for a while and write a certain body of material. And then one of us would get a girlfriend, and the other guy would move out. And that guy would break up with his girlfriend and be ready to move back in, and then the other guy would have a girlfriend. But the music always came first. I think we wanted it that way. I mean, it would have been nice—we wanted to have relationships with girls and have the band, too, but it just didn't seem possible. We were wedded to the muse or that vision—whatever it was and however murky it might have been.

Do you feel optimistic about working together again?

FREY: Well, we're going to see. It will be interesting. There's certainly a lot to write about.

HENLEY: I think we've matured a great deal. We have a better perspective on the world and our place in it. I mean, I want to stress that we had a *real good time*. We're pointing out the low points, but we had a great fucking time.

Your interviews about the Eagles always seem to emphasize the downside of things, but on a day-to-day basis, it had to have been fairly enjoyable.

HENLEY: Shit yeah! I mean, we were living . . . this was the dream that we all had. This is why we came to California. It just got bigger than we ever expected it to. It kind of scared us, I guess.

FREY: We tried to maintain that underdog frame of mind.

HENLEY: But it was hard to be an underdog when you're selling 12 million records [*laughs*].

FREY: Led Zeppelin might argue with us, but I think we might have thrown the greatest traveling party of the Seventies. It was called the Third Encore. Almost every night when we were on the road, we would throw this fabulous mixer. We'd hand out 3E buttons, and we'd invite all the key radio people and as many beautiful girls as we'd meet from the airport to the hotel and whatever. We had our own sound system, and we played Motown and blues records and had this terrific party every night.

How were you able to get up the next day?

FREY: You got to bed at four or five, and you get up at noon or one o'clock. If you're playing multiple nights, you don't travel and you don't sound-check. The Eagles—we didn't really have to sound-check very much.

Who did you see as your competition in those days?

HENLEY: Fleetwood Mac was the competition, but it was a friendly competition.

FREY: I thought about competition more in the earlier days. You know, once you become successful, you realize that you're competing with yourself. Somebody else making a good record can't keep you off the charts. We used to have these T-shirts that said *song power*, because we felt that was what we had going for us. There was, even in the early Seventies, too much emphasis on packaging. There was already dry ice and smoke bombs. I looked at Jethro Tull and some of those bands as the people we were competing against.

Bands that were about spectacle?

HENLEY: Yeah. We were deliberately minimalist, to a fault, probably. We were accused by one critic of loitering onstage—which pissed us off then. Now we can laugh about it. That's what's great about being forty—that shit's funny now.

Did you feel at any point like your identity was wrapped up in being one of the Eagles?

HENLEY: I guess I still think of myself, in some part of my mind, as being that. There is still in most cities, no matter how popular I am as an individual artist, a bunch of guys in the audience who at some point will start going, "Ea-*gles*, Ea-*gles*, Ea-*gles*." Some nights I get pissed off and say, "We'll get to that in a minute, but right now I'm up here. It's my name that's on the ticket." But, I mean, it's certainly something we're both proud of. We accomplished a lot. We were also a socially responsible band. We did our part to give something back to the community and charities of various kinds.

FREY: We didn't get to do quite enough, I think.

HENLEY: No, we didn't, again because there was a lot of disagreement.

FREY: This is something that disappointed Don and me toward the end of the Seventies. A couple of things happened. First of all, we did a bunch of benefits.

HENLEY: We got some flak for that. We learned at the very end of our career that it's not really a good idea to do benefit concerts for individual politicians. For causes, yes, but for individual politicians, it's not really a good idea—for us or for them. I mean, we've had various drug busts, and politics is so ruthless now that the opponent can always drag that kind of stuff up. And it's not good for us, either, because you have to maintain that outsider thing to some extent.

How did your political sensibility develop?

FREY: Linda [Ronstadt] started going out with Jerry Brown [*laughs*].

HENLEY: The first things we did were for the various American Indian tribes around California. It started out as an environmentalist/nature thing. We used to go camp out in the desert and do peyote rituals. The photo of us on our first album is one when we were ripped on peyote. So I think it started out with Indian folklore and myths, which is where the name for the band came from.

FREY: And then the antinuclear movement started.

HENLEY: Jackson Browne was influential on us in that respect.

Do you feel that politically, the Seventies suffered a hangover from the failed idealism of the Sixties?

HENLEY: Yeah, I'm still writing about it. The dream was unfulfilled. In the late Seventies, greed reared its ugly head. We turned from a society that was concerned with our brother and our fellow man into a society that was very self-centered, self-concerned, about money and power. That took us into the Eighties, but it really got started at the end of the Seventies. I guess it was a result of a disillusionment that the Sixties didn't quite pan out. For all the publicity about the baby boom generation and how we were going to change the world, we weren't in control. The same people who had *always* been in control were *still* in control. While we were out taking drugs and preaching flower power and having rock concerts and love-ins, people were running the country.

It sometimes seems that the Eagles are on the radio now as much as in the Seventies. How does it feel to be driving in your car and hear your songs?

FREY: It seems like all of our best songs have risen to the top—they're the ones that get played over and over again. You know, you get these printouts of your publishing, all the songs you've written, and of the Eagles songs, there are about eight or ten that just consistently do big numbers—and they also happen to be the ones I like. It just reminds you that maybe you are good at what you do and that what you did when you were young is still good now. That makes me feel good.

HENLEY: I feel good about it, too. It depends on the mood I'm in. Some days, "Hotel California" will come on the radio, and I'll turn it up and listen to it. Some days, I'll just turn it off or punch another station.

You are in the position of having lent an expression to the language: "Life in the fast lane."

HENLEY: Yeah, I wish I had a nickel for every fucking time somebody's used that.

FREY: We do! [*laughs*]

The Eagles had a hard time with the critics—a situation you didn't help by denouncing the New York Dolls from the stage in New York. Do you remember that incident?

FREY: God only knows what me, a microphone and a big PA could have done on any night. You know, it's hard to... we were—

HENLEY: Angry young men, using that anger to propel ourselves forward. I mean, it's not something we were really angry about. It's not like we lost sleep about the New York Dolls.

FREY: No, I think critics in New York were the real burr under our saddle. We became the symbol for that "laid-back, rich and don't-give-a-shit California lifestyle," you know what I mean? "These guys aren't struggling artists. Are you kidding?" Even when you're first coming out, they think you jump in your convertible and go to the beach, and then, when the sun goes down, you go to the club. We just had a problem with the New York critics. The New York Dolls were their flavor of the month, so that was probably why that came out.

HENLEY: The New York Dolls—where are they now? You know, all these so-called seminal groups—I don't get it. I don't understand what the big hoopla was about. We would just do things to irritate once in a while, but the resentment of us was part of a larger resentment—there always was a cultural rivalry between New York and L.A. New York has a certain amount of chauvinism about itself, and we fed the fires by talking back. Instead of ignoring it, we always had some rebuttal, which in retrospect was probably not a good idea. And then communications broke down completely. There was Irving Azoff's famous statement: "He is an Eagle and as such does not talk to the press."

FREY: That's when they started treating us nicer.

You spoke earlier about being educated by your success. What are the lessons of that education?

FREY: That you have to strive for perfection, but in rock & roll, you have to settle for excellence. We tried for three and a half years on *The Long Run* to make every note perfect, and we couldn't. Rock & roll is not supposed to be perfect. I mean, we would over-dub for days on guitar parts and things, when—

HENLEY: In retrospect, that's kind of silly. We spent too much time working on the album, when all one need do was listen to early Stones records to realize that all this striving for perfection is totally unnecessary. That's one thing. You learn a lot about human nature. We have more of a sense now of our place. I'm able to relax and enjoy it a lot more now and not take everything quite so seriously. Every time something bad happens, if you get a bad review or you have a bad performance, it's not the end of the world. Life goes on. You get perspective.

That's the part of rock & roll that is not talked about much. We get to travel a lot. You see a crowd of ten, twenty, thirty thousand people every night. You read local newspapers, and you really get an overview of what's going on in this country. Sometimes it's heartening, and a lot of times, it's frightening. You see that problems are widespread, and they're pretty much the same everywhere. If you spend any time touring the rest of the world, you can get a whole perspective of the globe and where this country stands in it. I mean, we've got a lot of work to do here. The underlying problem is greed and self-centeredness and the lack of a sense of community. Not enough people give a shit—that worries me.

What do you feel is the Eagles' legacy?

FREY: It's hard for me to say. We've left this collection of records, this body of work. In the end, I think our work mirrored the times, and that's what remains. That's what people will probably enjoy. For some people, it will be nostalgia, and for other people, it's like archaeology, like me listening to records from the Forties. That's not nostalgic for me, because I was never there. We are fortunate enough to be one of the bricks in the building.

HENLEY: I'm delighted that we have a history. We made all those albums, and we stayed together that long, which was a long time for a rock & roll group, even amidst all the turmoil.

It changed my whole life, didn't it? It's what I always wanted to do. I went to college for four years and studied, but I never had any intention of doing anything except this. It just worked out from certain twists of fate or something. I used to wonder about all that stuff: "Why me? Why not somebody else?" But we did work hard, and we were very determined.

Do you ever feel your past as an Eagle is a burden?

FREY: I think if you had asked Don and me that question two or three years after the band broke up, we'd have thought about it a lot more than we do now. For us, we're lucky enough to have gone on and done a few other things, so it's just part of us now. I don't see it as a problem. It was a problem maybe when I was thirty-two and making my first solo record. I've enjoyed the last ten years as much as I enjoyed the Seventies.

What's your sense about the future?

FREY: I just decided to be open to the possibilities. I think anything is possible. Some things seem possible that wouldn't have seemed possible a few years ago, related to maybe working with some of the guys again. Those possibilities are starting to show up.

HENLEY: Glenn and I were of like mind about several things, and now that we're older and more mature, we can apply what we've learned. If we do have another go-around, I think we can do a lot of positive things—for the environment, for the homeless, for any number of elements of society that need help where the government may have abandoned them. I mean, rock & roll now for me is not necessarily an end in itself. It's a means to some other end, to trying to improve the world and the community. I think rock & roll has always been that from the standpoint of rebellion, but I'd like to build upon that and make it a little more adult. I mean, let's face it: There's not going to be anarchy in this country—or even in the U.K. So let's get with the program and start affecting some real change and get something done, besides just yelling and screaming about it.

From an artistic standpoint, you've been able to say what you want to say in your solo work and still reach a very sizable audience. Why do you want to work with the Eagles again?

HENLEY: It won't change what I write about. It will increase the audience, which is the good part. I would get a lot more ears turned toward what I have to say. I'll probably write exactly what I would have written anyway.

People long for the past because it's so much safer than the future. The future is so uncertain, but the past is very concrete. We're living in very uncertain times. Even with the end of the Cold War, there are other considerations now: the economy, global warming, ozone depletion, widespread pollution of all kinds, and now this war in the Middle East has just flared up. There's a comfort people take in going back—I don't know if it's healthy or not. It's like people want to take the Seventies and pole-vault them over the Eighties and put them in front of them.

There are also a lot of young people who weren't there the first time around.

HENLEY: Yeah, they're at my concerts. It's odd. I could understand it in terms of the Beatles or somebody like that: "I missed the Sixties—I want to know what it's all about." But the Seventies? I guess I'm too close to it.

But you know, music is not in great shape right now, as far as I'm concerned. Music is not very musical anymore. People don't even have to be musicians anymore. They can borrow other material and just do what they want over it. I just got a tape from some local record company. They used part of one of our songs from the Seventies and just rapped over it. I resent that—go make up your own fucking music. They don't even have to make up their own grooves anymore. Man, I think that's bad for art, bad for music.

george clinton

By DAVID FRICKE

To most people, funk is a style of music, the sassy, electric Seventies stepchild of classic R&B. To George Clinton, it is "anything it need to be to save your *life*. . . . You can get so frustrated in life that you just want to jump out the window," he declares with a messianic gleam in his eye. "Funk tells you, 'Go ahead, man, but nobody gonna pay you any attention if you do.' It's a way of getting out of that bind you get in, mentally, physically."

"It's loose—it ain't that fuckin' serious," he continues, running a hand through his trademark coiffure—shoulder-length braids laced with long strands of Day-Glo thread. "To me, funk is 'Okay, let's start jammin',' and people just follow."

He should know. Clinton has been promoting "party" politics onstage and on record for more than three decades with the expanded family of singers, musicians and associated celebrants that originally composed his two main groups, Parliament and Funkadelic, and that now operates simply as the P-Funk All-Stars. During the Seventies, Clinton transformed black popular music with a propulsive, flamboyant mélange of locomotive polyrhythms, screaming Hendrixian guitars, sharp R&B vocal harmonies, acid-damaged rapping and jazzy brass that married the anarchic spirit of psychedelic rock with the good-foot properties of James Brown's down-home soul. (To fortify the funk, Clinton hired a number of former J.B. sidemen, including Fred Wesley, Maceo Parker and William "Bootsy" Collins, who went on to solo fame.) Over that already explosive mix, Clinton preached his singular gospel of mind expansion and sexual liberation, using a potent mix of ghetto realism, ribald wit and P-Funk slang. For visual sizzle, he took the glitter-rock look totally over the top, culminating in the 1976–77 Mothership Connection tour, which featured Clinton descending from an enormous spaceship.

The result was a long series of musically visionary and commercially successful albums by both groups—among them, Parliament's *Up for the Down Stroke* (1974), *Mothership Connection* (1976) and *Funkentelechy vs. the Placebo Syndrome* (1978) and Funkadelic's *Free Your Mind and Your Ass Will Follow* (1970), *Maggot Brain* (1971) and *One Nation Under a Groove* (1978). By the early Nineties, the entire P-Funk catalog was being sampled silly by young rap stars like De La Soul, Digital Underground, Jungle Brothers and Public Enemy, while the black-rock movement spearheaded by Living Colour and Fishbone took Clinton's original electric R&B concept to a new futurist plane.

Born in North Carolina, Clinton formed the original doo-wop version of the Parliaments as a teen in the mid-Fifties in Plainfield, New Jersey, where he ran his own barbershop. During the mid-Sixties, Clinton landed a staff writing gig at Motown Records, where, he admits, he picked up a lot of his tricks. "I learned how to write with clichés, puns and hooks," he says. "So when I got Parliament-Funkadelic, I just went stupid with it. Instead of one or two hooks, we'd have ten hooks in the same song and puns that were so stupid you could take 'em three or four ways."

The Parliaments finally went Top Twenty in 1967 with the gritty soul classic "(I Wanna) Testify." When Clinton became embroiled in a court battle over rights to the Parliaments' name, he simply realigned the group, bringing the backing band up front and calling it Funkadelic. In 1970 he won the legal battle and started recording Parliament (he dropped the *s*) and

Funkadelic, beginning a decade of extraordinary productivity that included numerous splinter groups and off-shoot productions signed to a multitude of record labels. Financial and legal complications forced him to put P-Funk on ice for a few years, but he returned to the charts in 1983 with the hit single "Atomic Dog."

Being a crucial influence on rap and pop music in the 1990s didn't take up all of Clinton's time. Fifty at the time of this 1990 interview, he was working on a new solo album for Prince's label Paisley Park and was featured in the film *Graffiti Bridge*.

Clinton has continued to tour, doing marathon four-hour shows with P-Funk for his still-growing rainbow coalition of fans. "It's like a religion," he says proudly. "At the same time, though, I'm sayin' it ain't nothin' but a party."

How do you feel about the resurgence of interest in and rampant sampling of the old Parliament-Funkadelic records?

I love it. In time, everything comes back around, and I was getting ready to fight nostalgia, make sure that people weren't coming from that point of view. And I didn't even have to fight it, because with sampling, it sounds like brand-new music. When De La Soul's record got real big, this lady we know, her son is ten years old, and she kept telling him that "Me Myself and I" was really P-Funk. And he said, "You think everything is James Brown and P-Funk!" So she went and got a copy of "(Not Just) Knee Deep" [*Uncle Jam Wants You*, 1979], and since De La Soul used so much of it on the track, he heard it and fell in love with it. The lady says she can't keep the kid out of her records now.

And now you got M.C. Hammer using "Turn This Mutha Out" ["P-Funk (Wants to Get Funked Up)," *Mothership Connection*]. Kids come up to me and say, "Man, he's ripping you off. They payin' you for this? That 'Humpty Dance': Ain't that yours?" Yeah, it is [*laughs*].

The remarkable thing about the P-Funk revival is that the young black rappers have picked up on the continuing relevance of the lyrics of those records, not just the musical grooves.

I like Public Enemy especially because they're using the philosophy. Like, *America Eats Its Young* [Funkadelic, 1972] sounds just like what they're saying today. Those songs sound like they were made today for today. We were talking about heroin and Vietnam. Today you could just substitute cocaine and South America.

According to P-Funk legend, your idea for a fusion of modern R&B, psychedelic rap and freakout ritual was the result of a gig the Parliaments played with Vanilla Fudge in 1967.

That was one of the first gigs we did when we went out on the road with "Testify." It was a show at a college in upstate New York. We did three nights with Vanilla Fudge and the Box Tops, and we had to use the Vanilla Fudge's equipment, because we didn't have any. And goddamn! That shit was so *bad!* It was extremely loud. So I went out and bought Jimi Hendrix's *Are You Experienced?*, Cream's album, a Richie Havens record and Sly's *Whole New Thing*. I gave them to Eddie [Hazel, guitarist] and Billy [Nelson, bassist] in the band. They were just fifteen, sixteen at the time, and the second night we used the Vanilla Fudge's equipment, we knew what to do with that motherfucker.

Was Hendrix a big influence on Funkadelic?

He was it. He took noise to church. With that feedback, you could almost write the notes of that feeling down. His music, like the Beatles', was way past intellectual. That shit was in touch with somethin' else. Once I saw what he was doing, I knew what to do with it on our thing.

There's a review of a show Funkadelic did at Ungano's, in New York, in 1970, in which the group is described as "a black soul version of the Stooges." Was that an apt description?

It was like the Stooges! I had a head with a dick shaved onto it right down the middle, with a star on the side and a moon on the other, and bald all around that. I was crawling all around the floor sticking my tongue out. We were James Brown on acid, the Temptations on acid, the Stooges—that's how people described us. Because we didn't just get costumes and look like hippies. We really were silly! When we got into town for a gig, I'd get to the Holiday Inn, take the Holiday Inn towel, cut four holes in it, and that was my diaper. I'd take the sheet off the bed, use that. Or take the drapes down and use them. We got away for three years without having to pay for costumes.

But even in the early Seventies, it was one thing to be white and crazy onstage, like Iggy Pop or Alice Cooper. It was quite another to be black and crazy. You must have seemed pretty scary to some audiences.

1
6
1

We were ten crazy niggers. With Jimi Hendrix, it was cool because it was him and two white boys. People don't go for ten niggers doin' that shit—pullin' off your clothes and runnin' around—but we had a hard-core following. The pimps used to tell us, "The whores won't work when you come to town." The slogan was "Pimps, whores and hippies." That was the audience we'd get.

On early Funkadelic classics, like "Mommy, What's a Funkadelic?" and "Free Your Mind and Your Ass Will Follow," you created the trademark P-Funk style of long, spacey jams topped with bluesy, socio-cosmological rapping. Were those tracks first developed onstage?

That was what the whole stage show was about, the chants and all. In fact, most of the stuff I said on those records I said onstage first.

But there was actually a strong social- and political-activist slant to P-Funk's peace-love-and-acid shtick.

I'd hung around Boston and Harvard for a long time, got into debates with people about B.F. Skinner and Timothy Leary. The shit was really political. It wasn't just being free and love and peace. The Vietnam War was really fucking things up. And the dope thing— I was from a place where everybody was a junkie. "Maggot Brain" and things like that were all about "How you gonna straighten yourself out when the things you're using, the drugs, your brain, are all fucked up?"

When you reactivated Parliament in 1974 with the album *Up for the Down Stroke,* how was it going to be different from Funkadelic?

No psychedelic guitars for Parliament and no horns for Funkadelic. We broke those rules a couple of times, but for the most part, that was the main difference. Funkadelic was the rock & roll band, with guitars dominating, the crazy stream-of-consciousness lyrics. Parliament was going to be as close to structure as we could get. I later used a lot of Funkadelic theory to do Parliament, but it was more structured. There were melodies, real songs, a straightforward message.

Parliament also took David Bowie's Ziggy Stardust look to new extremes with the wild, spangled suits, huge, stacked-heel boots and the spaceship you used on the Mothership Connection tour.

David Bowie was one of my favorites. He always had concepts. He was never the same two times out. There was the Beatles with their concept *Sgt. Pepper,* the Who with *Tommy,* David Bowie and Sly. That's

where we were coming from. By the time I got the name "Parliament" back, I knew the psychedelic thing was all but gone, so I went with glitter. When it came to *Mothership Connection,* I knew I had a hit record ready to go, so I bought the spaceship for the stage show, using all the record royalties to pay for it. And when we went glitter with Parliament, it was all structured. No matter how crazy it looked, it was really thought-out.

What did you think of your main competitors at the time, the other black superstar bands, like Earth, Wind & Fire and the Ohio Players?

The Ohio Players, I'd known them for a long time, back when we started Funkadelic. They were one of the hottest club bands around. But to me, all of them, when they got pop, they were just doing watered-down versions of Sly.

During the mid-Seventies height of Parliament-Funkadelic, you released as many as three albums a year between the two groups, not to mention splinter projects like Bootsy's Rubber Band, the Brides of Funkenstein and the Horny Horns. How did you manage to cut so many records so fast?

We would just go into the studio and cut. I would be in one studio, and to keep people out of my hair, I would tell 'em to go up to another studio and make something. We had so many people wanting to do things that we had to buy a studio just to keep 'em cutting. Every time I sent people somewhere else to work, they'd come back with two or three tracks that I could use.

And it helped keep all those important people together. And they got a payday; they got a session check or put out an album themselves. The one talent I had was the ability to keep people together. I knew how to keep personalities in place, how to use them. That is still the most important thing I do in P-Funk. I can get anything out of anybody. And I'm talking about some of the craziest motherfuckers in the world that nobody else wants to deal with.

How did you feel about disco, which started peaking commercially just as P-Funk went into its Eighties chart slide?

To me, disco was like fucking with one stroke. You could phone that shit in. Disco itself was funk, but all they did was take one funk beat and sanitize it to no end. It's irritating. I loved Donna Summer's records, but too much of it . . . The slogan behind "(Not Just) Knee Deep" was "Let's rescue dance music from the blahs."

^ The Mothership has landed!
MICHAEL OCHS ARCHIVES/VENICE, CA

Could you hear any P-Funk influence in the early rap hits by the Sugar Hill Gang, Kurtis Blow or Grandmaster Flash?

Sequence, that girl group on the Sugarhill label, they used "Tear the Roof off the Sucker" [from *Mothership Connection*]. Right from the giddyap, they were using my records. Early on, I knew rap was gonna stay, because so many people got so irritable about it. It reminded me of '55, when rock & roll first came along. "'Wop-bop-a-lu-bop'—what the hell's he saying? Gets on my nerves." Public Enemy gave rap class. They, to me, are like Bob Dylan. What he did for rock & roll, they're doing for rap. And Eric B. & Rakim are like Jimi Hendrix, as far as technique.

What about Prince? Can you spot your influence on him?

He's the cleverest, man. Even though there is an essence of what we do in his thing, he can do that with any music that's out. With "Raspberry Beret" and that whole album [*Around the World in a Day*], he did the same thing with the Beatles that he's done with us. He can sound a lot like us, but he's got a whole lot of other shit going.

What does he actually take from P-Funk?

Just the nerve, mainly. You can't pinpoint a lick or two. He doesn't copy that close. He's too good for that. His version of what we do is more like the nerve and his style of doing business.

How about Michael Jackson?

He's the baddest motherfuckin' performer there is. I wish he would let somebody like Prince produce him. Anybody else would end up just producing him the same way. Nobody would take him *out*.

If you were going to produce a Michael Jackson album, what would you do?

I would do him *literally* James Brown, because he can do that unlike anybody else. I knew him when he was eight, nine years old, when he was singing our song "Testify." I saw him do stuff like "Papa's Got a Brand New Bag" and "I Got You." I would just get Fred [Wesley], Bootsy and all them, just do a James Brown record with him, because he's got that world audience, and somebody has got to make him give them a fresh version of his shit, like it's supposed to be done.

How do you feel about the rise of slick, crossover crooners like Freddie Jackson and Peabo Bryson?

It's watered down. There's nothing fresh about that. They're just trying to redo the old soul stuff. But that's okay, because it just leaves more room for the real funk when it comes along.

What effect do you think the sound and ideology of P-Funk will continue to have on black popular music, especially with AIDS, crack and the homeless problem devastating black communities?

Our obligation is to survive, to show that it's possible to survive no matter what the fuck is going on. Because if you give up, if you just go ahead and keep shootin' dope knowing that needle could have AIDS, it's too late to think. You're already past the ability to make a decision, if you've just given up. Hopefully, our survival will inspire people so that they can make these decisions, to want to live and contribute.

163

daryl hall's
favorite philly soul songs
of the seventies

1 **"Love Don't Love Nobody,"** by the Spinners

2 **"One of a Kind (Love Affair),"** by the Spinners

3 **"Sadie,"** by the Spinners

4 **"Back Stabbers,"** by the O'Jays

5 **"Love Train,"** by the O'Jays

6 **"For the Love of Money,"** by the O'Jays

7 **"Me and Mrs. Jones,"** by Billy Paul

8 **"Break Up to Make Up,"** by the Stylistics

9 **"The Love I Lost,"** by Harold Melvin and the Blue Notes

10 **"If You Don't Know Me by Now,"** by Harold Melvin and the Blue Notes

11 **"Sideshow,"** by Blue Magic

1
6
4

the ramones

By CHUCK EDDY

The April 1977 issue of *16* magazine had teen icons the Bay City Rollers on the cover. Inside, in her "Music Makers" column—amid textual analysis of the Sylvers and David Soul—a writer named Mandy answered the question "What is Punk Rock?" This was, no doubt, the first time many young Americans had heard this curious phrase. "Punk Rock is a term being applied to lots of different groups!" wrote Mandy. "Most Punk Rock groups have one thing in common—a good, loud, exciting hard rock sound, and a tendency to keep songs fairly short." Actually, that's *two* things they have in common. Regardless, nobody has explained it better since.

Two months earlier, Mandy had gushed over "I Wanna Be Your Boyfriend," the new Ramones single, calling it "super romantic and sexy." "I Wanna Be Your Boyfriend," like another Ramones song called "Now I Wanna Sniff Some Glue," was in the grand tradition of "I wanna" records, dating back through the Stooges' "I Wanna Be Your Dog" to the Beatles' "I Wanna Hold Your Hand." Like other punk bands, the Ramones presented themselves as a return to what had once made rock & roll great, before it became soggy and serious and slick and stagnant. Punk set out to revive what it saw as simplicity, chaos, danger, irony, fun. So, throughout the middle Seventies, at such New York venues as the Mercer Arts Center and Max's Kansas City and CBGB, bar bands and art bands full of dropouts and prep school misfits and failed poets from Forest Hills and Rhode Island and Detroit ruled the roost, often glorifying being down and out, a condition that more than a few such scenesters consciously selected. They wore unusual haircuts and jumped up and down a lot. Most of these groups— the Mumps, Tuff Darts, Psychotic Frogs, Laughing Dogs—aren't even footnotes anymore.

In 1976, the Ramones, one of the best and most famous of these New York bands, toured England and instigated an explosion. The Sex Pistols—vermin that had found their artistic calling while killing time at a respected bondage-and-rubber outlet called Sex, owned by a Situationist huckster named Malcolm McLaren—had played their first show in November 1975; a year later, their singer snarling as though he were burning himself at the stake, they issued "Anarchy in the U.K.," their first single. Within months, it seemed every other disgruntled resident of the United Kingdom under the age of twenty had joined a band and released a punk single of his or her own. (The *her* was important—like no rock before, punk inspired women to develop their own voices.)

The New York bands had sung with their tongues in their cheeks, but in the U.K., punk was played as if far more were at stake than the future of rock & roll—the future of their nation, perhaps, or the human race. England, then, was where most of the enduring punk recordings—the early Pistols singles, the first Clash album, the Vibrators' *Pure Mania*, the Adverts' *Crossing the Red Sea*, X-Ray Spex's "Oh Bondage Up Yours!"—came from.

In 1977, people thought this stuff might take over the world, or at least the Top Forty. In England, at least for a while, it did. Back in the U.S.A., it didn't even come close. In both countries, though, bands playing original material appeared in every borough, suburb and hamlet, having learned from the Ramones and Pistols that "anyone could do it" (which turned out to be a bald-faced lie, but what the heck).

Every town had its own punk-rock club; in 1982, *Volume: International Discography of the New Wave* listed more than sixteen thousand records by more than seventy-five hundred bands on three thousand labels, as well as thirteen hundred fanzines. Eventually, the music split into scores of factions, encompassing everything from Marxist avant-funk to revivalist rockabilly to power pop and techno-disco. Of the sound's originators, one congregation of stubborn souls insisted on remaining true to punk as it was played in 1977, and until the late 1990s, the Ramones were still among them.

"There's some of us here today that still fuckin' *remembuh rock & roll radio!*" Joey Ramone shouted in 1990 from a concrete stage, lamenting the passing of the Animals and Murray the K, beating a horse that's been dead for decades. With the rest of his band, Joey was wrapping up the Cincinnati installment of 1990's Escape From New York, a summer package tour also starring Debbie Harry, Talking Heads spinoff Tom Tom Club and former Heads keyboardist Jerry Harrison (the last two units billing themselves collectively as Shrunken Heads), graduates all of the Bowery punk milieu of the mid-Seventies.

Joey, still a string bean in 1990, exuded a warped charisma none of the thousand punk frontmen he inspired can touch. Behind him, bedecked with that classic Ramones emblem—an American eagle clutching a baseball bat in one talon and an apple-tree branch in the other—was a canvas sheet painted to look like a brick wall. The canvas could represent the urban hell from which this band supposedly sprang, or the Phil Spector Wall of Sound they electrocuted into a wall of noise, or the wall whose collapse they celebrated in their beloved Germany in 1989. Or what it may represent is the wall that held the Ramones at square one, the wall that kept them, and so very much of the music they fathered and grandfathered, safe.

To Joey's left was C.J. Ramone, a bassist who moved around more than any of his proud pinhead siblings; onstage he was the new king of the Ramones' leg-spread stance. C.J. wasn't born till 1965. Too young to remember rock & roll radio, he grew up on the Ramones and the Dead Kennedys and Metallica; he knew only one other punk rocker at his high school. When Dee Dee Ramone defected to rap, C.J. figured he'd never attend a Ramones show again, but then the band hired him to take Dee Dee's place. C.J. was AWOL from the marines at the time. Joey says C.J. had the right attitude, but guitarist Johnny Ramone says he makes the band look young. That was a priority.

The Escape From New York tour was *not*, the principals emphasized, a nostalgia show, but when ? and the Mysterians played Bookie's Club 870 in Detroit in 1980, *that* was certainly nostalgia, and ? was a punk before CBGB punks were punks, and "96 Tears" came out in 1966, and *The Ramones* came out in 1976, and fourteen years is fourteen years, right? Johnny, clad in the band's best shag and a U.S. Army Special Forces T-shirt, insisted the Ramones weren't relics in 1990, because "we never stopped putting out records, and when I watch us on videotapes from five or ten years ago, I find out we're better now than we were then."

And they've got a point—to a point. Though there were a few well-bred waistline casualties who looked as if they had closed up the office early for the day, this 1990 Cincy crowd wasn't mostly old New Wavers out for memories; it was kids out for kicks, scrubbed suburban brats in Smiths and 7 Seconds and Faster Pussycat T-shirts. The teenybopper girls in Cure and Depeche Mode T's were way more lively than the rad boys in Misfits and Danzig T's, but every last member of the crowd was involved, screaming at lung tops while standing on seat tops.

The Ramones maintained a very loyal audience, and all the way back to "Sheena Is a Punk Rocker," Joey's songs suggested that he loves his disciples as much as they love him. "They know that we care about them," he has said. Their audience evolved over the years, from post-Warhol art students in the early days to gobbing mohawk wearers of yore to post-metal high-school students, but all along it was a self-classified community of misfits— "Gabba gabba we accept you we accept you one of us," goes the Ramones anthem "Pinhead."

In concert, the Ramones played the "hits" like "I Wanna Be Sedated," because that's what the fans screamed for. They played them like seasoned pros; the problem was, standing against seasoned professionalism was what once made this a great band.

And an important one, too, obviously. British punk can be read as a reaction to the dole queue and impending Thatcherism, but inasmuch as Ameripunk meant anything, it meant putting a generation of old farts out to pasture. At least that's what it meant if you're to believe most of the zillion words that have been written about it since—that the music had grown overblown and impersonal and corporate and soft, that the stars were all either blow-dried bores or black-tied jet-setters sniffing powder in the back of limos, blah blah blah. Punks defined themselves, or were defined, as the opposition; the New Wave audience identified itself as an "alternative." Drummer Marky Ramone has said how "in those days, there were a lot of stuffy people who took rock way too seriously." So punk rock, starting with the Ramones, changed the rules. It redefined *success*.

What does this formulation ignore? First, punk rock didn't just "happen." In New York, at least, it was a direct offshoot of glitter rock and typified by the New York Dolls, who were inspired by the British glitter of David Bowie, who was inspired in turn by New York's Velvet Underground, which also largely inspired mid-Seventies Cleveland bands like Rocket from the Tombs and the Electric Eels, both of which also drew on late-Sixties Detroit bands like the Stooges and the MC5, which were inspired by the Stones and the Doors... and so on.

Yet, in the early Seventies, while Joey Ramone was biding time at Slade and Black Sabbath shows and not finding them impersonal in any way he can remember, Marky Ramone was still Marc Bell, drumming for a band named Dust. As late as 1975 and 1976, AC/DC's *High Voltage* and Aerosmith's *Toys in the Attic* and Ted Nugent's "Free for All" were uniting punk volumes with punk tempos with punk attitudes with better-than-punk rhythm sections. Furthermore, unlike the bands the Gotham media were falling in love with at the time, these bands were selling records—to high-school kids, of all people!

So was punk rock really new? Who knows! The Ramones combined old stuff, mainly power chords and bubblegum-surfboard harmonies, but they did it in a brand-new way. "Our music was structured like nothing else was ever structured before it," according to Johnny. "Ballroom Blitz," by the Sweet, had gone Top Five the year before the suspiciously similar

"Blitzkrieg Bop" hit the racks, but the Sweet never had the Ramones' singleness of purpose. In Ramones rock, there was no respite, no letup; the slightest change—a hand clap, a falsetto, an echo, a three-second Farfisa or a twenty-second guitar solo—felt cataclysmic.

And nobody else had ever celebrated the fuck-up-at-life disease the way the Ramones did—nobody ever sang anything like "Sitting here in Queens / Eating refried beans / We're in all the magazines / Gulping down Thorazines" before. "We've always had this trademark," Joey has said. "I just figured it was some kind of chemical imbalance." They gave a voice to the junk-food anomie of postaffluent American adolescence—like Chuck Berry or *MAD* magazine, only sicker.

The Ramones still don't understand how this linked them with Blondie and Talking Heads and Television and Patti Smith. "I never thought we had anything in common with those bands," according to Joey. "We were the only hard-rock group there." But Talking Heads bassist Tina Weymouth has claimed that all the bands were making music that hadn't been made before, that "the Ramones were an art band, too, in their own way." To be that "spontaneous" in 1976, to record your album in a week for $6,400, to adopt a common last name and common leather-jacket-and-ripped-jeans uniform, to create such cartoonish personas—to do all these things required a degree of meticulous thought unheard-of in the land of AC/DC and Nugent and even Kiss. "What set the Ramones apart from all the hardcore bands that came later was their discipline," according to Weymouth. They chose to be primitive.

And boy, did the idea ever catch on. "I bet the Ramones influenced more bands than anybody else on the scene today," C.J. said in 1990. Between speed metal and the Sex Pistols and hardcore and the whole idea of do-it-yourself, which spawned the whole idea of local scenes, which spawned the whole idea of postpunk independent labels, C.J. may be right. Consider, too, all the onetime punk rockers who wound up as stars, invariably playing something other than punk rock—Billy Idol, the Beastie Boys, Belinda Carlisle, Neneh Cherry, Debbie Harry, Joan Jett, various members of Guns n' Roses. And then think of the Ramones T-shirts you'll find on the chests of guys in Def Leppard and Poison; then the Megadeth and Skid Row covers of the Pistols—sometimes it seems heavy metal simply absorbed punk outright. Then, by the mid-1990s, a whole new crop of bands had successfully taken up the punk rock mantle, Nirvana, Green Day, the Offspring and Rancid among them. With these bands, punk rock went platinum.

But back in 1990, the Ramones were into their fifth van in umpteen years (a Chevy with transmission problems) and had just released their twelfth album, *Brain Drain*, with its characteristic mix of a song about not fighting on Christmas, a Freddy Cannon cover, some leaden playing, some heartfelt crap, even some bubble-headed rock poetry in "Punishment Fits the Crime." "We try to maintain what the Ramones are known for—hard, fast, crazy music," Joey said at the time. Johnny agreed, "In this ever-changing world, the Ramones stay the same."

I think their tour manager, Monte Melnick, put it best: "The song Ramones the same."

billy idol's
top ten punk songs of the seventies

1 **"Raw Power,"** by Iggy [Pop] and the Stooges

2 **"Frankie Teardrop,"** by Suicide

3 **"Anarchy in the U.K.,"** by the Sex Pistols

4 **"Human Fly,"** by the Cramps

5 **"Public Image,"** by Public Image [Ltd.]

6 **"Love in a Void,"** by Siouxsie and the Banshees

7 **"Roadrunner,"** by Jonathan Richman [and the Modern Lovers]

8 **"Rock 'n' Roll Nigger,"** by Patti Smith

9 **"White Riot,"** by the Clash

10 **"Beat on the Brat,"** by the Ramones

1
6
9

ozzy osbourne's
favorite hard rock of the seventies

There really wasn't an abundance of heavy metal in the Seventies, so I made a list of hard-rock bands. Actually, it pisses me off that anyone with long hair and a mustache and a guitar is classified as heavy metal. I mean, everything from Bon Jovi to Metallica goes under heavy metal.

As far as I'm concerned, there was a much healthier situation for rock & roll in the Seventies than in the Eighties, when it became like a factory, a music factory—churn the bands out, make them stars for a week and then they die.

1 *Mountain Climbing,* by Mountain. When I first came to the States in 1970, we supported Mountain. In England, we would just go to a bar, plug in and play, and then in America, when I saw the way it was really done, it bowled me over. Rock & roll could have its own private jet, and it just blew me away.

That whole Mountain album with "Mississippi Queen"—it's ageless. It still sounds fucking great today.

2 **"Whole Lotta Love,"** by Led Zeppelin. I still get goose bumps. That middle section— fucking unbelievable! Those early Zeppelin albums were incredible productions. Nobody seems to do it anymore. I'd never heard anything like that before.

There's so many people trying to imitate Zeppelin now. I really don't understand it, because you'd think with technology...If you consider that when I was in Black Sabbath, we recorded our first album in twelve hours on a four-track machine. Now you go to a live show and find out the band's been lip synching all night long.

3 **"Bohemian Rhapsody,"** by Queen. The production is just incredible. It sounds better today than it did when it first came out. Some bands just go and scream through the ceiling.

I like a little bit of a melody, because if you're walking down the road, you're not going to start whistling the drum text or the guitar text. You hum the melody.

4 **"Only Women Bleed,"** by Alice Cooper. People are still recording that now. I toured with Alice in the early Seventies. At that time, he did strange things, weird theatrical stuff onstage. Alice is a lovely guy, great person.

5 **"Frankenstein,"** by Edgar Winter. I wasn't into his music, but there was this one track called "Frankenstein," this incredibly heavy riff. It was ballsy.

6 **"Smoke on the Water,"** by Deep Purple. That has to be one of the all-time classic heavy-metal riffs. That and "Iron Man" are the first songs everyone learns how to play. It shows you how fucking simple *we* were. For example, the original title for *Paranoid* was *War Pinks*. If you look at the album, there's a guy with a pink suit and a shield. We were in the studio and—I distinctly remember this—we needed three and a half minutes to finish the album. So we all got a bit stoned, and in three minutes, we wrote "Paranoid." It's just a stupid song that's spanned the time. I still play it some onstage 'cause kids want it.

It's simplicity very often that wins the day—one or two chords. AC/DC is just basic rock & roll, but they do it so fucking well.

7   **"Ballroom Blitz,"** by Sweet. It's a well-structured song. It doesn't go on too long, goes straight to the point, gets the fucking message across and goes.

8   **"Cum On Feel the Noize,"** by Slade. There are so many superstar bands who've not lasted five minutes because they've not got a good fucking melody. In England, Slade were like the Beatles for about two years, and then Quiet Riot released "Cum On Feel the Noize." It wasn't as good as the original by any stretch of imagination, but it went to Number Five in America. [Slade's] Noddy Holder is a real close friend of mine, and he's got a tremendous voice.

9   **"The Boys Are Back in Town,"** by Thin Lizzy. Everything Thin Lizzy did was just great. [Leader] Phil Lynott was just great. I'm amazed that he never really took off in America. People probably know that song because Bon Jovi did it.

10 **"Bang a Gong,"** by T. Rex. I remember seeing T. Rex in 1967, playing next to Jimi Hendrix in England. That's when it was called Tyrannosaurus Rex. What a tragic end. Marc Bolan was an all-out rock star. [Vocalist and songwriter Bolan died in a car accident in 1977.] He had a great look.

the eighties

By ANTHONY DeCURTIS

Who could have foreseen the brutal superficiality and greed of the Gimme Decade? In November 1980, Ronald Reagan was elected to his first term as president of the United States. A little more than a month later, on December 8, John Lennon was shot to death outside his apartment building in New York City. Each of those two events had its own all too real causes and consequences, but each has also come to bear the weight of symbol: Each is a lens through which the mood and the manners of the Eighties, the cultural climate of the decade that followed, may be read.

Some say the Sixties died at Altamont; others say the Sixties died at Kent State. In any case, whatever vestige of Sixties-style visionary thinking and progressive politics managed to survive the Seventies—when, after all, the Watergate revelations and Nixon's resignation at least partly vindicated Sixties radicalism and inspired a brief resurgence of idealism among the young—who can deny that the election of Ronald Reagan proved to be the fatal blow to the Sixties dream? Even the liberal values of the Great Society, which were little more than an extension of the civilizing efforts of FDR's New Deal, were anathema to Reagan— let alone the wild utopian urges that were meant to transport us to the Gates of Eden, the road of counterculture excess that would lead us to the Palace of Wisdom.

The generous collective impulses of the Sixties may ultimately have yielded to the Me Decade hedonism of the Seventies, but who knew that the next stop would be the pinched privatism, the smug selfishness, the glib pragmatism, the grim status consciousness, the greed masking as taste, the brutal superficiality of the Eighties? Who knew that the hung-over sybarites of the Me Decade would transform, as if in the course of a nationwide Night of the Living Dead, into the desperately sober workaholics of the Gimme Decade?

Could there possibly have been a place for the likes of John Lennon in such a world? The point is not that Lennon was a saint, too good to live among the gleefully solvent sinners of the Eighties. It's just that he was too ungovernable, too unlikely to play by the rules, too interested in the margins to succumb to the savage mainstreaming of those ten years. The willful experimentalism, loopy romanticism and smiling politics that Lennon represented—this was a man, you will recall, who believed that bed-ins and planting acorns could bring about world peace—are not virtues that would have carried much weight in an era during which greed was the ultimate good. The characteristics that define the personality of Lennon's assassin, Mark David Chapman—an obsession with Lennon's media image to the point of obliterating the reality of Lennon the person, a worship of Lennon's power and celebrity so intense that it shaded into violence and hatred, a need to destroy the ideal he could not himself attain—are far more central to an understanding of the decade.

Like the killings at Kent State, Lennon's death struck at the very souls of a generation and made idealism seem senseless, even dangerous. The vacuum left in those souls was filled in the Seventies with a craving for pleasure that could be kindled in a moment and extinguished just as quickly, pleasure not as a means of self-discovery—not even to be enjoyed for its own delicious sake—but as a distraction from numbness, a way to feel *something*, however briefly. Money and possessions—things that could be counted, measured, and used and that, for those reasons, provided the illusion of certainty—filled the vacuum in the Eighties. That so many of the people who wept and lit candles to mourn John Lennon's death eventually fell into step with the unforgiving individualism of the Age of Reagan is only one of the innumerable contradictions of the decade.

Musically, the Eighties got off to an unsteady start indeed. The punk explosion of the Seventies had succeeded in stalling the alienating superstar juggernaut that had defined the earlier years of that decade, but punk itself became too self-infatuated and failed to gain much of a popular audience. Progressive artists like Talking Heads and Elvis Costello had found a niche, but many of their contemporaries had either burned out or simply fallen by the wayside. In the early years of the decade, the economy was poor, video games—a technological harbinger of things to come—had seized the imagination of the young and record sales were down significantly. It hardly seemed as if music mattered at all.

Then an event occurred that would energize the music scene once again and set in motion all the forces that would go on to shape the popular culture of the Eighties. On May 16, 1983, before a viewership of nearly fifty million people, Michael Jackson performed his Number One single "Billie Jean" on *Motown 25: Yesterday, Today, and Forever*, the television special that commemorated the twenty-fifth anniversary of Motown Records. After that, for better or worse, nothing was the same.

To that point, Michael Jackson's *Thriller*, which had been released on December 1, 1982, and had hit Number One during Christmas week, seemed as if it were going to be a successful record in the manner of *Off the Wall*, Jackson's fine previous solo album, which was released in 1979 and had sold more than six million copies. Jackson's electrifying performance of "Billie Jean" sent fans streaming into record stores, though, where they often purchased another album or two before leaving, giving the music industry a much-needed economic shot in the arm.

Thriller would go on to sell some fifty million copies worldwide, making it one of the best-selling albums in history, but its significance is far greater than even this astonishing number would indicate. It must be remembered that Jackson's appearance on the Motown special was not exclusively, or even primarily, a musical performance. Jackson lip synched to a recorded track—the better to execute his breathtaking dance steps, including the mind-boggling Moonwalk—and there were no musicians onstage even to create the illusion that a band was playing. For imagery, atmosphere, costuming and choreography, Jackson drew on the video he had made for "Billie Jean"—a prescient strategy that would go on to become conventional wisdom for artists like Madonna, Paula Abdul, Jackson's sister Janet and a host of other acts in the coming years. In a decade in which visuals meant as much as music, and live performance aspired to mimicking the static perfection of videos, Jackson's rendering of "Billie Jean" on *Motown 25* was a watershed.

Just about a month or two before *Motown 25* aired, MTV had broken its de facto boy-cott of black performers and begun showing Jackson's "Billie Jean" and "Beat It" clips. In the "Beat It" video, Jackson's audacious fusion of heavy metal—Eddie Van Halen played guitar on the track—and black street-gang imagery proved forward-looking, and Jackson and MTV proved to be a peerless match.

Founded in 1981, MTV had been flexing its muscles for a couple of years, finding a youthful audience primarily for a seemingly endless series of visually striking British bands of questionable talent like Duran Duran, Thompson Twins, and Men Without Hats and, to far more desirable effect, shaking up radio's monopoly on hitmaking. Still, MTV's standing was sufficiently precarious at the time that, rumor had it, CBS Records pressured the network into showing Jackson's videos by threatening to pull the clips of all its other acts. By the end of the decade, MTV's preeminence was so thoroughly established that such a threat would have been tantamount to filing for bankruptcy.

Quite apart from its considerable musical merits, *Thriller* defined both a strategy and a standard for success in the Eighties. The Beatles, Bob Dylan and the Rolling Stones had liberated recording artists from the tyranny of the hit single in the Sixties and established the album as a means of making an artistic statement. That tyranny returned in spades in the Eighties. Artistic statements or not, albums were seen as little more than collections of singles in the wake of *Thriller*'s seven Top Ten hits—and this was as true of *Born in the U.S.A.* and *The Joshua Tree* as of *Like a Virgin*, as true of *Purple Rain* as of *Forever Your Girl*. You might be a brilliant songwriter and a stunning musician, but after *Thriller*'s groundbreaking videos and the apotheosis of MTV, you'd better be something of an actor, too—or at least a pretty face.

And about those sales figures: A gold record—earned by sales of more than 500,000 records—might have impressed people in the Sixties and Seventies, but those days were long gone. After *Thriller*, platinum sales—earned by selling a million or more copies—were a prerequisite for stardom. Except for rare prestige acts—performers whose recognized status as important artists made them valuable to record companies despite their poor sales—the notion that you could have a productive career selling a few hundred thousand albums with each release was dead.

To a greater degree than ever before, marketing—the creation and selling of an image—became an essential component of an artist's success. Videos, video compilations, long-form videos, corporate sponsorships, product endorsements, T-shirts, book deals, interviews,

television appearances, movie tie-ins, songs for soundtracks—all that began to envelop what was once considered a rebel's world, the world you chose because you had no other choice or you hated the idea of working for the man, because you wanted independence and freedom and nothing less, because you wanted that greatest of all possible goods, that most sublime of all possible states: to be a rock & roll star. Being a rock & roll star became a *job*, and true to the Eighties ethic, you'd better be willing to put in the hours and produce—to smile and make nice with the powers that be—or you might as well go back to the bars.

By the mid-Eighties, rock & roll was well on its way to becoming terminally safe. Joining a rock band had become a career move like any other, about as rebellious as taking a business degree, and if you got lucky, more lucrative. Your accountant was likely to be as hip as your lead singer. And far from resisting the marketing demands made of them, artists seemed eager to sell out, to lease their songs to sell products, to put their dreams in the service of commerce.

Then just as it seemed that rock & roll was incapable of offending anyone, Tipper Gore discovered the line about masturbation in "Darling Nikki," on Prince's *Purple Rain* album, and founded the Parents' Music Resource Center (PMRC). The drive to place warning stickers on albums was under way. Due to Gore's influential standing and that of her colleague Susan Baker, wife of then–Secretary of State James A. Baker III, Senate hearings were held in which members of Congress pondered the meaning of rock lyrics. Rock & roll was the first target in the war on the arts that would soon escalate.

Eventually—and predictably—the controversy over lyric content and the effects of popular music on young people centered on the two musical forms that, despite their massive sales, still retained something of an outsider's edge: rap and heavy metal. Given how polarized our society became during the Reagan years, it is impossible not to see elements of racial and class prejudice in that development. While both genres have very much entered the mainstream, the core audience for rap is still black, and the core audience for metal still consists largely of working-class whites. These constituencies are typically not given much credit for being able to tell the difference between dramatic situation in a song and the realities of their own lives.

For that matter, the performers who speak to those constituencies are not capable of that distinction, either. If Eric Clapton—who is white and, better yet, English—covers a Bob Marley song and sings about shooting the sheriff, it's understood that he's an "artist" and doesn't really mean it. He can enjoy a Top Ten hit unhindered by questions about his motives or the effect on his listeners of the song he is singing.

Meanwhile, if the members of N.W.A., who are black, rap about a violent confrontation with the police, as they did on their blistering 1988 album *Straight Outta Compton*, they are presumed to be too primitive to understand the distinction between words and actions, between life and art. Their reward is organized boycotts and FBI harassment. In the case of 2 Live Crew, the reward is arrest and potential imprisonment. In many ways, the response that those groups have ignited—along with the legal difficulties endured by Ozzy Osbourne and Judas Priest—lends validation to the provocative content of much rap and heavy metal. The closest parallel to this persecution is the Nixon administration's effort to deport John Lennon in the Seventies because of his activism and the political content of his music.

But if rock & roll succumbed to the ethos of greed that characterized the Gimme Decade, and if it is still struggling to find the conviction to battle the incursions of bluenoses, it also helped restore a semblance of social consciousness to a period that, for the most part, borrowed its attitudes toward the less fortunate from Ronald Reagan and Margaret Thatcher. It took Bob Geldof, the charmingly brash leader of a failing Irish rock band, for example, to focus the attention of the entire world on the famine in Africa with Band Aid and Live Aid.

In response to a statement Bob Dylan made during his performance at the Live Aid concert in Philadelphia, John Mellencamp, Willie Nelson and Neil Young organized a series of concerts to assist struggling farmers in America's heartland. U2 headlined a series of shows in 1986 that helped bring a little-known London-based human rights organization called Amnesty International to the forefront of political awareness in the United States. Bruce Springsteen, Sting, Peter Gabriel and Tracy Chapman carried Amnesty's banner around the world—often to countries with frightening human rights records—two years later.

Those high-profile actions were not universally celebrated, however. They occasionally drew criticism—some of it justified or at least understandable. The big show could be seen as a kind of quick fix, and the quick fix, preferably as executed by internationally known celebrities, was a very Eighties phenomenon—as was the sense of boredom and even resentment that just as quickly set in when the quick fix inevitably failed to work.

Consequently, it was important that mammoth gestures on the order of Live Aid and the Amnesty tours were backed up by hundreds of artists like Jackson Browne, KRS-One, Living Colour, R.E.M., Simple Minds and 10,000 Maniacs. These performers consistently played benefits and supported causes in quotidian ways that demonstrated that problems do not disappear because a bevy of superstars fill a stadium and move their fans to dial an 800 number.

If rockers looked beyond the borders of their cities and countries and addressed the larger issues in the world around them, they also looked beyond their aesthetic borders for inspiration in their music. Talking Heads, led to African rhythms by their producer Brian Eno, stunned the music world in 1980 with the release of *Remain in Light*, an album whose relentless drive and thematic reach set the stage for similar experiments by other artists. Peter Gabriel's solo records and performing bands through the Eighties borrowed a host of sounds from musicians around the world. Gabriel returned the favor by establishing his Realworld label, distributed by Virgin Records, in 1989 to bring what had become known as world music to the West.

Certainly the most commercially successful—and controversial—cross-cultural fusion was Paul Simon's *Graceland*. Released in 1986 in a charged political atmosphere, the album drew critical raves but also incited a firestorm of protest because Simon had visited South Africa to record the album, violating the cultural boycott declared by the United Nations and the African National Congress, the organization leading the struggle against apartheid. The debate that ensued was bitter and prolonged. The musical merits of the album often seemed beside the point as the discussion centered on the proper role of artists in the political battles of their time. Undoubtedly, the experience was unpleasant for everyone involved, but it

provided further evidence of popular music's vitality and its ability to comment on and even enter the essential struggles of the age.

In addition to his political activism in support of Amnesty International and efforts to help preserve the rain forests, Sting broadened his musical palette in the Eighties, leaving behind the Police to work with jazz musicians like saxophonist Branford Marsalis and pianist Kenny Kirkland on his two groundbreaking solo albums, *The Dream of the Blue Turtles* and *…Nothing Like the Sun.* Onstage, Sting's bands played like *bands*—a virtual miracle of the decade in which improvisation, not to mention playing instruments at all, was held to an absolute minimum so as to make sure musicians did not fall out of time with prerecorded accompaniment or computerized lighting cues.

Springsteen, U2 and R.E.M. also played an essential role in preserving the human element in rock & roll at a time when technology threatened to overwhelm flesh and blood. Springsteen ran the gamut from the stark, acoustic balladry of *Nebraska* to the booming rock & roll of his massively popular breakthrough album, *Born in the U.S.A.,* all the while keeping the lives of his characters in rich focus with all the skill of a masterful short-story writer. U2 came roaring out of Dublin in 1980 with a message of faith and passion that eventually reached an audience of millions with *The Joshua Tree* in 1987. The anemic British synth-pop that U2 blew off the international stage early in the decade with fervent albums like *Boy* and *War* is now, for the most part, a dim memory.

Just as U2 put Dublin on the pop-music map, R.E.M. emerged from Athens, Georgia, in 1981 with the independently released single "Radio Free Europe"/ "Sitting Still" and gradually built an audience through relentless touring and an inspiring refusal to compromise with the more absurd edicts of the music industry. Throughout the Eighties, R.E.M. stood as a model of how a young band could remain true to its own idiosyncratic vision and still reach large numbers of listeners.

By the end of the Eighties, rap—which got its start in the mid-Seventies in the South Bronx and took the country by storm in 1986, when Run-D.M.C. (with the help of Aerosmith on the smash single "Walk This Way") and the Beastie Boys each racked up multiplatinum albums—was bearing much of the brunt of criticism for how soulless music had become. Indeed, rap's reliance on prerecorded rhythm tracks and sounds borrowed—some would say stolen—through sampling continues to make the genre all too vulnerable to such charges.

Nevertheless, at a time when most pop songs featured lyrics that were hardly worth any attention at all, rap placed words and the human voice at the very center of its sound. All talk about the irresistibility of hip-hop beats aside for the moment, what could possibly be more human than the insistent, demanding voices that came blasting out of tracks like Grandmaster Flash and the Furious Five's "The Message," Run-D.M.C.'s "King of Rock" or Public Enemy's "Bring the Noise"? Among its many other contributions to music in the Eighties, rap gave the big lie to the view—so common among rockers and some tediously hip rock critics—that lyrics don't matter.

A black rocker in the tradition of Jimi Hendrix, Prince was perhaps the artist who moved most gracefully amid even the most dangerous currents of the Eighties. Before it became fashionable—or even fashionably controversial—Prince shattered sexual stereotypes in 1980 with *Dirty Mind*, a bold rock-funk fusion that boasted songs about incest, oral sex, and troilism and a cover that featured Prince himself in black bikini underpants, all without seeming the slightest bit sensational. The urgent staccato riff that drove that album's title track—the essence of Minneapolis funk—would prove to be one of the most influential sounds of the decade. His work was a major target of the censorship brigade, but Prince never condescended to enter the fray, even mustering, presumably on the basis of his spiritual beliefs, some sympathy for his tormentors.

Prince also managed the visual demands of the decade with flair, offering up both a ter-rific feature film, *Purple Rain*, and a string of exciting videos. Shifting styles in ways that only rarely seemed contrived, he set certain trends, trailed after others, followed daring statements with vapid ones and, at a time when many artists were all too willing to pander, did pretty much whatever the fuck he pleased. It was heartening.

The Eighties more or less ended in January 1989 when Ronald Reagan left office. The vicious presidential campaign of 1988—in which the Republican Party gleefully played on white racial fears, wrapped its candidate, the insipid George Bush, in the flag and used McCarthyite rhetoric to make even the most centrist views seem seditiously un-American—now seems like the last dying gasps of cynical Eighties values.

As often happens, the uncertainty of the future sent people scurrying to the past for reassurance. This tendency achieved a certain crazed extreme in 1989, a year that spent most of its time trying its damnedest to be 1969—or at least an airbrushed version of 1969, blur-ring all the wrenching complexities of that year. Twenty years after Altamont, the Rolling Stones filled stadiums around the country and were the most popular show on the road. Nearly twenty years after the breakup of the Beatles, Paul McCartney dusted off a healthy bunch of Beatles songs and launched a highly successful American tour. Twenty years after they sang about how you "got to revolution," the members of Jefferson Airplane reunited for a series of shows so impossibly lame that it seemed like a Las Vegas lounge act's rendition of the greatest hits of the Summer of Love. And, of course, the twentieth anniversary of Woodstock inspired endless commentaries about the days of peace, love and granola in the mud.

Looking to the past, though, does not need to be an act of escapism or nostalgia, particu-larly in a country that is so extremely in need of a meaningful sense of history. An appreciation of the Sixties would be better served by allowing that decade's lessons to be enacted, not simply packaged and sold back to us as a sitcom. Those lessons are simple and important: the belief that we are not simply individuals but part of a larger culture that requires our most earnest efforts and ideas. The conviction that the worlds within and outside of ourselves are subject to transformation, that our actions can shape the future, that what we choose to do matters deeply. The insistence that America has a place for our best selves, and to the degree it doesn't, it must be changed. The notion that music can help formulate a vision toward which we can aspire.

And if we must look back to Woodstock, remember that Jimi Hendrix, the man who closed the show that last morning, once wondered what would happen if six turned out to be nine. What if.

my favorite eighties recordings

By SINÉAD O'CONNOR

1   *Straight Outta Compton,* by N.W.A. It's definitely the best rap record I've ever heard. Of course, I can see why people might be offended by the lyrics, but as a human being and not as a public figure, I'm not offended at all. I realize from reading interviews with people like Ice Cube, when they explain that they're not talking about women in general but about particular women they know, it makes a lot of sense.

I think the sound of the record is brilliant. I really like hard-core hip-hop and reggae stuff, so it's right up my flight of stairs.

2   *No Guru, No Method, No Teacher,* by Van Morrison. Of his records, this is the one that to me feels the most obviously spiritual. If you're fed up or in any way confused and you listen to this record, it makes you feel better. I like the strings. I just love Van Morrison. He's my hero. You can just listen to it and listen to it—it's really hypnotic.

3   *Infidels,* by Bob Dylan. This is really special to me because I was always mad into Bob Dylan when I was growing up. When *Infidels* came out, I nearly died 'cause it's so good. In particular, I like "Sweetheart Like You" and "Jokerman."

4   **"Apartheid Fe Conquer,"** by Shelly Thunder. Reggae is my favorite music. This song in particular is really upsetting, really sad.

5   **"One Blood,"** by Junior Reid. A song that just says that we're all in the same race and we can all be friends and need to stop creaming each other and blowing each other away. He's a reggae guy—he did the rap on the Soup Dragons record [see below].

6   **"Love Me Baby,"** by J.C. Lodge and Tiger. Ragamuffin is my favorite reggae style, and that's what they do. Lodge also did a record called "Telephone Love," which I really like.

7   *Money Mad,* by London Posse, and

8   *Give It Up,* by NSO. Two brilliant London bands. I like rappers with London accents. I think they're really wonderful.

9   **"Ghetto Heaven,"** by the Family Stand. Because it reminds me of someone.

10 **"I'm Free,"** by Soup Dragons. That's just how I feel at the moment.

my favorite eighties recordings

By SUZANNE VEGA

Most of these are records that I listen to as opposed to records that I think are important. I decided that rather than put the ones that I admire from a distance, I'd choose the ones I played a lot.

(In no particular order)

1 *Pirates,* by Rickie Lee Jones

2 *Synchronicity,* by the Police

3 *So,* by Peter Gabriel

4 *Hatful of Hollow,* by the Smiths

5 *Murmur,* by R.E.M.

6 *The Dreaming,* by Kate Bush

7 *Staring at the Sea,* by the Cure

8 *Lincoln,* by They Might Be Giants

And then some other ones I also liked, the second tier:

9 *In My Tribe,* by 10,000 Maniacs

10 *I'm Your Man,* by Leonard Cohen

11 *A Walk Across the Rooftops,* by the Blue Nile

12 *Learning to Crawl,* by the Pretenders

When I listen to some of these records, I feel something corny like, "These are the people that helped define the time." Then there are others who you feel would be themselves no matter what. Rickie Lee Jones, to me, is someone who does not define the Eighties but is very much herself and would be regardless of what was happening at any particular time. Whereas when I hear the Cure, it brings back a whole piece of my life and what I was doing at that time. They feel very much, to me, of their time. I hope that's not insulting; I think it's just as well if an album brings back 1984, like the Smiths record.

The Police write with an edge, which is something I was always attempting to do. I don't think it's perceived that way, but in 1981, when I was first trying to write with an edge, I listened to the Police and Prince records. Those records, I think, are melodically terrific.

Chrissie Hynde is just a person who's very consistent and will probably continue to write in her own style. Every single song on *Learning to Crawl* is one that you'd recognize, and each song has its own character.

The beginning of the Eighties were very different from the end. It just seemed to do an about-face right in the middle. It started off ironic and ended up *really* sincere.

bruce
springsteen

MIKAL GILMORE

On the night of November 5, 1980, Bruce Springsteen stood onstage in Tempe, Arizona, and began a fierce fight for the meaning of America. The previous day, the nation had turned a fateful corner: With a stunning majority, Ronald Reagan—who campaigned to end the progressive dream in America—was elected president of the United States. It was hardly an unexpected victory. In the aftermath of Vietnam, Watergate, the hostage crisis in Iran and an economic recession, America developed serious doubts about its purpose and its future, and

to many voters, Reagan seemed an inspiring solution. When all was said and done, however, the election felt stunning and brutal, a harbinger of the years of mean-spiritedness to come.

The singer was up late the night before, watching the election returns, and stayed in his hotel room the whole day, brooding over whether he should make a comment on the turn of events. Finally, onstage that night at Arizona State University, Springsteen stood silently for a moment, fingering his guitar nervously, and then told his audience, "I don't know what you guys think about what happened last night, but I think it's pretty frightening." Then he vaulted into an enraged version of his most defiant song, "Badlands."

On that occasion, "Badlands" stood for everything it had always stood for—a refusal to accept life's meanest fates or most painful limitations—but it also became something more: a warning about the spitefulness that was about to visit our land as the social and political horizon turned dark. "I wanna spit on the face of the badlands," Springsteen sang with an unprecedented fury on that night, and it was perhaps in that instant that he reconceived his role in rock & roll.

In a way, his action foreshadowed the political activism that would transform rock & roll during the 1980s. As the decade wore on, Springsteen would become one of the most outspoken figures in pop music, though that future probably wasn't what he had in mind that night. Instead, Springsteen was simply focusing on a question that, in one form or another, his music had been asking all along: What does it mean to be born an American?

Well, what does it mean to be born in America? Does it mean being born to birthrights of freedom, opportunity, equity and bounty? If so, then what does it mean that many of the country's citizens never truly receive those blessings? And what does it mean that in a land of such matchless vision and hope, the acrid realities of fear, repression, hatred, deprivation, racism and sexism also hold sway? Does it mean, indeed, that we *are* living in badlands?

Questions of this sort—about America's nature and purpose, about the distance between ideals and its truths—are, of course, as old as the nation itself, and finding revealing or liberating answers to those questions is a venture that has obsessed (and eluded) many of the country's worthiest artists, from Nathaniel Hawthorne to Norman Mailer, from John Ford to Francis Coppola. Rock & roll—an art form born of a provocative mix of American myths, impulses and guilt—has also aimed, from time to time, to pursue those questions, to mixed effect. In the 1960s, in a period of intense generational division and political rancor, Bob Dylan and the Band, working separately and together, explored the idea of America as a wounded family in albums like *The Basement Tapes, John Wesley Harding* and *The Band*; in the end, though, artists shied from the subject, as if something about the American family's complex, troubled blood ties proved too formidable. Years later, Neil Young (like the Band's Robbie Robertson, a Canadian obsessed by American myths) confronted the specter of forsworn history in works like *American Stars 'n' Bars, Hawks and Doves* and *Freedom*. Yet, like too many other artists or politicians who have come face to face with how America has recanted its own best promises, Young finally didn't seem to know what to say about such losses. In some ways, Elvis Presley, a seminal figure for Springsteen, came closest to embodying the meaning of America in his music. That's because he tried to seize the nation's dream of fortune and make himself a symbol of it. It's also because once Presley had that dream, the dream found a way of undoing him—leading him to heartbreak, decline, death. American callings, American fates.

Bruce Springsteen followed his own version of the fleeting American dream. He grew up in the suburban town of Freehold, New Jersey, feeling estranged from his family and community, and his refusal to accept the limitations of that life fueled the songwriting in his early, largely autobiographical LPs. Indeed, records like *Greetings From Asbury Park, N.J.; The Wild, the Innocent & the E Street Shuffle;* and *Born to Run* were works about flight from dead-end small-town life and thankless familial obligations, and they accomplished for Springsteen the very dream that he was writing about: That is, those records lifted him from a life of mundane reality and delivered him to a place of bracing purpose. From the outset, Springsteen was heralded by critics as one of the brightest hopes in rock & roll—a songwriter and live performer who was as alluring and provoking as Presley and as imaginative and expressive as Dylan—and Springsteen lived up to the hoopla: With his 1975 album, *Born to Run*, Springsteen fashioned pop's most form-stretching and eventful major work since the Beatles' *Sgt. Pepper's Lonely Hearts Club Band*. For all the praise and fame the album won him, it couldn't rid Springsteen of his fears of solitude, and it couldn't erase his memory of the lives of his family and friends. Consequently, his next LP, *Darkness on the Edge of Town*, was a stark and often bitter reflection of how a person could win his dreams and yet still find himself dwelling in a dark and lonely place— a story of ambition and loss as ill-starred and deeply American as *Citizen Kane*.

With *The River*, released in 1980, Springsteen was still writing about characters straining against the restrictions of their world, but he was also starting to look at the social conditions that bred lives split between the dilemmas of flight and ruin. In Springsteen's emerging mythos, people still had big hopes, but they often settled for delusional loves and fated family lives. In the album's haunting title song, the youthful narrator gets his girlfriend pregnant and then enters a joyless marriage and a toilsome job in order to meet his obligations. Eventually, all the emotional and economic realities close in, and the singer's marriage turns into a living, grievous metaphor for lost idealism: "Now, all them things that seemed so important," sings Springsteen, "Well, mister, they vanished right into the air; / Now I just act like I don't remember; / Mary acts like she don't care." In *The River*'s murky and desultory world, people long for fulfillment and connections, but as often as not they end up driving empty mean streets in after-midnight funks, fleeing from a painful nothingness into a more deadening nothingness.

The River was Springsteen's pivotal statement. Up to that point, he had told his tales in florid language, in musical settings that were occasionally operatic and showy. Now he was streamlining both the lyrics and the music into simpler, more colloquial structures, as if the realities he was trying to dissect were too bleak to support his earlier expansiveness. *The River* was also the record with which Springsteen began wielding rock & roll less as a tool of personal mythology than as a means of looking at history, as a way of *understanding* how the lives of the people in his songs were shaped by the conditions surrounding them and by historical forces beyond their control.

This drive to comprehend history came to the fore during the singer's remarkable 1980–1981 tour in support of *The River*. Springsteen had never viewed himself as a political-minded performer, but a series of events and influences—the near-disaster of the Three Mile Island nuclear reactor and his subsequent participation in the No Nukes benefit, at New York City's Madison Square Garden in September 1979—began to alter that perception. Springsteen read Joe Klein's biography of folksinger Woody Guthrie and was impressed with the way popular songs could work as a powerful and binding force for political action.

In addition, he read Ron Kovic's harrowing personal account of the Vietnam War, *Born on the Fourth of July*. Inspired by the candor of Kovic's anguish—and by the bravery and dignity of numerous other Vietnam veterans he had met—Springsteen staged a benefit at the L.A. Sports Arena in August 1981 to raise funds and attention for the Vietnam Veterans of America. On one night of the Los Angeles engagement, Springsteen told his audience that he had recently read Henry Steele Commager and Allan Nevins's *Short History of the United States* and that he was profoundly affected by the book. A month earlier, speaking of the same book, he had told a New Jersey audience, "The idea [of America] was that there'd be a place for everybody, no matter where you came from . . . you could help make a life that had some decency and dignity to it. But like all ideals, that idea got real corrupted. . . . Didn't know what the government I lived under was doing. It's important to know... about the things around you." Now, onstage in Los Angeles, getting ready to sing Woody Guthrie's "This Land Is Your Land," Springsteen spoke in a soft, almost bashful voice as he told his audience, "There's a lot in [the history of the United States]... that you're proud of, and then there's a lot of things in it that you're ashamed of. And that burden, that burden of shame, falls down. Falls down on everybody."

In 1982, after the tour ended, Springsteen was poised for the sort of massive break-through that people had been predicting for nearly a decade. *The River* had gone to the top of *Billboard's* albums chart, and "Hungry Heart" was a Top Ten single; it seemed that Springsteen was finally overcoming much of the popular backlash that had set in several years earlier, after numerous critics hailed him as rock & roll's imminent crown prince.

After the tour, though, the singer was unsure about what direction he wanted to take in his songwriting. He spent some time driving around the country, brooding, reading, thinking about the realities of his own emotional life and the social conditions around him, and then he settled down and wrote a body of songs, accompanied for the most part by his ghostly sounding acoustic guitar. He later presented the songs to Jon Landau and the E Street Band, but neither Landau nor the musicians could find the right way to flesh out the doleful, spare-sounding new material. Finally, at Landau's behest, Springsteen released the original demo version of the songs as a solo effort, entitled *Nebraska*. It was unlike any other work in pop-music history: a politically piercing statement that was utterly free of a single instance of didactic sloganeering or ideological proclamation. Rather than preach to or berate his listeners, Springsteen created a vivid cast of characters—people who had been shattered by bad fortune, by limitations, mounting debts and losses—and then he let those characters tell the stories of how their pain spilled over into despair and sometimes violence.

There was a timeless, folkish feel to *Nebraska's* music, but the themes and events it related were as dangerous and timely as the daily headlines. It was a record about what occurs when normal people are forced to endure what cannot be endured. Springsteen's point was that until we understood how these people arrived at their places of ruin, until we accepted our connection to those who had been hurt or excluded beyond repair, America could not be free of such fates or such crimes. "The idea of America as a family is naive, maybe sentimental or simplistic," he said in a 1987 interview. "But it's a good idea. And if people are sick and hurting and lost, I guess it falls on everybody to address those problems in some fashion, because injustice, and the price of that injustice, falls on everyone's head. The economic injustice falls on everybody's head and steals everyone's freedom. Your wife can't walk down the street at night. People keep guns in their homes. They live with a greater sense of apprehension, anxiety and fear than they would in a more just and open society. It's not an accident, and it's not simply that there are 'bad' people out there. It's an inbred part of the way we are all living: It's a product of what we have accepted, what we have acceded to. And whether we mean it or not, our silence has spoken for us in some fashion."

Nebraska attempted to make a substantial statement about the modern American sensibility in an austere style that demanded close involvement. That is, the songs required that you settle into their doleful textures and racking tales and then apply the hard facts of their meaning to the social reality around you. In contrast to Springsteen's earlier bravado, there was nothing eager or indomitable about *Nebraska*. Instead, it was a record about people walking the rim of desolation who sometimes transform their despair into the irrevocable action of murder. It was not exulting or uplifting, and for this reason, it was a record that many listeners respected more than they "enjoyed." Certainly, it was not a record by which an artist might expand his audience in the fun-minded world of pop.

With his next record, *Born in the U.S.A.*, in 1984, though, Springsteen set out to find what it might mean to bring his message to the largest possible audience. Like *Nebraska, Born in the U.S.A.* was about people who come to realize that life turns out harder, more hurtful, more close-fisted than they might have expected. In contrast to *Nebraska*'s killers and losers, however, *Born in the U.S.A.*'s characters hold back the night as best they can, whether it's by singing, laughing, dancing, yearning, reminiscing or entering into desperate love affairs. There was something celebratory about how these people faced their hardships. It's as if Springsteen was saying that life is made to be endured and that we will all make peace with private suffering and shared sorrow as best we can.

At the same time, a listener didn't have to dwell on these truths to appreciate the record. Indeed, Springsteen and Landau designed the album with contemporary pop styles in mind, which is to say it was designed with as much meticulous attention to its captivating and lively surfaces as to its deeper and darker meanings. Consequently, a track like "Dancing in the Dark," perhaps the most pointed and personal song Springsteen has ever written about isolation, came off as a rousing dance tune that worked against isolation by pulling an audience together in a physical celebration. Similarly, "Cover Me," "Downbound Train" and "I'm on Fire"—songs about erotic fear and paralyzing loneliness—came off as sexy, intimate and irresistible.

Yet, it was the terrifying and commanding title song—about a Vietnam veteran who has lost his brother, his hope and his faith in his country—that did the most to secure Springsteen's new image as pop hero and that also turned his fame into something complex and troubling. Scan the song for its lyrics alone, and you find a tale of outright devastation: a tale of an American whose birthrights have been paid off with indelible memories of violence and ruin. But listen to the song merely for its fusillade of drums and firestorm of guitar, and in a political climate in which simple-minded patriotic fervor has attained a startling credibility, it's possible to hear the singer's roaring proclamation—"I was *born* in the U.S.A."—as a fierce, patriotic assertion. Indeed, watching Springsteen unfurl the song in concert, slamming it across with palpable rage as his audience waved flags in all sizes, it was possible to read the song in both directions. "Clearly the key to the enormous explosion of Bruce's popularity is the misunderstanding [of the song 'Born in the U.S.A.']," wrote critic Greil Marcus during the peak of Springsteen's popularity. "He is a tribute to the fact that people hear what they want to hear."

One listener who was quite happy only to hear what he wanted to was the syndicated conservative columnist George Will, who, in the middle of the 1984 campaign that pitted Walter Mondale against Ronald Reagan, attended a Springsteen show and liked what he saw. In a September 14, 1984, column, Will commended Springsteen for his "elemental American values" and, predictably, heard the cry of "Born in the U.S.A." as an exultation rather than as a pained fury. "I have not got a clue about Springsteen's politics, if any," Will wrote. "But flags get waved at his concerts while he sings about hard times. He is no whiner, and the recitation of closed factories and other problems always seem punctuated by a grand, cheerful affirmation: 'Born in the U.S.A.!'"

Apparently, Reagan's advisors gave a cursory listening to Springsteen's music and agreed with Will. A few days later, in a campaign stop in New Jersey, President Ronald Reagan declared, "America's future rests in a thousand dreams inside your hearts. It rests in the message of hope in songs of a man so many young Americans admire: New Jersey's Bruce Springsteen. And helping you make those dreams come true is what this job of mine is all about."

It was an amazing assertion. Clearly, to anybody paying attention, the hard-bitten vision of America Springsteen sang of in "Born in the U.S.A." was a far cry from the much touted "new patriotism" of Reagan and many of his fellow conservatives. Yet, there was also something damnably brilliant in the way the president sought to attach his purpose to Springsteen's views. It was the art of political syllogism, taken to its most arrogant extreme. Reagan saw himself as a definitional emblem of America; Bruce Springsteen was a singer who, apparently,

<springsteen and the E Street Band live
LARRY HULST/MICHAEL OCHS ARCHIVES/VENICE, CA

extolled America in his work; therefore, Springsteen must be exalting Reagan—which would imply that if one valued the music of Springsteen, then one should value (and support) Reagan, as well. Reagan was manipulating Springsteen's fame as an affirmation of his own ends.

A few nights later, Springsteen stood before a predominately blue-collar audience in Pittsburgh and, following a rousing performance of "Atlantic City," decided to respond to the president's statements. "The president was mentioning my name the other day," he said with a bemused laugh. "And I kinda got to wondering what his favorite album might have been. I don't think it was the *Nebraska* album. I don't think it was this one." Springsteen played a passionate version of "Johnny 99," a song about a man who commits impulsive murder as a way of striking back at the meanness of the society around him—a song he wrote, along with other *Nebraska* tunes, in response to the malignant political atmosphere that had been fostered by Reagan's social policies.

Springsteen's comments were apt: Was *this* the America Ronald Reagan heard clearly when he claimed to listen to Springsteen's music? An America where dreams of well-being had increasingly become the province of the privileged and where jingoistic partisans had determined the nation's health by a standard of self-advantage? When Reagan heard a song like "My Hometown," did he understand his own role in promoting the disenfranchisement the song described?

Reagan's attempt to co-opt Springsteen's message also had some positive side effects. For one thing, it made it plain that Springsteen now commanded a large and vital audience of young Americans who cared deeply about their families, their futures and their country and that Springsteen spoke to—and perhaps *for*—that audience's values in ways that could not be ignored. The imbroglio also forced Springsteen to become more politically explicit and resourceful at his performances. After Pittsburgh, he began meeting with labor and civil rights activists in most of the cities he played, and he made statements at his shows asking his audience to lend their support to the work of such activists. He also spoke out more and more plainly about where he saw America headed and how he thought rock & roll could play a part in effecting that destiny. One evening in Oakland, when introducing "This Land Is Your Land," he said, "If you talk to the steelworkers out there who have lost their jobs, I don't know if they'd believe this song is what we're about anymore, and maybe we're not. As we sit here, [this song's promise] is eroding every day. And with countries, as with people, it'd be easy to let the best of yourself slip away. Too many people today feel as if America has slipped away and left them standing behind." Then he sang the best song written about America, in as passionate a voice as it had ever been sung.

None of this was enough. In November 1984, Ronald Reagan was reelected president by an even more stunning mandate than the first time. It seemed plausible that many (if not most) of the millions of fans of voting age who made *Born in the U.S.A.* such a huge success cast their votes for the man to whom Springsteen so obviously stood in opposition. Perhaps it nettled him, but Springsteen was finally facing the answer to the question he had been asking during the length of the decade: To be born in America, to be passionate about the nation's best ideals, meant being part of a nation that would only believe about itself what it wanted to believe. It also meant that one still had to find a way to keep faith with the dream of that nation, despite the awful realities that take shape when that dream is denied.

In 1984, America had not had enough of Ronald Reagan, or it would not have reelected him. It had also not had enough of Bruce Springsteen: After an international tour, he returned to the States a bigger, more popular artist than ever. It may seem like a contradiction that a nation can embrace two icons that differed so dramatically, but the truth is, Reagan and Springsteen shared an unusual bond: Each seemed to stand for America, and yet each was largely misunderstood by his constituency. Reagan seemed to stand for the values of family and improved opportunity at the same time that he enacted policies that undermined those values. Springsteen seemed to stand for brazen patriotism when he believed in holding the government responsible for how it had corrupted the nation's best ideals and promises.

To his credit, Springsteen did his best to make his true values known. In the autumn of 1985, he embarked on the final leg of his *Born in the U.S.A.* tour, this time playing stadium-size venues that held up to a hundred thousand spectators. Playing such vast settings was simply a way of keeping faith with the ambition he had settled on a year or two earlier: to see what it could mean to reach the biggest audience he could reach. It was also an attempt to speak seriously to as many of his fans as possible, to see if something like a genuine consensus could be forged from the ideals of the rock & roll community. Of course, the gesture also entailed a certain risk: If Springsteen's audience could not, or would not, accept him for what he truly stood for, then in the end he could be reduced by that audience.

In some surprising respects, Springsteen's ambition succeeded. At the beginning of the stadium swing, many fans and critics worried that he would lose much of his force—and his gifts for intimacy and daring—by moving his music to such large stages. If anything, however, Springsteen used the enlarged settings as an opportunity to rethink many of his musical arrangements, transforming the harder songs into something more fervid, more moving, more aggressive than before, yet still putting across the more rueful songs from *The River* and *Nebraska* with an uncompromised sensitivity. If anything, he made the new shows count for more than the election-year shows, if only because he recognized that addressing a larger audience necessarily entailed some greater responsibilities. In Washington, D.C., on the opening night of the stadium shows, Springsteen told a story about a musician friend from his youth who was drafted and who, because he did not enjoy the privilege of a deferment, was sent to Vietnam and wound up missing in action. "If the time comes when there's another war, someplace like Central America," Springsteen told his audience of fifty-six thousand, "then you're going to be the ones called on to fight it, and you're going to have to decide for yourselves what that means. . . . But if you want to know where we're headed for [as a country], then someday take that long walk from the Lincoln Memorial to the Vietnam Veterans Memorial, where the names of all those dead men are written on the walls, and you'll see what the stakes are when you're born in the U.S.A. in 1985." For the last dates of the tour, at the Los Angeles Memorial Coliseum, he added Edwin Starr's 1970 hit "War" to the show, coming down hard on the lines "Induction, destruction; / Who wants to die?"

Later, at the end of the last show in L.A., Springsteen stood before his band, his friends and his audience and said, "This has been the greatest year of my life. I want to thank you for making me feel like the luckiest man in the world." Indeed, Springsteen had begun the tour as a mass cult figure; he was leaving it as a full-fledged pop hero, a voice of egalitarian conscience unlike any that rock had yielded before, with a remarkable capacity for growth and endurance.

In short, Springsteen seemed to emerge from the tour occupying the center of rock & roll, in the way that Presley or the Beatles had once commanded the center, yet the truth was, in the pop world of the 1980s, there was no center left to occupy. Rock was a field of mutually exclusive options, divided along racial, stylistic and ideological lines. In fact, by the decade's end, even the American and British fields of rock—which had dominated the pop world thoroughly for a quarter century—were gradually losing their purism and dominance as more adventurous musicians began bringing African, Jamaican, Brazilian, Asian and other musical forms into interaction with pop's various vernaculars. In modern pop, America no longer overwhelmed the international sensibility.

In any event, Springsteen seemed to step back from rock & roll's center at the same moment that he won it. In 1986, he assembled a multidisc package of some of his best performances from the previous ten years of live shows, a box set intended to be a summation of his artistic growth and his range as a showman. It was the most ambitious effort of his career but also the least consequential. It didn't play with the sort of revelatory effect of his best shows or his earlier albums, and it didn't captivate a mass audience in the same way, either. Then, the following year, Springsteen released the album *Tunnel of Love*. Like *Nebraska, Tunnel of Love* was a more intimate, less epic statement than its predecessor, a heartbreaking but affirming suite of songs about the hard realities of romantic love. Maybe the record was intended to remind both Springsteen and his audience that what ultimately mattered was how one applied one's ideals to one's own world, or maybe the songs were simply about the concerns that obsessed Springsteen most at that time.

At the end of the decade, Springsteen was on tour again. Reluctant to continue playing oversize venues, he returned to the arena halls where he had done some of his most satisfying work in the years before and restored a more human scale to his production. It was another election year, and while he still spoke out about issues from time to time, Springsteen seemed wary of being cast as merely a rock politician or statesman. Perhaps he realized that America's political choices just couldn't be affected very tellingly from a rock & roll stage, or maybe he was simply discouraged by what he saw around him. To be sure, there was plenty to be disheartened about: It was a season when Oliver North enjoyed status as a cultural hero.

At the same time, Springsteen remained committed to the idea of turning the rock & roll audience into an enlightened and active community. After the Tunnel of Love tour, he headlined Amnesty International's Human Rights Now! world tour in the fall of 1988. Along with Live Aid, the Amnesty tour was one of the most ambitious political campaigns in rock's history. The fact that it could occur at all and could reach an audience that was both massive and ready was in some ways a testament to the sort of idealism that Springsteen had fought for throughout the 1980s.

Which is to say, despite the currents of history, Springsteen kept faith with a difficult quest. In the midst of a confusing and complex decade, he wrote more honestly, more intelligently and more compassionately about America than any other writer of the era. And after he did so, he set about the business of tending to his own life. An act like that is neither a retreat nor a failure. Instead, it is a way of refusing to be broken by the dissolution of the world around you. It is a way of saying that, sooner or later, you have to bring your dreams of a better world into your own home and your own heart, and you have to see if you can live up to them. All in all, that isn't such a bad way to finish off one decade. Or to begin another.

MILLI VANILLI: **fab morvan** (left) >
and **rob pilatus**
WARING ABBOTT/MICHAEL OCHS ARCHIVES/VENICE, CA

the rise of robopop

By DON McLEESE

Call it robopop. It had the face of Michael Jackson, the finest surface that thousands of dollars and hours of surgical molding can buy. It had the moves of Paula Abdul, the choreographed athleticism of health club aerobics. It had the flash of the video soundstage, a cathode-ray fantasyland. It had the beat of the computer pulse, sequenced, sampled and synthesized to rigid precision. It had the artistic vision of Milli Vanilli. It had the soul of a new machine.

In the 1980s, the dawning of the Digital Era made robopop inevitable, as computer technology revolutionized the very nature of recorded sounds itself. By transferring sound from the province of analog grooves to the realm of binary code, the all-pervasive computer showed how easy it could be to attain a certain type of perfection, a perfection based on the precision of ones and zeros.

Over the course of the decade, computer technology redefined every aspect of popular music, from the way it was created to the way it was consumed. The changes it wrought were so fast and so sweeping that it might be hard to remember that the sequencing and sampling that now dominate studio recording were unknown at the dawn of the decade, that the digital synthesizers introduced in 1980 were affordable only to the privileged few, that a marketplace ruled by the vinyl LP had no inkling of the compact disc.

The rise of computer technology makes it easy to romanticize rock's past, as if a sound that emanates from a Synclavier or a Yamaha DX7 necessarily has less integrity than one from a Fender Strat. There are music fans who couldn't live without their compact discs yet dismiss computers in the studio as inherently sterile.

But rock, throughout its history, has consistently been infatuated with the newest toys and gadgets, employing them as little more than entertaining gimmicks (wah-wah pedal as wah-wah pedal, Mellotron for the sake of Mellotron) until creativity could match strides with the new technology. Before rock even began, critics charged that almost every technological advance diminished music's human element, that the introduction of a microphone desecrated the purity of the human voice, that the electric guitar compromised the touch or the feel of its acoustic predecessor.

The problem with the technological revolutions of the 1980s is that the changes came so fast and furious that both artists and audiences did not have sufficient time to catch their breath, get their bearings and find the proper balance for the human element in this brave new world of sound. In the hands of a visionary artist such as Prince, computer technology opened new dimensions of one-man-band possibility, while Peter Gabriel—among others who embraced the new technology—demonstrated that machine-made music can beat with a decidedly human heart. Though sampling became equated in the minds of many with recycling (or ripping off), a master sampler like producer Hank Schocklee fashioned a sonic universe complete unto itself, and playful populists like Deee-Lite used sampling to create an audacious music pastiche. In the early Eighties, the precision of computer technology complemented the impeccable rhythmic diction of the Human League and Spandau Ballet; by the end of the decade, digital advances helped spawn the sonic guerilla warfare of Public Enemy.

Then again, the more possibilities that technology opens, the more limited the musical imagination can seem in comparison. The technology born in the Digital Decade inspired M.C. Hammer to move from point A to point A, as the push of a few buttons turned Rick James's 1981 hit "Super Freak" into "U Can't Touch This," the smash of 1990. The Digital Decade made chart-toppers (and, in the case of Milli Vanilli, Grammy winners) out of performers who couldn't sing, write or play. If digital technology could enable the producer to play God, it could also reduce popular music to a big computer game.

The strict precision that the computer age permits can make the human component in music seem messy, unpredictable, anachronistic. If that mess and unpredictability, that urgency and immediacy, were once part of what rock fans valued in their music, the digital development of the 1980s would eventually reprogram the robopop audience itself. Whereas earlier generations thrilled to power chords, the Eighties audience mesmerized itself with beats per minute, preprogrammed rhythms, tape loops. At times it seemed that there were listeners who only knew the sound of a drum or a horn section through its sampled simulation, who became so accustomed to synthesized sounds that those sounds seemed more real than the real thing. There were concertgoers who wanted nothing more than a video in the flesh, who weren't concerned with how much of the performance was canned—taped or otherwise preprogrammed—or with the possibility of any spontaneity getting lost in the process.

With the advent in the early Eighties of sampling, sequencing and MIDI (musical instrument digital interface) networking, the analog synthesizers of the Seventies soon seemed like horse-and-buggy relics. Though technological warhorses like the Mini-Moog and ARP Odyssey put their "space drool" and outer-limits atmospherics all over the so-called progressive rock of that decade, such self-styled futurism was itself an anachronism by 1980. With the introduction of the digital synthesizer, effects that previously took hours of patching and experimenting could now be stored in memory and made available in the studio or onstage at the push of a button. Where sounds that emanated from Seventies synths were recognizably synthetic, the synths of the Eighties could sample (record and store in digital form) any impulse from the entire realm of sounds and play that impulse as if it were a musical instrument.

Such possibilities were available at the beginning of the decade, but the Synclavier, introduced in 1980, and its competitor, the Fairlight, were so high-priced that the technology was out of reach except to the most expensive studios and the reigning aristocrats of progressive rock. With the introduction of the Yamaha DX7 in 1983, the price of synthesized digital technology dropped from a quarter mil for the basic Synclavier to two thousand bucks. While the DX7 didn't offer the all-encompassing musical workstation of the Synclavier, it afforded a populist explosion that made the new technology as available as cheap guitars had been to Sixties garage bands. The mid-Eighties breakthrough of MIDI allowed the networking of a series of rhythm machines from a single control, while the new sequencers offered multi-track memory that permitted manipulation never possible with analog tape. The immaculate precision of digital synths, drum machines and MIDI networking soon dominated the concert circuit as well as the recording studio, rendering musical excitement a matter of planned special effect instead of spontaneous inspiration.

Over the course of the Eighties, digital technology became a populist phenomenon rather than the province of music's elite and tech-minded experimenters. Like the groundswell that was rock & roll in the mid-Fifties, the most exciting developments within the musical revolution of the Eighties found barriers breaking, walls crumbling. The very definition of what constituted a musical property came up for grabs, as remixers turned what had previously been a finished product into sonic raw material, and samplers wrenched old sounds into new contexts. Computer language, and the rhythms that derive from it, has a universality that vigorously stirred the melting pot of world-beat possibility while making the very concept of cultural purity even more antiquated than before.

The shortcuts that digital technology offers, however, have a tendency to subvert the spirit that rock has long prized. The computer makes the myth of the rock band seem anachronistic, as the programming that MIDI permits makes the use of musicians unnecessary. While there's no question that a creative spark is lost when musicians stop playing together, computers make it tempting to sidestep the disorderliness of human interaction. As for the development of one's own sounds, sampling makes it all too easy to steal someone else's. Through years of devotion, Keith Richards learned just what it takes to sound like Chuck Berry. A contemporary sampler can sound just like Keith Richards (or, in a more likely choice, Jimmy Page) with push-button ease.

Just as quickly as popular music moved toward a bloodless perfection, however, it began to retreat from it by the end of the decade. The cyclical nature of musical trends is such that the rise of robopop made music that offered an alternative to such mechanization sound fresher than ever. In the latter half of the Eighties, the Cowboy Junkies turned their back on multitracking and recorded their gorgeous album *The Trinity Session* in a church, using a single microphone. Tracy Chapman and Bonnie Raitt showed that the human voice and the human heart offered a quality beyond the reach of computer programmers. Eventually, producers began employing technology to recapture what technology had lost, combining the warmth of natural sounds with the control that digital technology permitted.

While popular music swings between embracing technological possibility and rejecting it, there's no turning back in the marketplace, where the Eighties experienced the most profound revolution since the triumph of rock & roll music itself. In 1980, the vinyl LP still enjoyed a three-to-one advantage over the cassette, but the death of vinyl was all but inevitable. Within three years, the popularity of the portable Walkman pushed prerecorded tape ahead, and the computer-age compact disc was introduced. By 1988, the CD itself was selling twice as many units as vinyl, the cassette nearly seven times as many.

1
9
3

‹ The opposite of robopop, **tracy chapman**
© AL PEREIRA/MICHAEL OCHS ARCHIVES/VENICE, CA

It's a sign of the times that the vinyl record—a format that meant so much to so many—was so quickly discarded, but the durability of digital technology made the CD difficult to resist. While the shoddier sound of the cassette epitomized pop music as a disposable commodity, the CD was a keeper, seemingly immune to surface noise or the other ravages of wear that plagued vinyl LPs. While analog still has its adherents—who maintain that vinyl has a warmth and ambience that can't be captured by binary logic and that the CD isn't nearly as durable as promised—the battle for vinyl was a lost cause at the end of the Eighties.

The Digital Decade didn't see the end of a revolution but the beginning of one, as popular music began to explore the possibilities of computer technology. If all music can be transformed into the ones and zeros of binary logic, the computer can be a tool of consumption as well as creation, eventually blurring the lines between the two.

If the Eighties saw pop music committed to building the perfect beast, the challenge we face now is for the soul of the artist to survive amid the skills of the computer programmer. The same technology that reduced hitcraft to robopop in the Eighties has opened boundless new vistas in music, in both its sound, such as the introduction of electronica, and its delivery, via the Internet. Regardless, while new technology inevitably renders the technology of an earlier era obsolete, it is the human quality of popular music—a great singer, a great song, a great idea, a great emotion—that remains timeless.

madonna

By PAUL EVANS

1
9
4

You can't imagine the Eighties without her. Exploding onto the scene with her self-titled debut when the decade was a toddling three-year-old, she seized ears (and eyes) at once. The name alone was provocative: She came on as a hot tramp calling herself after Jesus' mom. She was all kinds of goddesses (and gods), however, from the get-go: Aphrodite in a rocket-tip bra; a media Athena sprung full-blown from the head of the decade's Jupiter, publicity; mercurial in her moods and costume changes; Dionysian in her promise of redemption through excess (perfect for a time when cocaine, cash and pre-AIDS sex all offered a profane paradise). She was Artemis, too, the Wild Woman, and even a hint of warrior Ares heightened her dangerous allure, as she battled, sweating, exultant and shameless, toward the top of the charts. Eventually, she became the world's most famous woman, beating out even Mother Teresa and Princess Di. From the start, she took our breath away.

Born Madonna Louise Ciccone in 1958, she grew up a dreamer in suburban Detroit, her dad a Chrysler engineer, her beloved mother dying when she was six. A dance-crazed kid, she studied the art at the University of Michigan; moving to New York City in 1978, she trained with the Alvin Ailey troupe. She sang and played drums—rhythm would be her music's signature—in a pop band, the Breakfast Club (très Eighties!). She danced and sang backup for Patrick Hernandez ("Born to Be Alive"); hung out in the disco demimonde; heated up hot spots like Danceteria. There, she performed her music on the rooftop and on the dance floor. A DJ played tapes of tunes she'd co-penned with an ex-beau; he then hooked her up with Sire Records. Boom! She hit big, her self-titled first album soaring to Number Eight and spawning dance instaclassics—"Lucky Star," "Borderline," "Burning Up," "Holiday," "Physical Attraction," "Everybody." Each was both a manifesto and a mirror—her music celebrated an underground demographic of urban ambisexual, multiracial artiste club kids and style queens; it was also all about her. As a madonna, then, for misfits, she'd arrived, complete with a glamorously disreputable fan base. She was ready for mainstream crossover. She was ready for world domination.

It came soon enough—and yes, this revolution would be televised. By far the sharpest of the video pioneers, she understood better than anyone since Bowie the importance of image. With Michael Jackson ex-manager and *Thriller* svengali Freddie DeMann (his real name) urging her on, she released breakthrough clips speeding onto the new avenue of stardom, MTV. She threw down "Borderline," a valentine to black-white love; she gave up "Lucky Star," with its extreme close-ups of the singer's belly button, soon a trademark as recognizable as her voice. (A decade later, girl-next-door sexpot Shania Twain employed the same titillation strategy to shake up country audiences and cinch her own pop crossover.)

With her second album, *Like a Virgin* (1984), its title again a twisted reference to her name (the Blessed Virgin Mary), and its Number One–charting title track, Madonna made the decade her own. At the time, out of French philosophy had come postmodernist thought, its point men (Derrida, Foucault) insisting that the only culture left to the end of an exhausted century would be a knowing hodgepodge, traditional elements ironically, campily,

funkily recycled. Originality, these thinkers claimed, was over, a delusion. Postmod's high-art turn was Eighties architecture—Corinthian capitals "wittily" affixed to steel-and-glass skyscrapers. The street version, of course, was rap, the art of sampling. Unconsciously (and thus even more effectively), Madonna became the movement's It Girl—she recycled Marilyn and Forties glam lingerie, toyed with jive jazz on the *Dick Tracy* soundtrack, appeared on MTV in *Amadeus*-wear, recalled the buoyancy of early Sixties pop with a hit like "Cherish." Her high-profile romances—a rocky marriage to mini-Brando Sean Penn, a tryst with Old Hollywood god Warren Beatty—recalled the screen divas of yesteryear, Liz Taylor and her many men, Lana Turner and hunky rascals. Even her embrace of porno chic—mainly with her *Sex* photo book, Madonna embracing S&M and every manner of kink—could hardly be deemed original ("sex sells" being the world's oldest schtick). Rather, her originality presumably consisted in this: Here was a woman exploiting *herself*.

By mid-decade, she'd starred in *Desperately Seeking Susan*, a movie that made ubiquitous in malls a look Madonna had outgrown the minute the film hit marquees. She'd racked up hits—"Crazy for You" (Number One), "Material Girl" (Number Two), "Dress You Up" (Number Five). She'd flopped alongside Penn in *Shanghai Surprise*; their divorce soon followed, a tabloid field day. *True Blue* (1986) stirred controversy with "Papa Don't Preach" and its plea that unwed mothers keep their unborn babies. Politically, that message was hard to decode, forming part of a larger continuing Madonna riddle: Feminist—is she or isn't she?

Bored briefly, perhaps, by notoriety, Madonna pursued legitimacy on Broadway in David Mamet's *Speed-the-Plow*, before returning to the business of shock. *Who's That Girl* (and its accompanying flop film) broke no new ground in 1987; *Like a Prayer*, two years later, was an earthshaker. Typically, it was the title-track video—burning crosses, a sexy, black Jesus—that compelled the biggest brouhaha (the Vatican railing, Pepsi canceling the star's corporate sponsorship), and with her last album of the decade, Madonna proved herself still more than capable of delivering the bad-girl goods.

Much more, of course, was still to come. A concert movie, *Truth or Dare* (with Warren Beatty's brilliant speculation that Madonna basically lived for the camera), a star turn as a de facto dictator in the big-budget *Evita*, high-profile (unwed) motherhood, tireless AIDS activism, her claim to mogul status as CEO of her own Maverick Productions (which would release the record-breaking U.S. debut of Alanis Morissette). More magazine covers, more movies, more sex, more music (none of it less than capable; less and less of it groundbreaking). More more.

Yet, with all the transformations, Madonna would always personify the Eighties—sound and image, a video incarnate, the essence of style-as-substance.

metal mania

By J. D. CONSIDINE

On May 29, 1983, Rob Halford saw the future.

It was Heavy Metal Sunday at the second US Festival, and Judas Priest—along with Triumph, the Scorpions and the headliner, Van Halen—was facing the biggest crowd of the festival, the biggest heavy-metal audience anyone had ever seen. "By that time, the whole country had kicked into heavy metal and hard rock," Halford says with pride. "It went across the board. It was a new generation. Suddenly, everybody looked at this music and said, 'Yeah, this is exactly what I want. It talks about what I want out of life.'" Halford heard America singing, and the song was Priest's "You've Got Another Thing Comin'."

Of course, heavy metal wasn't exactly a novelty in 1983. By the time Judas Priest made it to the US Festival, America's head bangers, earth dogs, rivetheads and other assorted metal maniacs had been pumping their fists in the air for more than a decade. "I kept having people say, 'I bet you're happy with the resurgence of heavy metal,'" says Ozzy Osbourne, another US Fest alumnus. "Well, it had never been any different for me, because I'd done sell-out concerts for years. I was one of the forerunners of this form of music, I suppose you could say."

If the music wasn't exactly new, its prominence was. Although bands like Aerosmith, Black Sabbath (Osbourne's first band), Deep Purple and Kiss were major attractions in the Seventies, their success seemed small-scale by Eighties standards. After all, the Eighties were the decade in which Michael Jackson's only serious competition on the charts was Def Leppard, whose *Pyromania* was 1983's second-best-selling album after *Thriller*. Meanwhile, records by Guns n' Roses, Mötley Crüe, Quiet Riot and Van Halen topped the album charts and dominated the Top Forty. Even more underground acts like Metallica and Anthrax managed to sell in the millions.

"The way I see it, we're like the Stones of the Eighties," says Leppard's Joe Elliott. "I'm not trying to say we're as good as the Stones; I just mean we represent that sort of musical area— a rocking band that has hits. We didn't want to be an album-track band. We always wanted to be as big as Zeppelin—but we wanted more than 'Kashmir.' We wanted 'Satisfaction.'"

Heavy metal earned its place in the sun by no simple means. Radio deserves some of the credit for bringing the music's kickass attitude into the mainstream, particularly after album-oriented rock stations, which programmed some metal, gobbled up much of the traditional, more pop-oriented Top Forty market; likewise, MTV lent the music new urgency and not only broke bands like Guns n' Roses and Living Colour but even managed to make Twisted Sister's Dee Snider something of a household name.

Yet, in a perverse way, what really sparked this heavy-metal explosion wasn't radio or video at all, much less the US Festival. In truth, much of the music was reaction against punk rock. "We hated the punk movement," says Steve Harris of Iron Maiden. "We hated it even more when we couldn't work because of it. When punk was happening, it was really difficult to get gigs unless you had Day-Glo hair and played out of tune." Harris's resentment is understandable. Despite the prominence of bands like Black Sabbath, Deep Purple, UFO and Uriah Heep in the early Seventies, once the Sex Pistols declared "Anarchy in the U.K.," it was open season on heavy rockers. "It was like punk rock was year 0," says Ian Astbury of the Cult. "We were told that everything that happened before punk was...*forget* about it, you know? It was 'bourgeois,' it was 'decadent,' it was 'hippie.'"

Metal may have been unfashionable in postpunk Britain, but its audience "never really went away," as Harris says. "There were always fans there; we proved that when we started playing gigs and would get packed houses everywhere. It's just that the press didn't really write about these rock bands, us included. But we started building up a following. A bit of buzz started happening about the band, and it just went from there; record companies started coming to check us out, and..." He pauses, not wanting his band to sound like an overnight sensation. "Actually, it took about four and a half years before we got signed," Harris says. "But the reason I think it happened was that there were other bands that were starting to pull in punters."

It wasn't a scene; it was more of a spontaneous heavy-rock underground. "We weren't aware of Def Leppard, and they probably weren't aware of us," says Harris, "because Leppard is from up in the Sheffield area, which was a long way from us in London. Saxon as well was from up north. Tygers of Pan Tang were from Newcastle. All over Britain, there were bands in the same position as us, and none of us knew that we all were doing the same thing—until it started getting in the press."

Once the press did catch on, there was no turning back. *Sounds* called it THE NEW WAVE OF BRITISH METAL, and suddenly dozens of eager young bands swarmed onto the scene: Sledgehammer, Saxon, Angelwitch, Dark Star, Venom, Tractor, Ethel the Frog, Tygers of Pan Tang. The floodgates had been opened. If this sudden outpouring was without precedent in Britain, it was, as a young Lars Ulrich would discover, without parallel in America. Newly transplanted to Los Angeles from Denmark, the future Metallica drummer had arrived in America as a would-be tennis star. Things didn't quite work out as planned. "In Denmark, I

‹ **def leppard**
MICHAEL OCHS ARCHIVES/VENICE, CA

was actually somebody in tennis," Ulrich says, laughing. "But in L.A., I didn't matter even on the block where I lived."

So Ulrich turned to his second love: music. Here again, though, L.A. was nothing like Denmark. At home, he and his fellow metalheads were aflame with the new wave of British metal, he says, "whereas in America, most of the hard rock—apart from exceptions like Van Halen and Aerosmith—was very much tailored toward FM radio; bands that over here were considered heavy bands, like Kansas and Styx and REO Speedwagon and Journey, were being laughed at in Europe."

Stunned that his favorites were "completely unheard-of" in America, Ulrich became all the more obsessed with metal. "I wanted to get a band together in America that had some of those qualities that I didn't see anywhere," he says. Ulrich found an early ally in James Hetfield, a guitarist and devoted Black Sabbath fan. Sabbath was the band "everyone was scared of," says Hetfield. "My friend in school would say, 'Oh, my mom won't let me listen to that stuff!' There was a mystique about it. When Lars brought some of that other stuff over, it was like hitting the jackpot. We started jamming on those kind of things. That's how we clicked together."

Ulrich and Hetfield weren't the only California kids disgusted with the state of American hard rock. "Rock & roll was at a standstill in the late Seventies and early Eighties," says Nikki Sixx of Mötley Crüe. "Zeppelin, Deep Purple, Black Sabbath, the Stones and, I hate to say, Aerosmith—they were considered dinosaurs. Like Black Sabbath: What was the difference between one album and the three before it? The music business was just *boring*."

Complaining about the corporate-rock status quo had become quite fashionable on the L.A. music scene in the early Eighties, but the bands getting the most attention for their antidinosaur stance—"skinny tie" bands like the Knack, the Pop and the Plimsouls—weren't the answer, either. For street kids like Nikki Sixx, what mainstream rock lacked most was attitude, the sound of life lived on the edge. Mötley Crüe cut its teeth on bands like the New York Dolls ("A glamour, pouty attitude, but they had the punk edge," says Sixx) and the Sex Pistols ("They had the pop edge and the gnarly teeth at the same time").

The Crüe hit the scene with what Sixx describes as "a punk-pop first album. . . . It wasn't a premeditated assault on the music industry," Sixx says. "It was enough of a shock, I guess, to start a new trend, but we didn't see it as anything other than fun. Our goals were amazingly low. We didn't know from stadiums and eleven-truck tours. We knew about 'What if we could headline the Whisky on a weekend?' 'How many chicks can we drag back to our pad tonight?' Those were our goals. In those days, I don't think we were as much a musical entity as we are today. It was lifestyle—lifestyle on 10, you know?"

Mötley Crüe wasn't the only band to glamorize the notion of heavy metal as "lifestyle on 10." Van Halen, for instance, conveyed a similar message to Poison's Bret Michaels. "Even though bands like Aerosmith and Kiss and AC/DC had an influence on me, Van Halen were the ones who said, 'This is living,'" Michaels says now. "It had that big an effect on my life."

Yet, as Michaels and his band mates found their way from workaday Harrisburg, Pennsylvania, to L.A.'s glamorous Sunset Strip, they learned that attaining that nothin'-but-a-

good-time lifestyle wasn't half as important as keeping the promise alive. That was why Poison took Mötley Crüe's postglam approach to such cosmetic extremes. As Michaels puts it: "We were living in the streets and trying to act like we weren't dirty. We were the kids without the money trying to look like we were glamorous. We wanted to be the jewel in the rough." And really, was that so much different from the Sex Pistols claiming to be the "flowers in the dustbin"?

As forms of musical rebellion, punk and metal had a lot in common: loud guitars, heavy attitude, the utter disdain of society at large. They parted company, though, on where that rebellion should lead. Punk's worldview lunged toward a gleeful nihilism of boredom and no future, but metal somehow clung to its underdog optimism. Sure, life sucked, the music seemed to say, but that's not the whole story. Above all, metal reminded its listeners that, good times or bad, the bands and the fans were all in it together. Whether it was Van Halen's smirking assertion that "everybody wants some; / I want some, too" or Judas Priest's triumphant insistence that "united, united, united we stand; / United we shall never fall," metal provided a comforting solidarity in the face of adolescent alienation and middle-class ennui.

"On one level, metal has always been about male bonding," says Living Colour's Vernon Reid. "It's like 'I am a Viking' fantasies or 'No one's going to tell me what to do, how to live my life.' And for a lot of people, it's a rite of passage. They get to a certain point and cut their hair or do whatever. I mean, it's really about the style more than the substance: 'You can have your teenage freakout as long as you come home and straighten up. If you cut your hair, you can go home again.'"

In the postpunk Eighties of Metallica and Anthrax, however, that began to change. "Metallica, and in another sense Guns n' Roses, has this idea of post-Vietnam music," says Reid. "It's the music of people who grew up looking at the Vietnam War. For a lot of these bands, it's like Metallica's 'Disposable Heroes'—there is no going home."

Given the accelerated disintegration of the American family, "no going home" was often the literal truth for young metal fans, and it was no accident that some of the era's strongest bands—Guns n' Roses in particular—emerged from the ranks of L.A.'s street kids and throwaway teens. Yet you didn't have to be a runaway to relate to the feelings of dislocation, terror and excitement that mingled in the likes of "Paradise City" or "Welcome to the Jungle." In fact, what made the notorious "One in a Million" so disturbing wasn't its slurs against blacks and gays but the emotions that fueled them; hearing the song was uncomfortably like stumbling across a scared and angry stray, its ears back and teeth bared.

Needless to say, these messages did not go over well with the powers that be. As metal's resonance among Reagan-era teens grew ever more apparent, Reagan-era moms began to voice their distress. Rather than address the issues—the fact that heavy metal not only spoke to the simmering discontent its listeners felt but provided an alternative source of personal pride and cultural identity—parents' groups like the PMRC homed in on the more superficial forms of subversion: dirty language and devil lyrics. Apparently, the fact that the members of Poison and Twisted Sister wore makeup or that Ozzy Osbourne once bit off the head of a live dove made metal a genuine menace to society.

"My reputation wasn't very wholesome," says Osbourne. "If it was me who had done Madonna's video with three burning crucifixes, it would never have got out of the box! I mean, I did deserve a lot of it, because I was fucking reckless for, like, fifteen years. I didn't give a fuck. It was like, 'You don't like Ozzy? Fuck you.' But I can't complain. Whether you loved me or hated me, I still got popular for a spell. Same as Alice Cooper—for whom I have a lot of admiration—in his day, same as a lot of people. Guns n' Roses were the bad boys [in the mid-Eighties]. For some reason, everybody likes a villain. Everybody likes the bad boys."

Maybe so, but not everyone enjoyed being a bad boy. Take the members of Iron Maiden, who were accused of being Satanists simply because they recorded a song called "The Number of the Beast." Says Harris: "At first, we thought it was quite humorous, because we'd never had any of that bullshit thrown at us before, but after a while, we thought it was boring. I mean, if we had wanted to, we could have planted people outside our shows with placards and burning crosses. If we wanted to stir up some shit, we could've, but we didn't want to. We thought, 'That's not the right way for us.' We wanted to break through on the strength of our music, not hype or publicity stunts. In the end, it became annoying, because people kept wanting to talk about this Satanism bit all the time—which is crazy. I mean, we're very obviously not Satanists, but a lot of people just take it on face value, from the album cover and the song title, and, you know, put two and two together and come up with five."

Some came up with even worse. Before the Eighties ended, both Ozzy Osbourne and Judas Priest had been accused of inspiring teen suicides. The suit involving Osbourne's "Suicide Solution" was thrown out before it got to court, but Judas Priest wound up spending a month in a Reno, Nevada, courtroom in early 1990 defending itself against charges that subliminal messages allegedly planted within the band's album *Stained Glass* triggered the suicide of a Nevada teen. Halford, though, has no regrets; if anything, he sees the persecution of Judas Priest as a testament to metal's vitality. "I think a lot of political groups were becoming concerned about how much power was being generated by the acceptance of this music by millions of adolescent Americans," he says now. "What we went through in Reno— we considered that simply an attack on our artistic expression. It was nothing to do with real belief in subliminals.

"However, the fact remains that here is a music that steadily grew through the Eighties, that more and more people identified with and got a great deal of pleasure out of," Halford continues. "I suppose some of the more radical bands—Metallica, Megadeth, Slayer, Anthrax—certainly do have a stronger cutting edge that might be considered more of a threat by certain groups and organizations. I think through the advent of these kinds of bands, we've found a much stronger attack on us from all quarters.

"But at the end of the day, it's just a part of growing up," Halford says. "It doesn't hurt you. In fact, it's a very productive experience. You're surrounded by the people who feel the same way you feel and have the same dreams and aspirations you have, the same problems you have. This business of metal unifying the bands with their audience is more important now than it has ever been.

"It was a bit ironical that four Englishmen had to come over here and help defend the American Constitution," Halford adds, "but we were happy to go through it. And now that it's passed, we just want to get on with doing what we always wanted to do: play heavy-metal music and have a good time."

kings of rap

By ALAN LIGHT

Russell Simmons and Rick Rubin brought rap to maturity—and to the mainstream. Together, they founded Def Jam Records, rap's first really influential label, and were responsible for such landmark recordings as Run-D.M.C.'s multiplatinum breakthrough, *Raising Hell*, and the Beastie Boys' debut, *Licensed to Ill*, which went on to sell more than eight million copies. In the 1980s, Simmons's Rush Artist Management handled virtually all of rap's major stars, from Public Enemy to De La Soul, while Rubin produced many of rap's essential releases.

In the late Seventies, Simmons began promoting rap parties in New York City. At the decade's turn, he started managing artists, including the influential Kurtis Blow. He also managed his own brother Joe, who was billed as Kurtis Blow's Disco Son, D.J. Run, until Joe hooked up with Darryl McDaniels and Jason Mizell, two of his boyhood friends from Hollis, Queens, and found his permanent rap identity as part of Run-D.M.C. Russell produced the first records by these early rap stars. While all that was going on, Rubin was a high-school student in Long Island, playing in a punk band and just discovering the new, exciting, unfamiliar sound of rap.

The two men began working together in 1984, when the Def Jam label was introduced with "I Need a Beat," the debut single by the sixteen-year-old LL Cool J. Rubin was running the label out of his New York University dorm room; he became so successful that CBS approached Def Jam with a big-money distribution deal in 1985. Rubin sent a Xerox of his first paycheck home to his parents by way of explaining that the record business was his new career. The check was for $600,000. He was twenty years old.

LL Cool J's 1985 album, *Radio*, and Run-D.M.C.'s 1984 Profile Records debut, *Run-D.M.C.*, heralded a new, stripped-down sound—a striking, funky contrast to the disco horns and rolling bass lines of earlier rap records. The production credit on *Radio* read "Reduced by Rick Rubin." Skeptics continued to say that rap was a novelty, a fleeting fad, and when rapping and break dancing began turning up in exploitation movies and television commercials, it looked like they might be right.

In 1986, though, Run-D.M.C. and Aerosmith recorded a cover of Aerosmith's 1976 hit "Walk This Way" that silenced all doubt about the music's staying power. It was rap's first Top Five pop single, and it dominated radio for that whole summer. Run-D.M.C.'s Raising Hell tour sold out arenas across the country, and rap faced its first national scandal when gang violence broke out at several shows and a number of cities prohibited the group from appearing.

Just a few months later, rap's pop potential exploded even further, as the party anthems of the white, bratty Beastie Boys brought the music to a new, suburban audience. The Led Zeppelin hooks Rubin employed for the Beasties' tracks also introduced the pop market to the concept of sampling, a technology that would be taken to its greatest heights by Def Jam's next major signing, Public Enemy, who eventually set in motion the forces that would mark the end of the Simmons-Rubin era at Def Jam. Rubin left the label and moved to Los Angeles, where he founded Def American Records and turned his attention back to hardcore and speed-metal bands. He gave the world Slayer's "satanic" lyrics and Andrew Dice Clay's malicious comedy albums. In 1989 Rubin returned to rap—and to the headlines—by signing and producing Houston's "horror rappers," the Geto Boys. In 1993, Rubin dropped *Def* from the name and released albums by Johnny Cash, the Jayhawks and Donovan.

Meanwhile, Simmons created a second label, OBR, for his beloved R&B artists and signed an agreement with CBS that gave Rush Artist Management six additional labels, the biggest subsidiary deal of its kind. He signed a movie-development deal and later produced such films as Eddie Murphy's *The Nutty Professor*. In the Nineties, his interests remained diverse—he founded the popular clothing line Phat Farm as well as the 360HipHop.com Web site, and he worked with the magazine *One World* and the television show *One World Music Beat*.

Rap's first pop hit, "Rapper's Delight," by the Sugar Hill Gang, entered the Top Forty in the first week of 1980. Ten years later, in 1990, the year's biggest-selling album was M.C. Hammer's *Please Hammer Don't Hurt 'Em*, at that time with more than five million copies sold. Despite the astronomical sales, though, rap continued to retain a serious level of street credibility.

The 1980s were ultimately about the expansion and diversification of rap, not its commercial co-optation. With roots in rap's outlaw origins and sights on its pop aspirations, aware of the style's history but obsessed with innovation, Russell Simmons and Rick Rubin tell the story of the rap decade better than anyone. I spoke with each of them at the dawn of a new decade, in 1990.

russell simmons

In 1980, you were still promoting parties, I guess. Rap wasn't really being recorded yet.

In 1980, I had my first Kurtis Blow record, "Christmas Rappin'." We had it on the shelf for 1979 Christmas. It came out around December 12th and had already burnt out half the places by January. The followup was Kurtis's "Breaks."

When you did "Christmas Rappin'," if someone told you that in ten years, rap would have Number One albums, five-million-sellers, would you have believed that?

No! Only an artist would tell you he believes that dumb shit. You have no idea. The only thing I know now is that LL Cool J's going to sell at least a million. I *know* that. Even if shit goes backwards or haywire or we go into a recession, if they're really big, they're going to sell a million. That second million is the hard one.

russell simmons ›

AL PEREIRA/MICHAEL OCHS ARCHIVES/VENICE, CA

You had been pretty successful promoting shows and parties around New York. Why did you make the move from promoting to managing?

You have a management company because you're the only person that understands the artist and what they really do. As a manager, that's what you hope to contribute, that input in developing the career that a record company doesn't have. One of the reasons I started Def Jam was because no one would help me develop my artists the way I wanted. I had a group like the Beastie Boys on an independent company. That's why I sold to Columbia, because I wanted to get the group to the next step. The reason I do a lot of things is to get the group to the next step, more so than to get the company to the next step. I think that works best.

You've never sold less than gold on a Def Jam rap release. Is there a model for Def Jam artists?

I think that the original Run-D.M.C. record, the first Public Enemy record, first LL, too—each of these records doesn't sound like anybody else's record. You create your own musical identity and do something special. The first Run-D.M.C. album had records on there that didn't sound like anything that had been made, ever. Each artist needs to have something special—and their own look, their own marketing, their own ideas. That's why it takes so long to find Def Jam artists.

With those groups, there was a reality that other rappers didn't have—D.M.C.'s glasses, LL's Kangol—

I try to develop images that people can relate to and appreciate because they can be like them. That's a basic difference between myself and a lot of other managers and marketing people. People *can* be these people that I make. It's a *big* difference.

Look at what rappers used to look like. They'd get a record and throw on sequins, leather—rock & roll shit. What the fuck? What you know about that—some old shit that's not accessible, that shows we're stars? It reinforces an artist's image and ego. They always think it's good because you get off a plane in a purple suit and orange hat—"Oh, shit, there's a superstar! I seen his clown ass on TV yesterday." And here comes LL Cool J getting off the plane behind him in a Kangol and a pair of sneakers. What we try and do is get what's real from them and sell that.

The early Def Jam records don't sound like rap records anybody had made before, either.

I'd like to take credit for the company being all that, but I think something like the early LL stuff was very influenced by Run-D.M.C. and not as revolutionary. No one had made a black or R&B record sound as loud and abrasive as "Jam-Master Jay," ever. There were four records on *Run-D.M.C.*, if you played them for an A&R director, whose job is to hear hits, they would have been offended: "Where's the music? Why is there a beat and no music? Why do you say you're finished?"

The Beastie Boys album *Licensed to Ill* was special like that. It had a different perspective. The way black kids who grew up with James Brown and his stuff, the Beastie Boys used Led Zeppelin. They used what they liked about Run-D.M.C. and some rap groups, and what they didn't like, they made fun of. They made it cool. It was very honest.

What was the idea behind trying to make spare and abrasive records?

It was just because everybody wasn't doing it. "Sucker M.C.'s" was not a hard record to sell to a kid on the street, but it was a very hard record to sell to a producer or to the industry. There was no standard to compare it with. Radio stations weren't waiting to play it, but every kid knew that they liked it when they heard it.

How much do you have to do with the sound?

I wrote "Sucker M.C.'s"—the beats, the whole shit. I had a lot to do with the shaping of the Def Jam projects, but I didn't actually produce any of them. I helped a lot, but Rick was one of the most talented producers I ever met. He could still walk in and make a very different-sounding, special rap record that would set a trend. He wasn't just listening to other people's records and copying them. But as much as he created new stuff, he was influenced by a lot of stuff, and Run-D.M.C. was his biggest influence, without question, for the Beasties and the first LL album.

How much did his leaving affect Def Jam?

Well, we don't have Slayer anymore—that's how much it affected us. We wouldn't have put out a ballad like [LL Cool J's 1988 hit] "I Need Love." Rick's a little boy. He's very hardcore and didn't grow up listening to R&B. I don't like a lot of real accessible things, either, but when I hear "Psychedelic Shack" in *Terrordome*, I'm happy 'cause I know the song.

^ PARTNERS IN CRIME: **run–d.m.c.**
AND **the beastie boys**
LAURA LEVINE/MICHAEL OCHS ARCHIVES/VENICE, CA

In 1985 or whenever, all those break dance movies and commercials seemed to make things level off—

Well, video changed things. It used to be enough just to put a good record out. Now that's all over. Before "The Breaks" came out in 1981, there wasn't going to be no rap records on radio: "Fuck that! We ain't playing no more, we don't like that, we don't give a fuck." "Breaks" came and changed all that. It died out again— "We ain't playing no rap!"—and "The Message" came. Within a week, they were playing that motherfucker. Blew up in the streets and sales and everything. As long as people keep breathing new energy into the music, new artists with new ideas, they'll play it.

Is there such a thing as oversaturation? Does Young M.C. doing ads for Taco Bell make any difference to rap?

It's up to Young M.C. We'll see what happens to him when his new album comes out, see if anybody gives a fuck. It's hard to think that they give a fuck *anyway*. But it's all just thin air. Taco Bell and all that is fine: big, bigger, commercial, successful, but can he sell any tickets? Any T-shirts? That's what matters—tickets and T-shirts.

Does it affect the whole rap business?

Not rap fans. "I used to like Young M.C., but now I see him on TV too much"—no, those are people who don't know nothing nohow. It ain't gonna matter to people who like N.W.A. when they see Young M.C. on TV. It's gonna make them like N.W.A. *more*. That ain't gonna affect the whole industry 'cause a couple acts went out like suckers.

Major labels are stepping up their involvement in rap. What's the impact?

They're putting out a lot of bullshit records. They don't matter. All the bad records don't matter. All the bad videos matter some, because video shows are not as smart as hip-hop programmers. Red Alert ain't gonna play a bad rap record. Chuck Chill-Out is not gonna play a bad rap record. But *MTV Raps* will give some fucked-up MCA rapper one play and take up somebody else's time. Bullshit artist, bullshit record, decent video: play it. Decent videos get on in place of your record that's *good*. *That's* the problem.

At the beginning, were you able to foresee how lucrative a commercial property rap would become?

I didn't know where it was going to go. I knew that I believed in it, loved it, devoted all my time to it. It's all I thought about and worked on. I thought maybe I'd make a living at it. I didn't know that I'd get rich. Who would've thought I'd be fucking the girls I'm fucking now?

Things happen one day at a time. You work hard toward your artists playing Vegas one day and being big superstars and being around for thirty years. But you don't know if every artist is going to be around that long. Kurtis Blow doesn't have a recording contract. But Bobby Womack didn't have the run LL's had; LL's never had less than a platinum album. Al Green never had the run Run-D.M.C. has had. They're eight years in the game now, and every record Run's put out is platinum. People say, "Well, we've never seen a rapper with longevity." What the fuck? Prince's last flop sold four hundred thousand, and the last Run-D.M.C. flop sold *a million three*. Run-D.M.C. is guaranteed to sell more records next time than Prince is guaranteed to sell. Prince might come out and sell five million—he's more likely to sell five million than Run-D.M.C.—but he's also more likely to sell three hundred thousand than they are.

You once said that "the people most threatened by rap are middle-class adult blacks." Given all the recent high-profile controversies centering on the music, is that still the case?

Life and *Time* and *Us* and *People* and ROLLING STONE have done many stories on rap. *Ebony*, *Essence* and *Jet* don't even barely acknowledge it. Until recently, they hadn't done any stories on it. It's not only rap; it's just this whole black thing—"What's acceptable? What do we spoon-feed to the black community?" That's why N.W.A. is important—the idea of artists with attitudes. Drastic as N.W.A. is, they're reporting something real in the community—their frustrations, what makes them happy, things that should be told in music.

In 1986, there were cities banning the Run-D.M.C. tour after violence at some of the group's concerts. Do you think that sort of activity is related to banning or arresting rappers now?

Not at all. Banning records is much scarier. The reason they didn't want another show in Long Beach, California, is because gangs would go to the shows and fight. People that ban shows can always point to something, but banning records is different. Okay, some kid listened to Slayer and hung himself. If you watch *Rambo* a lot—and you're fucked up—you might shoot somebody. But we go see *Rambo* because it lets off tension, it's a fun thing, it's exciting. I listen to N.W.A. and get a real good feeling; I don't feel like shooting nobody. I feel like being nice to people because I'm happy about the music.

rick rubin

What was your initial attraction to rap?

When I was in high school, I was listening to a lot of progressive punk rock, from the Ramones to Talking Heads. All the other white kids in my high school were listening to the Doors, Led Zeppelin, Pink Floyd. It was frustrating not having any community to be a fan with. Meanwhile, there was this exciting thing going on in rap that also had a wide appeal to its audience. I liked rap but might not have been as interested if people had accepted the Ramones and the Talking Heads at first.

Did rap immediately make musical sense to you, or were you just reacting to that sense of community?

Musically, I always liked it. Even when I've liked so-called metal stuff, it was AC/DC and Aerosmith rather than Judas Priest and Iron Maiden. It's always been boogie influenced, and I always listened to things like James Brown, so the music made sense to me from the start.

When I started at New York University in 1981, I went to rap shows every week. I found that the records didn't reflect what was going on in the clubs. In the clubs, they were playing Billy Squier and Aerosmith and James Brown, funkier beats than what was happening on the records. The records were glorified disco records. At the clubs, the DJ was really the key musician. At that time, scratching was the coolest part when you went to a rap club, but there was no scratching on records.

How did your first rap record come together?

Of the DJs at the time, Jazzy Jeff was my favorite, and we became friends. I asked him if he wanted to make a record, and we made "It's Yours," with T. LaRock MC'ing. The whole idea was to really bring the scratching up front. We did what a DJ did in a rap club.

What else did you set out to do differently?

I think my biggest contribution to rap was the structured-song element. Prior to that, a lot of rap songs were seven minutes long; the guy would keep rapping until he ran out of words. "It's Yours" separated it into verses and choruses.

I made "It's Yours" and was planning to release it on an independent label myself, which was going to be called Def Jam. Then I met Arthur Baker, and he put it out on Streetwise Records. It took about nine months until it caught on.

That's when I met Russell Simmons. He was shocked that I was white and had made that record. I was really excited about meeting him, because he had made a bunch of records I liked. We became friends.

By then I was already working with the Beastie Boys and had made "I Need a Beat," with LL Cool J. I brought the LL record to Russell, and he loved it. I said, "Let's start a record company," and he said, "I don't want to. I've got a bunch of artists, and I'm going to make a production deal with a major label."

I said, "Look, you already think this record is a hit. Here's what we're going to do: I'll produce all the records. I'll do the business. I'll run the company. You'll be my partner, okay?" And he said okay.

After you started Def Jam in 1982, were you really running the label out of your NYU dorm room?

Yes. In that situation I produced 7 twelve-inches. And then CBS came to us because we had sold so many twelve-inches and offered us this big-label deal.

What was your reaction to that offer?

I never made a record thinking it was going to sell. For me, it had always been a hobby. I was planning on going to law school. They offered us this deal, and here was an opportunity to not have to go to law school.

If there's one pivotal moment, it would seem to be putting Aerosmith in the studio with Run-D.M.C. for "Walk This Way" on *Raising Hell*. How did that come about?

The whole *Raising Hell* album was finished, and that song was not on the record. I called Russell and said, "We need something else. I want the group to cover a song, and I'm going to go through my record collection and find the right song."

Until then, it was a good rap record but not a monumental leap forward. I thought the way the vocals worked in "Walk This Way," it was already pretty much a rap song. It would be cool to have a high-profile rap group doing a traditional rock & roll song and not having to change that much. I think a lot of people thought of rap as so completely alien to music at the time, and here they were doing a cover that I knew would sound like a Run-D.M.C. song, but people could say, "Wow, I understand this!"

Tell me about your first encounter with Public Enemy.

Well, there was no such thing as Public Enemy when I first got involved. There was a tape that Chuck D had made when he was a DJ at the radio station at Adelphi University. It was well written and unusual sounding. His voice was amazing. I got Chuck's number and called to tell him I thought we should make a record. He said he was too old, he had a family, he had a straight job, and rapping was for kids. Chuck was a college graduate with a grown-up life. I wrote down his number on a Post-it Note and stuck it up on the wall next to my phone. I called him every day for close to six months, telling him that we had to make a record together. It got to the point where he told his wife that if I called, he wasn't in.

I remember being actively excited about Public Enemy, and Russell hating it. The first album was done, and I played it for Russell, and he said, "Rick, I don't know why you're wasting your time with this garbage. This is like black punk rock. You make hit records; you made pop records with the Bangles. How can you waste your time on this garbage?" I think he's since come around.

Did you sense the commercial impact that the Beastie Boys' album would have?

I never would have guessed, but I remember going to Al Teller, who was the president of CBS Records, and explaining to him that if the record was presented the right way, the potential was unlimited. Bottom line: The record was good enough to live up to anything that happened around it.

Why did you stop doing rap records?

Musically and businesswise, Russell and I were moving in different directions.

Had things gotten difficult at Def Jam?

Musically, our tastes were different for a long time. While at Def Jam, I was responsible for LL Cool J, the Beastie Boys, Public Enemy. At that time, Russell had brought in mostly R&B stuff: Oran "Juice" Jones, Alyson Williams. We each ran our own team, really, but then strings were starting to cross over, and when he would question what I was doing—"Why are you doing Public Enemy?"—it was becoming frustrating.

Why did you go back to hardcore rather than something closer to your Def Jam artists?

I've always just signed whoever I liked, and I had stopped listening to rap around the time of the first Public Enemy album. That community had turned in on itself. There wasn't progressive stuff going on; there were just people trying to get paid. Every once in a while, a Hammer comes along, and there's a feeding frenzy—every major in the world wants to sign anybody who can rap. Same thing as Guns n' Roses. Labels don't know why Guns n' Roses is good, so this other band that kinda looks like them must be just as good. It creates an atmosphere that creates artists who don't really care. You have a situation in L.A.

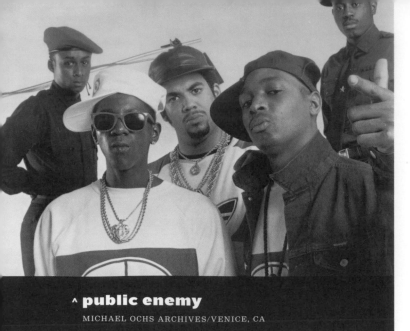

^ **public enemy**
MICHAEL OCHS ARCHIVES/VENICE, CA

where bands are getting together to get signed, as opposed to getting together to make great music.

You're back in the news with the Geto Boys' record. What does the response to their record and this whole national wave of censorship indicate to you?

I think a record's responsibility is to entertain its audience, and their record does that very well. Beyond that, I don't think there are any responsibilities. I don't think a heavy-metal record can make somebody commit suicide, and on the other side, I don't believe a rap record that says, "Don't do drugs; stay in school," is going to work, either. Records don't have the power. It's strictly entertainment.

The reason these groups—Guns n' Roses, 2 Live Crew—have gotten to where they are is because they weren't telling people something that didn't already exist. Same with Dice, same with the Geto Boys—all they do is talk about things that are going on. They may not be pleasant, but they're real. You can't paint a pretty picture—all you can do is hold up a mirror. Art has always reflected culture. That's all it ever does. It doesn't change culture. That

Andrew Dice Clay sells out Madison Square Garden two nights in a row could say some very bad things about what's going on in the world today, but it doesn't say anything about him. By getting rid of him, you don't get rid of the problems. We should be aware and be scared, but it can't be swept under the carpet, which is what Hollywood and the record industry try to do. It's never going to work, because the problems are in the world, not in the art.

Could any record disturb you?

Is there a record that I think should not be made? No. There are a lot of records that I wouldn't buy. The thing that pisses me off the most are records that are made with the idea of product, as opposed to somebody who cares about making a musical statement of some kind.

Are there still rap records you can get excited about?

The Ice Cube record is very good; he genuinely cares about making great records. Digital Underground genuinely care. That's about it. If I'd heard either of those and been able to sign them, I would have. But the community in rap really let me down. I felt like rap had left me more than I had left rap. For the most part, I just stopped listening.

Was that an inevitable result of commercial success?

The major record labels saw the success we had at Def Jam and said, "We want a part of it." That's going to be the death of rap: All these major labels spending three hundred thousand dollars on substandard rap albums. Then, when they don't sell because they're lousy, the labels will say, "Oh, rap is dead. Next." And that'll be the time to get back into it.

my favorite eighties recordings

By CHUCK D

All these records still get a crazy response.

1 **"Peter Piper,"** by Run-D.M.C. For the rhythm, the timing and Run-D.M.C. for stomping the rest of the competition. The story line is dope, the rhythm is moving. This record still doesn't fail.

2 **"Freedom,"** by Grandmaster Flash and the Furious Five. The rhymes are sharp and crisp. This was the first rap record that I was flabbergasted over. The rappers are tight and accurate, and the groove keeps moving. It's eight minutes long but doesn't feel like it.

3 **"Sucker M.C.'s,"** by Run-D.M.C. The first rap record that sounded like what you really wanted to hear—like a real rap party. The beats are large, bigger than everybody else's.

4 **"Funky Beat,"** by Whodini. A great intro and a mighty sound. The perfect complement for Ecstacy's voice, which I always liked. A great arrangement, too.

5 **"You Know I Got Soul,"** by Eric B. and Rakim. Rakim has the greatest rhyme style— it influenced me a lot. The rhythm moves fast, but the rhyme is taking its time. They had it together from their first record, "Eric B. Is President," but this one was just outta there.

6 **"Atomic Dog,"** by George Clinton. Pure funk. This is every rapper's favorite record East, West, North or South. When you heard it, you just had to move. It showed that Clinton's funk was never going to die.

7 **"Rock the Bells,"** by LL Cool J. LL at his finest. Nobody does a record in concert better than this one; he takes it to an even higher level. The beat's fast, and LL is rocking it at breakneck speed. It also has that go go feel to it.

8 **"The Show,"** by Doug E. Fresh and the Get Fresh Crew. I didn't like this record at first, but it's contagious. A fantastic arrangement—that's what got me. A great story line, and Slick Rick and Doug E. Fresh make for a great contrast.

9 **"It Takes Two,"** by Rob Base and DJ E-Z Rock. Great groove and great opening line. This one caught me the first day it was out and kept me all year long.

10 **"Poetry,"** by Boogie Down Productions. For KRS's rhyme style. This and Rakim, like "You Know I Got Soul," are the records that influenced me to come up with my own style. KRS is taking his time while the beat moves and grooves.

r.e.m.

By DAVID FRICKE

R.E.M., possibly the most commercially successful and critically applauded new American rock band of the Eighties, was born as the rock & roll clock struck 1980. It was in late January of that year, in the small, swinging college town of Athens, Georgia, that guitarist Peter Buck, singer Michael Stipe, bassist Mike Mills and drummer Bill Berry rehearsed together for the first time. The following April 5, they made their concert debut—without a name—at a free beer blast in the old, converted Episcopalian church where Stipe and Buck lived.

Playing a mixture of hip covers and their own hastily written originals, the future members of R.E.M. lurched through their set with lusty abandon fully in keeping with the Athens art-and-party tradition already established by the B-52's and Pylon. R.E.M. was destined for greater things. That show marked the beginning of the band's remarkable and sometimes troubled passage from local notoriety to mainstream acceptance and, with it, the rise of America's postpunk underground.

"I hate to hark back to 'the good old days,' because they weren't," Buck says with an ironic chuckle. "But it was a real interesting time. I lived in a town where a lot of stuff was going on, and no one knew that it was different for a town to have a scene: 'Oh, everybody plays in bands, and everybody has a friend who made a record.'"

R.E.M. did not single-handedly change the face of U.S. rock in the Eighties; the band shares that honor with the likes of X, Black Flag, the dB's, Hüsker Dü, the Minutemen, Mission of Burma, Sonic Youth, the Replacements, the Dream Syndicate and, of course, R.E.M.'s fellow Athenians. R.E.M. was in the thick of the fight from the very start, however. The band revitalized the independent recording scene with the success of its stirring 1981 vinyl bow, "Radio Free Europe"/"Sitting Still," issued on the tiny Hib-Tone label. *Murmur*, the group's 1983 debut album, set *the* standard for new American guitar rock, with its masterful blend of gauzy, lyrical impressionism and driving folk-rock passion. With the support of college radio and the fanzine press, R.E.M. was also instrumental in creating an alternative club circuit that catered to the growing market of young fans disgruntled by arthritic AOR programming and formulaic arena-rock spectacle.

"We played cheap, *anywhere*," Buck says proudly. "We'd always get more people every time we went back. We were fairly decent, and if nothing else, our show was a nice way to spend an evening for a dollar."

The venues, of course, became bigger; the ticket prices went up. R.E.M. first cracked the platinum barrier in 1987 with *Document* and again in 1988 with *Green*, and in 1996, when the group's contract came up for renewal, the band negotiated a then-unprecedented $80-million deal with Warner Bros. Records. In 1999, drummer Bill Berry amicably left the band after recovering from a brain aneurysm, and the group has used various musicians since.

At the time of this 1990 interview, Peter Buck had become an in-demand freelance producer specializing in young, outlaw bands. He continued to be an insatiable record collector and a keen observer of the American underground—or what, in his opinion, is left of it. Buck was interviewed in Bearsville, New York, while working on R.E.M.'s *Out of Time*.

"Now Athens is a real professional scene," says Buck. "People move down to form a band, they do a demo tape, make an independent single, tour the East Coast—same places we used to play, if they're still in business.

"In those days, there were different ways to do it," Buck says. "Pylon would only play New York and Georgia. They never went up and down the East Coast unless they had to. They just didn't want to tour.

"We, on the other hand," he adds, laughing, "had nothing better to do."

When R.E.M. started rehearsing in January 1980, what were your ambitions and expectations? Did the dawn of a new decade have any particular new meaning for you?

I never thought of it that way. To me, the Seventies ended in 1977. You have to remember, growing up at the time I did, there wasn't anyone who made records like us. Rock & roll was full of superrich guys that had mustaches and were ten years older than me. I was twenty-one, and it didn't make any sense to me.

So for you, the punk uprising of 1977–78 was the demarcation point.

That was the beginning of the Eighties for me, because there was a realization that there were ways to work outside the music business. In my scene, it was predominantly white kids doing it, but I think it was liberating for everybody. I never lived in New York, and I wasn't there when they invented rap and scratching, but I started listening to that in 1979, '80, and I went, "Wow, this is really interesting." For me, the Seventies were over, and I was really glad, too.

Did you see the Sex Pistols' U.S. debut show in Atlanta?

Yeah. I gave my mother the money because she had a credit card; you needed a card to reserve the tickets. Then I got down there, and they'd sold all the tickets. I was with this crazy guy, a friend of a friend who didn't know anything about the Sex Pistols. But he was so incensed—I was supposed to be in there—that he kicked the door in, and we got in. He got to see the whole show. They caught me and dragged me out. I saw one song, but it was pretty great.

No one really got it. There were guys with big bell-bottoms, beards and safety pins three feet long.

When I went to see all the weird bands in Atlanta in 1975, there wasn't a dress code. Mostly people wore whatever weird clothes they had laying around. And there were people doing odd stuff—the Fans, the Brains, the B-52's when they started. Then all of a sudden in '77, you suddenly had all these guys in brand-new leather jackets with safety pins in them.

Even in the beginning, the Athens scene exhibited a remarkable diversity. Where did R.E.M. fit into the mix?

The point was, nobody sounded like a punk band. There were the B-52's, who made up their own rules. Pylon was a weird, angular dance band. The Method Actors were a two-piece psycho-funk band. And then there was us. We were sort of considered the "pop" band, which was weird, because we're not all that poppy. Then, when we went out of town, everybody thought we were really weird.

Like the Seventies independent singles by Patti Smith and Television, the Hib-Tone 45 of "Radio Free Europe" was a major turning point for the underground record industry. Were you surprised by the success, and influence, of the single?

It was mindboggling. It was supposed to be a demo tape, so we could get jobs, and we met this guy who said he'd put it out. It wasn't very good mastering; we were all young, and we didn't know what the hell we were doing. We sent 200 promo copies literally to any magazine we thought of. We sent one to *Women's Wear Daily*—I swear to God. Then we started getting letters from people at record companies.

Did you feel there was an audience out there for R.E.M.?

It wasn't so much that there was an audience for us but that there was a lot of dissatisfaction. We weren't sure where our place in the business was or even if we had one, but we did realize something was going on when there seemed to be so many people, the *smart* ones in town, who would come up and say things: "Have you heard this band or that record?" Sometimes the towns we went through didn't have any bands of their own, or the local new wave band would do Cars covers, but people would go see that because, "well, at least it isn't Eagles covers." And in every town, no matter how small or how weird, there would always be from twenty to a hundred people who would say the same thing: "The radio around here sucks." The idea that we were kind of successful meant that there were other people who felt like we did.

When you started touring, what were some of the other cities and scenes that impressed you?

Minneapolis was very good to us from the beginning. We played to twenty people on Thanksgiving 1981, and every one of them came up to us afterwards and invited us to their house for a party. Nashville was always real good. There was stuff going on in Washington, D.C.

But there were clubs everywhere. There was a place in Greensboro, North Carolina, called Friday's. It was a pizza parlor, and the guy had bands play. It was an L-shaped room; you could see through the bar to the ovens, with the guy with the long stick with pizzas on it, and see us, too. He'd charge a dollar, we'd get 150 people in there, and we'd get the door. People would let us sleep on their floor. There were clubs like that in every city.

Even in New York, the audiences at your early gigs were mostly made up of rock critics who loved the single.

The first time, it was *all* rock critics. We opened for the Bloods at the Pilgrim Theater, and the P.A. broke halfway through the third song, so we played instrumentals, and we took requests. People were laughing, shaking their heads and thinking, "This is really unprofessional."

Critics and fanzines helped an awful lot. At the time, there were not a lot of ways to hear this music. When radio is confused and there isn't a way for something to be heard, it becomes a point where words mean a lot more. Today you have MTV. You hear about Pussy Galore on MTV. But in those days we were considered so out there by that area of the business that there was no way we were going to be heard of.

Did you consider yourselves "underground"?

It's an oft-abused phrase, but there was a definite difference between the showcase clubs and the dumps we played—and the dumps were more fun. Also, it wasn't just something that was only for rock & roll bands. Dwight Yoakam used to play a lot of the same clubs in L.A. that we used to play.

Underground is such a weird term, because *above-ground* is dead most of the time, anyway. Most of us were out of the public eye, and that was fine. There were these alternatives—the small clubs, the independent record stores. None of us expected it to ever be anything but this small alternative. Until three or four years ago, I never heard any of these bands say,

"Man, I really want a hit single. I want to sell a lot of records." That just wasn't considered, because it didn't seem possible. What you hoped for was to make enough money to make another record.

When you made *Murmur*, how did you cope with the business of recording professionally, with its emphasis on technology and "name" producers?

We wanted to use Mitch Easter and Don Dixon as our producers, and I.R.S. said, "It would be nice if you tried this guy Stephen Hague." Okay, he was a nice guy; he just wasn't what we needed. When we eventually did *Murmur*, every song on it was a first take, but Hague had us do songs thirty-five times, and then he'd put together an edit of, say, the chorus from the thirteenth with the bridge from the twenty-ninth. I got to the point where I didn't know what we were doing. Two days in the studio, and we didn't even finish one song.

We like technology, too. Every record I've ever done, I overdubbed guitars. But the one thing people were always interested in then was a big drumbeat and synchro stuff, and I never really got that. For us, the early records were essentially uptempo folk songs. What do you mean, "a big drum sound so they can dance to it"? They're not gonna dance to this.

How did you feel about your synth-pop contemporaries, like Soft Cell and the Human League?

I loved "Tainted Love." "Don't You Want Me" is a great song. Some of my favorite music is totally manufactured. On some of my [recent] favorite records, like Public Enemy's [*Fear of a Black Planet*], there's actually nobody playing on them. I know guys who can make a record with just a computer. Michael [Stipe] is working with the Boogie Down Productions guy, KRS-One. They tap a key, sample some stuff. Great—you can make records really cheap. And it's put the technology right in the hands of the kids. That's what punk was all about. Punk was never about buying a leather jacket and singing songs about Ronald Reagan. It was about liberating yourself from the strictures of the music industry.

Yet, you were forced to operate within certain strictures of the music industry when you signed with I.R.S. Records.

When we were looking for a label, I.R.S. was the one we wanted. They had the Buzzcocks at the time, the Cramps, the Fall, Wall of Voodoo. They were doing a lot of the kinds of records I was listening to, and it was the perfect label for us. It was small enough so

that we could go and talk to people and tell them what we wanted. And they helped us with marketing things, like touring. We'd just go, "Let's go out and play," and they'd say, "Why don't you play here, because your records are doing well on the radio?" Things that I never would have thought of. They didn't really leave us alone, but they didn't suggest really stupid things, either.

By the time R.E.M. finally cracked the Top Ten with "The One I Love," in 1987, your I.R.S. deal was almost up. Was the label frustrated by your inability to get hit singles during the preceding years?

Not necessarily. We made those records for so little money that they made tons of money off of us. Maybe not the first day, but *Murmur* cost twenty-five thousand dollars. It's gold now.

They would have liked hit singles, but we didn't come up with any. We talked about it, and sometimes Jay [Boberg, president of I.R.S.] had good input. We would never have put "9-9" on the first record if he hadn't said, "I really like that song; would you please record it for me?" That was a cool thing to say, because it obviously wasn't going to be a single. Sometimes he'd say, "If you remix this, it will have a lot better chance to be on the radio," and I'd go, "They're not gonna play this anyway." But they never put a lot of pressure on us. I mean, every album we made sold more than the one before it. You can't say anything bad about that.

Yet the success of "The One I Love" and "Stand" showed not only that you were quite capable of making hit singles but also that both AOR and Top Forty radio had become more receptive to your sounds and style.

Radio changed a lot. At the time we had a hit single, Los Lobos had hit singles and Tracy Chapman had a hit single. Who would have thought in 1982 that the biggest hit of '87 or '88 was going to be a black woman with a guitar doing songs about social injustice? There were a lot of us plugging away. Black and white and folk and rap and pop and jangling guitar—we all changed, a little bit, the way people looked at what could get on the radio. Radio is so much more open now than when I was young. I mean, [Depeche Mode's] "Personal Jesus" sold a million copies.

R.E.M. has long been seen as the archetypal Eighties college-radio band. How important was college radio to the band's survival and success?

In the beginning, it was very important, because we weren't getting on radio anywhere else. It never made us rich, but it got us to the point where we could play and know that in most cities a hundred people were gonna show up. The playlist was a lot more open then. College stations I go to now are fairly button-down. It's become more of a training ground for AOR radio. There's some great radio stations, but I get really tired of turning on the radio and hearing only major-label releases. We're on a major label—I have nothing to say about that one way or the other—but college radio turned into fun music for college kids who wanted to hear the new Depeche Mode. I always think that you should be able to learn something by listening to college stations.

The albums *Murmur* and *Reckoning* also triggered the rise of the "college radio sound," with a host of bands making records with jangling guitars, oblique lyrics and moody, pseudo-Stipe vocals. Were you flattered by the imitations or annoyed?

Well, you know, it goes in phases. There was a year and a half where I heard a lot of *Murmur*-esque bands. I mean, whenever anyone says a band sounds like R.E.M., they don't say they sound like *Green*. It's the first record, because that was a kind of different thing.

Two years after that it was the Replacements, and I still see a lot of Replacements bands. [In 1990] it's Sonic Youth. That's what white, middle-class kids are playing: noise-influenced kinds of songs, textured noise stuff. It comes and goes. We had our two years of being imitated.

You've also outlasted many of your original contemporaries, like X, Hüsker Dü and the Dream Syndicate. Where did they go wrong, and how did you beat the odds?

I have no idea. I can never understand why X wasn't the biggest band in the world. They had great everything—really great songs, they looked great. They were really literate, but you could also just sit there and bang your head and not pay attention to the lyrics. But I actually bumped into John Doe not long ago, and he said it was the dreaded *p* word: *punk*. They were seen as punks, and it doesn't matter what their influences were, whether it be Hank Williams or French symbolist poetry. They're seen as punks in leather jackets.

I don't think we were ever hindered with that scary image. Our image was four guys who don't have an image. We don't have to fight against any past, any looks. I think the problem with a lot of our contemporaries is that when they wanted to sell records, a

lot of them made really big mistakes. I don't think the Dream Syndicate or Hüsker Dü did that, but a lot of our contemporaries, they made their first record, and then they made the second record that they hoped would sell. Then they made the third record where they were really frightened and didn't know what to do. I couldn't tell you how many people I know that made three records, and the third record has nothing to do with what made the band good the first time. Musically, our records are fairly different, but we're still the same songwriters.

How would you describe the musical and emotional dynamics at work within R.E.M.?

What holds us together as a force is working together as songwriters and players. We write songs together and play them together. We haven't ever been in a position where someone's been pissed off about making less money or not having his songs on the record. We're the only band I know that fights *not* to be in our own videos.

We have a real socialist democracy. We sit around tables and vote just about as much as we write songs. We vote on where we're going to play, where we're gonna make the record, who's gonna produce it. We each have equal say and input when we bring songs into the studio. Everything is a total compromise between the four of us.

How do you break a tie?

We have a "rule of no." If we can't make up our minds, then we don't do it. It has to be all four in one direction. If one person really thinks that something is wrong and is passionate about it, even if we think he is wrong, we agree with him. Like on the new record, we were playing with something where there's a little sample in it. I like it when people sample records. Mike [Mills] is against it. He really hates that idea. So we're not gonna make samples of our own stuff to use, because he feels strongly that it's wrong.

Has the band ever come close to splitting up?

Yeah, several times, but it's just like any marriage: It's when you don't talk about stuff that things get bad. Me and Mike have wrestled on the ground before. We've thrown things at each other and cursed and broken things, but I argue less with the three of them than I do with my parents.

The thing is, we have to be able to look at ourselves in the mirror. You can't really be in a band unless you say at the end of the day, "Everything we did today is okay by me." I hate those meetings.

Sometimes they'll go on for four hours, and we still haven't made a decision, and sometimes we'll change our minds three times, but you have to do that. I wouldn't want to do it any other way.

I play with other people all the time, and I realize how fucked up other bands are. There's one guy making decisions, and the rest of the guys don't like it. I wouldn't want to do that. We're still making good music, but aside from that, if we make a really dud record sometime, it's the four of us deciding it.

In recent years, the band has become more outspoken on social and ecological issues. How did growing up in the Reagan decade affect your personal political agenda?

It's not like we, as people, were not interested in that kind of stuff, but it was kind of like being in a deep freeze. I like America. I live here. I felt totally out of step. It just seemed like a real coldhearted decade. And you go, "Well, I'm a rock & roller guy. This is silly, for me to make any kind of statement." But after a while, you realize, "Well, this is my country, too."

I still don't think the president has anything to do with me. I vote in every election, but I always feel defrauded in everything but a local election. But locally, we do all kinds of stuff. We go to city council meetings and vote on things. There are things in Athens that are different now because of people like us.

For example?

Historical preservation. We have curbside paper recycling, which is pretty cool. Members of the city council who we have involved ourselves with have been very good about trying to protect what is nice about the town. You try to do what you can locally and do the food bank stuff—all the things that make a small town.

Do you ever have problems deciding which issues to publicly support as a band?

Michael is involved with People for the Ethical Treatment of Animals; we're not. I agree with a lot of their goals, but I wouldn't feel comfortable supporting them, because I'm wearing suede shoes. I eat meat, you know? I am against most testing on animals, but I have some friends who have AIDS, and I'm not gonna say you should stop using animals for AIDS tests.

So we talk that kind of stuff out. Generally, it's not like we espouse revolutionary platforms. I don't think recycling and helping the homeless is such a shocking agenda. We're gonna do some of the vote stuff. That's probably the main thing people need to realize, that they have the power to vote, and if

that doesn't work, they always have where they spend their money.

How would you describe the rock underground of 1990?

I think that the underground is so overground now that the *real* underground is people who haven't really made a record yet. We've never heard of them. I keep up and get a lot of fanzines. I go see bands, and there are bands that are just brand-new, and they have a "career." They have a T-shirt merchandising guy, and they have a tour-booking agent. It's a little more career oriented than when we were starting out. As far as underground, I don't know if that means anything anymore. That's the bad thing about what's happened to college radio: There isn't an us-and-them dividing point.

Can you tell whether your original audience has grown with you or away from you over the years?

I think my peer group still listens. I really don't think we've done anything that has really alienated an audience. We were never young guys in hip clothes on the cover of teen magazines and singing about young love, and here, all of a sudden, it's the end of the Eighties, and we're *this* kind of band. We've grown steadily and changed, and I'm sure there's a lot of people that listen to Dylan that bought his first or second record.

Do you think the success of R.E.M. helped changed the major labels' attitude toward the likes of Sonic Youth and the Butthole Surfers?

I think there's enough people who grew up with us that were college-radio programmers and who are now in A&R. I bump into people all the time who work at record companies, and so many of them say, like, "I was in college when *Murmur* came out," and now they're doing A&R. I think that's great, because the A&R people are always the ones who love what's going on. They're the ones who want to sign bands.

In a way, R.E.M. is engaged in its own A&R campaign. The band has always taken great unknowns out as support acts—like Camper Van Beethoven and 10,000 Maniacs—and you've done production work for bands like the Feelies and Run Westy Run.

If I like a band, I'll take them in the studio and work for free. I don't go in and say, "Let's make a hit single." It's more like, "What is this band about?" I did a record with Charlie Pickett; it was this kind of deranged Johnny Thunders blues band. And they'd worry about something being out of tune. I'd just say, "Don't worry about it. It sounds fine. You're not the Doobie Brothers. I guarantee you, nobody is going to return this record and say the guitar is out of tune."

I'm not really sure the things I've done have sold anything because of my name, but if I enjoy it, and if it helps kids in bands and it encourages them, great. If for some reason, I couldn't write songs anymore or play in a band, I would produce a record a week—or every other week.

What were your favorite Eighties bands?
I'm just like every other old-timer, in a way. To me, it's colored by who really made your head spin the first time you saw them. My favorite bands? I just remember moments.

What were some of the moments?
We worked with the Replacements a couple of times—before they started getting really drunk all the time. They were just wonderful. Hüsker Dü—the first time I saw them was a great experience. Another really cool moment was seeing the Dream Syndicate. I think they even put out a live EP from it; it was live upstairs at a radio station. We saw the Plugz in Los Angeles, and it was great. In Washington, at the Bayou, the Gang of Four put on probably one of the top three shows I ever saw. I'll never forget that. That was the great thing about the Eighties, that it was *moments*. I'd be so shocked to discover a great band in a place I never thought I'd see one. Who would have known that Minneapolis was just full of really great bands?

What were the biggest disappointments?
I didn't enter the music business with any illusions whatsoever. I hate to sound like Mr. Positive, but I was pleasantly surprised by how many people were nice and had their heads screwed on straight. I was ready for big, fat guys with chains around their necks, and I met some of those, but more often, I met people who really cared about music and did the best they could. One of the things that always moved me was, you'd go into town and there were always a few people keeping the flame going. They might be schoolteachers or janitors or work in a record store, but when I get to this town, I'll call this guy and he'll tell me what band's great, so I can see them.

What are your hopes for the Nineties?
We went through a decade where politically it was the most backwards and screwed-up decade imaginable. A lot of things socially were going wrong. Racism seemed to be on the increase. But things came together in a kind of a nice way musically. A lot of the stuff that deserves to be on the radio *is* on the radio.

A lot of bands that you wouldn't necessarily think have a lot in common have worked together. Like the Amnesty [International] tour. For all the imprecise talk about what good it was, it got lots of different music together onstage, and that's kind of where it all ends up for me. A lot of people I respect mutually are playing well, making good records and working together. Some of those boundaries are down a bit.

That's my hope for the Nineties: a lot less formal and, musically, a lot more people working together and not paying attention so much to boundaries—because they're not my boundaries.

the eighties according to
michael stipe

I've been calling the Eighties the Reagan–Garfield era. They're over. That's probably a good thing. We can all praise our various gods for that.

Musically, we saw punk rock becoming more commercialized, black music on the upswing. Personally, I think we came out a little bit ahead. I feel a kind of weird nostalgia. Will people start wearing those same clothes three years after they wore them the first time? But I think that kind of immediate nostalgia is a reflection of the kind of impact American culture has had on the world—that things happen at such an accelerated pace, these clipped parts of our lives. This immediate nostalgia is a really creepy thing.

I don't want to put too much emphasis on those ten years—the decade as a discrete unit—but people tend to, and it seems to work too well. It's really odd that those numbers can change things that much. As we move toward the end of the century, that makes a huge difference. I'm optimistic about the Nineties. I think a lot of people will spend the next decade educating themselves and finding out how the world is run.

The last ten years seemed like thirty. Maybe the next ten will seem like sixty.

Some favorite recordings of the Eighties:

1 Anything by Arvo Part

2 *Mesopotamia*—the B-52's

3 Anything by the Cramps

4 *Wings of Desire* soundtrack

5 *Doolittle*—the Pixies

6 *Armed Forces*—Elvis Costello and the Attractions (from 1979)

7 *Margin Walker*—Fugazi

8 *Songs of the Free*—Gang of Four

9 *Surprise Surprise Surprise*— Miracle Legion

10 *Talking With the Taxmen About Poetry*—Billy Bragg

11 *Psychocandy*—the Jesus and Mary Chain

12 *Stutter*—James

13 *Ghetto Music: The Blueprint of Hip Hop*—Boogie Down Productions

14 *Diesel and Dust*—Midnight Oil

15 *Viva Hate*—Morrissey

16 *I Will Not Be Sad in This World*— Djivan Gasparyan

17 *Sign o' the Times*—Prince

18 *Wave*—the Patti Smith Group (from 1979)

19 *All Hail the Queen*—Queen Latifah

20 *What Makes a Man Start Fires?*— Minutemen

21 *God*—Rip Rig and Panic

22 *The Elephant Man* soundtrack

23 *In My Tribe*—10,000 Maniacs

24 *Fiyo on the Bayou*—the Neville Brothers

25 *Le Mystere des Voix Bulgarer*— the Bulgarian State Female Vocal Choir

26 *Rain Dogs*—Tom Waits

27 *Under the Big Black Sun*—X

28 *Gyrate*—Pylon

217

michael jackson

By MIKAL GILMORE

In the 1980s, when I was pop-music critic for the *Los Angeles Herald Examiner*, I wrote more about Michael Jackson than almost any other single pop figure of the time. I almost wish I hadn't. In the pages that follow, I'll try to trace and explain some of what it was that caught me about Jackson and what it was that eventually left me feeling disillusioned and saddened about him.

The first piece ran in the *Herald* on April 11, 1983. It appears here with only slight editing:

Everywhere this last season I've heard this animating sound. It begins with taut, maddened, funk-infused guitar lines that scramble against the upsweeping curve of a string section in a heady depiction of emotional panic. Then a high-end, sensually imploring voice enters the fray and imposes elegance and resolution upon the panic: "What do you mean," the singer moans breathtakingly. "I AM the ONE / Who will DANCE on the FLOOR in the ROUND." The song is Michael Jackson's "Billie Jean," and it has suddenly, surely become one of the most ubiquitous—and exciting—breakthrough singles in recent pop history.

Whenever a song becomes as madly popular as "Billie Jean," it can be fun to examine the reasons why: Is it simply the appeal of the music's exacting but impelling sound? The fine phrasing and tremulous emotion at play against one another in the singer's voice? The allure of the artist's personality or celebrity?

In the case of "Billie Jean," it is a bit of all of these things. Clearly, since a string of brilliant childhood triumphs with the Jackson 5 (the last great 1960s-style Motown group), the now-twenty-two-year-old Michael Jackson has long been one of soul *and* rock's most stirring singers. But it wasn't until 1979's *Off the Wall* that he stood out as a mature, stylish vocal force in his own right. For that reason, as much as for the memorable songwriting of Stevie Wonder, Paul McCartney and Rod Temperton, or the ravishing production of Quincy Jones, the record proved one of the most consistently exuberant (and popular) black pop works of the last ten years.

It came as a surprise, then, that at first few listenings, Jackson's long-awaited followup, *Thriller*, seemed somewhat disappointing. Quincy Jones—whose elegant but edgy arrangements on *Off the Wall* exalted Jackson's evocative vocalizing in much the same manner that Nelson Riddle's graceful, rousing work once enlivened Frank Sinatra—had taken to displaying both dominating and overprudent instincts in his recent work. As a result, he seemed to restrict Jackson on much of *Thriller* to a catchy but somewhat tame brand of dance-floor romanticism.

Indeed, the boldest sounding tracks on the album were ones Jackson himself had the strongest hand in writing, producing and arranging: "Wanna Be Startin' Somethin'," "Beat It" and "Billie Jean." After hearing these songs find their natural life on radio, it became evident that they were something more than exceptional highlights. They were in fact the heart of the matter: a well-conceived body of passion, rhythm and structure that defined the sensibility—if not the inner life—of the artist behind them.

These were instantly compelling songs about emotional and sexual claustrophobia, about hard-earned adulthood and about a newfound brand of resolution that seeks to work as an arbiter between the artist's fears and the inescapable fact of his celebrity. "Wanna Be Startin' Somethin'" had the sense of a vitalizing nightmare in its best lines ("You're stuck in the middle . . . / And the pain is thunder . . . / Still they hate you; you're a vegetable . . . / They eat off you; you're a vegetable"). "Billie Jean," meantime, exposed the ways in which the interaction between the artist's fame and the outside world might invoke soul-killing dishonor ("People always told me . . . 'Be careful of what you do 'cause the lie becomes the truth'," Jackson sings, possibly thinking of a debilitating paternity charge from a while back). And "Beat It," in many ways the album's toughest song, was pure anger: In its relentless depiction of violence as an enforced social style, it conveyed terror and invincibility almost as effectively as Grandmaster Flash and the Furious Five's "The Message."

But the ultimate excitement here is that "Billie Jean" is merely a first step. When Michael Jackson performed the show a couple of weeks ago at Motown's twenty-fifth anniversary bash (in what was one of his first public acts as a star outside and beyond the Jacksons), it was startlingly clear not only that he is one of the most thrilling live performers in pop music but that he is perhaps more capable of inspiring an audience's physical and emotional imagination than any single pop artist since Elvis Presley—and I don't know anyone who came away from that occasion with a differing view.

There are simply times when you know you are hearing or seeing something extraordinarily fine and exciting, something that simply captures all the private hopes and dreams that you have ever wanted your favorite art form to aspire to and that might unite and inflame a new audience. That time came for those of us who saw Jackson onstage that night, and now every time I hear "Billie Jean," I have a vivid image of one of rock & roll's brightest hopes. "Billie Jean" is the sound of a young man staking out his territory—a young man who is just starting to lay claim to his rightful pop legend.

From there, things went up—far up—and then far down. *Thriller* went on to place an unprecedented seven singles in *Billboard*'s Top Ten and also became the then-biggest-selling album in pop history (over 35 million copies, or something like that). At the 1984 Grammys Michael Jackson captured eight awards, including Best Album and Best Record of the Year. Then, a few months later, it was announced that Michael would be setting out on a nationwide tour with his brothers, the Jacksons. By that time, the massiveness of Jackson's fame was already starting to work against him—and the controversies that started surrounding the Jacksons' Victory Tour (as it was billed) only made matters far worse. For one thing, there were fears that Jackson's popularity would attract such large crowds that something horrible might result—something like the crowd rush that occurred at a 1979 Who show in Cincinnati, where eleven young people were trampled to death or smothered. Also, there were charges of greed: The Jacksons were charging as much as thirty dollars a ticket and had also accepted the multimillion-dollar sponsorship of the Pepsi company.

The tour began in Kansas City, Missouri, in July 1984, and days before the group ever hit the stage, things had gone weird and awry. At times—what with the tireless histrionics of promoter Don King (who said that anybody who saw the Jacksons' show "will be a better person for years to come") and the manner in which local politicians and sports officials ingratiated themselves with the Jacksons' organization—it was easy to forget that this was primarily to be a musical event, featuring one of the more popular and captivating performing groups in pop's recent history.

Unfortunately, that fact seemed lost even on the Jacksons. When the group finally took the stage at Kansas City's Arrowhead Stadium, amid curls of purple smoke and crimson laser beams, some of the reporters were eyeing the crowd for signs of the much-predicted hysteria. We never found them. Instead, what we saw was an overwhelmingly white, affluent-looking audience of forty-five thousand fans—largely parents and children—exhibiting a kind of polite exhilaration at the vision of Jackson going through his trademark, impossibly adept maneuvers. It was good, of course, that there was not mob hysteria (in fact, I doubt if there was so much as a scratch in the audience that night), but it also would have been nice had there been something of real excitement taking place onstage. But on this night, Michael and his brothers—Marlon, Jermaine, Tito and Randy—didn't work as effectively as a cooperative unit as they did on their 1981 tour. For that matter, the best collaboration I saw that whole night came from a clique of about five black and white children standing in the aisle near my seat, dancing in joyful abandon with one another, trading quick, sharp, fancy moves in a fun and funky exchange, mimicking the action they saw onstage (or rather, on the large screen *above* the stage). When I looked closer, I realized they were all wearing the souvenir Michael-style sunglasses that were being sold at the arena, and then I realized that for these kids, this was truly a transfixing dream that no amount of critical scrutiny might ever obscure or alter.

Well, good for them, because for some of the rest of us, the whole thing really wasn't that much fun. Much of the press that came to Kansas City wanted *something* to be critical of, and the Jacksons had unwittingly served that interest with the displays of apparent greed and incompetence that preceded the tour. Worse, they delivered a show that didn't work, a show that proved too susceptible to the allure of spectacle, as if an epic display of technology and stagecraft might also count as substance and excitement. Simply, the group was overwhelmed by its own trappings, forced into a position in which it attempted to connect with the audience through predictable displays of pyrotechnics and flashy mechanics rather than by force of their own performing matter. (The audience, it must be said, seemed to enjoy it all: Musical art and physical mastery be damned, give us the bomb!) It was frustrating to watch a performer as resourceful as Michael Jackson succumb to such a grandiose and ultimately unimaginative interpretation of his art.

The problem was, Michael Jackson should never have done the 1984 tour in this way. He was unquestionably beyond the Jacksons by this time, and he seemed constrained in his role as a frontman for a group he truly no longer felt a part of. By all rights and reason, Michael should have been working a stage alone. After all, his best performances worked as public declarations of intensely private fears; that's the quality that gave his art whatever anxious depth it possessed at that time. The 1984 tour was to be Jackson's way of paying off—and breaking off—family ties, but what it would cost him, in a way, was that moment he had finally captured, after a lifetime of waiting.

A month later, I was in New York City to attend the New Music Seminar during the same week in which the Jacksons were playing several dates at the city's Madison Square Garden. By this time, the skepticism and suspicion that had greeted the tour's start in Kansas City had turned into outright hostility in some quarters, most of it directed at Michael Jackson himself. On more than one occasion, when Jackson's name would be cited during panels at the New Music Seminar as somebody who had helped dispel some of the racial barriers in the 1980s pop scene, the notion was met with jeers.

This is what is called backlash, and in the case of Michael Jackson, it was not a simple or pretty matter. To be honest, some of the anger directed at Jackson had to do with the press's notion that somehow Michael and his brothers were simply the latest case of pop-cultural hype, a charge that was also frequently leveled at Elvis Presley and the Beatles in the early stages of their mass fame. Clearly, there is a big difference between what Michael Jackson represented to his audience (an instinctual physical and emotional savvy meant to turn personal fear into public celebration) and what Presley and the Beatles represented to theirs (good, old-fashioned youth-cultural disruption). Yet, all these artists shared one thing: They bound together millions of otherwise dissimilar people in not just a quirk of shared taste but also a forceful, heartfelt consensus that spoke to common dreams and era-rooted values. In 1984, it wasn't yet clear whether Jackson would go on to have the continuing momentum or epic sweep of Presley and the Beatles, but at the time, I thought it likely that his mass popularity represented something more significant than the incidental mass appeal of such artists as Peter Frampton or the Bee Gees. Looking back, I think I was both right and wrong, and I'm not sure which likelihood today disturbs me more.

I remember a friend telling me, during that New York visit, "If Jackson had never gone out on this tour, I would still resent him, and so would other people. The awful thing is, Jackson consciously wanted the biggest audience in the world, but he didn't want to give them anything too revealing or risky."

This was true: Michael Jackson wanted it all, and got it. It is obvious, in retrospect, that *Thriller* was designed with mass crossover audiences in mind. Jackson put out "Billie Jean" for the dance crowd, "Beat It" for the white rockers, and then followed each crossover with crafty videos designed to enhance both his intense allure and his intense inaccessibility. But as a ploy, was that really such a bad thing? Was it, for that matter, any different from what Elvis Presley did with his hillbilly–blues–rock & roll crossover music and what he accomplished in his Dorsey Brothers and Ed Sullivan TV appearances? In fact, wasn't Presley initially a song-and-dance cat, somebody who took his personal fearfulness and made a public passion out of it, and won intense mass affection as a result? Didn't Presley, too, set out to capture the biggest audience in the world, and isn't that still (at least for some people) one of the most evident dreams pop can aspire to? Why, then, did we need to condemn Michael Jackson for his popularity?

The truth is, by the mid-1980s, some music partisans just weren't terribly fond of the idea of Presley- or Beatles-sized popularity anymore. That, plus the notion that Jackson didn't, for some, really fit the modern definition of a pop hero: He wasn't somebody with literary or sociopolitical aspirations or dreams of sexual revolution. But as one thoughtful friend pointed out to me, there was an even touchier problem about Jackson's success, one that made the temporary vexations of the Jacksons' tour seem paltry. "What turned me off to him," this critic told me, "was his eagerness to trade his former black constituency for an overwhelmingly white audience. Plain and simple, he doesn't want a black identity anymore. He records with proven white stars like Paul McCartney and Mick Jagger, and he's allowed the tickets to be priced so high for this tour as to exclude the majority of working or young black fans in this country. Just look at the makeup of these audiences—*barely* ten percent black. But what really drove the nail into the coffin is that Jackson appeared at the White House with Ronald Reagan. That announced to everybody that he'd divorced himself from the concerns of the black audience at large."

I couldn't argue with that one. Certainly, it would have been better if Jackson had refused the invitation to the White House in protest of the administration's antiblack policies. It would have been nicer if he had openly repudiated Reagan. Still, many of our best pop stars have made some unworthy choices, including Elvis Presley and James Brown aligning themselves with Richard Nixon.

Interestingly enough, about the only person I heard defend Jackson during my New York visit was James Brown, and it almost cost him the affection of a fawning music business audience. The moment came at the New Music Seminar during the artists' panel that featured Brown, among others. A member of the audience asked the panel what an artist's responsibility is to his fans, given the outrageous prices the Jacksons had imposed on their following. Brown agreed that the ticket price was unrealistic, regardless of the tour's supposed overhead costs, but went on to say that he didn't think it fair to excoriate Michael Jackson or his brothers on the basis of their bad business sense. "It's a mistake—let's hope it doesn't happen again—but believe me, these are good people. Give them another chance."

Cries of angry disagreement shot up from the floor. The mood in the room became riled, like that of a piqued political caucus. But Brown stood his ground. "You don't really know what Michael had to go through to make this tour happen. I won't stay here and let you attack somebody who isn't present to defend himself."

What Brown didn't mention is that he had reportedly declined Michael Jackson's invitation to sing with the group at Madison Square Garden because he privately felt the ticket prices would exclude any real soul audience. He could have scored big and easy points with the NMS crowd by divulging that, but it was a testament to his integrity, and to his respect for the difficulty of Michael Jackson's position with the press and public, that he kept his censure measured and made his defense sound reasoned.

Of course, it would have been even better if Jackson had expressed more concern for the audience who sustained him during his singular rise to pop stardom. Like Presley before him, though, Michael Jackson was now in uncharted territory, and every move he made would map out either his redemption or his ruin.

The Jacksons' tour came to its close in early December 1984, with six sold-out performances at Los Angeles's Dodger Stadium. I almost skipped the whole thing. I was weary of all the arguments and vitriol surrounding Michael Jackson by this time, plus I'd already seen the show in Kansas City and Manhattan, and the experience hadn't been worth either trip. But on the tour's last night, I went. It was my job.

As it turned out, this was the only Victory Tour show I saw that had a good dose of something that the other dates had lacked: namely, Michael Jackson's unbridled passion. Let me say it without apology: It was a hell of a thing to see.

Pass it off, if you like, as Jackson's possible sense of relief at leaving the long debacle behind, but from his wild, impossibly liquid-looking glides and romps during "Heartbreak Hotel" (still his best song), to the deep-felt improvisational gospel break at the end of the lovely Motown ballad "I'll Be There," and the fleet-tongued, raw-toned scat-rap exchange he shared with Jermaine at the end of "Tell Me I'm Not Dreaming (Too Good to Be True)," Michael accomplished as much as was likely possible that night—short of kicking his brothers offstage and setting Don King afire. At moments, he seemed so refreshingly lively and acute that it almost worked against him. What I mean is, watching Jackson at this peak is a bit like watching pornography—something so provoking it can rivet you and seem incomprehensible (maybe even unbearable) at the same time. Which means a little goes a long way, and a lot can seem plain numbing.

In any event, on that last night I thought, "Maybe there's hope for the guy after all."

Four years later, I was on the Michael Jackson Road again, writing coverage for Rolling Stone of the opening dates of his first solo tour. Jackson had a recent album to promote, *Bad,* and once again he was nominated for some key Grammy Awards. But in 1988, Jackson was up against some hard competition. Artists like U2 and Prince had fashioned some of the most ambitious and visionary music of their careers—music that reflected the state of pop and the world in enlivening ways. By contrast, Jackson's *Bad* seemed mainly a celebration of the mystique and celebrity of the artist himself.

More important, in 1988, there was suspicion among many critics and observers that Jackson's season as pop's favorite son might have passed. When Jackson arrived in New York to attend and perform at the Grammys and to give a series of concerts at Madison Square Garden, he was met with some bitter hints of this possibility. In the 1987 ROLLING STONE Readers and Critics Poll, Jackson placed first in six of the readers' "worst of the year" categories (including "worst male singer"); in addition, the 1987 *Village Voice* Critics Poll failed to mention *Bad* in its selection of 1987's forty best albums. This was a startling turnaround from four years before, when Jackson and his work topped the same polls in both publications.

Plus, Jackson still had a knack for grand gestures that often seemed overinflated. I remember one morning in a Manhattan disco, where Michael Jackson stood smiling uneasily before a throng of reporters and photographers. The occasion was a large-scale press conference, convened by Jackson's tour sponsor, Pepsi, to commemorate a $600,000 contribution from the singer to the United Negro College Fund. The philanthropy of the event was somewhat overshadowed by Pepsi's other purpose: namely, to premiere Jackson's flashy, new, four-episode commercial for the soda company, which would make its TV debut the following night, during the broadcast of the Grammy Awards at Radio City Music Hall. All in all, it was an odd excuse for a press gathering, and Jackson looked uncomfortable with the stagy formality of the situation. Not surprisingly, he was willing to say little about the occasion, nor would he take any questions from the nearly five hundred journalists who were crowding the room. In short, like most Michael Jackson press conferences, the event proved little more than a grandiose photo opportunity—and yet it had all the drawing power of a significant political function. In a sense, it's easy to see why. It's as close to Michael Jackson as most members of the press will ever get, and though many reporters remain put off by the singer, they still find him fascinating and are quite happy to ogle his transfixing, part-beautiful, part-grotesque countenance.

But why Jackson would find it necessary to endure an occasion like this is another story. According to one associate (who, like most people around Jackson, would prefer not to be quoted for attribution), high-profile media galas like this—or the following night's Grammy program—have a special significance for the singer. "You have to keep in mind," the associate told me, "what happened to Michael during the 1980 Grammy Awards. His album *Off the Wall* had sold over 6 million copies. In effect, Michael was the biggest black artist America had ever produced. He fully expected to be nominated for the Album of the Year and Record of the Year awards, and he deserved to. But instead, he won only one award: Best Male R&B Vocal.

"That experience hurt Michael, and it also taught him a lesson. You could be the biggest black entertainer in history, and yet to much of the music industry and media, you were an invisible man. That's why he aimed to make *Thriller* the biggest record of all time, and that's why he has aligned himself with Pepsi. Pepsi gave him the biggest commercial-endorsement contract that anybody has ever received, and to Michael, the more accomplishments to your name, the more people have to recognize you. That's what an event like this is all about. Michael still wants the world to acknowledge him."

The next night, as the Grammy show progresses, things go better and worse than expected. The good news is that Jackson turns in an inspired performance that also serves as a timely reminder of an almost forgotten truth about him: Namely, that whatever his eccentricities, Jackson acquired his fame primarily because of his remarkably intuitive talents as a singer and dancer, talents that are genuine and matchless and not the constructions of mere ambition or hype. Moreover, it is also plausible that in certain ways, Jackson's phenomenal talent may not be completely separable from his eccentricity. That is, the same private obsessions and fears and reveries that fuel his prowess as a dancer and songwriter and singer may also prompt his quirkiness, and perhaps without all that peculiarity, he would be far less compelling to watch.

In a sense, Jackson's opening moments on the Grammy telecast—in which he delivers a slow-paced, Frank Sinatra–inspired reworking of "The Way You Make Me Feel"—are exemplary of his famed quirkiness. He seems self-conscious and strained pulling off the song's cartoonish notion of streetwise sexuality, and his overstated hip thrusts and crotch snatching come off as more forced than felt. Yet when the music revs up, all the artifice is instantly dispelled. Jackson seems suddenly confident and executes startling robotic hip-and-torso thrusts alongside slow-motion, sliding mime moves that leave the audience gasping.

But it is in his next song, the social-minded, gospel-influenced "Man in the Mirror," that Jackson defines for himself some surprising new strengths. It is a deceptively straightforward delivery, yet its simplicity prompts Jackson to an increasingly emotional performance. By the song's middle, he isn't so much singing or interpreting as he is simply surrendering to the song. At one point—spurred on by the majestic vocal support of Andrae Crouch and the New Hope Baptist Church Choir—Jackson breaks into a complex, skip-walking dance step that carries him across the stage and back. He then crashes hard to his knees in a posture of glorious, testifying abandon, sobbing fervently as Crouch comes forward and dabs the sweat from his forehead, then helps him back to his feet. It is a moment that reminds some viewers of James Brown's famous stage routine, but in truth, Jackson has taken the move from the same sources that Brown appropriated his from: archetypal gospel shouters like Claude Jeter and James Cleveland.

A few minutes later, as Jackson takes his seat in the front row alongside producer Quincy Jones, his triumph comes to a fast, sobering end. As many observers expected, U2's album *The Joshua Tree* takes the Album of the Year award, and before the evening is out, Jackson will also lose all the remaining awards that he is nominated for.

Perhaps Jackson's most telling response comes during an uproarious incident when Little Richard, presenting the Best New Artist award, playfully castigates the academy for neglecting him throughout his career, stating, "You-all ain't never gave me no Grammys, and I been singing for *years*. I am the *architect* of rock & roll." Jackson is among the first spectators to his feet, bouncing up and down and clapping hard.

Maybe it's only the hilarious spirit of the moment, but maybe it's something more. In a way, Jackson is Little Richard's vengeance. He is the brilliant, freakish black prodigy who would not tolerate being snubbed, and so he figured a way to win pop music's attention and acclaim. But as the late James Baldwin once wrote, "[Michael Jackson] will not swiftly be forgiven for having turned so many tables, for he damn sure grabbed the brass ring, and the man who broke the bank at Monte Carlo has nothing on Michael." On this night, Jackson may have learned the hard lesson behind Baldwin's words: What can be won big can also be taken away—and losing it is sometimes harder than never having had it in the first place.

Jackson's Grammy losses serve to raise expectations for his Madison Square Garden shows, which get under way the night following the Grammys with a benefit performance for the United Negro College Fund. Some of his supporters speculate that Jackson intends to use the concerts to redeem his reputation by putting on the most impressive and assertive shows of his career—and that is precisely what he does. In contrast to the tour's opening shows a week earlier in Kansas City, Missouri, where he had often seemed overwhelmed by glitzy and relentless staging, Jackson seems not merely involved and animated but often flat-out magnificent in his New York shows.

But it is during the two songs toward the show's end, "Billie Jean" and "Man in the Mirror," that Michael Jackson's greatest strengths—as well as his greatest problems—as a live performer are displayed. "Billie Jean," in fact, conveys both at once. When Jackson first performed the song in public—during his startling appearance on the 1983 *Motown 25* TV special—he was still close to its meanings, to the fear and anger that inspired the song. In addition, he was performing it as the first public declaration of his adult independence, as if not only his reputation depended on it but also his future. Now, though, with all its letter-perfect maneuvering and moonwalking, "Billie Jean" seems less like a dance of passion than a physical litany of learned steps, less like an act of personal urgency than a crowd-pleasing gesture. Even so, "Billie Jean" is still a marvelous and bewitching thing to behold.

But as Jackson demonstrated the night before at the Grammys, his live version of "Man in the Mirror" is an act of living passion. In fact, it now seems a more personal and heartfelt song for Jackson than "Billie Jean." Back in 1983, the latter song seemed like his way of negotiating with the world, a way of attracting the world's curiosity in the same motion that he announced that he was afraid of being misinterpreted or used up by that world. But with "Man in the Mirror," a song about accepting social and political responsibility, Jackson may be trying to integrate his way back into the world, or at least to embrace his place in it a bit more. It is hardly an easy peace that Jackson seeks. After all, at the end of the song, he retreats back into his *real* world, a very private and isolated place. What's more, it may be that the world no longer loves or wants him as much as it once did. After watching Jackson on nights like this, however, when his power and passion are so undeniable, the idea of his audience rejecting him amounts to a sad loss on everybody's part.

We all know what happened next. In 1993, he began the year by playing at a preinaugural gala for President Clinton, and a month later, he gave a lengthy TV interview to Oprah Winfrey, in which he tried to dispel the rumors about his eccentricities, plastic surgery and the lightening of his skin (the latter, he said, was the result of a skin disease, vitiligo).

Then, in August, Jackson was hit with public charges that he had sexually abused an underage boy. The police raided Jackson's house, looking for evidence; his sister LaToya claimed that Michael often spent the night with young boys in his room; Jackson was forced to cancel a worldwide tour that was under way; and Pepsi ended its long relationship with the singer. In early 1994, lawyers for both Jackson and the boy's father announced that the matter had been settled out of court for an undisclosed sum. The criminal investigation was eventually dropped, and Jackson steadfastly maintained his innocence, despite the settlement that he had agreed to. In 1997, Jackson had his own child; unfortunately, the event became fodder for bad jokes and trash reporting.

Whether the charges were true or not, Michael Jackson had fallen, from a very big height. In light of the rumors, his earlier peculiarity began to take on an even deeper creepiness for many people. Michael went on to marry, then divorce, Lisa Marie Presley, Elvis Presley's daughter. To some people, it seemed as if the Presley name had been just another big prize for Michael to claim for his own, in the same way, a few years before, he had bought much of the Beatles' song catalog.

For my part, I guess I should own up to what I once thought of him, that Michael Jackson was an artist of immense talents and possibilities, and I should also own up to what I think of him now, that he is a man of even *more* immense hubris and tragedy.

I'm not sure it was all his fault. He had an intensely strange, unkind and horribly coerced childhood, and later, when he would finally win his dream, he would also win intense hatred for realizing that dream. As a result of both of these things, perhaps Michael Jackson had long been living in a no-win dimension. At the same time, he seemed unwilling to learn from his fall; he seemed unwilling to be seen as anything less than a demigod. He allowed statues to be built of himself, and he insisted that *his* had been the most injured innocence of all. Michael Jackson may yet again make music that is pleasurable to hear, but I don't think it can ever really matter again. He lives in a trap, as critic Dave Marsh once pointed out, and while much of it is of his own doing, no doubt some of it is of our making, as well. He is among the best proofs I've seen in my lifetime of William Carlos Williams's famous perception: "The pure products of America go crazy," and rock & roll's America has had few purer products than Michael Jackson.

Still, I'll never forget that night back in March 1983, when onstage in Pasadena, California, at the Motown anniversary show, Michael Jackson gave his first solo public performance, vaulting into that astonishingly graceful, electrifying version of "Billie Jean." Dancing, spinning, sending out impassioned, fierce glares at the overcome audience, Jackson did a powerful job of animating and mythologizing his own blend of mystery and sexuality. I'd never seen anything quite like it—maybe I never will again—even if so much of what followed after that night was simply Michael Jackson's moonwalk to his own ruin.

my favorite eighties recordings

By ROBERT CRAY

(In no particular order)

1 **"Fed Up With Music,"** by A.C. Reed. I like A.C. Reed as a performer. I've seen him do this song, and I think he's just great. The part of the song where he talks about "One hit song, I'd be a star like the Rolling Stones" is just great. I've known a lot of people who have felt that real frustration in trying to get a hit, and so I think it is a great song.

2 **"I Can't Win,"** by Ry Cooder. I like Bobby King and the singing in that song. It reminds me of a nice, old R&B ballad. And, of course, it's got great guitar work on it.

3 *Bring the Family,* by John Hiatt. It's really difficult to pick a particular song by him— I like everything he's been doing lately. I think this is when everybody started listening to him again. He knocked that album out in a few days—that's just incredible.

4 *Hot Number,* by the Fabulous Thunderbirds. I've always loved the T-Birds. I picked this album, but I really like all of them. They just do so much good stuff.

5 **"Damn Your Eyes,"** by Etta James. I [once] saw her sing this on *The Tonight Show*, and I thought she just tore it up. It's a great song, a great ballad.

6 *Toots in Memphis,* by Toots Hibbert. Toots is way too funky. I've been listening to him for years and years. He wants to be Otis Redding really, really bad, and it was great finally hearing him sing Otis's songs. I like listening to this when I'm out driving around.

7 **"Do I Love Her,"** by Taj Mahal. I like the groove on this—it's a serious groove. I also like that he's talking about Muddy Waters and Howlin' Wolf, and then he does the Wolf imitation—Taj does the best Wolf imitation around. People need to know more about Taj, because he hasn't been on the scene in a big way for a long time, but Taj is one of my favorites.

8 **"To Know Someone Deeply Is to Know Someone Softly,"** by Terence Trent D'Arby. I don't think too many people liked this album, and I didn't like a lot of stuff on it, but I thought this melody was just gorgeous. I like the way he sings it. There's a lot of great stuff on his first record, but I'm a fool for real pretty melodies, and I think this is just a great melody.

9 *Cold Snap,* by Albert Collins. Collins is one of my favorite guitar players, and I think this whole LP is just a bunch of great songs. Again, I could have chosen any of his records.

10 **"End of the Rope,"** by Lonnie Brooks. I've wanted to do this song for a long time and just haven't gotten around to doing it yet. A great lyric in that song, and a great ballad.

my favorite eighties recordings

By DAVID BYRNE

(In no particular order)

1 **Shahad (The Khazana Collection),** by Mehdi Hassan

2 **Amour Fou/Crazy Love,** by Kanda Bongo Man

3 **"Symphony of Sorrowful Songs,"** by Henryk Mikolaj Górecki

4 **Yellow Moon,** by the Neville Brothers

5 **Creuza de Mä,** by Fabrizio de André

6 **"Ojala Que Lléva da Café,"** by Juan Luis Guerra y 4:40

7 **Fear of a Black Planet,** by Public Enemy

8 **Estrangeiro,** by Caetano Veloso

9 **King of America,** by Elvis Costello

10 **Rum, Sodomy & the Lash,** by the Pogues

11 **"Abusadora,"** by Wilfrido Vargas

12 **3 Feet High and Rising,** by De La Soul

13 **Greatest Hits Vol. 2,** by Celia Cruz

229

the nineties

By ROB SHEFFIELD

Once in a blue moon, a record comes along to define a decade—no, a generation. A record that wraps yellow tape around everything that came before and stakes a claim on everything to follow. A record that maps out a new canon of rock & roll mythology. Such a record came out in late 1990, introducing the bold, new voice that would dominate the era. The group that made the record exploded out of nowhere to change the face of music, and its all-too-brief career raised the hopes of everyone who'd given up on the future of rock, daring us to dream all over again. No doubt about it: We can all remember the first time we heard C+C Music Factory's "Here We Go, Let's Rock & Roll."

You remember C+C Music Factory's "Here We Go, Let's Rock & Roll," don't you? Come on, it was a Number Three hit—you know, that group who did the "Everybody dance now" song, with Zelma Davis, the model who "visualized" the vocals? Well, maybe you *don't* remember, but C+C sealed their place in rock history one fateful afternoon in the summer of 1991, when rapper Freedom Williams passed out onstage (from "exhaustion," of course) in the middle of a stadium show, and his voice kept booming out of the speakers while he lay there unconscious. Thanks to the miracle of lip synching, the show went on—they could have pumped the poor guy's stomach without missing a beat—but the Eighties died right then and there, and so did the whole music factory that had made 1990 the worst year for recorded music since the invention of magnetic tape. Pop artifice is a wonderful thing, but incompetent pop artifice is something else, and with C+C, the industry had finally reached the point where it couldn't even churn out quality garbage. Even those of us who were card-carrying Bananarama and Pet Shop Boys fans had to scoff at what was left of the Eighties machine and sneer, "Here we go. Let's rock & roll." Or to put it another way: "Here we are now! *Entertain* us!"

Nirvana came along a few months later, blowing up the music factory with the opening guitar lick of "Smells Like Teen Spirit," but the world was already changing around them. In 1991, the *Billboard* charts began using SoundScan technology. Previous charts had been compiled via informal, unverifiable phone surveys of record-store employees, who, er, wouldn't *dream* of cooking the books to help out their friends at the big labels. SoundScan forced the charts to reflect what people were actually buying, and without SoundScan, the big stories of the Nineties don't exist. Sure, Nirvana would have been a hit anyway, but would *Nevermind* have bitch slapped Michael Jackson and Guns n' Roses out of the Number One slot? If you believe that, David Geffen probably has a great deal to offer you on a few hundred thousand unopened Ratt CDs.

After that, the Nineties were a whole new ball game. Grunge happened. Rave happened. Alanis happened. Gangsta rap happened. You remember those two kids with the backwards pants, the ones who sampled the Jackson 5 and outrocked Michael himself in "Jump," maybe the greatest summer hit in the history of the universe? They happened, too. Lollapalooza happened. So did Lilith Fair and the Macarena. Elton happened, but then, doesn't he always? Puffy happened all over us. Here we went. We rocked and rolled. We sucked in the century. We got drunk, we got weak, we got lost, we got crazy with the Cheez Whiz. None of it made a damn bit of sense. And we won't stop, 'cause we can't stop.

In the wake of SoundScan, things got seriously tweaked, as the radio swarmed with con artists, sex puppets, guitar monsters, leather-clad pleasure speculators, fly-by-night disco scammers and other pop visionaries. It was excellent. Records started debuting at Number One and then tumbling off the chart right away. (Hello and goodbye, Skid Row.) Fads came and went before we had a chance to get sick of them. (*Bonjour et adieu*, Kris Kross.) The boom-bust cycle accelerated like never before—the rise faster, the heights dizzier, the fall steeper. (*Ave atque vale*, P.M. Dawn.) Careers that would have taken years in the pre-Sound-Scan era played themselves out in a matter of months. Nobodies like Billy Ray Cyrus, the Spin Doctors, Third Eye Blind and Paula Cole went megaplatinum their first day at the rodeo but then, just as suddenly, found themselves up the hootie without a blowfish. A few years after spending fourteen weeks atop the *Billboard* album chart, all M.C. Hammer had to show for it was debt, bankruptcy, some brightly colored pants and a basement full of PROPER! IT'S HAMMER TIME! keychains and yo-yos.

The great center of Eighties pop fell apart. The Eighties crossover superstars saw their audiences disappear and had to start over as cult artists. Michael Jackson made some god awful records, married Elvis's daughter, settled a child-molestation suit out of court, sampled *Fiddler on the Roof* and got to know his chimps better. Prince went off the deep end and changed his name to The Artist Formerly Known as Prince. Unfortunately, he was soon just The Artist Formerly Known, settling into a routine of haphazard albums with two or three good songs apiece. His best song of the decade was a truly bizarre gospel-metal cover of Joan Osborne's "One of Us," buried on the third disc of the otherwise flaccid 1996 set *Emancipation*. Bruce Springsteen went solo, but without E Street drummer Max Weinberg, he got outflanked by Garth Brooks and Eddie Vedder. Richard Marx withered away. Lionel Richie is now reportedly living in Miami Beach under the name "Mrs. Hyman Roth." Madonna, one of a kind as always, prospered by playing to the dance and Adult Contemporary markets simultaneously. Hall and Oates, though, couldn't get arrested in the Nineties. George Michael, on the other hand, could, and for using the other hand. (Hey, sex is natural, sex is fun, sex is best when it's one.)

These artists struggled because the Eighties mainstream no longer existed. In the Nineties, the center could not hold, and there wasn't a single Top Forty station in the country playing the whole Top Ten. Rock & roll decentralized like crazy, splitting up into factions of hip-hop fans, indie-rock fans, jam-band fans, alt-country fans, Tejano fans, contemporary Christian fans, Swedish reggae fans and countless other audiences. It was never easier to avoid music you didn't like. Radio was so micro-niched that you could listen for hours a day without getting jolted out of your own little demographic bubble. Celine Dion, Mariah Carey, Whitney Houston and Michael Bolton racked up plenty of Number One smasheroos, but nobody outside the presold schlock market ever heard them. Meanwhile, Garth Brooks sold sixty million records without a pop hit—unless you tuned into the country station, he never crossed your radar.

In a way, this was a loss; there wasn't anything like the public fun of a *Thriller*. But there was more great music out there than any human being could possibly process in a mere ten years, and there were more ways of getting access to it (or, if you were a musician, releasing it) than ever before. It was too late to keep 'em separated: It was time to come out and play, go zooming around the dial to hear new kinds of fun getting invented. There was no hope of keeping up with everything, but there was so much funky stuff in the air, every music scene had its own self-sufficient fan base.

That's why the Nineties spiritually belonged to weirdos. Consider a few quintessential Nineties career artists: Beck, Phish, Indigo Girls, Ani DiFranco, the Roots, Sarah McLachlan, KRS-ONE, Moby, Cornershop, Alison Krauss, the Flaming Lips, Los Lobos, Superchunk, Primus, k.d. lang, Emmylou Harris. In any other decade, these folks would have been way too weird for stardom, and some entered the decade with the washed-up major-label sales figures to prove it. Yet they each built—or rebuilt—long-haul careers in the Nineties, mostly by working hard on the road, keeping the overhead low and conceding that there was a firm limit on the number of converts they were going to reach. Since there was no percentage in straining for big-budget platinum, let alone going into debt to gamble on it, they settled for steady gold or less. A few fluked into platinum now and then, but it did them no harm as long as they remembered it was temporary and paid off their credit cards. None of these folks ever had a Number One hit, but they all probably kept more money than C+C Music Factory did, and it's a safe bet they even enjoyed the job, playing music that they themselves might actually want to listen to. Is there anyone alive who honestly enjoys each one of these acts? Not a chance, kid. Is it good news anyway that they all kept making their music? Hell yes, and anyone who disagrees probably thinks the Beatles sold out when they left Liverpool.

One of the best American rock band of the Eighties, the Replacements, spent their final years deliberately making records that they knew were bad but that they hoped would get played on the radio. Needless to say, it didn't work. Not too many Nineties artists fell into this trap, just because the radio had become too fragmented for a winner-take-all jackpot. There was little commercial incentive for anyone to make a bad record, and so the decade's finest artists simply made the records they wanted to make and figured the right audience would find them. When Moby tried to make hit records, he was a bore. When he said the hell with it and made himself an indie-label vanity recording of antique blues voices remixed into techno spirituals, 1999's *Play*, he stumbled onto a slow-building international smash that kept him touring for over a year. That was the way the cookie crumbled in the Nineties, and boy, did that cookie crumble, as whole careers were built on the narrowest of audience margins. Like the late, great Jerry Garcia used to say, one man gathers what another man spills.

It was the decade for arty guitar bands, maybe the best ever. The year 1991, once promised in *Planet of the Apes* as Year One of the ape revolution, instead turned out to be The Year Punk Broke. Nirvana came along to rock high school parking lots from coast to coast, fusing Hüsker Dü's "Whatever" to the Replacements' "Never Mind" as Kurt Cobain's yowl seethed with angst and wit and compassion. Spandex metal died out overnight—grunge was the word. *Paris Match* editorialized about "le grunge," while the tabloid TV hit *Cops* introduced one Seattle episode with the unforgettable tag line "Tonight . . . in the city where Pearl Jam was born . . . the cops are taking out the grunge!" At your local drugstore, you could purchase a fifty-cent tube of Grunge Gunk, labeled as the "Alternative Hair Styling Mud." What a time to be young and in love.

When Nirvana kicked the door down, they brought romance and adventure back to guitar rock, and the airwaves were suddenly full of terrific new bands trying to rise to the challenge of the new audiences opening up everywhere. We started hearing from "underground" singer/songwriters like Hole's Courtney Love, Nine Inch Nails' Trent Reznor, PJ Harvey and Liz Phair. Green Day, the Offspring and Rancid revitalized garage-style punk rock. The Breeders sang the joys of sex, cars and summer, rocking with all the subtlety of a divine hammer and crashing the Top Forty anyway. Beck's "Loser" skated to glory on a hot-wired blues guitar riff and a cheap beatbox.

Across the ocean, Brit-pop bands threw off the mantle of mediocrity, as brilliant chancers like Pulp, Oasis, Stereolab and the Verve took their bows. Pavement's Stephen Malkmus, the great guitar romantic of the decade, murmured painfully beautiful ballads about the kinds of girls he liked in the August sun. The Lemonheads' Evan Dando, the first blush of fame still pink upon his celebrity skin, spread his loving arms across the land. The Beastie Boys took yoga classes, bought some cool sneakers, respected women and almost accidentally evolved into six or seven of the world's greatest rock & roll bands.

Some people worried that all this mass appeal would kill off indie rock at the grassroots level. They were wrong. More bands than ever learned how to put out their own records, and more indie bands than ever were worth hearing. Underground bands like Sleater-Kinney, the Auteurs and the Silver Jews weren't auditioning for MTV; they were just exploring their guitars with a sense of romance and adventure that wouldn't have been possible in 1990, when indie rock was just a collegiate parlor game. Some of the decade's finest indie records, like Dump's *International Airport*, never came out on CD; others, like the Secret Stars' 1994 Shrimper debut cassette, never even went vinyl. Riot grrrls like Bikini Kill, Bratmobile and Excuse 17 were the decade's truest punk voices, giving the drummer some and expressing feminist aggro that didn't have to hide behind a come-on. Bikini Kill's classic 1993 single "Rebel Girl" even featured a duet with Joan Jett on the girl's playground classic "Miss Mary Mac," which spoke volumes about where their sense of punk-rock daring came from.

Like so many previous rock & roll moments, this one slowed down when the drugs took over. Kurt Cobain had better taste in Vaselines import twelve-inches than Mötley Crüe did, but he had the same taste in drugs, ending up another junkie suicide in 1994. Countless other bands got stalled or stopped dead by heroin: the Breeders, Meat Puppets, Smashing Pumpkins, Stone Temple Pilots, and the list goes on. It's still difficult to connect Kurt Cobain's death with his voice, to square his pathetic, isolated decline with his voice's lust for human contact. In adult love songs like "Heart-Shaped Box" and "All Apologies," or in the soulful marital tableau of *MTV Unplugged in New York*, you can still hear Kurt's fierce, vital passion as he pledges devotion to a lover who has married him and buried him, a lover he will never let go, no matter what. And although the heroin got him instead, the music still tells a more interesting story. The surviving Nirvana members decided to keep a respectful, loyal silence on the subject of Kurt's death; amazingly, and admirably, they've managed to stick to it, a tribute to the power of their friendship that itself stands as the most eloquent statement of what Nirvana's music was all about.

Meanwhile, as the audiences kept expanding and subdividing, it was a gas to see silly genre names multiply faster than domain names to define musical styles that had barely begun to exist yet. This was especially true of techno, the European dance music that hit big in the States with all-night raves, toxic drugs and white people in silly hats. Techno offered up a new subgenre every few weeks, each one touted by heavily sedated adepts as the future: drum and bass, trip-hop, post-rock, hardstep, quickstep, macro-dub, illbient trancebeat, intelligent breakbeat, international house of pancakes, speed garage, speed racer, camptown races, doo dah, doo dah. Before long, the scene was as complex and dull as Seventies progressive rock, with a new generation of Rick Wakemans manning the turntables to make their own *Tales From Trip-Hopographic Oceans*. Most of the music was too chemically zonked to matter outside its highly specialized drug culture. But that didn't stop the Chemical Brothers, DJ Shadow, Daft Punk and other brave spirits from creating excellent mood music. Compared to the psychedelic soul of Massive Attack's "Protection" or μ-Ziq's "The Fear," most of techno's crimson kingpins sounded like twentieth-century schizoid men.

Country boomed in the Nineties, making rich men out of Garth Brooks, basically a rhinestone Phil Collins, and Tim McGraw, the son of former Mets reliever Tug "I Never Smoked Artificial Turf" McGraw. The real star of the show, though, was Shania Twain, a Canadian showgirl bride who got her professional start singing "Y.M.C.A." in a revue called Viva Vegas before changing her name from Eileen and becoming the Shania the world needed her to be. If any artist summed up the Nineties, she did, ignoring the Nashville machine and indulging her own truly strange fantasies along with her husband, former Def Leppard producer Mutt Lange, who poured some sugar on her and cranked up the disco drums. No fussing about roots for Miss Shania—she wouldn't have known a mandolin if it bit her on the leg, but that shamelessness is what made her the great glam-rock poseur of her era. America was the only market in the world where *Come On Over* was decorated with steel guitar twang; abroad, it was sold as a straight electric-boogie record. Indeed, when Eurotrash disco troupers Real McCoy covered her hit "(If You're Not in It for Love) I'm Outta Here," it sounded *exactly the same.*

Hip-hop entered the decade still reeling from the success of N.W.A.'s gangsta rap, which razed every other style of the music. Nongangsta rap basically ceased to exist. The rigid code of rules that gangstas were afraid to break (the usual bullets, blunts and bitches over the usual ascetic G-funk trudge) drained all the musical and sexual imagination out of hip-hop, especially for party people of the nongangsta persuasion.

But interesting things were brewing. The Wu-Tang Clan built themselves an elaborate mythology, making up new aliases for each other from track to track, fronting as Chinese kung fu masters or Italian mobsters, inventing new languages for the urban horror around them to the broken beats of the RZA's ominous avant-wacko production. Virtually all the Wu-Gambinos made solo albums, peaking with the brilliant trilogy of Raekwon's *Only Built 4 Cuban Linx*, GZA's *Liquid Swords* and Ghostface Killah's *Ironman*. The Fugees took similar polyglot inspiration from the Caribbean and the movie house in *The Score,* as the hip-hop nation broadened enough for capos and bohos, poets and pimpresarios. As the Fugees' Pras Michel put it in 1996, summing up the broad reach of the new hip-hop: "Back in the early Eighties, niggas was break-dancing to Duran Duran and Culture Club. There was no discrimination. Remember the Eighties British invasion? I don't give a fuck who you are, man, can't nobody front on that shit. Everybody was listening to that, straight up. That's what we grew up with."

By the mid-Nineties, hip-hop was bringing the noise to a radio dial that sounded livelier than ever, thanks to R&B smoothies like Babyface and R. Kelly, beat wizards like Timbaland and Teddy Riley, and a renaissance of brilliant pop schemers like Puffy, Biggie and Missy, not to mention Scary, Sporty, Grumpy, Dopey, Nanny, the Professor and Mary Ann, plus who-ever sang "How Bizarre." Puff Daddy's Bad Boy empire culminated in the Notorious B.I.G.'s *Life After Death,* a tender, brutal, floridly emotional, hysterically funny statement of musical bravado that dominated the radio during this long and glorious pop moment. Unfortunately, Biggie wasn't there to hear it. In March 1997, he was murdered by an unknown assailant with a handgun outside an industry party in L.A. His murder came just six months after the similarly unsolved execution of his West Coast gangsta rival Tupac Shakur in September 1996. Their deaths tragically signaled the limits of gangsta toughness as a musical pose, but the commercial and creative clout of hip-hop just kept on to the break of dawn.

A host of specialized package tours began crossing the nation, after Lollapalooza had defied all industry logic with a hugely successful tour of arty guitar bands in 1991. It ran every summer until 1997 and inspired plenty of inheritors, moving in on increasingly specific slivers of the audience: H.O.R.D.E. (Hacky Sack hell), Lilith Fair (female singer/songwriters), Warped (moshing hockey players) and Smokin' Grooves (too *crunk* to fuck). By decade's end, most fans had stopped bothering with stadium shows, as ticket prices soared and conditions declined. Some bands soaked the faithful for over a hundred bucks a ticket; for that kind of money, you should get dinner, a deep-muscle massage and Joe Walsh to pick up your dry cleaning, not to mention a working bathroom.

The decade's real road warriors were the hippie jam bands. Unlistenable to outsiders, hypnotic to their masses of presold hard-core fans, these guys played entirely different sets every night, improvising to their hearts' content and encouraging tapers. The Dave Matthews Band became international superstars with their virtuosic Grateful Heads—Talking Dead fusion. Phish, the cult band of all cult bands, blended Frank Zappa's sense of rhythm, Captain Kirk's sense of humor, the Three Stooges' grasp of Eastern metaphysics and Sun Ra's personal hygiene into a four-ring prog-rock circus. Love 'em or hate 'em, they were the band who took the most outrageous advantage of the new freedoms that the Nineties opened up. In the Eighties, Phish would have been lucky to break even, but in the Nineties, they proved that extremism in the defense of liberty was no vice, and not a bad way to make a shitload of money, either.

In the midst of all this chaos, some of rock & roll's oldest voices found themselves reinvigorated. Free from the restrictions of Eighties big bam boom, veterans like Leonard Cohen, Joni Mitchell, Tom Waits and Randy Newman made music on their own staunchly unfashionable terms. After wasting most of the Eighties trying to adjust to trends that had nothing to do with him, Bob Dylan shocked everyone with *Time Out of Mind*, rasping in the voice of a drifter who'd seen the whole world without ever being impressed.

Neil Young, long assumed to have taken up permanent residence in the Sugar Mountain Retirement Home, came back strong as rock's unquestioned elder statesman, topping himself with great new songs like "Harvest Moon," "Over and Over" and "Big Time." His 1995 collaboration with Pearl Jam, *Mirror Ball*, was largely just a fun throwaway, but it also included "I'm the Ocean," a song neither he nor anybody else could have dared in the Eighties. Over a powderfinger guitar riff, Neil rants about growing old in a world he gave up trying to understand long ago, but a world he's still passionately attracted to, as Kurt Cobain, O.J. Simpson, Bill Clinton and other rock stars battle it out in his soul. The song ends with Neil in a Cutlass Supreme, stuck in the middle of the intersection, trying to turn against the flow, and leaves him stranded there in a hailstorm of guitar noise.

If there was a better song written about love, death and grief in the Nineties, nobody else had the chutzpah to release it. Like the rest of us, the Neil Young of "I'm the Ocean" found the decade painful, dizzying, scary. It took us out of the blue. It took us into the black. It was stupid and contagious. It was also more fun than it had any right to be.

my favorite nineties recordings

By MOBY

(In no particular order)

1 **"Anytime,"** by Brian McKnight

2 **"Unfinished Sympathy,"** by Massive Attack

3 **"...Baby One More Time,"** by Britney Spears

4 **"Hurt,"** by Nine Inch Nails

5 **"Poison,"** by Prodigy

6 **"Spice Up Your Life,"** by the Spice Girls

7 **"Playing With Knives,"** by Bizarre Inc.

8 *Roots,* by Sepultura

9 **"My Heart Will Go On,"** by Celine Dion

10 **"Mo Money Mo Problems,"** by Notorious B.I.G.

lollapalooza

By DAVID FRICKE

According to the definition printed on the back of the official tour T-shirt, a *lollapalooza* is "something, or somebody, very striking or exceptional; also, a big lollipop." To the sellout crowd of surf dudes, skate punks, metalheads, bat-cave belles and just plain curious folks at Irvine Meadows Amphitheater, near Los Angeles—many of whom are wearing that shirt—the Lollapalooza Festival has certainly been an all-day sucker of future-rock fun. Opening under a hot afternoon sun with the torrid angst & roll of the Rollins Band, featuring ex-Black Flag throat Henry Rollins, the day's action has zigzagged all over the so-called "alternative music" map: the bull-elephant grunge-guitar stomp of the Butthole Surfers; L.A. rapper Ice-T's brilliant double play of hardcore gangster verse and the heavy manners of his punk band, Body Count; Nine Inch Nails' dentist-drill disco attack; the sociopolitical slamming of Living Colour; Siouxsie and the Banshees' gothic pop; and finally, the epic art-thrash wail of the headline act, Jane's Addiction.

But from the festival's inception, Jane's singer Perry Farrell—the principal brains and balls behind the Lollapalooza Festival, the most successful and provocative package tour of the summer concert season—wanted this movable feast to be more than just nine hours of college-radio fuzz 'n froth, a portable Woodstock for the black-lipstick-and-nose-ring set. So just before Jane's Addiction's final encore, a fervent reading of the *Ritual de lo Habitual* ballad "Classic Girl," Farrell makes a little speech to the adoring horde.

"This is it, homeboys. Youth revolution!" Farrell declared in a high, weedy voice. "Last chance. Let's get on with it!" Later, as the last line of the song—"Yeah, for us, these are the days"—hangs in the cool night air, Farrell looks at the seething mosh pit at his feet and dives in headfirst. By the time security pulls him out, he already regrets opening his yap.

"When I said it, I really shrank," Farrell confesses the next day while the industrial dance din of Nine Inch Nails rattles his dressing-room trailer. "Because I felt like, 'Right, these guys could give a shit.' I'm sad to say I came offstage feeling like 'This isn't gonna happen; they are just too happy with life.'

"But I don't believe we can have mass rioting in America too soon," Farrell insists. "And maybe I shrank out there. Maybe I felt a little bit alone. But not naive; because you gotta give it a try. Maybe there's one guy out there who could be a political leader of some kind, who heard that and thinks, 'Right on: that guy onstage has something there.' You gotta give it to a guy for tryin'. And I'm tryin'."

If nothing else, the Lollapalooza Festival (which climaxed August 29, 1991, in Seattle after playing to almost half a million people in twenty-one cities) is a tribute to Perry Farrell's entrepreneurial nerve and up-the-mainstream attitude. "This is a pioneer tour," says Ice-T. "All the groups in their own way have pioneered a certain form of music. And the fact that none of us get played on the radio—to be able to pack arenas and all, it shows people want to hear this. It's also a very educational experience. Everybody's taking a pill they're not used to."

That's certainly true of the arts-and-issues sideshow at every venue, a Farrell idea rooted in his belief that it'll surely take more than a Big Rock Show to defang the conservative menace. Experimental artists, some chosen by Farrell himself and his wife, Casey Niccoli, display

their work on the grounds, while national and local activist groups run voter registration drives and talk turkey with the fans about the environment, censorship, abortion rights and handgun control, among other things. At Irvine Meadows, the art show is disappointingly small, a meager handful of weirdo sculptures and hangings. A few days later in San Francisco, a city with a tradition of multimedia events going back to the original Trips Festivals, though, the art scene is a gas, an outdoor cornucopia of huge, vivid canvases and interactive pieces like the *Piano Bell From Hell*, a pyramid of battered, old piano parts that people can bang on, play or kick at will. And in both cities the kids are transfixed by the demonstration put on by Body Manipulations, a bohemian crew specializing in "piercing, brandification and scarification." Farrell even tried to get representatives from the military and the National Rifle Association to take part. Not surprisingly, both groups declined. A U.S. Army spokesman replied to this invitation by saying, "Why should I bother getting into a pissing match with a bunch of left-wing rock & roll punks?"

Farrell would have liked nothing better. "Look, it's very easy to dance a dance that everybody knows," says Farrell. "But to be thrown things that are not that easy and familiar... this whole thing has a bit of tension," he says excitedly. "White kids listening to rock & roll are not exactly accustomed to hearing Ice-T or even Henry Rollins or the Buttholes. And people who listen to Ice-T exclusively don't know shit about us."

Gibby Haynes of the Butthole Surfers figures the kids don't know shit about revolution either. "They've got the Sixties backwards," says Haynes. "You look at the Sixties: The changes started with issues and worked themselves back into the music. The music was not the catalyst. And judging from the kids at Irvine, there ain't gonna be no revolution out of this. Maybe they'll change something like putting less vanilla in vanilla wafers."

Farrell is willing to take that risk. "This is an experiment," he says. "This is not a shoo-in. The Who is not going to fly in on a helicopter. And you want to hear some bullshit about Woodstock? Jimi Hendrix played, and everybody split on him. People smashed fences down, ruined this guy's farm and parked all over the place. It wasn't exactly Eden.

"The memory of it, the *myth*, is something else," Farrell continues. "I'm lucky because I have that, times twenty-one. I have twenty-one chances to get it right."

There are two good reasons why the Lollapalooza Festival has defied the summer's recession-fueled box-office blues—doing sellout or near-sellout business at many stops on the itinerary—while hastily organized copycat packages like A Gathering of the Tribes, the Sisters of Mercy–Public Enemy–Gang of Four Tour and the heavy-metal smorgasbord Operation: Rock & Roll have done so-so or shut down altogether. One reason is the ten months of planning by Farrell and his Lollapalooza brain trust: Jane's manager Ted Gardner, the band's drummer, Stephen Perkins and the group's booking agents, Marc Geiger and Don Muller.

The other, according to Gardner, is that "every one of these bands is a legitimate headliner on their own." So were most of the other two dozen acts on the original wish list for the tour, including the Pogues, Nick Cave and the Bad Seeds, the Jesus and Mary Chain, Fishbone, the Sugarcubes, the Red Hot Chili Peppers, the Pixies and Public Image Ltd. (Cave and the Peppers would join future Lollapalooza bills).

The original spark for Lollapalooza was England's annual Reading Festival, a three-day pageant of international postpunk stars and hot U.K. indie-chart bands. Jane's Addiction was scheduled to play last year but cancelled due to illness (Farrell's voice gave out). Farrell, Gardner, et al. went as spectators and came away so jazzed by the event they decided to mount a traveling version stateside, headlined by Jane's Addiction and booked into outdoor amphitheaters.

At that point, Farrell went into overdrive, becoming involved in everything from choosing the bands and judging artwork for display to arranging for free condoms to be distributed at the show (some of which ended up being inflated into big penis-shaped balloons and batted around the audience). "I was very reluctant to play to a large crowd," Farrell says. "So I told Marc, 'If I'm going to do something of that size, I want to surround myself with other great bands and great things on the grounds—food, books, art—to make it worth the money.' I'm very proud of my band. I think we're great. But I don't think it's worth twenty-five bucks to see a flyspeck."

Some of his schemes didn't pan out, like the illusionist he wanted to use during Jane's Addiction's set. For L.A., Farrell arranged for a cheerleading squad to come on during one number—except the cheerleaders showed up without pom-poms, which disappointed him so much that he nixed the idea. "The sound, lights and trucking were the easiest parts of this," notes Ted Gardner with a weary smile.

Picking the bands just turned out to be a matter of natural selection. Siouxsie and Living Colour shared the same booking agency as Jane's, and the Rollins Band had opened for Jane's on two earlier tours. Ice-T was already tight with the band, having traded epithets with Farrell on a hard, heavy remake of Sly Stone's "Don't Call Me Nigger, Whitey" featured in the long-form video *The Gift*. "For two people who do such different music," says Ice-T, "if you listen to the records, we're damn near saying the exact same shit." That's especially apparent at the second Irvine Meadows show, when he and Farrell reprise their Sly duet with electrifying results.

Guitarist Paul Leary of the Butthole Surfers says Jane's Addiction guitarist Dave Navarro "claimed in an interview that he was going to kill himself on tour if not for a tape of the Butthole Surfers that he listened to on his Walkman over and over again." So the Buttholes were in, although they were bemused to find skittish newspapers abbreviating their name to the *B. H. Surfers* in tour ads. "If my sixty-eight-year-old mother can say 'Butthole Surfers,'" cracks Leary, "what's the problem?"

Trent Reznor, the singer and leader of Nine Inch Nails, wasn't sure at first if he fit into the music mix or the tour's outdoor setting. "I feel like everyone's got a semipositive vibe, and we're the negative Antichrist onstage," says Reznor. "I'm not out preaching 'Be nice to your neighbor' or 'Save the whales.'" Also, Reznor confesses, "we've just mastered the art of playing in a club." His fears were confirmed at the first date in Phoenix, when the Nails suffered a recurring power outage that effectively killed the bass and keyboard tapes they use in the show. And let's face it: Dry ice at four in the afternoon is deeply bogus; in L.A., the band looked like it was having a hell of a barbecue onstage. The Nails proved their worth at the concession stands, though, where they rivaled Jane's Addiction in their T-shirt sales.

Without question, the most striking juxtaposition of sound and vision on the bill is that of Ice-T and Living Colour. Ice hits the stage with his posse, firing a pistol in the air and shouting, "Fuck the police!"; Living Colour rams its message of cultural celebration and racial responsibility home with avant-metal ferocity. The two acts actually have the makings of a mutual admiration society going. "Living Colour broke down barriers no one was supposed to ever break down," Ice says. (In San Francisco, he was out in the crowd, head banging to "Cult of Personality.") As for Ice's own black rock-and-rap band, Body Count, Living Colour drummer Will Calhoun says: "The concept is smokin'. Rappers should use more live musicians, leave the James Brown and P-Funk records alone."

But the two acts hit a major impasse over Ice's liberal use, in front of a largely white audience, of what Calhoun dryly refers to as "the *N* word." Onstage, Ice uses it without apology but with pride. "People get on me because I use the word *nigger*," Ice says before going into "Straight Up Nigga" from his latest album *O.G. Original Gangster*. "In my category, all of yous are my niggers." The crowd, predominantly white, goes bananas. Later, during an interview, he sums up the difference between Living Colour and Body Count by saying with a laugh, "Living Colour is black. We are niggers."

In San Francisco, Living Colour guitarist Vernon Reid responds with a special introduction to the song "Pride": "In Africa, there are no niggers. And I will die before I become a nigger for your entertainment."

"That word is about reduction," Reid contends. "It means that for 400 years, anything you could possibly imagine is justifiable. A lot of gangsta rap talks about 'this is real, this is what's on the streets,' but is that a reality we can live with and grow with? Absolutely not."

Even Ice admits that if he gets anything out of this tour, he'd like it to be the demolition of a stereotype or two: "All I want them to do is come out and say, 'I like him.' Not get the message, not understand a word I'm saying—just think, 'Those black guys on the stage I used to be scared of, I like 'em.' I want to come out and say, 'Peace.' If I can do that, that's cool."

Trent Reznor, on the other hand, has more modest expectations. When asked what he figures he'll get out of the festival, he looks down at the sheet-white hospital pallor of his skinny arms and says with a smile, "Skin cancer."

A week into the tour, and the asshole factor, as the Butthole Surfers' Paul Leary puts it, is nowhere to be seen. "I was a little worried that with all these bands on the tour, it would turn into the Battle of the Tremendous Egos," says the band's drummer, King Coffey. "But all things considered, it's been pretty cool."

It's still a little early for forming lasting friendships, and it's unlikely that some parties will ever really get along. The Buttholes can't help but cackle at the *veddy* English Banshees lounging around the dressing area après gig in fluffy bathrobes. The Banshees, in turn, probably wouldn't find anything amusing about the Buttholes' endless store of uproarious road stories involving bodily functions. But Vernon Reid has been rapping with Trent Reznor and talking guitars with Dave Navarro. Perry Farrell sat down with Siouxsie over pizza the other night. And the Buttholes are looking forward to playing basketball with Ice-T's crew.

Everybody, however, is totally in awe of Henry Rollins. His fierce stage act is the talk of the tour, and there are often more musicians watching from the side of the stage—Ice-T, Farrell, members of the Banshees and Living Colour—than there are kids in the seats when he hits the stage. "Henry Rollins is not about whether the audience is into it or not," says Vernon Reid. "It's about how *he's* into it."

More than any other act on the bill, Rollins embodies the street-hardened rebel moxie that Lollapalooza aspires to. As guitarist Chris Haskett, bassist Andrew Weiss and drummer Sin Cain fuse jagged riffs and choppy rhythms into a punk-jazz-metal firestorm, Rollins—in raggedy shorts and bare feet—anchors his rock-solid physique in an attack crouch, veins popping out of his neck like steel pipes as he rails against convention, complacency and fascist authority. "Next time someone convinces you that they know what you think and they strip you of your self-respect," he announces at one point, "pull this out of your pocket. This is called 'Brick' "—which is exactly what the song feels like when it hits you.

"It's the blues," Rollins says of his music. "If anything, we're an industrial-strength, urban-blues-band assault unit. I'm fueled by rage, and if I don't do music and writing and a lot of physical working out, I get very depressed and very destructive. I'm not a musician. I'm the kind of person who just ended up onstage, and it was perfect for a freak like me."

As a teenager in Washington, D.C., Rollins used to work out his frustrations via street violence "with other boneheaded males." In 1981, he found a more productive outlet as the singer for the seminal L.A. punk outfit Black Flag. Since forming the Rollins Band in 1987 (soundman Theo Van Rock is the fifth member), he has recorded and toured relentlessly, sweating out his "unadulterated crystalline hatred" onstage. In his spare time, he also runs his own publishing company, 2.13.61. (his birth date), and gives spoken-word performances.

Rollins recently signed with a major label, but his no-nonsense gigging ethic remains the same. "When we do work, you get destroyed," he writes in his press bio. "That's just the way it is." And to prove it, the Rollins Band careens through a daredevil medley at one Lolla- palooza show that includes Rollins's own "Fireman," the anarcho-hippie anthem "Do It" by the Pink Fairies, a voodoo crawl through Canned Heat's "On the Road Again" and "Ghost Rider" by Suicide. There is scattered applause in the crowd; the musicians, managers and roadies in the wings just stand there, mesmerized.

"The way I relate to people and music now is just 'Let's do it; let's let it happen,'" Rollins later says with a shrug. "If you put your soul into it all the way, like James Brown, people will see it and feel it. And today, I was all the way *there*."

Perry Farrell's first Lollapalooza Festival is barely under way, and already he's thinking about the next one. He's thinking small, too—more intimate surroundings, a more adven- turesome crowd, a mix of "real bizarre stuff"—because the next time, Jane's Addiction won't be around to top the bill and draw the mainstream teens. After this tour and a handful of extra Jane's dates in Australia and Hawaii, the band is breaking up, much to Farrell's relief. "Musicians have a funny thing that follows them—their past," Farrell says backstage that afternoon. "An actor doesn't have to play the same roles over and over. An artist doesn't have to paint the same picture. I, if I stay in Jane's Addiction, will have to sing 'Mountain Song' or 'Jane Says' or 'Ocean Size' every night. To try to fit Jane's Addiction into what I want to do next is like trying to fit a square peg into a round hole."

It's too bad he doesn't find Stephen Perkins's bold tribal drumming and Dave Navarro and Eric Avery's thundering guitar-bass crossfire malleable enough for his purposes. At the three Lollapalooza shows at Irvine Meadows, Jane's is in blistering form, rampaging through "Stop!" and "Three Days" as if the band had just stepped out of the garage. With his closely cropped hair, oversize, red woolen suit and jittery, stick figure dancing, Farrell looks even more extreme and dangerous than when he had braids and wore an S&M bodysuit—like a psycho-ward cross between Mr. Natural and Groucho Marx.

"I'll probably feel a little sad when I don't have it anymore," Farrell says of Jane's. "But that will just make me work really hard to do something that will top Jane's Addiction. I like pushing. Singing a Jane's song now, the band could fall asleep and play it. To be able to *conquer* that shit, that makes you bigger. To drop Jane's, man, and break that fear barrier—'Can I top this?'—that's what gives a man power and courage. My problem is, I think ahead, to the point where I get really annoyed with the present. I can't wait to get the hell out of things."

And into something else. Farrell is annoyed that his Lollapalooza ideal has been neces- sarily compromised by using an existing rock concert infrastructure. He intends to bag that at the first opportunity. "There is so much you can do with this," he says. "In the proper envi- ronment, I can entertain people, I'm sure of that."

"But," Farrell concedes, "this is reality we're talking about. I have only so much clout and so much time. And this is a great start."

kurt cobain

By GREIL MARCUS

If you look back over the last ten years, you can, if the notion appeals to you, choose an artist who most shadows these times: the Coen brothers, Oliver Stone, David Lynch, Bill Pullman or Jim Carrey in the movies; Mike Judge on TV; Tupac Shakur as an icon in the life-proves-art game; Dr. Dre, Puff Daddy or Master P as entrepreneurs and empire builders; Bill Clinton as fast-talking, slow-walking, good-looking Mohair Sam. You can regret those who had a chance to speak in a new voice and lost it, or simply let it go: the Geto Boys, Snoop Doggy Dogg, Sinéad O'Connor. I could make a better case for the music of PJ Harvey, the Pet Shop Boys, Corin Tucker in Heavens to Betsy and Sleater-Kinney, Bob Dylan or David Thomas. Yet, if Kurt Cobain, speaking through Nirvana, had done nothing but write and record "Smells Like Teen Spirit" and make it a hit, he might still be a step ahead, even though he left the decade to its own devices before it was half over.

In the time he took, Cobain used the decade up—and in a sense "Smells Like Teen Spirit" used his music up even as it announced it. You can hear every other song Nirvana made in what this one song asked for, in what this one song was convinced it would never get. From the first time they heard it, for every time afterward—in the two-and-a-half years between the tune's entry into the charts, in the fall of 1991, and Cobain's suicide, in the spring of 1994, and in the years since—more people than myself or maybe you have felt the chill of the slow, transparent, chiming notes that are the repeated signature of "Smells Like Teen Spirit." You hear all that is lucid, simple and unrushed—a between-past-and-future suspension of time lovely enough to convince you that the world itself has paused to listen—pulling against the desperation and hurry of everything else in the performance, the everything else that finally sucks up those brief prophecies of clarity and wipes them out.

Still, those silken notes hang in the air, a mourning for the failures of the past, the suggestion of a future to be made or lost, a sense of starting over stopped in its tracks, remaining as an echo that rebukes you for your own failures. The song is big, loud, ambitious, definitively unsettling and a definitive release, with the singer as sure of what he means as he is that it's a waste of time to explain it to anyone who might hear him.

In the world called up in "Smells Like Teen Spirit," there was room for small, quiet, perfect Nirvana tunes like "Something in the Way" and huge, rolling screams like "Tourette's," for sterile manifestos like "Serve the Servants" and fabulous shaggy-dog stories like the band's bootlegged cover of the Doors' "The End" (the Oedipal tragedy here reduced from eleven minutes to two, and set entirely in a Belgian waffle house)—room, in other words, for anyone who felt the song stake its claim to a moment it insisted couldn't last. "A denial! A denial! A denial!" Cobain said as he ended the song, in a voice that tested the body more than the soul, over and over, again and again: "A denial! A denial!" Of what? Of what you want most, of what you know you can't have. But as the sound pulls against its words, the song says something else: if you can have something as good as this, why can't you have what you want most?

There is a great, whole drama taking place in Nirvana's music, a drama that holds its shape, a drama that is also small and odd, a drama made with costumes but not masks. Kurt Cobain plays all the roles here; band mates Krist Novoselic and Dave Grohl are the chorus, standing off to the side, free to comment on the action but not implicated—positioned, as

‹ **kurt cobain**
KEVIN MAZUR

2
4
5

the drama hits its notes and runs its course, neither to reap the glory for the deeds performed nor pay for the crimes enacted.

You can see it in the opening and closing footage of Kevin Kerslake's 1994 video documentary *Live! Tonight! Sold Out!!*, with Cobain appearing onstage in chopped reddish hair, a scruff of beard on his chin, a cigarette in his mouth, wearing nothing but a grossly overstuffed Frederick's of Hollywood–style black slip. Behind the drum kit, Grohl is stripped to the waist, typical metal-drummer attire, except for a black bra; Novoselic is literally the straight man, a telephone pole with short hair and a Kmart cotton shirt hanging out of his pants. This is true grunge: not some music-business catchphrase, but dirt. The self-portrait Cobain presents is vaguely repulsive before it's anything else; before it's silly, the ultimate fulfillment of the Beavis and Butt-Head dream Nirvana acted out better than any other band; before it's disturbing, before it's confirming, before you dismiss it with a laugh or scratch at it under your skin.

Grohl and Novoselic look funny here, as if they're having a good time, amused with the show. On Cobain's face, and in the way he holds his body—if it's even his anymore—is an unreadable, unstable smear of sarcasm and self-contempt, a cheap joke on the audience's presumed gender politics and an absolute refusal of things as they are. Cobain offers male as female, rapist as rape victim, prom queen as the ugliest girl in school ("People just left me alone," Cobain told critic Jon Savage in 1993. "They were afraid. I always felt they would vote me Most Likely to Kill Everyone at a High School Dance"), guitar hero as cultural terrorist, pop star as star of the bad dream you'd be ashamed to have, let alone imagine the star himself of having, the THIS WAY OUT of the band's biggest hit always available, really the end of every song: *Oh well, whatever, never mind.* At the end of this particular concert, at

the end of the film, Cobain, his slip now more like a film of grime on his skin than a garment, his eyes dark and seeing something you're not seeing, crawls off the stage on his hands and knees like an animal.

The drama played out in Cobain's performance was a drama of abjection and abasement, of worthlessness and redundancy, a drama of surplus population, be it that of a solitary nobody who nobody liked or a generation the economy didn't need and the culture didn't want. "Raised in a home with six baby boomers, all I ever set out to do was find out why I felt so different," Gael Fashingbauer Cooper wrote in Minneapolis's *City Pages*, in a readers' forum published just after Cobain's death. "I celebrated their past through every trivia game and hundreds of history books, and one day it occurred to me that, however short it is, I might have a past of my own. Nirvana spoke to that, even if they had lives that were way more messed-up than your own, even if you never liked them."

This drama, an acting out of the truth that you can make your own history, that you have to, was taken to extremes—in the screams out of Cobain's throat you couldn't gainsay as effects, in the band's punk war against its own success. More commercially successful than any other punk band, Nirvana was also the band most infected by the folk virus: the suspicion that if what you do is accepted by a mass audience, then your work must be either devoid of content or a sellout, and you yourself the enemy you set out to destroy. And yet, the band made great drama even out of something as puerile as this—a doctrine inherited less from Johnny Rotten than Pete Seeger. There is a sequence in *Sold Out!!* when, through the milky, indistinct tones of what seems to be a tenth-generation bootleg video dub of "Love Buzz" as performed somewhere in South America, you see Cobain dive off a low stage into the crowd, which is pressing up against the stage as if it's bellying up to a bar. A guard roughly pulls

Cobain back, then smashes him in the head and knocks him down. As Cobain pulls his arms and legs into his chest, the guard stomps him. This wasn't staged, it was real—and yet there was a way in which this event *was* staged, because it was always present in the music. The glimpse you are given of the man inside the publicity, a defenseless loser named Kurt Cobain inside a star who happens to have the same name—something the thug in the guard has suddenly glimpsed, and just as suddenly acted upon—is shocking.

It's not as shocking as a *Sold Out!!* clip from *The Jonathan Ross Show*, apparently a U.K. TV variety program, however. A smiling Ross introduces Nirvana and "Lithium," musically a relatively moderate number in the group's repertoire; the band appears and, on this pleasant, orderly show, on a small, neat set, plays a harrowing version of "Territorial Pissings" instead. The band utterly explodes the context—which means that as you watch, nothing fits. More than that, what you're seeing is in some inarguable way *not right*. Every sound, every gesture, is wild, rough and scraping: scraping the paint right off the walls, scraping your knowledge that in a setting such as this everything is ritualized right out of your head. Even as you watch, you can't imagine this was ever on TV. It's too strong, the song too far outside of itself, the musicians too far outside of themselves, the performance too far outside of any rules for it to be brought back into the strictures of expectation and result, for it to be returned to the frame of reference within which entertainment rests. And because this is a play, staged inside the little theater of the TV show, its reality is paradoxically far more complete than the real-time event of the guard attacking the performer. The shock is total: a denial, and as a denial a violation, someone killing everyone at the high school dance, yourself included, no matter how much you say you always liked the song.

"Nirvana was about our distrust and dependence on popular culture," wrote Darin Smith of St. Paul, another contributor to the *City Pages* forum. "We hate it because it's shallow, sentimental and dishonest. There are more points of similarity between Mariah Carey and Eddie Vedder than there are differences. I wear the same dumb stare when I put my Walkman on... Kurt didn't offer any solutions, he just railed against the ugliness and made it his home. We got a cheap thrill from celebrating our wretchedness with him. He wasn't brilliant or even all that articulate, but I liked to scream along. He didn't want to be my voice, and I know there was nothing healthy about singing 'Rape Me' every day on the way to work, so maybe it's best that he's gone. Or maybe 'Rape Me' will feel even more compelling now." It does: so many of Cobain's last songs were draped in a curtain of noise, but today that curtain hides nothing. All the demands in the music—the demand to be heard, to be left alone, to come as you are and leave when you choose—stand out clearly, and all of those demands remain unsatisfied.

my favorite nineties recordings

By SHIRLEY MANSON of GARBAGE

1 *To Bring You My Love,* by PJ Harvey

2 *The Bends,* by Radiohead

3 *Nevermind,* by Nirvana

4 *The Miseducation of Lauryn Hill,* by Lauryn Hill

5 *Achtung Baby,* by U2

6 *Live Through This,* by Hole

7 *Dig Your Own Hole,* by The Chemical Brothers

8 *Fear of a Black Planet,* by Public Enemy

9 *Debut,* by Björk

10 *Maxinquaye,* by Tricky

live
in the nineties

By DAVID FRICKE

We hear it on radios and records, see it in films and on television and download it from the Internet. In its purest, most exciting and transportive form, though, rock & roll is a performance art—a live thing. A song or album can change your life; a great concert will change it on the spot. Nowhere does the collision of creative risk, emotional response and physical release that defines music in general—and rock in particular—mean more or feel better than in a room where player and audience meet, firsthand and in real time.

That was as true in the 1990s as it was at the birth of the music in the Fifties and at every revolutionary stop along the way. The following are accounts of these very different, powerhouse live shows during the 1990s.

PHISH
New Year's Eve at Madison Square Garden, New York City
December 31, 1995

"We listened to this show last night," Phish singer-guitarist Trey Anastasio says one afternoon in the summer of 1999, gesturing across a table in a New York hotel lounge at keyboard player Page McConnell. "The idea that we were playing this stuff at Madison Square Garden on New Year's Eve."

Anastasio sighs in astonishment and smiles, a bit sheepishly, as he looks at the song list in front of him: three long sets of whimsically tangled Phish originals; surging instrumental jams; a daffy buffet of Edgar Winter, Who and Collective Soul covers; fat chunks of a complex

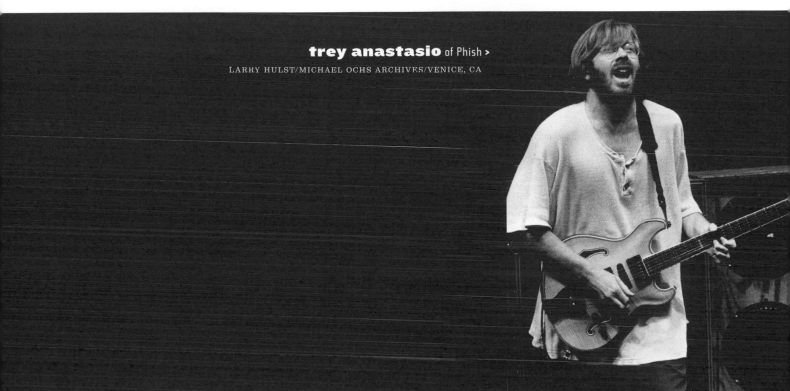

trey anastasio of Phish ›
LARRY HULST/MICHAEL OCHS ARCHIVES/VENICE, CA

Phish song cycle about the make-believe land of Gamehendge; and, at the stroke of midnight, a splashy visual prank involving a Phish time machine and a New Year's baby rising from a coffinlike crate to the strains of "Auld Lang Syne."

"Listening back, it struck me how bizarre it was, these operatic songs colliding with these inside jokes," Anastasio says. "But what I was happy about was that it sounded unique. It's a lot of different things. Another band would say, 'We don't do this, we don't do that.' We wanted to bring the whole megillah into the stew."

"But from the band's inception, this is what we were about: playing live," McConnell says. As for the audacity of booking the Garden—the most famous venue in America's largest city—on the biggest night of the year, he claims that "had just as much to do with the fans. We didn't think we *couldn't* fill it."

By the last night of 1995, Phish—Anastasio, McConnell, bassist Mike Gordon and drummer Jon Fishman—were six albums (five studio, one live) and twelve years into a career as the hottest cult band in America: an object of apostolic devotion from a young, neohippie congregation small enough to party happily at the fringes of the mainstream music industry but large enough to fill arenas nationwide. Phish had already packed the Garden once before, on December 30, 1994.

Then, with the death of the Grateful Dead's Jerry Garcia on August 9, 1995, and the de facto end of that band, Phish became, by popular consensus, the primary guardians of the vagabond idealism of the Deadhead life. With responsibility came reward: A year after Garcia's passing, Phish played to a two-day audience of more than 135,000 at the Clifford Ball in Plattsburgh, New York, and made waves on commercial radio for the first time with their seventh album, *Billy Breathes*.

Yet New Year's Eve '95 marked the end of the innocence—of the cozy, family ritual vibe and carefree stage deviltry born at Nectar's, the Burlington, Vermont, club where Phish enjoyed a carte blanche residency through the mid- and late Eighties. At Nectar's, Phish typically played three straight nights every month, three sets a night, and, Anastasio says, "We had time to kill. A lot of things grew out of that, little seeds that we planted that continued to grow, and when you hear this [Garden] show, they're all in there."

The Garden concert was, even by Phish standards, a feast of elaborate musical and theatrical conceits. There were episodic heaps of the Gamehendge suite: "The Sloth," "Colonel Forbin's Ascent" and "Fly Famous Mockingbird" in the first set, "Lizards" and the startlingly punkish "Axilla II" in the second. Phish returned to the Who's 1973 opera *Quadrophenia*, which they had played in its entirety the previous Halloween, for a note-perfect blast of "Drowned" and a graceful, solo-McConnell reading of "Sea and Sand."

Fishman appeared in a king-size diaper as the Infant New Year, and the rest of the band (with a Fishman ringer) played mad scientists fiddling with a huge time travel contraption, complete with Tesla coils, for the latest in a financially ballooning tradition of Phish New Year's Eve spectacles. (In 1994, the group flew over a Boston audience on a giant hot dog.) The Garden date also marked the finale of a chess tournament, on a giant board, that Phish played with fans during intermissions throughout the fall '95 tour. The final score: a 1-1 tie.

The music, though, is the real reason why New Year's Eve '95 was designated the Number One "Phan Pick" in the 1998 Phish concert encyclopedia, *The Pharmer's Almanac*. A first-set streak through the hairpin hooks and eccentric rhythm math of "Punch You in the Eye," "The Sloth" and "Reba" highlighted the pop cheer with which the band treats even Anastasio's knottiest melodies. The second set was even more exhilarating: a high-stepping sequence of "Lizards," "Axilla II" and "Runaway Jim" bookended by long instrumental digressions in "Drowned" and the Gordon original "Mike's Song," bearing the unmistakable imprint of the Dead's free-fall jam aesthetic.

< THE BEASTIE BOYS,
FROM LEFT TO RIGHT:
**adam horovitz,
mike diamond**
and **adam yauch**
EBET ROBERTS

"You know how you read interviews with Garcia, and he talked about how they started with formlessness, and that led to a whole new form? That form was a blueprint for us," Anastasio acknowledges. "At the same time, if you're really going to learn from them, you have to create your own form, and I feel like we did." The proof, on New Year's Eve '95, was in the taut, circular escalation of the improvising—the ebb and crash of riff and chorus—in "Mike's Song" and, in the third set, "Weekapaug Groove," the latter then rolling into a glassy McConnell piano reverie that slowly, gently became "Sea and Sand."

This show was a turning point for Phish—and the turn itself was not easy. "We started to butt our heads against the wall right after this concert," Anastasio says. "We felt like this gumbo of styles and attempts at writing grandiose, symphonic jokes, all mixed together, was getting in the way of what we thought we were capable of playing—a much more fluid music."

Two months after the Garden, Phish began work on *Billy Breathes*—"which was this real quiet, introspective album," Anastasio says. He pauses, then laughs: "We grew up."

Still, he retains a fondness for the pocket-history high jinks of this show. "More than half of the night," Anastasio points out, "is unrecorded material that we had been playing and developing and that was completely unknown to the world at large. It was known only to our fans."

He adds, "I felt like I knew everybody in the crowd." He sighs again in amazement. "Which was one more level of the inside joke: 'Hey, we're all at the Garden. Ha, ha, ha.'"

THE BEASTIE BOYS
Hello Nasty U.S. Tour
July–September 1998

Most pop, rock and rap acts go on tour to promote a new record. Mike Diamond, Adam Yauch and Adam Horovitz of the Beastie Boys booked their 1998 shows for a slightly different reason: to force themselves to finish their fifth album, *Hello Nasty*—the trio's first since 1994's *Ill Communication* and nearly three years in the making.

"We set a date for doing late-spring festivals in Europe," Diamond (Mike D) explains. "We were working for months, doing six-day weeks, twelve-hour days. We had to give ourselves a certain date by which [*Hello Nasty*] had to be done, or we'd keep tinkering with songs forever. In a sense, the touring was integral to finishing the record," Diamond says, only half in jest.

Hello Nasty's warp-drive spin through funk, punk, metal, Bronx playground scratching, electro-Seventies pop and three-way rhyme spray was, in turn, the blueprint for the B-boy playtime theater of the group's '98 road show, the Beasties' most artistically complete, viscerally focused production. Decked out like real beat doctors and rhythm mechanics in metallic blue lab coats and Day-Glo–hued jumpsuits, Diamond, Yauch (MCA) and Horovitz (Ad-Rock) worked America's big rooms from the very center—on a round, slowly revolving stage outfitted with TV monitors, real instruments and the hyperactive decks of DJ Mix Master Mike. For an hour and a half, with no rest stops, the three rappers barked verse in military unison, slippery crossfire and fearless freestyle. The Beasties also played Afrofunk instrumental sets; blew through nuggets from their teenage hardcore years, such as "Egg Raid on Mojo"; and, in encores, dumped a whole lotta Led Zeppelin over *Ill Communication*'s "Sabotage." In his review of the August 12 show at Chicago's Rosemont Horizon, Greg Kot of the *Chicago Tribune* clocked the Beasties at twenty-nine songs in eighty-five minutes.

The Beasties—abetted by keyboard ace Mark Nishita (Money Mark), percussionist Alfredo Ortiz and hardcore segment drummer Amery Smith—also changed their set list every night. The band variably opened with *Nasty*'s "Super Disco Breakin'," "The Move" or "Body Movin'," with "Time to Get Ill," from the '86 smash *Licensed to Ill*, sometimes thrown into rotation. Last-minute alterations were often made in midshow. "Rarely is there a night when we will not change something on the set list as we go," Diamond says.

Thanks to Mix Master Mike, the pace and character of the music could also radically shift in midtune—much to the Beasties' surprise. "We would never know, night to night, song to song, which beat Mike would drop next," Diamond claims. Once, while the group was in the middle of "Egg Man," from the '89 album *Paul's Boutique*, Mike suddenly veered back to *Licensed to Ill*'s "Brass Monkey," then into Gary Numan's "Cars," all within eight bars.

Native New Yorkers raised on both the heavyweight glitz of classic-rock arena gigs and the humid crush of early-Eighties hardcore-punk and hip-hop club shows, the Beasties asked themselves a simple question before designing their live Nasty blowout: In Diamond's words, "How do we subvert the actual environment of the arena, play with it, mess with it, so that it's not these little ants onstage far, far away?" Diamond says the group briefly considered using multiple stages—"We'd pop up and do a hip-hop set on one stage, with a DJ on another"—but dropped the idea as impractical.

Instead, the Beasties fattened the fun of rapping in the round with hot threads and what Diamond calls "visual sampling," a staccato combination of live performance close-ups and kinetic custom images compiled by video director Josh Adams. According to Diamond, Adams's work was so good that the Beasties were frequently tempted to turn their backs to the audience and just dig some TV—like the sock puppets that lip synched "So What'cha Want" and the Seventies basketball footage that accompanied "Root Down."

The martial look of the Beasties themselves was the result of two previous experiments in sartorial coordination: a guerrilla punk-rock club tour under the name Quasar and the 1997 Tibetan Freedom Concert in New York, where the Beasties wore brightly colored jump-suits. After that, Diamond says, "we got addicted to uniform catalogs and uniform stores. We actually had to spend a lot of time debriefing our crew about how what we wore onstage was actually uniforms, not costumes. The terminology was very important."

ROLLING STONES
Bridges to Babylon Tour
September 1997–February 1998

There was no bridge on the first night. A long, retractable span shooting out from the main stage over the fans to a small, bar band–style performance space in the thick of the crowd, the bridge was the central, eye-popping contraption in the Rolling Stones' Bridges to Babylon sta-dium pageant. The device was not ready, however (it buckled in early tests), when the Stones hit the kickoff riff of "(I Can't Get No) Satisfaction" at Chicago's Soldier Field on September 23.

So, at just past the halfway mark of the two-and-a-half-hour show, when the Stones moved out to the satellite stage for a little loose boogie, Mick Jagger, Keith Richards, Ron

‹ keith richards proves he can still rock as the Bridges of Babylon tour stops at Madison Square Garden, January 14, **1998**
KEVIN MAZUR

Wood, Charlie Watts and Darryl Jones truly walked among the people, cutting a path *through* the astonished audience. "It was Runways to Babylon," Jagger cracked dryly later, "rather than Bridges to Babylon."

In fact, the Stones had to make do without the bridge (Jagger's general estimate of its total cost: more than $1 million) for the first two weeks of the tour. "But in the end, it worked," Jagger says. "And it taught us a lot about concentrating not on the gimmick but on what are you going to do when you get out there?"

Bizarre but true: Even the Rolling Stones—still making a mockery of the old bullshit question "Is this the last time?" in their fourth decade of roadwork—need occasional remedial schooling in live rock & roll as a contact sport. They set an early high bar for arena-rock showmanship on their '69 U.S. tour (see the film *Gimme Shelter*—the bits before Altamont) and jacked up the lights, sound and fireworks when they went into outdoor stadiums in the late Seventies and early Eighties. For the American leg of their '89 Steel Wheels jaunt, the Stones rocked football fields from beneath a Godzilla-size rig that looked like Fritz Lang's idea of a New Jersey oil refinery.

The Stones were born in clubs, though—the tiny, dank R&B pubs of early-Sixties London—and they can't help going back: in spirit, theatrical flair and sometimes for real. Five nights before Soldier Field, the band held an open rehearsal at the Double Door in Chicago, shaking the wrinkles from some of the songs that would go into the big show's garage-jam segment: "Let It Bleed," "You Got Me Rocking," "The Last Time," Chuck Berry's "Little Queenie." On October 25, the Stones packed the intimate Capitol Theater in Port Chester, New York, for a half-hour live MTV telecast—and after the cameras were turned off, fired a second, extended blitz of hits for the lucky few in the room.

As big as the buildings and paydays were at most of the stops on the tour—which ultimately ran for two years around the world, drew more than five million people and grossed more than $337 million—the Bridges to Babylon production was, at least in its ideals, clubland writ mega. The repertoire, which changed often, was scripted in good, old four-sets-a-night fashion: a hello whirl of classics and a few fresh grinders (like the sleek, muscular "Out of Control," from the *Bridges to Babylon* album); a ballad sequence that often included the great drug prayer "Sister Morphine"; a hop on the bridge to the faux-bar stage; a final frisky sprint through the monsters ("Tumbling Dice," "Start Me Up," "Jumpin' Jack Flash").

The Stones even took requests—one a night from an Internet poll conducted before the concert. "'Under My Thumb' won a lot of times," Jagger says a tad wearily—so many times, it turns out, that the band stuck it in the regular show. "We thought, 'Fuck it—put it in the set. Otherwise, they'll keep voting for the same one.'" Other notable winners: "She's a Rainbow," "Waiting on a Friend" and "Starfucker."

For all of its disproportionate size and snazz, the physical Bridges set—the mock-Mesopotamian statues, the giant circular video screen overhead—was designed to pull your eyes down to the Stones themselves: Jagger in nonstop, rubber-limbed gymnastics; Richards cutting wiry, guitar-pirate poses; the eternally boyish Wood with cigarette hanging precipitously from his lower lip, pulling taut, fluid leads from his instrument; the unflappable Watts in flawless, living-rhythm form. "It was kind of old-fashioned, like a theater," Jagger says of the architecture. "The intention was to be operatic. The prosceniumlike appearance focuses attention on the center."

When the Stones unexpectedly returned to arenas in January and February '98, they squeezed the bridge and club stage into the reduced production. Jagger says the decision to get a little more cozy came well into the stadium run: "We had to do these shows in Europe [in '98], so we decided to stay on the road and do arenas." Oddly, he had trouble adjusting to the downsizing. "You have to *play* more," he explains. "It's more performing, in an odd way. You can see everybody. They can see everything you do. It was very hard work physically. We got used to playing stadiums, and I just got good at that.

"I also found that, to some extent, the audience didn't really want to hear unusual songs as much as I had imagined, because I could see their faces," Jagger adds with a droll laugh. "This wasn't me imagining it. I expected the audiences to be somewhat different. Some nights they were great: some nights they were a bit staid."

Yet, Jagger believes, there was more than begrudging respect for the new material drawn from the *Bridges* album. "We did better than we did on the Voodoo Lounge tour," he claims cheerfully. "We had three or four numbers that went down really well, and it wasn't only in the U.S. In Europe, they sing 'Saint of Me,' and I can't get them to shut up for the next number. They keep singing it over and over and over. I can't really complain."

Nor does Jagger apologize for the notorious leap in prices, to $300 for a premium seat, when the Stones went back into arenas, coolly noting the lavish cost of Knicks tickets at Madison Square Garden. He will concede, at least in hindsight, that real fans—the ones without the gold credit cards—are getting priced out of the live-rock experience: "There should be more seats at cheaper prices that are good ones, though people always talk about the top price. They never talk about the average price. The average price was high, but it wasn't $300." At the '98 Garden shows, you could sit right behind the stage for less than a fifth of that, and if it's any consolation, for a good part of every show, the other Stones play facing Watts, anyway.

"But people never want the cheap tickets, mainly because they're cheap," Jagger says. "People said to me on the streets, in clubs and cafes, 'I can't get a ticket to your concert.' I'd say, 'There are seats behind the stage,' and they'd go, 'We don't want to buy those.'

"But it's really not a bad seat."

backstage at lilith

By LORRAINE ALI

We're sitting in a traffic jam behind a VW van smothered with Deadhead stickers on a dirt road outside the Gorge Amphitheater, 141 miles east of Seattle in a Godforsaken place called George, Washington. It can only be described as a moldy desert dotted with a few agricultural fields and irrigation machines that resemble fragile dinosaur skeletons. Photographer Merri Cyr and I are on a mission: We will follow the Lilith Fair tour for its first five days, July 5–9, 1997, traveling like its artists do, down the West Coast in tour buses, planes and automobiles; then we'll disembark before it moves inward to spread its womanly goodness across the nation.

The fair is a thirty-seven-date extravaganza featuring a rotating roster of sixty-one female artists, among them Sheryl Crow, Shawn Colvin, Mary Chapin Carpenter, the Indigo Girls and Joan Osborne (Sarah McLachlan is the only constant performer). It's the summer's most popular tour, outselling Lollapalooza and H.O.R.D.E. It's also a statement by its creator, the Canadian singer/songwriter McLachlan, that sisters, most of whom play a wafty blend of coffeehouse folk, are doin' it for themselves. "Three years ago, promoters were really afraid to put two women on the same bill," said McLachlan in an interview. "With Lilith, we just wanted to prove that the concept can be done." They've succeeded. Hugely. Lilith has sold out large venues across the country and is projected to sell more than a half-million tickets ($1 from each ticket goes to women's charities). It has also raised the monetary consciousness of record moguls across the board by proving that an all-female tour can be viable, profitable and well-reviewed. There would be two more successful Liliths, in 1998 and 1999.

On this leg of the tour, the main stage features Suzanne Vega, then Paula Cole, Jewel, Tracy Chapman and McLachlan. The festivities will begin at 5:50 p.m. on the dot, after lesser-known artists do their thing on two smaller stages. But by 2:30, people are already pouring into the venue, which is perched on the side of a beauteous gorge carved by the Columbia River.

"I'm glad to see some men out there," says McLachlan during a special acoustic set that will kick off Lilith Fair. She is on the smallest of the three stages, known as the Borders Stage and sponsored by the bookstore chain. McLachlan, barefoot and standing next to a carefully placed bouquet of wildflowers, strums her guitar and lilts lyrics, her gauzy red skirt and apricot-tinged hair blowing in the breeze. The predominantly female audience—clad in bathing-suit tops, cutoff shorts and flowing hippie garb that exposes primitive goddess tattoos of suns, moons and stars—looks transfixed.

Lilith is as safe and nonoffensive as it gets. No one shows up drunk or shags groupies backstage ("There aren't any on this tour," says Cassandra Wilson, "at least not on my bus"). No one gets held up at airports for smuggling drugs in body crevices, and no one trashes a hotel room. Compared with Lollapalooza, H.O.R.D.E. and Warped, the Lilith Fair is this summer's tour equivalent of Glinda the Good Witch. Even the crowd members are well-behaved, apologizing when they bump into one another, drinking bottled water rather than beer and swaying in seats rather than starting up a mosh pit.

There's no Courtney Love brawling with members of Bikini Kill, no Salt-n-Pepa professing their need to shoop, no Liz Phair singing "Fuck and Run" (though Phair and rapper

sarah mclachlan

enthralls her audience, **1997**

EBET ROBERTS

Missy Elliott would eventually join Lilith in '99). Lilith's press release calls it "a reflection of women's evolving role in popular music," but as a wide range of people on the tour admits, its initial offering is too one-dimensional: there's nothing too risky or nongoddesslike. Instead, women are represented as a whole by Jewel singing "You Were Meant for Me," Tracy Chapman performing with a didgeridoo and McLachlan herself headlining all thirty-seven nights with a set that can be described as squeezably soft. It's all smiles and serenity.

"I don't really remember who's playing, but I came out to celebrate women in music," says one concertgoer at the Shoreline Amphitheater, just outside San Francisco. "There's been a boys' club for long enough—now it's time for us to start our own." I wonder whether everybody has forgotten about the last ten years in music, during which Hole, Björk, Alanis Morissette and TLC have eclipsed guys in the popularity and creativity departments.

But when you're steeped in Lilithland, you can forget about the world outside and simply celebrate womanhood by purchasing free-flowing skirts in the Village area, dining at health food stands with names like Wok on the Wild Side, and standing in harmony with other women in half-hour-long bathroom lines. Though the crowd is forced together as one, there's little sisterly fraternizing backstage. Like high school society, a pecking order quickly forms: Suzanne Vega is the cool and distant art chick, Paula Cole the down-to-earth best friend, Jewel the stuck-up one, Tracy Chapman the respected activist and McLachlan the peppy student body president who wears weird-colored eye shadow. The second-stagers—Mudgirl, Leah Andreone and Cassandra Wilson—are like the stoners in the smoking area, possessing the coolest clothes, attitudes and tattooed backup dudes. The Borders Stage's solo artists— Kinnie Starr and Lauren Hoffman—are the tagalong little sisters, still gawky, unpolished and apart from the social hierarchy.

Those extremes on the largest and smallest stages make the second stage the most interesting, with goofy punk-rock sets by Mudgirl (one of the few unsigned bands on the whole tour); weird, high-pitched Ani DiFranco yowls from Andreone; and a deadly cool set by jazz diva Wilson. When Vega starts up on the main stage, she does a spare set with just her bass player. It's detached, arty and beautiful and would have been devastatingly effective later in the evening. Her short set is a definite success with the audience, who get to sing the "*do do do do's*" of "Tom's Diner." Cole proves the most exhilarating—and sometimes ferocious—performer, shaking, dancing, whistling and making animal noises.

Then there's Jewel's set, during which she tells the audience how great it is not to be a waitress anymore. Meanwhile, a guy behind the mixing board, in a shirt that reads I LOVE THE SMELL OF DIESEL IN THE MORNING, keeps looking at his watch. Jewel's backing band, an odd group that looks totally disconnected from her and one another, appears no more enthusiastic. Jewel attempts Patti Smith's "Dancing Barefoot" all pouty and pigeon-toed, and sounds like, well, Jewel. The next four dates will consist of an unwitting game that people play sidestage while Jewel performs. It's called Is That a Cover or an Original? "I think that's Dylan's 'Tom Thumb's Blues,'" comments another artist's backup musician. "But I think she just did another cover, of Blondie's 'Call Me,'" says someone else. Meanwhile, I'm busy thinking how much her hit "You Were Meant for Me" sounds just like that sappy Seventies hit "Danny's Song" ("Even though we ain't got money...").

At this point I need ampage, screams, but Chapman comes out singing "Behind the Wall" a cappella, which echoes hauntingly across the stadium. Her set is spotless, perfect, supplemented by seven session musicians. (A big problem here: Most of the bands are precise yet robotic session guys, which results in little spontaneity on the main stage.) Chapman is a clear favorite with the fans and deserved so, with a confident delivery and commanding presence.

McLachlan comes next. A few more gauzy moments, and the show is over. Then begins my and Merri's nightly scramble for a ride. McLachlan, Jewel and Chapman send handlers to tell us we can't go on their buses (Vega and Cole don't have one yet), but Wilson offers to take us to Seattle. I wake the next morning in the Holiday Inn humming, "Tell me everything's gonna be all right. . . ."

According to Hebrew folklore, Lilith was Adam's first wife, but from there, the stories vary, depending on just whom you talk to. McLachlan says that Lilith didn't want to take orders from Adam, so she dumped his ass. Kinnie Starr says that Lilith wasn't subservient enough and was banished from the Garden of Eden. Even in the Old Testament, it's unclear just what she did to cause such a stir. Isaiah 34:14 says, "Wild cats shall meet with desert beasts, satyrs shall call to one another; there shall the Lilith repose and find for herself a place to rest." Somehow it's hard to imagine Jewel lying with desert beasts in her red spaghetti-strap dress ("Herb Ritts gave it to me"), but at the Lilith Fair, we use our imagination.

"What's cool is, no one here acts like a star," Jewel tells me in her dressing room on the San Francisco stop of the tour. "It doesn't matter how many records you sell, even though I've sold the most."

"When my album *Fumbling Towards Ecstasy* came out three years ago, a lot of radio stations said they couldn't play the single because they had another woman, Tori Amos, on their playlists," says McLachlan at a press conference; these will take place every day for the first five days of the tour. "Like, 'Go 'way—we've already got our token female this week.'" Maybe the fact that there's little airtime allotted to women explains the underlying sense of competitiveness at these press events, which resemble the uncomfortable alliance of a NATO meeting. Answers are filled with feminist-sounding words like *empowerment, community* and even *germination*, and the participants look as detached from one another as a seated row of subway riders. At the press conference in Los Angeles, however, there is a moment of unification when a reporter asks why the lineup isn't more diverse, with more rock and rap acts. McLachlan shoots back, "I think the lineup's very diverse." Andreone jumps in: "I've never seen so many different styles together." Vega, Kim Bingham of Mudgirl and Kinnie Starr remain silent.

In Salem, Oregon, we're supposed to meet McLachlan for an interview, and we wait by her dressing room door for five minutes. When she opens it, she says with a grin, "You're late—we have five less minutes now. I have to see Paula Cole play at 7:05, then from 7:30 to 8, I have to use my stair machine." I feel so rushed, I ask stupid questions that result in answers with *togetherness* and *community* in them, then go outside to watch Cole. There aren't a lot of performers hanging out watching others' sets, but when they do, they find, like it or not, that Cole is the one supplying and stealing the fire.

"There is a connectiveness with all the music on this bill," says McLachlan at one point, "just a vibe and energy. Everybody on this bill has a real gift of sharing." But Bingham of Mudgirl, the only slightly punk-rock band on the tour, doesn't exactly feel a oneness with the lineup today. "Our set was really disappointing," she says, slamming her guitar case shut behind the second stage. You can hear Vega starting up on the main stage. "It's like there were too many hippies out there, and they wanted something folkier. They just didn't get it. I guess we were too rock & roll." When I catch up with Vega, I ask whether she has been able to share with any of the artists. "I made an appointment to meet Tracy Chapman on Tuesday," she says. Today is Saturday.

Lilith's sponsors, all of whom have donated good amounts of money to women's charities, are divided by McLachlan into such categories as spirit, shelter, learning and wellness ("Socially conscious business is what we wanted," she says). Borders Books is in the learning category; Nine West Shoes in wellness (if you look good, you feel good).

I think of this earnestness as I share a plane ride from Salem to San Francisco with Paula Cole. She is discussing how the artists have been talking to fans online at Microsoft booths. "One person asked me what I most wanted to take home from this experience, and I said, 'Sarah's underwear,'" she says. "It went over like a lead balloon."

Remember, feminism is no joke. In the rare, uncomfortable interview I get with Chapman, all I want to do is break the Lilith seriousness with questions like, "What clothes do you bring on tour?"

"I can't believe I'm answering this," Chapman says with a tinge of embarrassment. "I guess mostly all black stuff. It's easier to match—like adult Garanimals." Then she cracks a smile. "Is that it?"

Irvine Meadows, near Los Angeles, is the only venue that sports a cigar booth, a Mercedes-Benz giveaway and celebrities. Sharon Stone and Fran Drescher mill around backstage, while Matthew Perry dines in the catered area. Again, Chapman begins a cappella with "Behind the Wall," and Stone bounces up toward sidestage like a teenybopper, as if to say, "Up with women!"

It is also in L.A. that the veneer begins cracking. Word leaks out that Wilson is upset because she wasn't asked to play the main stage; another artist complains that McLachlan has been stealing her quotes to use at press conferences. When Bingham goes onstage, she announces, "I know you're probably expecting something a little folkier, but instead what you're getting is 'Sautéed Onions,'" then launches into a power-punk number.

As the show draws to a close, however, all is serene and calm, just like womanhood should be. McLachlan brings out her female dog, Rex, who sits on a Persian carpet; her husband, drummer Ashwin Sood, is by her side. As the band stands in a warm circle and performs McLachlan's closing song, Rex lifts her leg, licks her crotch and falls asleep. And like the setting moon on a Celestial Seasonings box, Lilith Fair is done for the evening.

truth telling in the nineties

By KRS-ONE

The Nineties symbolized the changing of American music interests—a passing of the torch, if you will. This torch was passed from the rock & roll generation directly to the hip-hop generation in the form of an established music business with which hip-hop is now burdened, and privileged, to take to the next level. Those of us who grew up declaring, "I am hip-hop" never saw ourselves as rock & rollers. To participate in hip-hop, one simply had to *be* hip-hop. For millions of rejected, nonrepresented, inner-city people between the ages of eighteen and thirty-five, hip-hop is a lifestyle, a way to be, a life strategy, a style of living.

All those rap songs recorded in the Nineties came from real places. They tell the stories and express the aspirations of a forgotten and ignored sect of people commonly called "hiphoppas." Although we, hiphoppas, always communicated the truth amongst ourselves through music, it was in the Nineties that America was finally forced to recognize the reality of police brutality, racial profiling and government corruption—all of which appeared in our music before, during and after each unjust event. If the truth be heard and documented, let it be known to the future that hip-hop culture, with rap music as its diary, told the *truth* in the Nineties!

The Nineties will be of special interest to future generations if for no other reason than it was the decade rap music officially replaced rock & roll as the world's most popular youth music. Rock & roll, rest in peace.

What follows are my favorite recordings from the 1990s:

1 *The Chronic,* by Dr. Dre

2 *Nevermind,* by Nirvana

3 *The Low End Theory,* by A Tribe Called Quest

4 *Runaway Slave,* by Showbiz & A.G.

5 *Metallica* (Black Album), by Metallica

6 *50 MC's* mixtape, by Tony Touch

7 *The Final Taping of The Arsenio Hall Show,* featuring KRS-ONE, Mad Lion, Yo Yo, Wu-Tang Clan, Guru, A Tribe Called Quest, and others

8 *A Brief History of Time* (CD or cassette), by Stephen Hawking

9 *Lyricist Lounge Volume One,* by Various artists

10 *It's Dark and Hell Is Hot,* by DMX

beck

By MARK KEMP

"You gotta do the chicken thing again." Beck's manager interrupts the 26-year-old singer's lunch on the set of the British pop-music TV show *TFI Friday* and shuttles him out a back-stage door. It's a typically drizzly London afternoon in 1997, and Beck is here to perform his latest single, "The New Pollution," to a gallery of screaming English teens. First, though, he has to go outdoors to retape a skit in which he's been asked to scale the side of a massive soup vat and drop a whole raw chicken in it. There's no rhyme or reason to the routine—just one of those wacky British-comedy things—but Beck rises to the challenge, and the performance is Oscar-worthy, as he stands at the rim of the vat, a shit-eating grin on his face, and plops the soggy bird into the gooey yellow stew.

Later, after a few other, similarly bizarre segments, the show's bumbling host turns to the studio audience and announces, "Ah, heck, it's *Beck!*" Whereupon the singer, dressed in his familiar snug-fitting blue polyester suit and black dress shoes, appears on the stage moonwalk-ing, high-jumping, hip-shimmying, tambourine-shaking and head-bobbing to the tune's cool "Taxman" bass line and sax-drenched melody.

"I love British humor," Beck tells me later as we begin the first of two two-hour interview sessions in a room at the Royal Garden Hotel, high above London's Kensington Palace. "It's just so...*surreal*." He gazes out the window with an intensity that belies his youthful features—rosy cheeks, pouty lips, fine, wind-swept blond hair and doe eyes, which today have faint circles under them. The past three days have been pretty surreal for Beck, beginning with two Grammys he won back in New York, for Best Alternative Music Performance and Best Male Rock Vocal Performance. The following day, he took the Concorde to England for the *TFI Friday* gig as well as a *Top of the Pops* appearance and a concert performance later in the week.

"I feel lucky," Beck says of his Grammy coup. "It probably hasn't sunk in yet; it's only been a couple of days." When he speaks, Beck does so in slow, measured tones punctuated by long, thoughtful pauses. "I never had any expectations of winning a Grammy," he continues. "It wasn't something I was set on, that I was hoping and praying and starving for." He looks up with a gleam in his eye: "But it *is* incredible!"

Beck Hansen's journey to the Grammys is one of the odder tales in Nineties pop lore. He was born in Los Angeles in 1970, the son of a bluegrass musician father, David Campbell, and a mom, Bibbe Hansen, who briefly hung out with Andy Warhol's Factory crowd of the 1960s; his late grandfather Al Hansen was a member of the Fluxus avant-garde art movement of the Fifties and Sixties. Beck quit school in the ninth grade, and at age eighteen took a bus trip across the country. He spent about a year playing folk music on New York's Lower East Side before returning to Los Angeles in the early Nineties. In 1992, after performing regularly at local punk dives like Raji's and Al's Bar, Beck tossed off a folk-based hip-hop tune called "Loser" in the living room of a friend's home. A year later, Tom Rothrock, a local booster who had started an indie label called Bong Load Custom Records, released the song as a single.

What followed was nothing short of miraculous: Taste-making modern-rock radio stations from Los Angeles to Seattle began playing "Loser" in heavy rotation; the song became an instant smash, and major labels, in a bidding frenzy, began knocking at Beck's

door. By the time Beck released his first album for DGC, *Mellow Gold*, in 1994, "Loser" was already in the Top Forty, and its video was in MTV's Buzz Bin. The downside of all the hype was that Beck was being *characterized* as the Loser of his song. It didn't help that his tender features worked right into the myth or that the artful playfulness of his songs suggested to some a vacantness associated with the so-called Generation X. Despite the intelligence and wit in his music, Beck was designated King of Slackers. "It didn't seem like people understood what I was doing," he says. "It was like 'Is this guy for real? Is he making music that's worthy or valuable?' I felt like I was constantly having to prove myself."

Which is exactly what Beck did. The same year that *Mellow Gold* came out, he immediately followed it with the much stronger *One Foot in the Grave*, a mostly acoustic album of country blues, folk and warped pop released on the tiny independent label K. Then he put out the more experimental *Stereopathetic Soul Manure* on the punk label Flipside. In 1996, Beck dropped the bomb with his second DGC release, *Odelay*, a giant leap of artistic prowess for the singer. After its release, the album remained in the *Billboard* Top 200 for eighty-eight weeks, where it peaked at Number Sixteen, eventually selling double platinum. Meanwhile, the videos for his singles "Where It's At," "Devil's Haircut" and "The New Pollution" became MTV staples.

Beck's irreverent cross-pollination of styles—from hip-hop to country rock to funky Seventies soul— showed him to be one of the most innovative and forward-looking artists of the Nineties, as he continued his exploration of sounds with 1998's *Mutations* and 1999's *Midnite Vultures*. Though he is a member of a generation that looks skeptically upon honors associated with previous eras, it seemed pretty clear during our interview that winning two Grammys in 1997 made a genuine impression on him. When I mention that the Grammy voters seemed to be making an attempt to compensate for past cluelessness, Beck's stoic gaze turns to a smile.

"I do think they're opening the umbrella a little bit to include stuff that isn't standard Grammy fare," he says. "On the other hand, I think in my case, I'm somewhat of a traditionalist to them; I'm working from a place that maybe someone who came up on folk-rock or singer/songwriter stuff can relate to. Maybe that's it." He furrows his brow. "But maybe not, because other things that I do are just pure deconstruction, just dismantling the whole notion of songwriting."

I was talking to a friend after you won your Grammys, and she was telling me that when she heard the news, it felt like one more notch on the belt for her generation. It felt like validation— or vindication.

Yeah. Yeah. It's hard for us to be recognized and get our foot in the door, you know—just the dominance of the older generation—so I think it's amazing that I get to do that. If my generation was as dominant as the generation of the Sixties and the Seventies, it wouldn't be me against Sting and Bryan Adams, people who have been around for such a long time. How can we compete? They're twenty years ahead of us. It's hard to measure us against people who've got so much under their belts. And I think it's strange. Not that I'm criticizing them or anything; I mean, it *is* the way it is. But it's interesting, really, not being able to compete with my peers in the music world.

Do you feel like a rock star now?

To me, *rock star* conjures up something like a mystic: someone who sees himself as above other people,

someone who has the key to the secret that people want to know. The cliché of what a rock star is— there's something elitist about it. I never related to that. I'm an entertainer. I think of it as, you're performing for people. It's not a self-glorification thing.

I remember being really shocked after *Mellow Gold* came out and going on tour, and all these kids were there. It totally disturbed me. Who are all these young people? I'd been playing Mississippi John Hurt covers in coffee shops to a bunch of thirty-, forty-, fifty-year-olds. Then all of a sudden there were these teenagers. It was very surreal.

The word *cliché* is a sort of theme for you. It's as though you can't bear the thought of doing something that has been done in the past.

I think my whole generation's mission is to kill the cliché. I don't know whether it's conscious all the time, but I think it's one of the reasons a lot of my generation are always on the fence about things. They're afraid to commit to anything for fear of seeming like a cliché. They're afraid to commit to their *lives* because they see so much of the world as a cliché.

So I'm trying to embrace the world and all this stuff in a way that doesn't seem clichéd. [*Laughs*] I guess I'm creating the *new* cliché. I mean, there are things that are continuous through the ages, but we have this tendency to laugh at our parents and make fun of them, and I think that's healthy to a certain point, but I feel that it's also important to take it somewhere. Otherwise, you're stuck.

One thing that really bugs you is when people don't get the subtlety of the humor in your songs and performances.

They think I'm being a clown. I'll come out in a fringe Nudie rhinestone suit, and I'm doing it as a tribute to the late-Fifties George Jones or Webb Pierce. I've always loved the Nudie suit. I've always thought of it as one of the greatest clothing styles in any kind of music, but when I come out in one, people immediately say, "Oh, he's doing an Elvis." I mean, how simple-minded can you be? The reference is a little more interesting than just "doing an Elvis." It's like, you pick up a harmonica, and you're "doing a Dylan."

Your music is very uplifting. How can you be so optimistic in such a negative era?

There's some dark stuff on *Odelay*—I don't think it's all bubblegum—but I wanted it to feel good, too, in the way that any life-affirming music does.

I think of Brazilian music, because that's one of the main kinds of music that I listen to for my own pleasure. You've got a country there that's so riddled with poverty, and then there's this music that's so full of spirit. But it isn't just phony happy music—it's genuine. That's often the case in struggling cultures or among struggling people: The music does just the opposite.

If you have time to make really dark music, then it's a privilege. I've always felt that way. I didn't come from suburbia. I didn't come from a place where I had a lot of time on my hands. I couldn't relate to sitting around and complaining about being miserable. That didn't seem like an option to me.

What were your options growing up?

I was born in Los Angeles. My parents lived in a rooming house near downtown. My mom had just come from New York, and my dad was from up north. They were very young. My mom was eighteen or nineteen when they had me. Then, later on, we moved to Hollywood and lived just off of Hollywood Boulevard.

But you do come from a notable family. Your grandfather was a pioneering avant-garde artist, and your mother spent some time on the New York Factory scene of the Sixties. From the outside, that might seem like a privileged situation.

Oh, man! What can I say? [*Laughs, looking slightly appalled*] No, it wasn't a privileged situation. What I'm doing now is pretty sweet for my family, because there's been a lot of struggle for a long, long time. My grandfather was an originator of so many ideas, but he never had it together enough to present them. He never documented himself like other artists did. He was pushing all these ideas, but he struggled with being recognized.

He died in June 1995, before he was able to watch you take those Grammys. What do you think he would have said to you?

[*Gazes off*] I wish he'd been alive to see what's happened. He was around when "Loser" came out, and he was incredibly proud. He kept all the articles. He connected with the things I was doing with hip-hop because he came out of the hipster, Beat thing—using language as freestyle expression, coming up with the most outlandish combinations of slang and rhyming things. But he didn't get to see what I'm doing now.

Was he around much when you were a kid?

He was this strange phenomenon, you know, who'd come from out of nowhere. I remember he came to stay with us when I was about five, and he brought with him bags full of junk and magazines, cigarette butts, all sorts of refuse and materials that he would use for his art pieces. I had some old toys that had broken and didn't work stored in the back room somewhere. He found an old rocking horse, the kind you buy at Kmart, made out of plastic with springs on it, and he offered me five bucks for it—which, for me, was an unheard-of quantity of money. I immediately said, Yeah, he could have it, but I couldn't understand what he would do with it, what use he could have for it.

So I came back from school one day and saw this *thing* sitting at the side of the house, vaguely familiar but somehow completely unrecognizable. He had taken the thing and glued cigarette butts all over it, severed the head off and spray-painted the whole thing silver. It was this metallic, headless monstrosity. I think I was interested, but something within me recoiled as well. It was . . . it was so *raw*:

something so plain and forgotten suddenly transformed into this strange entity.

At the time, it was more of a curiosity to me. But in retrospect, I think things of that nature gave me the idea, maybe subconsciously, that there were possibilities within the limitations of everyday life, with the things that we look at that are disposable. Our lives can seem so limited and uneventful, but these things can be transformed. We can appoint ourselves to be, to be alchemists, turning shit into gold. So I always carried that with me.

How old were you when you found out that your mother had been a denizen of Andy Warhol's Factory scene?

I didn't really understand it until I was about sixteen or seventeen. I had gotten into the Velvet Underground's first record, and I pulled it out and started looking at it. My mom saw that I was into it and said, "I know them." I said, "Tell me about that stuff." I already sort of knew about it, but it hadn't really connected until then.

Was it exciting to you that your mother had a connection to the Velvet Underground?

You know, that time period—anything in the Sixties, but especially something like that scene—is always blown up into this larger-than-life thing. The whole Factory thing—it was really just Andy's scene. It wasn't really a life-impacting situation. I mean, [my mom] hung out a few times; she was on film. It was all about "Everyone's a star."

Was your father, who played bluegrass music, instrumental in your decision to make music?

He was just a musician for hire. He played violin. I heard him play here and there, but it wasn't like I went into the living room and people were jamming or anything. I just remember that he was always working. I liked what he played, but it wasn't like I went out and picked up an instrument and started playing myself. It wasn't until a lot later that I picked up an instrument.

Your music is about taking remnants from other periods and recycling them for a new era. And you grew up during a very transitional time in L.A.—the Seventies and Eighties—when developers came in and destroyed the face of old Hollywood.

Yeah, I spent my childhood watching the decline of Hollywood Boulevard, watching the dying embers—the final light of the Hollywood era—fade into decay. I remember certain relics of the Forties and Fifties Hollywood eras [being] still around when I was growing up. They had the lunch counters, shoeshines and family-owned businesses, which have now turned into rock-poster shops and bad souvenir shops.

We lived near Tiny Naylor's, which was a monument from the age of the Fifties drive-in coffee shops. It was just a megalopolis of hamburgers and milk shakes, that whole—you drive up, and the waitress puts the tray on your car. They still had that up into the Seventies. And right next to that was Ali Baba's, a Middle Eastern restaurant with belly dancers, and on top of it was a two- to three-story statue of Ali Baba.

Then in the early Eighties, all that was suddenly gone. The developers came in and tore it all down and turned it into giant condominiums and block apartments. I remember seeing L.A. just transformed within a couple years. All of a sudden there were mini-malls everywhere. The Eighties came and conquered, and it erased a lot of the heritage of that city. It's not the same city at all.

It was around that time that your mother and father split up, and your family moved away from Hollywood, back to the downtown area where you were born. How did that transition affect you?

I spent the rest of my childhood there, all my teenage years. By that time, it was a little Salvadoran neighborhood bordering on Koreatown. I was the white boy on the street. A lot of drugs, a lot of refugees from the Central American wars. It wasn't the safest place, but it was definitely a community. I remember walking to the bus in the morning to go to school, and there'd be roosters and chickens running through the street and mariachis passed out on the sidewalk. There was an anarchy there in the neighborhood, but still, it was a neighborhood.

It's just east of South Central. I remember meeting the Cypress Hill guys, and we were talking, and we realized we grew up within a mile of each other. They were saying, "Shit, man, we thought you were from England or something."

A lot has been made of the fact that at eighteen, you took a bus from Los Angeles to New York. What prompted that?

There was a special on Greyhound: You could go anywhere in the country for forty bucks. It must have taken at least a week to get there. I stopped off here and there, went through the South.

Any wild experiences on the road?

At some point in the middle of west Texas, the sun was going down, and I realized that all the straight people—all the working people—had gotten off the bus and everyone left was a drug fiend or an ex-con. I remember one of them whispering in my ear as soon as I fell asleep: He was going to slit my throat. I knew I was descending into the heart of America. I was discovering the heartland at that moment.

That sounds scarier than living in downtown L.A.

I don't know about that. At that point I'd seen some fucked-up shit: People machine-gunned on my front lawn; coming out in the morning and playing with the bandages when I was a little kid.

You saw someone machine-gunned?

No, it happened on my front lawn overnight. But back then it was nowhere near as bad as it is now. L.A.'s an incredibly violent place.

How did your journey across America fit into the evolution of your music? I mean, that's a pretty romantic thing to do—go across the country on a bus.

There was no romanticism left in it by that time. As a teenager, I'd read all the Beat literature; I'd read all about the folk revival of the Sixties. I knew that was all gone. It wasn't about that. I was intensely into the blues, country blues, but I knew it wasn't a romantic thing. [The blues] came out of hardship, misery. I think in the Sixties it *was* romanticized—the wise-old-bluesman thing—but I didn't really have any illusions about it. You spend about two minutes in the downtown L.A. Greyhound bus station, and your romanticism about taking a bus trip across America will be eradicated and exterminated immediately.

You mean to tell me that at eighteen, you felt absolutely no thrill in taking to the highway? I mean, now you have the benefit of hindsight: You've grown up, seen things and put things into perspective. But then, you were a teenager. Were you already so hardened that you didn't even get a rush from it?

See, I'd known that kind of thing. I quit school early, and I was working jobs, and I had already taken trips by myself. By the time I was sixteen, my mom was treating me like another adult. I was just someone else living at the house. I came and went as I pleased. I'd traveled through Europe on $150, you know, so . . . I was used to going somewhere with no means, not really knowing anybody, sort of making my way through it. I dunno, I *was* naive. I tend to trust people.

Why did you quit school?

I wanted to go to school more than anything. I would never want to give the idea that I left because I didn't think school was important. It was just the circumstances that I was in. We lived in a one-bedroom apartment, and it was pretty crowded in there. There were sometimes five or six people at a time when I was a teenager. I have a brother; he's younger than me. And when you're a teenager, you want space, you want time alone. Also, the part of Los Angeles where I was going to school, it wasn't exactly the safest.

Do you wish you had finished school?

Oh, yeah, definitely—more than anything. I envy my friends that got to go to college. I thought maybe I would work for a few years and save money to go to college, but that never worked out. I went to New York instead and was playing music. I thought I would eventually go back to school, but I never have.

What was it like when you arrived in Manhattan?

I remember getting to New York, and there was this anti-folk scene happening. I remember literally standing on the street and running into some people, and when they saw I had a guitar, they'd say, "There's an open-mike night—why don't you come?" And I was probably scared to death to play.

What did you live on?

I just trusted that I'd find somebody who'd let me crash here or someone who knew about a job, and I'd get a job for a while. I never pushed to get anywhere. I just always trusted that I would end up where I was supposed to go. That was always my belief, and that would happen to greater or lesser degrees. If I ended up in a weird place, I'd just make the best out of it, you know.

And so you made the best out of the anti-folk scene.

It was an insular scene, but there was a lot of space within there to do almost anything you wanted. I remember going in and getting as drunk as possible and getting up and playing a few tunes. We could take our cue from KRS-One, rewrite an old Woody Guthrie song, make it something totally different. It felt powerful because we didn't need guitars, amps, a practice space or anything; each person was a one-person band.

I guess you could say that was a time of realization—or *de*-realization, forgetting what you know and starting over. It was before all that Nineties alternative thing. It still felt like something was possible, that there was no way it was going to get turned into something commercial, that it would always remain true, that you wouldn't be able to work a formula out for it. There was a feeling that "We will not be fooled." It was innocent in the sense that it wasn't a post-post-post-post thing, you know?

Then you moved back to L.A., "Loser" happened, and you were suddenly introduced to the wonderful world of Innocence Lost: the power of celebrity in the Nineties. How have you dealt with all the attention?

The thing that frustrates me is just how simplified things can be made, cut down to the lowest common denominator. How can you sum up my life—or *any* life—in a paragraph in *USA Today*? It takes all the dignity and all the expansiveness out of it.

If you don't fit into someone's mission of what a musical personality should be in 1997, then they'll just make you into it. They airbrush out Neil Young's sideburns and give Patti Smith a nose job. People, music, everything in our culture—it's so disposable now. That was the most upsetting thing about a recent magazine cover I was on. I wasn't cool enough, so they just made me look the way they wanted me to look. They put makeup on me and made my hair a different color. They even *changed* the structure of my face! That's weird. It's fucked up. The bottom line is, they made me look like a junkie, but I'm not a junkie; I'm not self-destructive.

What gets me is that it's just too easy. I'm shocked when I see people take the easy way out. It's easy to be a rock musician with a drug problem because it's been done before. There's already a romance to that. It's already been applauded. It's like doing a cover of a song that was Number One years ago: It's a safe bet. There's nothing creative about it.

Some might say that you do the same thing with musical styles, using technology, dabbling in the past to create something new.

Yeah, but that's not really the same, because I'm not trying to get to the artifice; I'm trying to get to what it is. People have this conception that I put on different characters, but to me, there's a definite continuity in what I do. If there wasn't, it wouldn't work. If I was just trying on a bunch of silly outfits, then there wouldn't be any weight to what I do. I would be a dilettante. But I'm *not* a dilettante: I'm committed to what I do. There's nothing dilettantish about it.

You spend a lot of time crafting your sonic collages. How important are the words of your songs?

I couldn't sing my songs every night if I thought, "Oh, I just scribbled this down—it doesn't really mean anything." It's got to have some connection to me. It's weird that in America, almost every review I see says, "Oh, the lyrics are nonsense; they don't mean anything; they're not important; he's not really saying anything." I've written hundreds of songs, and I got bored of saying things the same way. I wanted to use the language differently.

But I didn't want to be pretentious or pompous in the way some songwriters suddenly decide, "Okay, now I'm a poet; I'm going to turn these lyrics into poetry." For me, the words still have to be funky, especially in the area of music I'm working in: It's not art music; it's not conceptual. The words have got to *feel* good, and they have to *sound* good; they have to fit the rhythm. That's the hardest thing. You got a melody, you got this thing that's musical, and you want to stick words on it. Words can really weigh something down. And if you put in the wrong words, I'm telling you, it'll ruin the music; it'll ruin the melody.

Dylan put a lot of thought into things like that— "Subterranean Homesick Blues," "Tombstone Blues"—and some of your more surreal songs, like "Loser" and "Devil's Haircut," remind me of that stuff.

Oh, yeah. A lot of Dylan's work, the music was writing the words, but there's meaning there, too—a lot of meaning. I would say that people are just being lazy if they can't find meaning in words like that. You know: Be creative! I don't want to fill out the picture. You fill in the blanks. That's the way it should be.

Like when you sing, "She's alone in the new pollution," you want people to really explore the lyrics, ask, "What the hell's he saying? What does that mean?"

Yes, but I'm not trying to confuse people. I want to communicate. A song like "The New Pollution"—I mean, *pollution*, it's a presence in our lives, and isn't it interesting to use a word like that, something with such horrible connotations, in the context of almost a love song? That's where you create friction. That's where you can start to get to someplace where you aren't dealing in the banalities of everyday, pedestrian rock lyrics. Not that I mean to be snobby about it— I can appreciate the good ol' song, and I still like to write that way sometimes.

Let's talk about "Devil's Haircut."

I would like to say that everyone should have their own idea of what that song means, from the most obvious—"Oh, gee, I got a bad haircut"—to something incredibly involved and academic. For me, I had this idea to write a song based on the "Stagolee" myth. The chorus is like a blues lyric. You can imagine it being sung to a country-blues guitar riff: [*sings like an old bluesman*] "Got a devil's haircut—in my mind." And all the images in the song—"Something's wrong: / My mind's fadin'; / Everywhere I look, / There's a devil waitin'"—it's a blues song. So that's where I wrote it from, and that's why I get frustrated when people say, "Oh, that's a bunch of gibberish." It's the way you perceive it. Maybe people just aren't patient enough to get into it.

Patience, observation, scrutiny—the loss of these qualities in our contemporary culture seems to make you sad.

Yeah, and each generation loses it a little bit more. They lose their ability to articulate their experiences. That's why the so-called Generation X is an easy target. Most of Generation X can't even defend themselves. They don't know how to put the words together to bring out their inner experience. That's a loss—a big loss. And then when somebody does come out full of angst, which is something commonly associated with this generation, it's written off simply as whining. As if it's not real. As if it's just made up. But it's not; it's more substantial than that.

Who is doing the writing off? The baby boomers?

Yeah, and there's a dominance to that generation that will always be there. It's a large group of people, and we can't really steal any of their fire. We're not allowed to. If we come out and we speak about things that enrage us or things we feel strongly about, it gets reduced to "whining" or "angst."

The interesting thing is, you're fairly old school in your own music and thinking.

I'm a traditionalist in a lot of ways. A lot of what my generation is into, what it represents, I'm totally against. I find that I connect much more with older musicians. I think a lot of my generation has been fed a culture that's just so disposable. I can see that a lot of it is very 1997—stuff that's very-of-its-time disposable. A lot of simple techno stuff—it's going to look stupid ten years from now. It might look fresh and new and exciting now, but it's going to look old and stale as time goes by.

In a 1968 ROLLING STONE interview, Eric Clapton was asked what he thought of the San Francisco music scene as compared with the British scene of the time. He said, "The English music market has been bred so long on immaturity, in the press and music papers, they are concerned with nothing else but Top Forty, and music doesn't really matter. . . . They could use, from San Francisco, a little more open-mindedness." Isn't that what you're saying about the current American alternative market?

The thing is, there *was* disposable culture in the Sixties. It's not just a Nineties thing. The pop thrill, the newest and freshest thing—there's a place for that. I recognize that need in our culture: the new thing, the new magazine, the new shoes that just came out that you dig for about five minutes before they get old, and then you throw 'em away and hop onto the next thing. But it seems to be so dominant today.

But it's funny that you would read that to me. I'm interested in seeing things that people said back then because so many things haven't changed. Like you see stuff Dylan said in the Sixties, and it doesn't seem like he's the institution that he is now. He was just another musician. And that kind of puts things into perspective. If you look back at stuff like that, you're more likely not going to get caught up in all the mess, all the hype.

What are some other things you'd like to do?

I enjoy making videos. I have a lot of ideas. I spent about five weeks of my life doing the video for "The New Pollution," and, damn it's a lot of work, but it's satisfying in the end.

It was a bit shocking to have this picture—something visual in my head—translated into existence. I'm used to being able to do that with sound—to have an idea and approximate it in a song—but not with an actual picture. It's frightening to take something that you dream or daydream or imagine, something you've conjured up in your thoughts from out of nowhere, and put it into existence on a screen. [*Laughs*] There's something *wrong* about that, something very disturbing when you can do that. It's a power that we shouldn't have, but it's exhilarating.

Did it come out the way you wanted it to—the Sixties go-go dancers, the hood ornament that comes to life, and the hair-metal band scene?

Oh, yeah. It's insane that it came out exactly the way I pictured it. It's a whimsical video. It's very silly; most of it's not serious at all, and I think that's what videos should be. I think videos should be more about just ruining everything you've built up in the music. I think you should just go and blow it all up by making a bunch of dumb, funny imagery.

Many of your songs are based in blues and rap . . . I think the big problem with music now is how segregated it is. In the early days there was such a connection between black and white music, and, of course, rock came right out of that marriage. Even in the Sixties, there was still such a warm connection— the Stones were totally into that culture. You don't see that kind of connection now. You don't see the big alternative band being as much into what somebody in the R&B world is doing, and I think that connection is what perpetuates popular music and keeps things fresh and ensures that there'll be a crop next year. Right now, we're mining the same old thing, we're growing on the same soil, and it's all worn out, and it's getting dusty, and it's going to blow away pretty soon.

tupac shakur

By MIKAL GILMORE

I don't know whether to mourn Tupac Shakur's death or to rail against all the terrible forces—including the artist's own self-destructive temperament—that resulted in such a wasteful, unjustifiable end. I do know this, though: Whatever its causes, the September 13, 1996, murder of Shakur, when he was twenty-five, robbed us of one of the most talented and compelling voices of recent years. He embodied just as much for his audience as Kurt Cobain did for his. That is, Tupac Shakur spoke to, and for, many who had grown up within hard realities—realities that mainstream culture and media are loath to understand or respect. His death left his fans feeling a doubly sharp pain: the loss of a much-esteemed signifier and the loss of a future volume of work that no doubt would have proved both brilliant and provocative.

Certainly, Shakur was among the most ingenious and lyrical of the Nineties generation of rappers, often pitting his dark-toned, staccato cadences against lulling and clever musical backdrops, achieving an effect as memorable for its melodic contours as for its rhythmic verve. In addition, his albums *2Pacalypse Now* (1991), *Strictly 4 My N.I.G.G.A.Z.* (1993), *Me Against the World* (1995) and *All Eyez on Me* (1996) ran the full range of rap's thematic and emotional breadth. In the first two albums alone, you could find moments of uncommon tenderness and compassion (the feminine-sympathetic portrayals in "Brenda's Got a Baby" and "Keep Ya Head Up"), astute political and social observation ("Trapped," "Soulja's Story" and "I Don't Give a Fuck"), and also declaration of fierce black-against-black anger and brutality (the thug-life anthems "Last Wordz" and "5 Deadly Venomz"). What made this disconcerting mix especially notable was how credible it all seemed. Shakur could sing in respectful praise and defense of women, then turn around and deliver a harangue about "bitches" and "ho's"—or could boast of his gangster prowess one moment, then condemn the same doomed mentality in another track—and you never doubted that he felt and meant every word he declaimed. Does that make him sound like a confused man? Yes—to say the least—but Shakur was also a man willing to own up to and examine his many contradictory inclinations, and I suspect that this quality, more than any other, is what made him such a vital and empathetic voice for so many of his fans.

Shakur was also a clearly gifted actor (his first performance, as an adolescent, was in a stage production of *A Raisin in the Sun*), though he wasn't especially well served by mediocre young-black–coming-of-age films such as *Poetic Justice* and *Above the Rim*. In his first, 1992's *Juice*, Shakur played Bishop, a young man anxious to break out of the dead-end confinements of his community and who settles on an armed robbery as the means of proving his stature, his "juice." Once Bishop has a gun in his hand, everything about his character, his life, his fate, changes. He shoots anything that obstructs him, including some lifelong friends. He kills simply to kill, as if by doing so, he will eventually shoot through the one thing that hurts him the most: his own troubled heart. "I am crazy," he tells a character at one point. "But you know what else? I don't give a fuck." Shakur speaks the final line with such sure and frightening coldness, it is impossible to know whether he informed his delivery with his own experience or whether he was simply uncovering a disturbing but liberating personal ethos.

tupac shakur ›

It was with his two final recordings—*Me Against the World* and *All Eyez on Me*—that Shakur achieved what is probably his best-realized and most-enduring work. The two albums are major statements about violence, social realism, self-willed fate and unappeasable pain, though it's as if they were made by two different, almost opposing sensibilities. Or they could be read as the combined, sequential statements of one man's growth, except in Shakur's case, it appears that the growth moved from hard-earned enlightenment to hard-bitten virulence. *Me Against the World* (released after he was shot in a 1994 robbery and during his imprisonment for sexually abusing a woman) was the eloquent moment when Shakur paused to examine all the trouble and violence in his life and measure not only his own complicity in that trouble but how such actions spilled into, and poisoned, the world around him.

On *All Eyez on Me*, released a year later on Death Row Records, Shakur gave way to almost all the darkness he had ever known—and did so brilliantly. Indeed, *Eyez* is one of the most melodically and texturally inventive albums that rap has ever produced—and also one of the most furious. Tracks like "California Love" and "Can't C Me" are rife with sheer beauty and exuberance, and even some of the more dangerous or brooding songs ("Heartz of Men," "2 of Amerikaz Most Wanted," "Life Goes On," "Only God Can Judge Me," "Got My Mind Made Up") boast gorgeous surfaces over their pure hearts of stone. On both albums, in song after song, Shakur came up against the same terrible realization: He could see his death bearing down on top of him, but he didn't know how to step out of its unrelenting way. So he stood there, waiting, and while he waited, he made one of rap's few full-length masterpieces, *Eyez*.

The hardest-hitting, most eventful song of the *Eyez* project—and possibly of Shakur's career—appears as the B side on the "California Love" single: a track called "Hit 'Em Up." According to many in the rap community, the song is an attack aimed (mainly) at Sean "Puffy" Combs's Bad Boy label, specifically at recording artist Biggie Smalls (the Notorious B.I.G.), who recorded for the label and who was gunned down in a drive-by shooting six months after Tupac met the same end. In the mid-Nineties, these figures had become archrivals of Marion "Suge" Knight, owner and cofounder of Death Row Records, and Shakur indicated that he suspected they were involved in his 1994 shooting. (In 1996, Knight, a suspect in Smalls's murder, was imprisoned for parole violation.)

As a result, "Hit 'Em Up" was much more than just a song—it was Shakur's salvo of revenge and warning. "I fucked your bitch, you fat motherfucker," he says, addressing Biggie Smalls as the track opens, referring to a rumor about B.I.G.'s wife and Shakur. But that boast is trite compared with what follows: "Who shot me?" he barks, and then answers, "But you punks didn't finish. Now you're about to feel the wrath of a menace, nigga." A minute later, Shakur steps up his rage a couple of notches. "You want to fuck with us, you little, young-ass motherfuckers?" he rails. "You better back the fuck up, or you get smacked the fuck up . . . We ain't singin', we bringin' drama . . . We gonna kill *all* you motherfuckers . . . Fuck Biggie; fuck Bad Boy . . . And if you want to be down with Bad Boy, then fuck you, too . . . Die slow, motherfucker . . . You think you mob, nigga? We the motherfucking mob . . . You niggas mad because our staff got guns in their motherfucking belts . . . We Bad-boy killers / We kill 'em."

I have never heard anything remotely like Tupac Shakur's breathless performance on this track in all my years of listening to pop music. It contains a truly remarkable amount of rage and aggression—enough to make anything in punk seem flaccid by comparison. Indeed, "Hit 'Em Up" crosses the line from art and metaphor to real-life jeopardy. On one level, you might think Shakur was telling his enemies, "We will kill you competitively, commercially," but listen to the stunning last thirty seconds of the track. It's as if Shakur were saying, "Here I am—your enemy and your target. Come and get me, or watch me get you first."

So: A man sings about death and killing, and then the man is killed. There is a great temptation for many to view one event as the result of the other. In Tupac Shakur's case, there are some grounds for this assessment: He did more than sing about violence; he also partici-pated in a fair amount of it. As Shakur himself once said, in words that *Time* magazine appropriated for its headline covering his murder: WHAT GOES 'ROUND COMES 'ROUND. Still, I think it would be a great disservice to dismiss Shakur's work and life with any quick and glib headline summations. It's like burying the man without hearing him.

Shakur's death has been cited as justification for yet another campaign against hardcore rap and troublesome lyrics, one of the perennial causes of the 1990s. In 1989, the FBI got into the act by contacting Priority Records to note the bureau's official distaste for ground-breaking group N.W.A.'s unyielding, in-your-face song "Fuck tha Police." In 1990, *Newsweek* ran a cover story titled "Rap Rage, Yo!" calling rap a "street-wise music," rife with "ugly macho boasting," and three years later, the magazine reiterated its disdain with a Snoop Doggy Dogg cover that posed the question: WHEN IS RAP TOO VIOLENT? In 1992, conserva-tive interest groups and riled police associations pressured Warner Bros. Records to delete "Cop Killer" from Ice-T's *Body Count* album (subsequently, Warner separated itself from Ice-T). And in 1995, moralist activists William Bennett and C. DeLores Tucker succeeded in pressuring Warner's to break the label's ties with Interscope Records, due to Interscope's support of a handful of hardcore rap artists, including Tupac Shakur. At the time of Shakur's death, some record executives were questioning whether any further associations with rap and its bad images would be worth the heat that labels would have to face.

It is true, of course, that certain figures in the rap community took their inflammatory rhetoric and violent posturing to an insane, genuinely deadly level. It was saddening and horrible to witness such lethal rivalry among so many young men with such innovative talent—especially when the artists and producers shared the sort of common social perspective that should have brought them together. Death Row and Bad Boy could have had a true and positive impact on black America's political life, but that couldn't happen when the companies sought to increase their own standing by tearing away at black opponents perceived as enemies. From such actions, no meaningful or valuable victories were to be had.

At the same time, there's nothing meaningful or valuable to be gained by censoring hardcore rap—or at least, that course would offer no real solutions to very real problems that much of the best (and worst) rap signifies. For that matter, such a course would only undermine much of rap's considerable contribution to popular culture. Rap began as a means of black self-expression in the late Seventies, and as it matured into the wide-ranging art form of hip-hop, it also became a vital means of black achievement and invention. In the process, rap began to report on and reveal many social realities and attitudes that most other arts and media consistently ignored—that is, rap gave voice and presence to truths that almost no other form of art or reportage was willing to accommodate. Works like N.W.A.'s "Fuck tha Police" and *Niggaz4Life* may have seemed shocking to some observers, but N.W.A. didn't invent the resentment and abuse they sang about. Nor did Ice-T, Ice Cube or the Geto Boys invent the ghetto-rooted gang warfare and drive-by shootings that they sometimes rapped about. These conditions and dis-positions existed long before rap won popular appeal (also long before the explosive L.A. riots of 1992), and if hardcore rap were to disappear tomorrow, these conditions would still exist.

What disturbed so many about rap—what it is actually deemed guilty for—is how vividly it represented the circumstances that the music's lyrics and voices illuminated. It wasn't pleasant to hear about murderous rage and sexist debasement—to many, in fact, rap came across as an actual threat. As one journalist and author friend told me when I recommended that he listen to Snoop Doggy Dogg's *Doggystyle*, "I don't buy records by people who want to kill me." Interestingly, some music fans didn't seem to brandish the same scrupulous distaste when rock groups like the Rolling Stones, the Sex Pistols, the Clash and several others also sang about murder, violence, rage and cultural ruin.

Tupac Shakur, like many other rappers, intoned about a world that he either lived in or witnessed—in Shakur's case, in fact, there was a good deal less distance between lyrics and life than is the case with most pop-music figures. Sometimes, Shakur saw clearly the causes for his pain and anger and aspired to rise above being doomed by that delimitation; sometimes, he succumbed to his worst predilections. Far too often, he participated in actions that only spread the ruin: He was involved in at least two shootings, numerous vicious physical confrontations and several rancid verbal assaults; he was also convicted and served time for sexual abuse. Moreover, he probably made a certain element of the rap world genuinely dangerous by embodying the ideal that "real" rappers had to live the lethal lives they sang about. In the end, perhaps Shakur's worst failing was to see too many black men and women with backgrounds similar to his as his real and mortal enemies.

Listen to Tupac Shakur before you put his life away, though. You will hear the story of a man who grew up feeling as if he didn't fit into any of the worlds around him, feeling that he had been pushed out from not only the white world but also the black neighborhoods in which he grew up. You will also hear the man's clear intelligence and genius: his gifts for sharp, smart, funny perceptions and for lyrical and musical proficiency and elegance. Of course, you will hear some downright ugly stuff—threats, rants, curses and admitted memories that would be too much for many hearts to bear. Mainly, though, you will hear the tortured soul-searching of a man who grew up with and endured so much pain, rancor and loss that he could never truly overcome it all, could never turn his troubled heart rightside-up, despite all his gifts and all the acceptance he eventually received.

In case anybody wants to dismiss this man's reality too readily, consider this: We are experiencing a time when many of our leaders are telling us that we are vulnerable to people who live in another America—an America made up of those who are fearsome, irresponsible, lazy or just plain bad, an America that needs to be taught hard lessons. So we have elected to teach these others their hard lessons. In years immediately ahead, as a result of recent political actions, something like one million kids will be pushed into conditions of poverty and all that will come with it, including some of the horrible means of recourse left to the hopeless. Imagine how many Tupac Shakurs will emerge from this adventure, all those smart kids who, despite whatever talents they will possess, will not be able to overcome the awfulness of their youth and who will end up with blood on their hands or chest, or both.

Indeed, what goes 'round comes 'round. The America we are making for others is ultimately the America we will make for ourselves. It will not be on the other side of town. It will be right outside our front doors.

a brief history of electronica

By NEIL STRAUSS

Ravers trace electronic dance music, or electronica, to the early techno singles of the late 1980s, although the music's roots stretch far deeper than that. Its branches are dense and knotty, multiplying in the mid- to late Nineties every few months with a new style, genre or subgenre. Unlike traditional rock-based music, electronica's lineage of twentieth-century popular music bypasses the blues, Elvis Presley and the Beatles in favor of avant-garde composers like Karlheinz Stockhausen, the early synth-pop band Kraftwerk and dub-reggae pioneer Lee "Scratch" Perry.

The following is a look at the origins and permutations of electronica and its thickest branches.

composers & inventors

The Italian futurist manifesto *The Art of Noises* gave birth to what became rave culture way back in 1913 by calling for a modern music pieced together out of the mechanical and electrical din of the city. With self-made noise boxes and compositions that incorporated the sounds of sirens, horns and whistles, the futurists were basically making techno music without the beat. As the century progressed, composers like Pierre Schaeffer and Pierre Henry began cutting and splicing magnetic tape to create collages out of natural sounds (an early version of sampling), while Stockhausen created a sophisticated electronic world music. Long before club DJs were using variable-speed turntables as instruments, the futurist Luigi Russolo and the American composer John Cage were incorporating as many as forty-two turntables into a single piece. Those maverick composers were later sampled or remixed in the music of such Nineties artists as Irresistible Force, DJ Spooky, Fatboy Slim, Coldcut and others.

minimalism

If early- to midcentury avant-gardists were precursors to electronic dance music's instrumentation, the minimalist composers who followed them in the Sixties and Seventies heralded the music's form. For La Monte Young, Philip Glass, Terry Riley and Steve Reich, that form was repetition, and through repetition came musical revelation, enlightenment or ecstasy. Minimalism may have led to the most vapid of New Age music, but it also led to the more substantial trance and ambient dance music.

To this category we must add Brian Eno, the innovative producer and pop musician who coined the term *ambient music* in 1978, putting out albums like *Music for Films* and *Ambient 1/Music for Airports*. In his gently pulsing electronic instrumentals, Eno composed complex music that could be listened to as simple background music, taking the pretension out of composition and setting the stage for contemporary ambient's laid-back textural drone.

kraut rock

The late 1990s saw the resurfacing of nearly every obscure (and not so obscure) German progressive-rock band of note: Kraftwerk, Can, Faust, Tangerine Dream and Cluster. The timing was no coincidence. In the late Sixties and early Seventies, these rockers picked up synthesizers

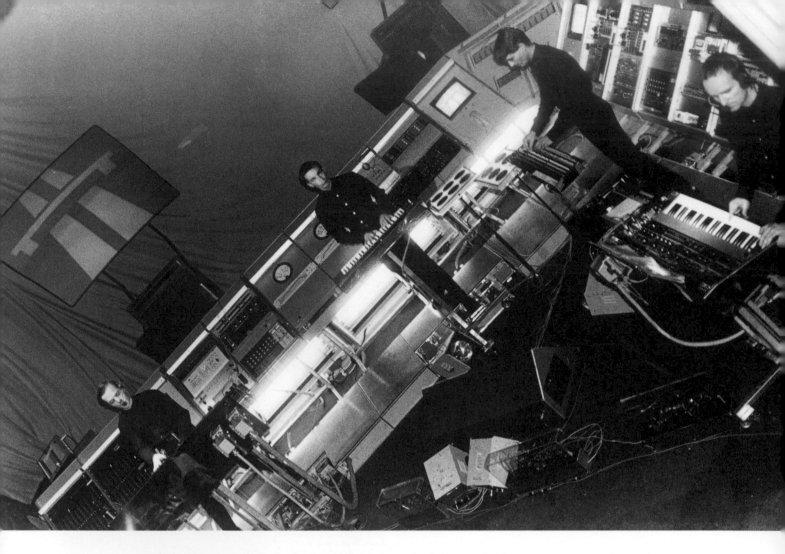

and oscillators and made rhythm-oriented psychedelic music about outer space, drug trips and technology—all of which remain among the central themes of electronic dance music.

Kraftwerk, in particular, may be the single most important electronica precursor. They also may be the style's original faceless musicians, maintaining an aura of mystique and letting robots fill in for them in photographs and onstage. Melding the city-as-symphony ideas of the futurists, the repetition of the minimalists, homemade sequencers and drum machines and an obsession with technology, Kraftwerk created spick-and-span machine pop that still sounds good. It was Kraftwerk's records that Afrika Bambaataa sampled to create one of rap's first big hits, "Planet Rock," and it was Kraftwerk that Detroit city kids were listening to when they came up with their own variant, techno.

dub

Using the recording studio as an instrument in the early Seventies, the pioneers of Jamaican dub (King Tubby, Lee "Scratch" Perry, and Sly and Robbie) worked backward. They took reggae hits and removed basically everything but the drums and the bass. They then replaced bits and pieces, adding reverberating vocal snatches, echoing guitar fragments and all kinds of spacey sound effects with little regard for narrative. Prefiguring the rave scene, dub and reggae culture revolved around mobile sound systems that traveled from city to city, while the presentation (vocalists singing over the DJ's turntable work) influenced early rap. In nearly every subgenre of electronic dance music—drum and bass, ambient, techno—there is a splinter that looks back to dub music as its chief inspiration, striving for a slow, stoned-out groove.

disco

Before *Saturday Night Fever* helped to complete disco's conversion from black and gay club music to mainstream pop, there was a lot of substance and innovation in the music. Just as electronica started to gain popularity in America when alternative rock went stale, disco emerged after progressive rock became too slick and bloated. Among disco's biggest influences on electronica are the driving electronic sweetening that producer Giorgio Moroder added to Donna Summer anthems and the quasimystical worship of the drum in songs like "Turn the

Beat Around." In fact, Hot Butter's instrumental "Popcorn" sounded like techno before the term became commonplace.

Just as important as the music itself was the way disco culture transformed club music. Early Seventies gay-club DJs gave birth to the art of mixing by seamlessly combining songs to create one long transcendent groove, and as an aid to DJs, the first twelve-inch singles with extended remixes were born in the mid-Seventies.

synth pop

Evolving out of punk in the late Seventies, new wave went through many permutations before it became the music we happily denigrate as the domain of skinny-tie–wearing, hair-spiking, synthesizer-wielding New Romantics. It was near this later stage of new wave's development, as synth pop, that the music laid down the roots for electronica. That period is marked by the romantic glide of New Order, Depeche Mode and Yaz, in particular. It also includes the many bands that inherited Kraftwerk's technology-obsessed legacy—Gary Numan, the Art of Noise (named for the futurist manifesto), D.A.F., Yello and the Yellow Magic Orchestra. Also included are the industrial dance bands that added a harder edge to electronics—Cabaret Voltaire, Throbbing Gristle, Ministry and Front 242. It is from new wave and its predecessors and mutations—punk, industrial, gothic—that the early rave audience was recruited.

electrofunk

In many ways, electrofunk took disco and replaced the diva with a robot.

Technology-friendly funksters like Zapp, Parliament-Funkadelic and Prince helped pave the way for early Eighties bands like Afrika Bambaataa, Uncle Jam's Army, Mantronix, Newcleus, George Kranz and World Class Wreckin' Cru (which included the young Dr. Dre), which built songs from synthesizers, drum machines, James Brown samples and human vocals synthesized through a Vocoder. Here was black music's answer to Kraftwerk, proving that funk could be played by machines just as effectively as rock could.

Also important in this era were the first break-beat records: albums of drum machine beats, samples and sound effects created solely for DJs to scratch and mix from. In the ensuing years, these records slowly took on a life of their own, forming the basis of everything from the big beat of the Chemical Brothers to the funky breaks of the Propellerheads to modern turntablism.

house

Chicago, 1984. The Warehouse is often pinpointed as the club where modern electronic dance music came to fruition. There, disco never died—it just went back underground. Marshall Jefferson, Steve "Silk" Hurley, Jamie Principle, Farley "Jackmaster" Funk and others removed the pop and fueled their tracks with piano riffs, Latin rhythms, dry kick drums and deep, deep bass. At the Warehouse, DJ Frankie Knuckles was the music's messenger, and to the delight of hyped-up clubgoers, he added his own sound effects and drum machine rhythms to club tracks. Meanwhile, at the nearby Music Box, dancers were flooding in to see how long DJ Ron Hardy could ride a single beat. Unlike most of the preceding styles, house music was still thriving at the end of the Nineties, not just because of overseas devotees of the Chicago style (like France's Daft Punk) but because of Chicago acts like Cajmere and DJ Sneak and spin-off genres like trippier, slicker progressive house and more soulful deep house.

techno (detroit)

If house was about the moment, techno was about the future, thanks in large part to the Electrifyin' Mojo, a DJ who spread Kraftwerk, New Order and Devo to Detroit's inner-city youth. The holy triumvirate of Detroit techno—DJs Juan Atkins, Kevin Saunderson and Derrick May—began making minimal, electronic tracks, using futuristic names like Cybotron, 3070 and Model 500. Over time, the music got faster, with more funk and house creeping into the mixes, leading to techno's first big hit, 1989's "Big Fun," by Inner City (an alias for Saunderson and the inspiration for Goldie's 1996 jungle hit "Inner City Life"). All of these DJs released innovative singles and albums, and they were joined by an equally talented crop of younger Detroit players like Carl Craig, Jeff Mills, Richie Hawtin and Kenny Larkin, many of whom began taking the music to increasing levels of abstraction.

acid house

The name of Chicago's Acid Trax house label may have meant many things: slang for sampling, a way to describe the squiggly sounds of the Roland 303 bass synthesizer or a reference to psychedelic drugs. When English DJs began to return home from Chicago with crates of these singles under their arms in the late Eighties, they created their own acid house, taking Chicago rhythms and adding television samples, sound effects and electronic noises on top. Fueled in large part by something else borrowed from America, the psychedelic drug ecstasy, English youth culture galvanized around this new music, with disparate classes and colors mixing and, in 1988, celebrating what they called their own Summer of Love. DJs like Danny Rampling and Paul Oakenfold in London, and bands like A Guy Called Gerald, 808 State and T-Coy in Manchester, were the genre's first proselytes, with Tim Simenon of Bomb the Bass, S-Express, M/A/R/R/S and Coldcut soon following their lead with major hits. Many of these DJs and musicians continued making music into the late Nineties, reinventing themselves with each passing trend.

techno (england)

This is where the name game begins. In 1989, for various reasons, rain began falling on acid house's psychedelic parade. Thugs, big-time drug dealers, tabloid exposés, police busts and, finally, parliamentary laws prohibiting unlicensed outdoor gatherings forced the scene back underground, where it was retooled and transformed into techno. This time the inspiration wasn't Chicago—it was Detroit, helped in large part by Neil Rushton of Network Records, which released in England the first significant compilation of Detroit musicians to be put out anywhere (including Detroit).

European hits like Human Resource's "Dominator," L.A. Style's "James Brown Is Dead," Opus III's "It's a Fine Day," Prodigy's "Charly" and the Smart E's' "Sesame's Treet" embedded themselves in the mind space of a generation. Since the era of huge raves was mostly over, the music went back into small clubs, which were able to gear the sounds—from spacier trance to frenetic hard core—more toward particular audiences. As the music became pop in England, it spread across Europe, then into Asia and finally back to North America, where hundreds of musicians previously ignored by the music industry (from Josh Wink in Philadelphia to the Crystal Method in Los Angeles) were signed to major-label deals.

ambient

Taking drugs or dancing all night at clubs, kids needed a place to come down. Thus, the chill-out room was born, where the ears (and mind) were stimulated while the feet were given a rest. Alex Paterson of the Orb dreamed up latter-day ambient music when he thought he heard something Eno-esque in a Tony Humphries dance mix in New York. Along with Jimmy Cauty of the KLF, he began mixing Eno and prog-rock records with train and barnyard animal sound effects at clubs. Soon dance music was freed from the tyranny of the beat, with song titles like the KLF's "3 A.M. Eternal" and the Orb's "Perpetual Dawn" cluing listeners in to ambient's proper setting. Other artists, such as Irresistible Force, Future Sound of London, the iconoclastic Aphex Twin and Germany's Pete Namlook, began pushing the music's envelope, and modern electronic dance music produced its first coherent single-artist albums.

The anything-goes aspect of ambient gave scores of older avant-garde musicians and composers an opportunity to reinvent themselves and find a younger audience. At the same time, burned-out rock musicians began spacing out, forming bands like Tortoise, Main, Seefeel, Trans Am and Experimental Audio Research, which often approximated the sound of electronic dance music using guitars, bass and drums.

jungle

A collision between inner-city kids in love with hip-hop break beats and acid-house DJs (like Fabio and Grooverider) who were in search of something faster, harder and darker, jungle began as England's dub-influenced answer to rap. Though early jungle hits included vocals by reggae MCs, the crux of the music is a deep, hair-bristling bass line and drumbeats that are cut up, rearranged, fed through effects and sped up to create a busy, complex, ever-changing rhythm. As soon as credibility, creative potential and cash flow were realized, around 1994, jungle was taken out of the ghetto and appeared in mainstream culture, where artists from David Bowie to U2 to Everything But the Girl began using it in their music. Like techno, jungle (which came to be called by its more PC name, *drum and bass*) splintered into specialty styles: fast jump-up, jazzy jungle, the more aggressive hard step and the Indian-influenced ethnojungle of Talvin Singh.

trip-hop

Trip-hop is the vaguest term here, perhaps because it is the only dance style in this list that was named by the press (the same people who brought you the umbrella term *electronica*). In its broadest definition, *trip-hop* is a catchall for more down-tempo experimental electronic dance music that doesn't quite fit into any trend, like the eclectic offerings of England's Mo Wax label. In the narrowest sense, it describes the music of Massive Attack, Portishead and Tricky, who all emerged from Bristol, England, in the early Nineties. Neutralizing hip-hop's aggression with elements of dub, movie soundtrack composition and a spacey production aesthetic that places vocals over heavy bass, trip-hop crossed into the mainstream, replacing Sade as the hip lounge music of choice.

tech step, digital hardcore, speed garage and beyond

Like an elusive, infectious strain of bacteria, dance music just keeps dividing and mutating, offering something for everybody: Hippies groove on Electric Skychurch; Jazzbos find solace in the fusion-style drum and bass of bassist-programmer Squarepusher and saxophonist James Hardway; For world-music lovers, there's the ethnotechno of Transglobal Underground and Banco de Gaia; Punks flock to Germany's extreme digital hardcore.

For those who prefer more dangerous and industrial-sounding jungle, there's the tech step of DJ Trace, Ed Rush and Nico. For artists and avant-gardists, there's New York's experimental illbient scene. And for fans who just want to go completely insane, there's Holland's high-tempo genre, gabba. As the twentieth century draws to a close, the permutations have only accelerated: Detroit disc jockeys combined techno, Miami bass, strip-club music, jungle and rap to make ghetto-tech (or booty house); in England, the influence of Manhattan club remixers helped launch speed garage and two-step, which spiced New York garage music with the flavor and intricacy of drum-and-bass and, as electronic dance becomes a worldwide sound, new genres are popping up in South Africa (kwaito), Brazil (baile funk music) and other countries. Finally, there continue to be styles so new that they exist almost exclusively on anonymous, white-label singles. In the twenty-first century, there will no doubt be even newer, more specific strains of electronica. For those who can't find a style they find appealing, they can simply create their own.

my favorite nineties recordings

By LUCINDA WILLIAMS

(In no particular order)

1 ***Time Out of Mind,*** by Bob Dylan

2 **Everything Neil Young released in the 1990s** [*Ragged Glory* (with Crazy Horse), *Weld* (with Crazy Horse), *Harvest Moon, Unplugged, Sleeps With Angels* (with Crazy Horse), *Mirror Ball* (with Pearl Jam), *Broken Arrow* (with Crazy Horse), *Year of the Horse* (with Crazy Horse)]

3 ***Sol Negro,*** by Virginia Rodrigues

4 ***Hundred Lies,*** by Malcolm Holcombe

5 ***Rhythmeen,*** by ZZ Top

6 ***Royal Memphis Soul*** (Hi Records box set), by various artists

7 ***She-Wolf,*** by Jessie Mae Hemphill

8 ***The Chess Box,*** by Etta James

9 ***The Best of Tony Joe White,*** by Tony Joe White

10 ***After Hours,*** by Nina Simone

contributors

LORRAINE ALI is an award-winning music journalist and Los Angeles native who recently relocated to New York City. Formerly a senior critic at ROLLING STONE, she is a senior writer at *Newsweek* magazine. She has also written for the *New York Times, Details, Spin, Entertainment Weekly, Us, Mademoiselle* and the *L.A. Weekly* and contributed to Rolling Stone Press's *Cobain* and *The ROLLING STONE Book of Women in Rock*.

J. D. CONSIDINE, the pop critic at the *Baltimore Sun* for more than a decade, is managing editor of *Revolver*. He has contributed to numerous Rolling Stone Press books, including *The ROLLING STONE Album Guide*.

ANTHONY DeCURTIS is a contributing editor at ROLLING STONE and the author of *Rocking My Life Away: Writing About Music and Other Matters*. He is the editor of *Present Tense: Rock & Roll and Culture* and coeditor of *The ROLLING STONE Illustrated History of Rock & Roll* and *The ROLLING STONE Album Guide*.

CHUCK EDDY is the music editor of the *Village Voice* and the author of *Stairway to Hell: The 500 Greatest Heavy Metal Albums in the Universe* and *The Accidental Evolution of Rock 'n Roll*. He lives in Brooklyn with his pet guinea pig, Eggplant.

GAVIN EDWARDS is the author of four humor collections (*'Scuse Me While I Kiss This Guy and Other Misheard Lyrics, He's Got the Whole World in His Pants and More Misheard Lyrics, When a Man Loves a Walnut and Even More Misheard Lyrics* and *Deck the Halls with Buddy Holly and Other Misheard Christmas Lyrics*) and one novel (*Dead Centerfolds*). He has written about music, comic books and life-threatening adventures for ROLLING STONE, *Wired, Playboy, Spin*, the *Village Voice* and *Details* (where he was an editor for many years). He lives in New York and spends his free time trying to get his cat to act less like Ike Turner and more like Dan Fogelberg.

PAUL EVANS has contributed to *The ROLLING STONE Album Guide, The ROLLING STONE Jazz and Blues Album Guide* and *The ROLLING STONE Encyclopedia of Rock & Roll*. A teacher and writer living in Atlanta, he has written for the *Washington Post*, the *Los Angeles Times* and other publications.

DAVID FRICKE is a senior editor of ROLLING STONE, having joined the magazine in 1985. He is also the American correspondent for *Melody Maker* and the author of *Animal Instinct*, a biography of Def Leppard, and has written liner notes for CD reissues of the Byrds, Moby Grape, John Prine, Led Zeppelin and the Velvet Underground.

KINKY FRIEDMAN, the former leader of the band the Texas Jewboys, is the author of fifteen mystery novels and ten country music albums. These days he travels the world singing the songs that made him infamous and reading from the books that made him respectable.

MIKAL GILMORE is a ROLLING STONE contributing editor and the author of *Shot in the Heart*.

MICHAEL GOLDBERG, the founder and editor-in-chief of insiderone.net, an online pop culture magazine; he writes a syndicated weekly music column, "The Drama You've Been Craving." He founded Addicted to Noise, the first Web music magazine, in 1994. From January 1984 until July 1993, he was an associate editor and senior writer at ROLLING STONE.

LEE JESKE began his career in New York City in the mid-Seventies. He has been an editor at *Down Beat* and *Cash Box* magazines, a producer at MJI Broadcasting and a music critic for the *New York Post*. His work has appeared in ROLLING STONE, the *New York Times*, the *New Yorker*, the *London Sunday Times*, the *New Grove Dictionary of American Music, CitySearch, SonicNet* and many other publications. He was the contributing editor of *Listen Up: The Lives of Quincy Jones*, and his liner notes appear on more than 100 albums. He lives in New York.

MARK KEMP is former music editor of ROLLING STONE and a former executive editor of *Option*. From 1997–2000 he was vice-president of music at MTVNetworks.kemp. He has written about music and other topics for magazines, newspapers, book collections and television, and in 1998 was nominated for a Grammy for his liner notes to the Phil Ochs box set, *Farewells & Fantasies*. He currently lives and works in New York City.

ALAN LIGHT is the editor-in-chief of *Spin* magazine. He is the former editor-in-chief of *VIBE* and a former senior writer at ROLLING STONE. He also edited the anthology *Tupac Shakur* (Crown, 1997) and *The VIBE History of Hip Hop* (Crown, 1999).

KURT LODER is MTV's chief news correspondent and a contributing editor to both ROLLING STONE and *Esquire*. He is the coauthor of *I, Tina* and author of *Bat Chain Puller*, a collection of his writing for ROLLING STONE. He is also a member of the nominating committee of the Rock and Roll Hall of Fame.

GREIL MARCUS is a contributing editor of ROLLING STONE. He is the author of *Invisible Republic*, *Lipstick Traces* and *Mystery Train*.

DAVID McGEE, a New York–based writer whose work has appeared in ROLLING STONE, *Spin*, *New Musical Express* and other publications, is the author of *Go, Cat, Go! The Life and Times of Carl Perkins, the King of Rockabilly*. He has also served as assistant curator for the Rock and Roll Hall of Fame and Museum.

DON McLEESE has been a popular music critic for the *Austin American-Statesman*, *Chicago Sun-Times* and *Chicago Reader*. A frequent contributor to a variety of publications and Web sites, he is associate editor for *Midwest Living*.

ROBERT PALMER, a longtime contributor to ROLLING STONE, was the first full-time pop-music critic for the *New York Times* and in his lifetime published five books, including *Deep Blues* and *Rock and Roll: An Unruly History*. Palmer held teaching posts at a number of universities, including Yale and the University of Mississippi; produced blues albums for Fat Possum; wrote, narrated and directed several films; and acted as chief consultant for a multipart television history of rock & roll jointly produced by PBS and the BBC. At the time of his death in 1997, at the age of fifty-two, he was working on two books, a memoir of his thirty-year career as a music journalist and an account of his years in Morocco.

STEVE POND is a former contributing editor at ROLLING STONE. His work appears in the *New York Times*, *Premiere*, *Playboy*, *GQ* and the *Washington Post*.

PARKE PUTERBAUGH is a music writer and longtime contributor to ROLLING STONE and a coeditor of *I Want to Take You Higher: The Psychedelic Era 1965–1969*. He has also served as a curatorial consultant to the Rock and Roll Hall of Fame and Museum.

HENRY SCHIPPER is an entertainment-business reporter who has contributed to ROLLING STONE, *Daily Variety* and other publications. He is also the author of *Broken Record: The Inside Story of the Grammy Awards*.

ROB SHEFFIELD is a ROLLING STONE contributing editor and writes the magazine's "Pop Eye" column.

NEIL STRAUSS is a pop music writer for the *New York Times*. He lives in Los Angeles.

acknowledgments

The editors of Rolling Stone Press would like to thank our Chronicle editor Sarah Malarkey and our literary agent Sarah Lazin for bringing this book to life. Others have been crucial to our efforts: ROLLING STONE's Jann S. Wenner, Kent Brownridge, John Lagana, Mary McDonald O'Brien, Evelyn Bernal, Joe Levy, Nelson Gonzalez, Tara Canova, Elizabeth Gorzelany and Maureen Cadigan; Azi Rad, Beth Weber, Aaron Kilber and Anne Bunn at Chronicle; Michael Ochs, Helen Ashford and Rena Smith; Ebet Roberts; Kevin Mazur; Stephanie Chernikowski; Laura Levine; Shirley Manson, KRS-ONE, Lucinda Williams and Moby; Sandy Sawotka; Karen Wiessen; Frank Callari; Susan Barbiesi at Borman/Moir Entertainment; the Temple of Hiphop; Ann Abel, Kim Curry, Becki Heller, Marcie Muscat and Heidi Pauken.

index